Event Management and Sustainability

Event Management and Sustainability

Edited by

Razaq Raj and James Musgrave

Leeds Metropolitan University, UK

CABI is a trading name of CAB International

CABI Head Office
Nosworthy Way
Wallingford
Oxfordshire OX10 8DE
UK

Tel: +44 (0)1491 832111
Fax: +44 (0)1491 833508
E-mail: cabi@cabi.org
Website: www.cabi.org

CABI North American Office
875 Massachusetts Avenue
7th Floor
Cambridge, MA 02139
USA

Tel: +1 617 395 4056
Fax: +1 617 354 6875
E-mail: cabi-nao@cabi.org

A catalogue record for this book is available from the British Library, London, UK.

Library of Congress Cataloging-in-Publication Data

Event management and sustainability / edited by Razaq Raj and James Musgrave.
p. cm.
Includes bibliographical references and index.
ISBN 978-1-84593-524-5 (alk. paper)
1. Special events--Planning. 2. Special events--Environmental aspects. I. Raj, Razaq.
II. Musgrave, James. III. Title.
GT3405.E92 2006
394.2068--dc22

2009003839

ISBN: 978 1 84593 524 5

Typeset by SPi, Pondicherry, India.
Printed and bound in the UK by MPG Books Group.

The paper used for the text pages in this book is FSC certified. The FSC (Forest Stewardship Council) is an international network to promote responsible management of the world's forests.

Contents

Contributors

Volkan Altıntaş graduated from Gazi University in Ankara, obtained an MSc in Tourism and Hotel Management at Akdeniz University in Antalya with a thesis on tourism and the European Union, and is currently is undertaking a PhD at Akdeniz University Institute of Social Sciences. His research areas are quality of life, tourism politics and local development. Volkan has been working as a research assistant at Akdeniz University Institute of Social Sciences since 2003. At the same time, he is a member of the Junior Researchers Team in the Center for European Integration Studies at Bonn University in Germany. Mailing address: Akdeniz University, School of Tourism and Hotel Management, Dumlupınar Boulvard, Antalya, Turkey; e-mail: altintas@akdeniz.edu.tr

Sean Beer is a researcher and teacher with extensive academic experience in the UK and abroad, backed up with considerable practical experience in agriculture, food, tourism, marketing and the rural economy in general. He is currently a Senior Lecturer in the School of Services Management at Bournemouth University. His principal research and teaching interests include the food supply chain, consumer behaviour, rural business, and society and development. Sean is a Rotary Foundation Scholar, a Winston Churchill Fellow and a Nuffield Scholar; he is a regular commentator on radio and television and is active in the community. Mailing address: School of Services Management, Bournemouth University, Dorset House, Fern Barrow, Poole, Dorset BH12 5BB, UK; e-mail: SBeer@bournemouth.ac.uk

Antonella Capriello (PhD, University of Turin) is an Assistant Professor in Marketing at the University of Eastern Piedmont. Her research interests concern event management, rural tourism, and strategic marketing for the hospitality industry. In 2006 she was a Visiting Scholar at the University of Brighton, UK and a Visiting Researcher at Sheffield Hallam University, UK. She received prizes from the Italian Academy of Management in 2007, the Piedmont Region in 2007 and the *International Journal of Contemporary Hospitality Management* at the International Conference in Alanya, Turkey in 2008. She is the author of over 40 publications including books, book chapters, articles and conference proceedings. Mailing address: Department of Business Studies and Environment, University of Eastern Piedmont, Via Perrone 18, I-28100 Novara, Italy; e-mail: antonella.capriello@eco.unipmn.it

Phil Clements is a Senior Lecturer and Course Leader at the UK Centre for Events Management, Leeds Metropolitan University, and has a wide range of experience as both an academic and a practitioner in the hospitality, tourism and events industry. His pragmatic approach to sustainable events management is based not only on academic interest and research, but also includes international exposure and involvement in tourism and events activity – from the tropical rainforests of Australia to high-profile sporting events such as the Sydney 2000 Olympics, the unique hospitality events of New Zealand, and tourist operations in the Mediterranean and the French Alps. Mailing address: UK Centre For Events Management, Leeds Metropolitan University, Civic Quarter, Leeds LS1 3HE, UK; e-mail: p.clements@leedsmet.ac.uk

Daphne Comfort is the Research Administrator of the Business School at the University of Gloucestershire. She is a geography graduate and her research interests are in new developments in retailing, sustainable development, corporate social responsibility and woodland management. She is currently working on a project which evaluates the nature and quality of the student experience. Mailing address: The Business School, University of Gloucestershire, The Park, Cheltenham, Gloucestershire GL50 2RH, UK; e-mail: dcomfort@glos.ac.uk

Maria Teresa Cuomo is a tenured Researcher and teaches Marketing and Systems of Market Analysis at the University of Salerno. Her numerous research interests range from marketing and market research to international management and finance. She has published several articles as well as numerous studies. She regularly participates at national and international conferences and is a Member of the PhD Joint Teaching Committee at the School of Economics. At present she is visiting at the Business School, Hull University, UK. Besides her commitment to academic and scientific research, she is also widely engaged in applied research and consultancy. Mailing address: School of Economics, Department of Business Studies and Researches, University of Salerno, Via Ponte Don Melillo, I-84084 Fisciano, Italy; e-mail: mcuomo@unisa.it

Lóránt Dávid was born in Hungary and graduated in History, Geography, European Studies and Tourism. He is Professor in Tourism at Károly Róbert College, Gyöngyös, and Honorary Associate Professor at Szent István University, Gödöllő, Hungary. He has longstanding teaching, publication and research interests in tourism, regional development and environmental studies. More recently he has been undertaking research on tourism management. He is the author and editor of more than ten books as well as over 100 journal articles and book chapters, and has been active in a number of international research and teaching associations. Mailing address: Department of Tourism and Regional Development, Károly Róbert College, Mátrai u. 36, 3200 Gyöngyös, Hungary; e-mail: davidlo@karolyrobert.hu

Ilaria Fava, PhD in Marketing and Management, is International Business Developer for Corporate Education at MIP Business School. Her research interests are in the field of marketing strategy, with a special focus on the convergence between marketing and supply chain, and in exhibition and convention management. She collaborates with the Sino-Italian Research and Training Centre on Exhibition & Convention Industry. Mailing address: School of Management, Politecnico di Milano, Piazza Leonardo da Vinci 32, I-20133 Milan, Italy; e-mail: fava@mip.polimi.it

Giuseppe Festa is Research Professor of Management at the School of Economics of the University of Salerno, where he is a Lecturer in Marketing. He is the author of numerous scientific works, mainly in the fields of health management and information technology management. Giuseppe is also a member of the Faculty of the PhD Course in Marketing and Communication and President of UNISCE, the Alumni Association of the School of Economics. As a consultant, he is Scientific Director of Consorzio ISMESS (Istituto Mediterraneo di Scienze Sanitarie) and External Verifier for the ECDL Health Certification c/o AICA (Associazione Italiana per l'Informatica e il Calcolo Automatico). Mailing address: School of Economics, Department of Business Studies and Researches, University of Salerno, Via Ponte Don Melillo, I-84084 Fisciano, Italy; e-mail: gfesta@unisa.it

Malcolm Foley has an extensive publishing record in the field of events and festivity. He also has significant international experience of consulting in festival and events development for various national government organizations including Singapore, Indonesia, Syria, South Africa and South Korea. Professor Foley has been a keynote contributor to international conferences on festivals and events, including conferences held in Montreal (Canada), Waikato (New Zealand), Queensland (Australia) and West Sumatra. His current academic focus is on achievement of the 'common good' in a shared power world as it applies to cultural activity in local communities. Mailing address: Caledonian Business School, Glasgow Caledonian University, Cowcaddens Road, Glasgow G4 0BA, UK; e-mail: mtfo@gcal.ac.uk

Kevin A. Griffin (BEd, MA, PhD) initially studied teaching, then tourism organization and then historic settlement, and worked in a number of Geography Departments in the Dublin/Kildare area. Since 2001 he has worked at DIT, where he is actively involved in teaching and researching a broad range of tourism topics with particular specialism in both heritage and sustainable tourism. Now Head of the Department of Tourism, his main research interests include tourism and sustainability, religious tourism/pilgrimage, heritage tourism, social tourism and teaching methodologies. Mailing address: Department of Tourism, School of Hospitality Management and Tourism, Dublin Institute of Technology, Cathal Brugha Street, Dublin 1, Republic of Ireland; e-mail: kevin.griffin@dit.ie

Maria Manuela Martins Guerreiro has a Bachelor's in Marketing, a Master's in Cultural Business Administration (University of Algarve and Université Paris-8) and a PhD in Management ('City branding: The case of European capitals of Culture', University of Algarve). She has been Assistant Professor of Marketing, Services Marketing and Human Resources Management at the Faculty of Economics, University of Algarve, since 1996. Her current research interests include marketing and branding places, cultural tourism, events management, and tourism destination images. Mailing address: Faculdade de Economia, Universidade do Algarve, Campus de Gambelas, 8005-139 Faro, Portugal; e-mail: mmguerre@ualg.pt

Emma Harvey (Director, SaltaSustainable and Senior Lecturer, International Centre for Responsible Tourism) is a sustainability consultant with a pragmatic, commercial approach and experience in 'greening' businesses, helping them to make carbon reductions and other environmental and social improvements. Recent clients include Wembley Stadium, the Live Earth global concert series, The Climate Group (a leading climate NGO), Virgin Atlantic, Enterprise Inns (a FTSE 2590 company with over 7500 public houses) and Divine Chocolate. Emma has a first class degree and a PhD in Psychology. She has 18 years' experience of managing a range of initiatives, from small and local to large-scale, complex projects. Mailing address: SaltaSustainable, 31 Victoria Street, Leeds LS7 4PA, UK and International Centre for Responsible Tourism, Leeds Metropolitan University, Civic Quarter, Calverley Street, Leeds LS1 3HE, UK; e-mail: emma.harvey@saltasustainable.co.uk and e.harvey@leedsmet.ac.uk

Claire Haven-Tang is a Senior Lecturer in the Department of Tourism, Hospitality and Events Management in the Cardiff School of Management at the University of Wales Institute, Cardiff (UWIC). Recent projects undertaken for the Tourism Training Forum for Wales, Capital Region Tourism, People 1st and Adventa include: exploring best practice in business and events tourism, labour market assessments, tourism industry training provision, and customizing sense of place. Her research interests include: destination development and tourism SMEs, sense of place, labour market and human resource development issues. She has co-edited a book (*Tourism SMEs, Service Quality and Destination Competitiveness*) with Professor Eleri Jones. Mailing address: Welsh Centre for Tourism Research, Cardiff School of Management, University of Wales Institute, Cardiff (UWIC), Colchester Avenue, Cardiff CF23 9XR, UK; e-mail: chaven-tang@uwic.ac.uk

David Hillier is Emeritus Professor in the Centre for Police Sciences at the University of Glamorgan. From 1994 to 2006 he was Head of Geography at Glamorgan. His principal research interest is in crime and the design of the urban fabric, and the work he has undertaken with Paul Cozens, now of Curtin University in Perth, Western Australia, has been widely disseminated by the UK's Home Office. David also has research interests in retail change, sustainability and urban regeneration. His work has been extensively published in a range of marketing, business and management, transport, planning and geography journals. Mailing address: Centre for Police Sciences, University of Glamorgan, Pontypridd CF37 1DL, UK; e-mail: dhillier@glam.ac.uk

Guo Jurong, PhD, is Associate Professor in Antai College of Economics and Management, Shanghai Jiao Tong University, where he directs the EMBA Office. Advisor for the training and consultancy in many Chinese groups, he is Executive Director of CCPIT–Shanghai Jiao Tong University E&C Research Center. Mailing address: Room 115, Building 1, Antai College of Economics and Management, Shanghai Jiao Tong University, 535 Fahua Road, Shanghai 200052, People's Republic of China; e-mail: guojurong@sjtu.edu.cn

Deborah Johnson is Head of the Tourism and Event Management Department, Faculty of Business, Cape Peninsula University of Technology. Since 1987 she has been involved in the tourism industry with tourism development and event management. She was responsible for pioneering the first event management qualification offered at a South African University of Technology. She is also involved with research linked to tourism and event management. Mailing address: Head of Department, Tourism and Event Management, Cape Peninsula University of Technology, PO Box 652, Cape Town 8000, South Africa; e-mail: johnsond@cput.ac.za

Eleri Jones is Director of Research in the Cardiff School of Management at the University of Wales Institute, Cardiff (UWIC). Her research interests are focused on innovation, information technology and human resource management in relation to sustainable tourism development. Professor Jones supervises an extensive international portfolio of research degree candidates, some in collaboration with colleagues from Africa and the Middle East. She is a member of the Welsh Assembly Government's Tourism Advisory Panel, which advises the Minister for Heritage. She has managed a number of European projects including BESTBET, a European Union-funded project looking at best practice in business and event tourism. Mailing address: Welsh Centre for Tourism Research, Cardiff School of Management, University of Wales Institute, Cardiff (UWIC), Colchester Avenue, Cardiff CF23 9XR, UK; e-mail: ejones@uwic.ac.uk

Ian Jones is an Associate Dean of Sport in the School of Services Management and Acting Head of the Centre for Event and Sport Research (CESR), Bournemouth University. His teaching interests are based largely around the sociology of sport, sports management and research methods for sport. He has published in a variety of sport- and leisure-related journals, was co-author of *Research Methods for Sport Studies* (Routledge, 2004), and also co-edited two volumes, *Leisure Cultures: Investigations in Media, Technology and Sport* (LSA, 2003) and *Serious Leisure: Extensions and Applications* (LSA, 2006). He is a member of the advisory board for the *Journal of Sport & Tourism*. Mailing address: School of Services Management, Bournemouth University, Dorset House, Fern Barrow, Poole, Dorset BH12 5BB, UK; e-mail: jonesi@bournemouth.ac.uk

Peter Jones is a Professor in the Business School at the University of Gloucestershire, previously serving as Head of the Department of Retailing and Marketing at Manchester Metropolitan University and as Dean of the Business School at the University of Plymouth. He has undertaken educational and commercial consultancy work in Norway, The Netherlands, Switzerland, Greece, Spain, India, Singapore, Indonesia and Malaysia. His current research interests are in corporate social responsibility and sustainability within the service sector of the economy. In the past Peter has published on the introduction of information and communication technologies within retailing and on urban fringe management projects. Mailing address: The Business School, University of Gloucestershire, The Park, Cheltenham, Gloucestershire GL50 2RH, UK; e-mail: pjones@glos.ac.uk

Lucio Lamberti, PhD in Management Engineering, is a Marketing and Business Economics Lecturer at Politecnico di Milano. His research interests are in the field of marketing, with a special focus on customer-centric management, territorial marketing and exhibition and convention management. He collaborates with MIP Business School and the Sino-Italian Research and Training Centre on Exhibition & Convention Industry. Mailing address: School of Management, Politecnico di Milano, Piazza Leonardo da Vinci 32, I-20133 Milan, Italy; e-mail: lucio.lamberti@polimi.it

David McGillivray is a Senior Lecturer in the Division of Cultural Business, Glasgow Caledonian University. His doctoral thesis applied a Foucauldian conceptual framework to the context of work–leisure relationships. His recent research investigations have focused on the events-led urban entrepreneurial strategies of developed and emerging global cities. He has also recently published on the sports fan experience of the Germany 2006 World Cup Fan Parks, applying a Foucauldian critical lens to consider this emerging events-related phenomenon. Commissioned research work includes an evaluation of the design and delivery of cultural entitlements in a Scottish rural environment. Mailing address: Caledonian Business School, Glasgow Caledonian University, Cowcaddens Road, Glasgow G4 0BA, UK; e-mail: D.McGillivray@gcal.ac.uk

Gayle McPherson is the Acting Head of Division, Cultural Business and a Senior Lecturer in Cultural Policy at Glasgow Caledonian University. She leads a team with interests in the consumption and production of festivals and events, both on a global scale and in enhancing community interests, and in using culture to develop the social economy. She has a particular interest in the social and cultural impacts and benefits of events on local communities. Commissioned research work includes the use of culture, as a planning tool, in deprived communities to develop social economy. Gayle co-wrote the 'Culture, Ceremonies and Education' element of the successful Glasgow 2014 Commonwealth Games bid and was the cultural advisor for over a year. Mailing address: Caledonian Business School, Glasgow Caledonian University, Cowcaddens Road, Glasgow G4 0BA, UK; e-mail: gmp@gcal.ac.uk

Júlio da Costa Mendes (Bachelor's in Business; Master's in Business; PhD in Management – Strategy and Organizational Behaviour) is Assistant Professor at the Faculty of Economics, University of Algarve, where he is Coordinator of the PhD programme in Tourism and in some Master's and Post-Graduation Degrees. His current research interests include integrated quality management in tourism destinations, competitiveness, events management, tourism destinations image, branding, marketing strategies, and customer satisfaction. Júlio supervises some academic research studies. He has made several conference presentations, both in Portugal and abroad, and has professional experience in public and private companies. Mailing address: Faculdade de Economia, Universidade do Algarve, Campus de Gambelas, 8005-139 Faro, Portugal; e-mail: jmendes@ualg.pt

Gerardino Metallo is Full Professor of Management and Business Development at the Faculty of Economics of the University of Salerno. His research interests range widely from business and finance issues, where he has published numerous works including *I circuiti finanziari tra localismi e globalizzazione: Verso un'integrazione* (Giuffrè, 1993), *Decisioni di investimento nell'impresa commerciale complessa* (Cedam, 1999) and *Finanza sistemica per l'impresa* (Giappichelli, 2007), to more general management, where he has published several articles in international journals and numerous other studies. Besides his commitment to academic and scientific research, Gerardino is also widely engaged in applied research and business consultancy. Mailing address: School of Economics, Department of Business Studies and Researches, University of Salerno, Via Ponte Don Melillo, I-84084 Fisciano, Italy; e-mail: gemetall@unisa.it

James Musgrave, BA(Hons), MSc, PGCE, is currently Course Leader for the MA in Responsible Events and is actively involved in the development of the new MSc distance learning programme and the undergraduate programme for the UK Centre for Event Management. At present,

James delivers modules at undergraduate and postgraduate levels, including Strategic Management and Management Principles. His research interests are in strategic management and sustainable management principles, transitional management, transportation, planning strategies and audit trails, specifically related to the events sector. James worked for Thomas Danby College as Programme Leader for the hospitality management programmes. Before moving into education, James had a successful career in hotel and consultancy management for a range of national and international companies, where he gained much of his strategic planning experience and developed his skills in training. Mailing address: UK Centre For Events Management, Leeds Metropolitan University, Civic Quarter, Leeds LS1 3HE, UK; e-mail: J.musgrave@leedsmet.ac.uk

Giuliano Noci is Full Professor of Marketing at Politecnico di Milano, Dean of the Degree in Management Engineering of the Como campus (Politecnico di Milano) and Scientific Director of the Marketing area in all of the MBA programmes at MIP Business School. His research interests are in the field of consumer marketing, territorial marketing and exhibition and convention management. He is Vice-President of the Sino-Italian Research and Training Centre on Exhibition & Convention Industry. Mailing address: School of Management, Politecnico di Milano, Piazza Leonardo da Vinci 32, I-20133 Milan, Italy; e-mail: giuliano.noci@polimi.it

Roselyne N. Okech is Assistant Professor in Tourism Studies at Sir Wilfred Grenfell College, Memorial University of Newfoundland. She holds a Bachelor's Degree in Commerce, a Master's in Tourism Administration from India and a PhD in Tourism from KwaZulu-Natal University, South Africa. Her research interests include ecotourism planning and management, cultural tourism in various communities in Africa and issues in sustainable tourism and events. She has written numerous articles appearing in *Anatolia*, the *Journal of Human Resources in Hospitality and Tourism*, the *World Journal of Tourism, Leisure and Sports* and *Tourism Today*, among others. She is also a board member of ATLAS-Africa. Mailing address: Tourism Studies, Memorial University, Sir Wilfred Grenfell College, 10 University Drive, Corner Brook, Newfoundland A2H 6P9, Canada; e-mail: Rnokech@yahoo.com

Mirko Palić, PhD, is a Lecturer in the Marketing Department at the Faculty of Economics and Business, University of Zagreb. He lectures in Marketing and Marketing Channels at undergraduate level. His research interests include retail marketing, marketing innovation and marketing metrics. He is author of over 20 scientific papers and is involved in a number of commercial research projects with leading Croatian companies. Dr Palić is also a member of relevant marketing associations such as CROMAR, CIRCLE and HUPUP. Mailing address: Marketing Department, Faculty of Economics and Business, University of Zagreb, Trg J.F. Kennedya 6, Zagreb, Croatia; e-mail: mpalic@efzg.hr

M. Chris Paxson, PhD, is an Associate Professor with the School of Hospitality Business Management at Washington State University. She currently teaches courses introducing students to the hospitality industry and in conventions and meetings management. Trained as a psychologist, Dr Paxson's research focuses on ageing and hospitality, management issues, teaching and learning, and survey methodology. Mailing address: School of Hospitality Business Management, Washington State University, Todd Hall Addition 470, PO Box 644742, Pullman, WA 99164-4742, USA; e-mail: cpaxson@wsu.edu

Razaq Raj is a Senior Lecturer and Teacher Fellow at the UK Centre for Events Management, teaching Financial and Strategic Management. He has published work on special events, financial management in events, information technology, events sponsorship, cultural festivals and events, sustainable tourism and religious tourism. He is Editor-in-Chief of the *World Journal of Tourism, Leisure and Sport* and has edited/written the textbooks *Religious Tourism and Pilgrimage Management: An International Perspective* (CAB International, 2007) and *Advanced Event Management: An Integrated and Practical Approach* (SAGE Publishing, 2009). Mailing address:

UK Centre For Events Management, Leeds Metropolitan University, Civic Quarter, Leeds LS1 3HE, UK; e-mail: r.raj@leedsmet.ac.uk

Neil Richardson has over 20 years' experience in sales management, marketing and customer service in the B2B sector, covering a wide spectrum of operational and strategic positions. Neil's teaching areas have included postgraduate modules such as for the Chartered Institute of Marketing and at Master's level. His undergraduate modules include consumer behaviour, sales management, retail marketing and digital and interactive marketing. Neil's research has focused on sustainable marketing and he has published a number of articles. He has also undertaken consultancy work for a diverse range of organizations. Mailing address: Faculty of Business and Law, Leeds Metropolitan University, Civic Quarter, Leeds LS1 3HE, UK; e-mail: n.richardson@leedsmet.ac.uk

Ian D. Rotherham is a Reader in Tourism and Environmental Change at Sheffield Hallam University in the Faculty of Development and Society. He has researched and written extensively on a wide range of environmental subjects and on aspects of tourism in relation to culture, nature and economic impacts. He leads ongoing research projects on wildlife tourism, nature-based and cultural tourism, and related issues of marketing, quality assurance and networking. The work includes international collaborations especially in Europe and in the USA. His UK-based projects include the potential role of tourism and related hospitality to aid the regeneration of rural areas and to engage local communities in the process. Mailing address: Tourism and Environmental Change Research Unit, Faculty of Development and Society, Sheffield Hallam University, City Campus, Sheffield S1 1WB, UK; e-mail: i.d.rotherham@shu.ac.uk

Deborah Sadd is a PhD scholar in the School of Services Management at Bournemouth University, researching the urban regeneration legacies associated with the hosting of mega-events and in particular leveraging the legacy for London 2012. She teaches on the BA Events Management and MSc Events Management programmes as well as undertaking guest lectures within the Sports Management programme. Her research interests include social impacts of events, urban regeneration opportunities from events and legacy planning – particularly on the wider opportunities to be gained from hosting the London 2012 Olympic Games, not just those for the local communities in London. Mailing address: School of Services Management, Bournemouth University, Dorset House, Fern Barrow, Poole, Dorset BH12 5BB, UK; e-mail: dsadd@bournemouth.ac.uk

Sarah Saeed-Khan (BA and BEd, University of Manitoba) worked in the events industry for over 13 years on events that received national media coverage, establishing her as a well-known figure within the industry in Canada. In the UK, Sarah has organized corporate events for a number of blue-chip organizations (M&S, ASDA), as well as various music festivals across the UK. Sarah is now a Senior Lecturer in the UK Centre for Events Management at Leeds Metropolitan University and has recently gained her MSc. Mailing address: UK Centre For Events Management, Leeds Metropolitan University, Civic Quarter, Leeds LS1 3HE, UK; e-mail: S.Saeed-khan@leedsmet.ac.uk

Zhu Shichang (BA, Fudan University and MA, Sydney University) is Full Professor of English and Dean of School of Foreign Languages of Shanghai Institute of Technology (SIT). Besides exhibition and conference industry analysis, his major research interests also include discourse analysis, pragmatics and stylistics. Mailing address: Shanghai Jiao Tong University School of Foreign Languages of Shanghai Institute of Technology (SIT), 800 Dongchuan Road, Shanghai 200240, People's Republic of China; e-mail: zhushichang1@yahoo.com

Andrew Smith is a Senior Lecturer in the School of Architecture and the Built Environment at the University of Westminster, where he leads an MA module in Events Tourism. He has published research in leading journals including *Urban Studies*, the *Annals of Tourism Research* and *European Planning Studies*. Andrew's work focuses on the regeneration and re-imaging of cities, particularly the use of sports events to assist these ambitions. His other publications concern city image change and the relationship between urban monuments and tourism marketing. His latest events research addresses social sustainability issues and, perhaps inevitably, the London 2012 Olympic Games. Mailing address: Centre for Tourism Research, School of Architecture and the Built Environment, University of Westminster, 35 Marylebone Road, London NW1 5LS, UK; e-mail: smithan@wmin.ac.uk

Cecilie Smith-Christensen is a Norwegian economist with a special interest in events and festivals as drivers for sustainable development. Since 2002 Cecilie has been based in South Africa, where she founded Event Research International (ERi), providing research services and capacity-building strategies promoting the concept of responsible events. Cecilie is currently Deputy Director of the Nordic World Heritage Foundation, a UNESCO Category 2 centre. Here she also heads the Tourism for Sustainable Development initiative. Cecilie holds a Master's Degree in Economics from the University of Oslo (1999), with specialization in development and environmental economics. Mailing address: Event Research International (ERi), Nedre Skogvei 8B, 0281 Oslo, Norway; e-mail: cecilie@eventresearch.org

Dimitri Tassiopoulos is an Associate Director at the School of Tourism and Hospitality of Walter Sisulu University, South Africa. Since 1993, he has been involved in various national and international tourism research projects of a multidisciplinary and multi-institutional nature, concerning entrepreneurship, agri-tourism, events, cultural and wine tourism, among others. Mailing address: School of Tourism and Hospitality (SCOTH), Walter Sisulu University, PO Box 1421, East London 5200, Buffalo City, South Africa; e-mail: dtassio@wsu.ac.za

Marija Tomašević Lišanin, PhD, is a full-time Professor in the Marketing Department at the Faculty of Economics and Business, University of Zagreb. She lectures in Marketing, Personal Selling and Negotiation and Sales Management at undergraduate level. Marija is also Head of the Sales Management specialized graduate study, a programme dedicated to all aspects of sales management with emphasis on key account management, business negotiation, category management and private labels, sales promotion management, customer relationship management and similar relevant topics. She is mentor to a number of postgraduate students who aim to make a contribution towards the development of marketing and particularly sales-oriented scientific research. Mailing address: Marketing Department, Faculty of Economics and Business, University of Zagreb, Trg J.F. Kennedya 6, Zagreb, Croatia; e-mail: mtomasevic@efzg.hr

Patrícia Oom do Valle (Bachelor's in Business; Master's in Business; PhD in Applied Quantitative Methods to Economics and Business – Statistics) is Assistant Professor at the Faculty of Economics, University of Algarve and Coordinator of the Master's in Marketing programme. Her current research interests are in applied statistics and modelling in the areas of integrated quality management in tourism destinations, events management, tourism destinations image, branding, marketing strategies, customer satisfaction, and environment behaviour. She is a Member of the research centre Tourism and Leisure. Patrícia has made several conference presentations, both in Portugal and abroad, and has published in quantitative methods and business journals. Mailing address: Faculdade de Economia, Universidade do Algarve, Campus de Gambelas, 8005-139 Faro, Portugal; e-mail: pvalle@alag.pt

Preface

Utilizing the United Nations Environment Programme (UNEP), the Commission on Sustainable Development (CSD), the World Tourism Organization (WTO/OMT), coupled with the International Olympic Committee (IOC) and industry leaders, it is apparent that the events industry generates a multitude of activities associated with varied events. These have both positive and negative impacts on interested stakeholders, the community and the environment.

Principles of sustainability refer to the environmental, economic and sociocultural aspects of event development, and a suitable balance must be established between these three dimensions to guarantee an event's long-term sustainability and legacy. The sustainable development and production of events requires strong management, political leadership and the informed participation of all stakeholders to ensure adherence and congruence to a sustainable philosophy and management. Thus, the editors of this book propose that sustainable event management should:

- provide realistic and long-term economic event development and production, ensuring that socio-economic benefits are distributed fairly to all stakeholders;
- provide continuous employment opportunities, entrepreneurial opportunities and distribution of event income within host communities, thereby contributing to the reduction of socio-economic disparity;
- consider the use of environmental resources that assist in event development and production, complying with essential management processes and conservation techniques to help safeguard natural heritage and the biodiversity of the surrounding community; and
- develop and produce events in conjunction with the host communities, protecting their sociocultural authenticity, built landmarks, traditions and cultural values by promoting intercultural understanding and tolerance.

Although these are not prescriptive rules and regulations that must be adhered to, sustainable event management should aim to provide high satisfaction to all interested parties in the development and production of events. It is worth noting that in order to achieve sustainable event management, a continuous and constant evaluation process is imperative.

With the aim of contributing to the field, this book first presents sustainable management theory, academic research and empirical case studies. This should give the reader some historical foundation, thus allowing him/her to understand the more philosophical and conceptual elements of the topic.

The book then gives a full and complete view of the concepts of sustainable management and how it relates to various sectors within the events industry. It illustrates the fundamental importance of local communities, businesses and interested stakeholders in relation to future events in regional, national and international locations. Historical and documented reports supplement this area. Next the book focuses on international governing bodies and national government strategic objectives as the cornerstone for sustainable development in the events sector. The relationship between these strategic objectives and on-the-ground operational responsibilities is presented using research by contributing authors and accredited organizations to add scope and depth to the publication.

The book is not intended to become a reference material for practitioners or appointed advocates. However, best practice case studies are presented within the book to highlight and explain particular sustainable management issues where necessary. The book is intended to support practitioners in their operational and administrative duties and to educate undergraduates/postgraduates within their industry sectors throughout the UK and on an international basis.

1 Introduction to a Conceptual Framework for Sustainable Events

J. Musgrave and R. Raj
Leeds Metropolitan University, Leeds, UK

This chapter explores concepts of sustainable development and focuses on the traditional elements of social, economic and environmental pillars within the context of planned events at different scales and levels. It examines the integration of principles of sustainability at all levels and stages of a planned event and the associated positive and negative impacts for different stakeholders. The aim is to provide a conceptual framework emergent from existing principles and guidance that will underpin the professionalism of sustainable event management.

Chapter outline

- Introduction
- What is Sustainability?
- Sustainability: a Multidimensional Theory
- Sustainable Event Management
- Principles of Sustainable Management in Events
- Sustainable Policy Guidelines
- Conceptual Framework for Sustainable Events Management
- Summary
- Key Questions

Introduction

There is compelling evidence that the topic of sustainability has gained widespread acceptance in many areas of society, with significant claims for the benefits of adopting the principles of sustainability as an integral part of development strategies, not least within the field of events. As DeSimone and Popoff (1997) suggest, sustainable management has emerged out of a necessity to continue to grow and prosper while working in partnership with surrounding communities, the environment and the economy. Fundamentally, sustainable event managers must be cognizant of the concept of sustainability and implement the principles within the organization and delivery of the event. The events industry benefits from easily accessible environmental and social resources, but as the industry grows to an estimated £11 billion in the UK (EIA, 2007), events and festivals will continue to generate both positive and adverse impacts on communities and cultures. Beyond the symbolic value of such claims is a requirement by academics and practitioners to determine, through empirical investigation, the approaches taken in identifying and implementing best practice, and to evaluate and measure the sustainable strategies implemented. A future glimpse suggests that the events industry will operate with imposed legislation and applications if the industry does not respond to the rationale of sustainability and operate within principles of sustainable management.

Issues of sustainable development have been around for centuries. The 19th-century economist Thomas Malthus was concerned with the production of food and suggested that supply would be outstripped by population growth, developing the idea that nature is not simply a never-ending resource (Brodribb, 1997). More formalized organization and documentation of these issues began with the formation of the Environmental Development Fund (EDF) in 1968. Moving quickly forward, in 1992, Agenda 21 called for all countries to develop national sustainable development strategies (NSDSs). In November 2001, a UN International Forum on National Strategies for Sustainable Development agreed guidance on NSDSs that proposes 'elements' of successful strategies for both developed and developing countries and economies (IISD, 2008).

There are formidable barriers when attempts are made to translate the principles of sustainability into action within events (Jones *et al.*, 2006), such as lack of reliable information, individual and organizational inertia, employee perceptions and the lack of using planning and performance standards. In essence, events are fragmented – made up of many stages, many suppliers, many performance indicators and many clients. Therefore any attempt at introducing a sustainable policy should be integral to all elements of the event. Undoubtedly the 'elements' of an event refer to pre-, live and post-event, and, as such, the life cycle and entirety of event management must be considered.

What is Sustainability?

Sustainability is embedded in loose terms to enable acceptance within varying scenarios and correlates to social will. The term 'sustainability' derives from a political and socially constructed terminology that supports the ubiquitous policy of 'sustainable development' (Dresner, 2002; Rogers *et al.*, 2008).

Sustainability is often referred to as 'sustainable development' and frequently adopts a discourse of social, environmental and economic parity between developing and developed countries. Although definitions of sustainable development are concerned with multilevel, worldwide issues, they are also influenced by local and national initiatives. Sustainability implies a link towards ecological impacts; namely, the consumption of natural resources and the deliberation of pollution and energy use, the concern for social inclusion and distribution of wealth, coupled with the economic themes of growth and longevity. The more affluent a society becomes, the more distant it is from the impacts of its lifestyle. Antithetically, the poor often lack the resources to be concerned with their immediate community. Policy makers need to be mindful of the interactions between the social, economic and environmental factors in order to provide a sustainable and achievable lifestyle.

The Bruntland Commission report for the World Commission on Environment and Development (WCED, 1987) defined sustainability as 'development that meets the needs of the present without compromising the ability of future generations to meet their own needs'. Additionally, *BS 8901:2007 Specification for a sustainable event management system with guidance for use developed* proposes that sustainable development is 'an enduring, balanced approach to economic activity, environmental responsibility and social progress' (BSI, 2007, p. 7). Within this framework is the realization that responsibility lies within the core activities of the event manager and considers all the support activities aligned to the planned events.

The International Institute for Sustainable Development (IISD, 1996) considers sustainability as a set of worldwide systems that highlight the cause and effect of actions and activities – personal and economic, national and local. Clearly the problems are complex, and worldwide problems cannot be solved by a single planning solution and probably not by any single action. Moreover, there is a continuous discourse surrounding the dichotomy of economic and environmental principles, and the suggestion that one principle takes priority over the other. Subsequently, social considerations are frequently given less attention. Within this book and within this chapter, equal consideration of all three principles – including the implementation of social frameworks – is fundamental to the concept of sustainable event management.

Sustainability: a Multidimensional Theory

Sustainability and sustainable development must be considered a multidimensional, plural concept that cannot be translated into fixed, predictable goals. The economic, environmental and social elements of sustainability are defined as follows.

- *Economic*. Although economic stability is traditionally concerned with the concepts of efficiency and effectiveness of generating profit from a business activity, the more radical suggestion is that economic growth cannot be infinite, and that limitations to resources and thus scarcity of these resources will impact on economic stability (Found *et al.*, 2006). As previously mentioned, the 'three pillar' principles are interwoven, and thus the economic transition towards a responsible direction must put economics within a social and environmental context; thus a natural capital. Accordingly, the more widely accepted definition in these terms suggests that sustainable economic development must maintain economic capital, while simultaneously improving quality of life and the environment to ensure stable economic growth.
- *Environmental*. The more widely associated issue concerns itself with the impact on biodiversity and the environment. Overexploitation and mismanagement of ecological systems, living organisms and the non-living materials of the surroundings impact on the welfare of the population and society at large. Effects range from supply disruption of raw materials and acceptance of reduced quality through to scarcity of food items, seen more recently with water availability and crop yield (WWF and SustainAbility, 2007). More worryingly, the exploitation of natural resources is irreversible and, to be truly sustainable, consumption must be within the biophysical limits of the overall ecosystem. By reducing waste and preventing ecological pollution and consumption of natural resources, the present generation can ensure that future generations do not regret the lack of action taken now.
- *Social*. Societal needs cannot solely be met by providing a stable ecological environment. Social and cultural stability goes hand-in-hand with the other pillars. Without investment and services to support a stable infrastructure, a cohesive society cannot exist. Jeopardizing community cohesion will ultimately jeopardize the economic and ecological make-up of society. Consequently, structured approaches and frameworks that assist in the creation of strong civil societies – including meeting the needs of individual groups and generating shared values, equal rights and equal access – are integral for sustainable development (UNCSD, 2007). Only by sharing the responsibility of creating such a utopian ideology of society can government, private industries and individuals create true social sustainability.

Within a business context, these three impacts have come to be known as the 'triple bottom line'. Within the notions of corporate social responsibility (CSR), the World Business Council for Sustainable Development (WBCSD, 1998) believes that the benefits of incorporating CSR can be felt not only by the business but also by its stakeholders. Clearly here philosophical questions related to the purpose of business are raised. Simply put, a business can be used to reinvest profits within the business itself, its staff and surrounding community, or as a means to serve return on investment of the shareholders and generate increased profit.

Sustainable Event Management

The nomenclature of events includes mega, special, social, major, hallmark and community events. Events are categorized by virtue of their size, scope and scale. Moreover, events can be categorized according to their type or sector, such as conferences and exhibitions, arts and entertainment, sports events, and charitable events. The APEX (Accepted Practices Exchange)

Industry Glossary of Terms (CIC, 2003, cited in Bowdin *et al.*, 2006, p. 14) defines an event as 'an organised occasion such as a meeting, convention, exhibition, special event, gala dinner, etc. An event is often composed of several different yet related functions.'

Events are explicitly linked to fundamentals of the human race – social and cultural values, and the more basic ladders of social inclusion, a sense of belonging and a sense of identity (Goodland, 2002; Garcia, 2003). It is evident that hosting an event creates vast impacts, as seen in Fig. 1.1. Dwyer *et al.* (2000) support the view that organizing and managing a planned event involves many component parts and many stakeholders. Often the decisions to organize and host events are taken from different stakeholder viewpoints. Good economic rationale is a strong indicator coupled with the social and cultural benefits to a destination, raising awareness of community/social issues, and enhancing the exchange of ideas, networking and business contacts. Often neglected and often ambiguous are the social elements of the three pillars of sustainability. The scope of any framework should encompass those working, participating and attending the event, consider social inclusion as a key principle to widening participation and encourage interest from all aspects of the surrounding community. Social inclusion within events should include (DCMS, 2001; Garcia, 2003; UK Sport, 2005):

- awareness of the needs of groups participating at the event;
- creation of a structured policy statement to ensure equity and equality for all; and
- induction and training of all staff and volunteers in the awareness, recognition and self-management of equity and equality for all.

Significantly, the move towards the creation of a number of published frameworks for sustainable event management has not only provided a sense of professionalism in light of contemporary concerns, but also highlighted best practice within the industry, advice and guidance, practical solutions and an inward sense of the importance of events in modern society.

There have been many major developments towards the events industry becoming sustainable. For example, in 1992 McDonough and Partners created the Hannover Principles, designed with sustainability principles in mind, for the Expo World Fair 2000. In February 1994, Lillehammer, Norway presented the first 'green' games in the history of the Olympics (Lesjo, 2000). The northern English city of Sheffield set out to develop the World Student Games as a catalyst for economic and social regeneration (B. Bramwell, 1995, unpublished paper), and the Sustainable Exhibition Industry Project (SEXI) set to reduce waste as a first step towards sustainable development within the exhibitions sector of events (MEBC, 2002).

Clearly, sustainable event management has evolved over a number of years, rather than being a concept born out of government strategies or academic posturing. The recent proposition to develop past and existing frameworks into a recognized standard is a natural progression. A conceptual framework that has developed and emerged out of the planning and management of events over the past decade is a necessity for a responsible events profession operating within the 21st century. Hediger (2000) proposes that a component of sustainable principles is to induce cultural change within society, and thus within the events sector. Therefore principles of transition management apply here (Presbury and Edwards, 2005), wherein sustainable event management is a problem for each generation and requires changes through successive generations via:

- a change in attitude;
- an increase in supply chain pressure;
- an increase in the awareness of the true cost of waste; and
- transparency of product life cycle.

Meadowcraft (1997, p. 37) states:

> Each generation must take up the challenge anew, determining in what direction their development objectives lie, what constitutes the boundaries of the environmentally possible and the environmentally desirable, and what is their understanding of the requirements of social injustice.

Principles of Sustainable Management in Events

The creation of a framework or set of principles that can be adaptive to changes in market requirements is crucial for successful

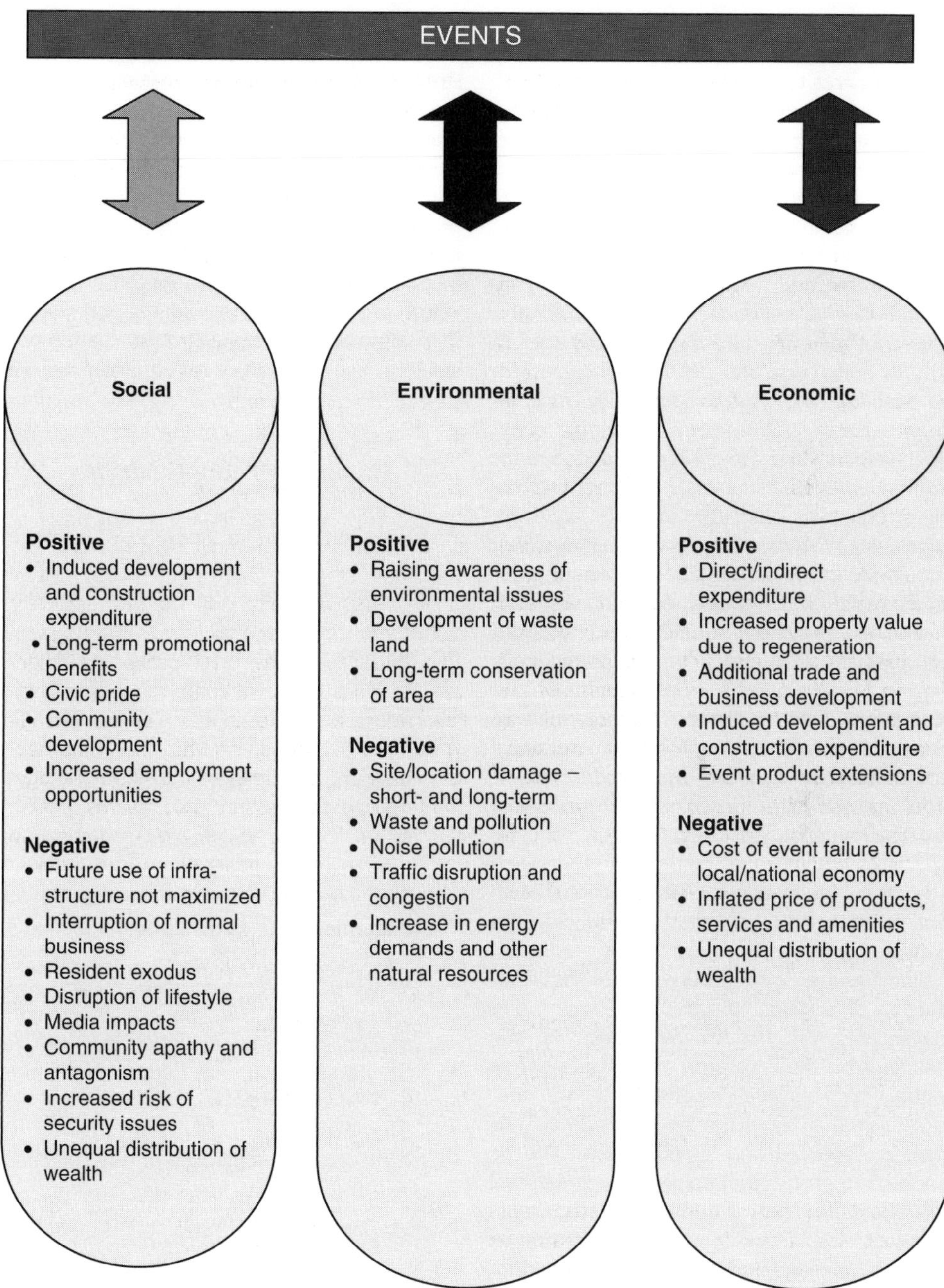

Fig. 1.1. The 'three pillar impacts' of events.

implementation within the events industry. A major challenge to achieving sustainable management practices is the incessant stress on the physical and ecological environments as the number of participants at events and festivals increases (DEFRA, 2007). Moreover, there is a requirement to develop a framework that fits with the internal and external events environment. Finally, a sustainable event management framework should enable alleviation of the impacts of hosting highly consumptive, resource-led events and incorporate achievable improvements to the 'three pillar impacts'.

Preparation in planning is paramount for the successful implementation and evaluation of any management plan. The nature of the events industry is such that constraints on time, contractual relationships, tight margins and the continuous pressure to produce unique experiences are second nature (MEBC, 2002). Any existing and/or new activity must consider the source of materials and the materials used in light of a life cycle analysis. If materials are to be used, then these are to be reusable, recycled or recyclable. Consequently, supply chain management and procurement negotiations are fundamental elements of aligning sustainability principles and the logistics of event organization. Sustainable event management should set improved targets, implement innovative practice and consult new technologies. It should also provide a holistic view of all event activities in an industry that is traditionally viewed as consumptive of materials and resources. Even so, simple actions such as event tickets, delegation packs and contractual communication can be distributed via electronic means or produced using recycled and reusable materials.

Business as usual cannot continue, and innovative design approaches and communication must become standard in the industry. Sustainable principles must provide a social, political and economic purpose for the introduction of sustainable systems (Downing and Ballantyne, 2007). An awareness of the demands on the ecological and social systems within which any event operates is a basic principle. An analysis of the resources used, how they are sourced and supplied must also be adopted to ensure that compliance is adhered to; where it is not, actions and steps should be taken. Absolute policy and processes must be designed and applied throughout all components and all stages of any event.

Elements of strategy can help establish basic project management thinking in any planned event. Designing a critical path and chain analysis will assist in understanding the resources, time and interactions of key activities between each stakeholder, in order for basic actions and continuous measurement, evaluation and improvements to be made (Van der Ryn and Calthorpe, 1991). The purpose of strategic thinking within sustainable events management is to ensure that any interventions are timely, gain the optimum influence and generate an understanding of the cause and effect of any action against all other stakeholders, resources and principles of sustainability. The act of measurement and evaluation as a sustainable management tool can be used to adjust processes and procedures accordingly. Evaluation and an emphasis on evaluation provide crucial opportunities for improvement.

Sustainable Policy Guidelines

As an absolute message of purpose, a sustainable policy and a sustainable plan can provide clarity to many different stakeholders. Equally, conformity and compliance of suppliers and procurement can be imposed as a requirement for success of implementation. There are numerous guides to sustainability principles within events; a few examples are given below:

- *Sustainable Events Guide* (DEFRA, 2007);
- *SEXI: The Sustainable Exhibition Industry Project* (MEBC, 2002);
- *The Hannover Principles: Design for Sustainability – Expo 2000* (McDonough and Partners, 1992);
- *BS 8901:2007 Specification for a sustainable event management system with guidance for use developed* (BSI, 2007);
- *Staging Major Sports Events: The Guide* (UK Sport, 2005); and
- *The Sustainable Music Festival – A Strategic Guide* (Brooks *et al*., 2007).

There are many practical tips throughout these published guides (see Table 1.1), such as a reduction in travel to decrease carbon emissions and improve the well-being of clients during the live event. However, incentivized strategies for participants, staff and the organization will provide instantaneous results and a more enthusiastic compliance towards the sustainable paradigm. For example, discounted train tickets offered to participants and the new market opportunities for low-carbon,

Table 1.1. Sustainable event guides and principles.

Publication	Key principles
DEFRA Sustainable Events Guide	Include sustainability clauses in contracts Use the 3 Rs – reduce, reuse, recycle Communicate electronically rather than by paper Be energy- and water-efficient Minimize the impacts of travel Consider the well-being of delegates, local community, suppliers and stakeholders Raise awareness and share best practice Be transparent
SEXI: The Sustainable Exhibition Industry Project	Waste hierarchy as applied to the exhibitions industry – research, re-design, reduce, reuse and recycle Monitoring, recording and reporting Influence cultural change, engage in community groups and adopt training sessions Project champions Increase efficiencies and profitability Environmental policies and responsibilities Sustainability reporting Offset emissions of carbon dioxide Off-site sorting Infrastructure Industrial symbiosis Materials and technology
Hannover Principles	Insist on the right of humanity and nature to coexist Recognize interdependence Respect relationships between spirit and matter Accept responsibility for the consequences of design Create safe objects of long-term value Eliminate the concept of waste Rely on natural energy flows Understand the limitations of design Seek constant improvement by the sharing of knowledge
BS 8901:2007	Identify capabilities Design roles and responsibilities Identify appropriate resources Develop knowledge, competencies and training Plan and manage operational activities Supply chain management Communication and coordination Documentation and record-keeping Monitor and measure performance Develop sustainable policies and systems for regular audits Human rights and equity Race, ethnicity and sport Ageism and disability in sport Social and religious inclusion Evaluation and recommendations
UK Sport	Adopt a green policy Carry out an 'environment scoping review' of venues and operations Establish environmental teams Define programmes and set appropriate targets Implement programmes

Continued

Table 1.1. Continued.

Publication	Key principles
	Monitor implementation and adjust programme accordingly Evaluate and publicize results Awareness of diverse groups within the scope of the event Create a structured policy statement to ensure equity and equality for all Induction and training of all staff and volunteers in the awareness, recognition and self-management of equity and equality for all
The Sustainable Music Festival – A Strategic Guide	Produce no waste – phase out all disposable food and beverage containers Use 100% renewable energy – implement an internal energy efficiency policy Develop strategic partnerships to access renewable energy Use resource-efficient transportation – sell a new ticket that includes transportation Review the location Work with sustainable stakeholders Identify key roles and responsibilities Create an atmosphere of inclusion and respect – create areas/access for under-represented people Drive societal change towards sustainability – start with one thing from artists, suppliers to attendees Generate ideas and raise awareness through electronic media

energy-efficient products and services, estimated at US$500 billion worldwide (Stern, 2006, p. xvi), will help create impetus with industry and consumers alike.

There are many more principle guides that can be linked to the events industry such as the Green Tourism Business Scheme (GTBS), The Eco-Management and Audit Scheme (EMAS) and ISO 14001. EMAS is essentially a voluntary scheme that distinguishes those companies that go beyond the scope of legislative compliance. ISO 14001 is an internationally accepted standard that provides organizations with a planned set of criteria required for implementation of an effective environmental management system (EMS). The standard addresses the continuing question of business purpose and the concept that business as usual cannot continue, thus creating a business ideology of balance between maintaining profitability and reducing environmental impact (BSI, 2007). The aim of the GTBS is to offer guidelines to businesses, such as conference venues, event sites and suppliers, on how to implement principles of sustainability without endangering quality of service and/or product. GTBS certification is dependent on the achievement of specific criteria and focuses on ten different areas, ranging from compulsory compliance to environmental legislation to social involvement and communication, transport strategies and innovate practices and use of technologies.

Conceptual Framework for Sustainable Events Management

From an analysis of existing models and other sustainable guides, the framework below (see also Fig. 1.2) provides an introduction to the fundamentals of sustainability, coherence and integration within the events industry. Equally, adopting such a framework presents a number of advantages in working towards sustainability that are implicit outcomes of adherence. Additionally, these principles represent the underlying philosophy for the way sustainable events should be considered, and symbolize a vision and overall direction, which must be

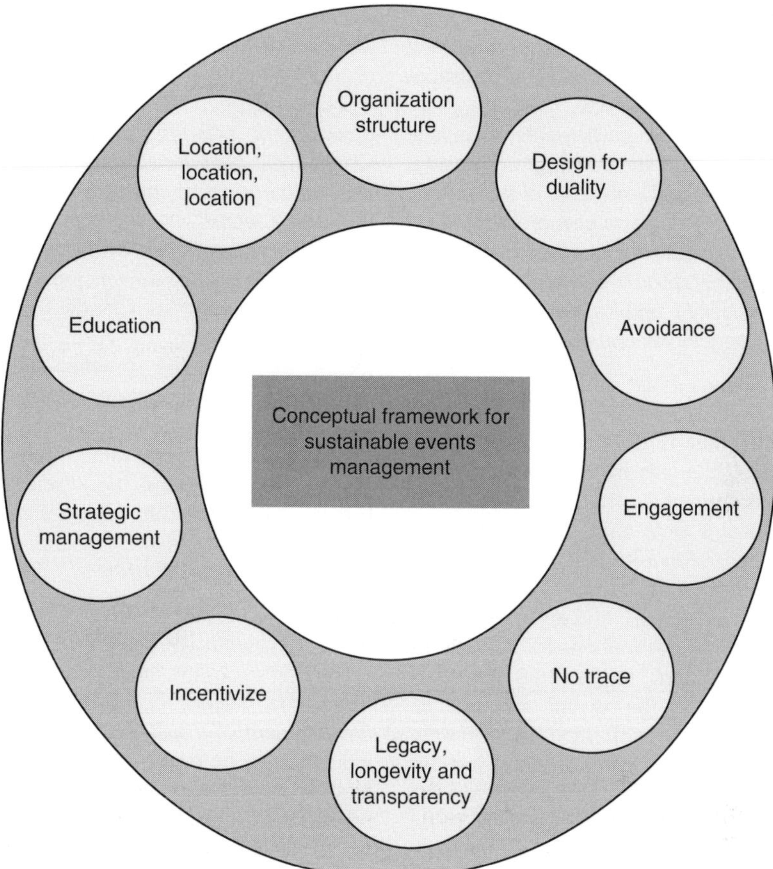

Fig. 1.2. The sustainable events management wheel.

accessible and realistic. A sustainable event policy must respect all ten elements of the framework as stated below.

1. *Organization structure*. Define roles, training, structured policies and procedures that foster positive attitude, compliance and understanding with suppliers, employers and other stakeholders, within a realistic time and budget.

2. *Design for duality*. Introduce new technologies and search for innovative approaches where services, products and facilities can be reused and/or recycled.

3. *Avoidance*. Establish baseline assessments and plan to reduce damage to surrounding ecological systems, disruption to surrounding communities and economic disparity.

4. *Engagement*. Invest time and resources in the culture of surrounding communities, create local partnerships and alliances, increase participation and access for all.

5. *No trace*. Work towards elimination of waste, reduction of energy consumption and a second-nature attitude towards product/service life cycle analysis.

6. *Legacy, longevity and transparency*. Measure, evaluate and inform all stakeholders of performance, actions taken and future investment.

7. *Incentivize*. Use strategic alliances to offer savings for compliance towards sustainability principles from all stakeholders, such as discounted rail schemes.

8. *Strategic management*. Create critical path and value chain analysis that will identify timely interventions, increase the influence of actions taken, and increase understanding of cause and effect against all other stakeholders, resources and principles of sustainability.

9. *Education*. Educate participants, suppliers, employees and the surrounding community about the purpose and principles of sustainability, sharing knowledge and best practice.

10. *Location, location, location*. Decide on a site/venue that provides accessibility, convenience, flexibility and/or compliance with sustainability principles and quality.

Previous debates have not paid particular attention to the nature of the events industry as a service that is continuously pulsating. For example, changes in visitor priorities to include environmentally friendly initiatives are a clear indicator of a shift in cultural buyer behaviour. Indicators also serve to guide consumers about the environmental and social quality of the destination, and are good benchmarks to stimulate destinations to compete on sustainability grounds rather than solely on price. Finally, within the current economic climate, year-on-year growth is expected to slow. The result is that many event organizations will only implement strategies to incorporate sustainability when it is commercially viable to do. However, changing the economic mindset and shifting entire business strategies to include sustainable principles – rather than unremitting percentage increases in profitability – will ultimately provide a well-considered, mature and stable business plan (Hamilton, 2003).

Token gestures only add mistrust to what many believe is an ideological principle. Littig and Griebler (2005) suggest that many individuals do not see the direct impact of their actions and therefore do not consider solutions to what is a social, personal and/or business dilemma. Many consider the concept of 'sustainability' an ethereal problem. Therefore, realistic ideas and solutions are crucial for acceptance of the ten key principles within events. Overcoming the problems of implementation is often associated with a lack of reliable information or trust ('green-wash'), boredom about the issues ('green fatigue'), perceived implementation costs and compliance. There is a need to measure and evaluate initiatives that recognize market forces within the events industry and that complement these and achieve sustainable results. The lack of use of planning and performance standards will only heighten the necessity for long-term government policies, such as the Climate Change Bill, and create imposed policies that will standardize and characterize operations in the events sector.

Events can operate within current budgets (Brown, 2003) while influencing individual and organizational inertia. Clearly there is finite achievement within the confines of existing technology, business practice and cultural acceptance, and practitioners must carry on pushing these parameters. Indeed, if the ignorance and complacency of short-term business strategy do not change, then the events industry will be forced into change, imposed by legislation.

Summary

Given the current economic instability, the development of a sustainable and harmonious industry may be overlooked in order to create a quick profit margin. However, it is this mindset and the overdependence on and draining of resources that impact the economic sustainability and success of events. While events do present opportunities, they can also entail risks, causing a disruption in the supply chain of key services, a reduction in the quality of services, a decrease in efficiencies and an increase in commodity costs. Sympathetic governments, local council and industry leaders must attain the knowledge to assess and withstand causes that stand as obstacles to sustainable development within the industry and ensure that weak market conditions are overcome. The primary risks are degradation of the natural and cultural environment, particularly those featured as hosts to mega and major cultural events. There are other risks to the host community, including economic disruption, as well as risks for investors, and even physical risks for participants and attendees. If commercialization continues to be the primary motivating factor in staging events, 'short-termism' will ensue resulting in no change in business practice.

Throughout this chapter there is an underlying premise that those involved in event management recognize the ethical responsibility involved in the planning and management of such events. Clearly this is not a given, and organizations must begin a top-down approach that creates long-term reductions in the adverse impacts on the surrounding environment of events. As the events industry evolves and moves further into the 21st century, the value systems of industry leaders that were once based on financial return must change to a value system based on community and moral judgement. The so-called 'paradox of profitability' will cease to be the driving force in the success of many event management companies and the current climate of social accountability will be the enduring remnant of a decade saturated in seminal social reports that reflect a more globally responsible paradigm.

Accepting responsibility for the impacts that events cause can create a new generation of event managers. Responsible events management will represent a holistic understanding of all core and support activities of planned events, raise awareness of the impacts of these activities and foster a strategic intent to reduce impacts, increase the effectiveness of actions taken and create a culture that continuously measures and evaluates these changes. By changing the mindset of the events business, from one that consumes resources to one that reduces the use of resources, the move towards responsible and sustainable event management can be achieved.

Key Questions

1. Sustainable event management attempts to implement the principles of sustainable development within the events industry. What are the implications within the events industry if there is no change in the way in which events operate?
2. What are the main differences between ISO 14001 and the BS 8901?
3. Using the conceptual framework for sustainable event management and your own experiences, how can an events manager implement BS 8901?

References

Bowdin, G., Allen, J., O'Toole, W., Harris, R. and McDonnell, I. (2006) *Events Management*, 2nd edn. Butterworth-Heinemann, Oxford, UK.

Brodribb, J. (1997) Mission Earth. *New Scientist Magazine*, 13 December, issue 2112, p. 49.

Brooks, S., O'Halloran, D. and Magnin, A. (2007) The Sustainable Music Festival – A Strategic Guide. Available at: http://www.thenaturalstep.org/en/system/files/MusicFestivalsGuidebook.pdf (accessed 16 March 2009).

Brown, L.R. (2003) *Plan B: Rescuing a Planet under Stress and a Civilization in Trouble*. Earth Policy Institute/ W.W. Norton and Company, London.

BSI (2007) *BS 8901:2007 Specification for a sustainable event management system with guidance for use developed*. British Standards Institution, London.

DCMS (Department for Culture, Media and Sport) (2001) *Staging International Sporting Events*. The Stationery Office, London.

DEFRA (2007) *Sustainable Events Guide*. Department for Environment, Food and Rural Affairs, London.

DeSimone, L.D. and Popoff, F. (1997) *Eco-efficiency: The Business Link to Sustainable Development*. MIT Press, Cambridge, Massachusetts.

Downing, P. and Ballantyne, J. (2007) *Tipping Point or Turning Point: Social Marketing and Climate Change*. IPSOS Mori Social Research Institute, London.

Dresner, S. (2002) *The Principles of Sustainability*. Earthscan Publications, London.

Dwyer, L., Mellor, R., Mistilis, N. and Mules, T. (2000) A framework for assessing 'tangible' and 'intangible' impacts of events and conventions. *Event Management* 6(3), 175–180.

EIA (Events Industry Alliance) (2007) Press Release: Bed Tax Put to Bed. Available at: http://www.eventsindustry alliance.com/page.cfm/T=m/Action=Press/PressID=50 (accessed 22 January 2008).

Found, P., Beale, J., Hines, P., Naim, M., Rich, N., Sarmiento, R. and Thomas, A. (2006) *A Theoretical Framework for Economic Sustainability of Manufacturing*. Cardiff Business School Working Papers. Cardiff University, Cardiff, UK.

Garcia, B. (2003) Securing sustainable legacies through cultural programming in sporting events. *Culture @ the Olympics* 5(1), 1–10.

Goodland, R. (2002) *Sustainability: Human, Social, Economic and Environmental Encyclopedia of Global Environmental Change*. John Wiley and Sons Ltd, Hoboken, New Jersey.

Hamilton, K. (2003) *Accounting for Sustainability*. Environment Department, The World Bank, Washington, DC.

Hediger, W. (2000) Sustainable development and social welfare. *Ecological Economics* 32(3), 481–492.

IISD (1996) *Global Green Standards: ISO 14000 and Sustainable Development*. International Institute for Sustainable Development, Winnipeg, Manitoba, Canada.

IISD (2008) *The Sustainable Development Timeline*. International Institute for Sustainable Development, Winnipeg, Manitoba, Canada.

Jones, B., Scott, D. and Abi Khaled, H. (2006) Implications of climate change for outdoor event planning: a case study of three special events in Canada's National Capital Region. *Event Management* 10(1), 63–76.

Lesjo, J.H. (2000) Lillehammer 1994: planning, figurations and the 'green' winter games. *International Review for the Sociology of Sport* 35(3), 282–293.

Littig, B. and Griebler, E. (2005) Social sustainability: a catchword between political pragmatism and social theory. *International Journal of Sustainable Development* 8, 65–79.

McDonough and Partners (1992) *The Hannover Principles: Design for Sustainability – Expo 2000*. William McDonough & Partners, Charlottesville, Virginia.

Meadowcraft, J. (1997) Planning for sustainable development: what can be learned from the critics. In: Kenny, M. and Meadowcraft, J. (eds) *Planning Sustainability*. Routledge, London/New York, pp. 12–38.

MEBC (2002) *SEXI: The Sustainable Exhibition Industry Project*. Midlands Environmental Business Company Ltd, Birmingham, UK.

Presbury, R. and Edwards, D. (2005) Incorporating sustainability in meetings and event management education. *International Journal of Event Management Research* 1(1), 30–45.

Rogers, P.P., Jalal, K.F. and Boyd, J.A. (2008) *An Introduction to Sustainable Development*. Earthscan Publications, London.

Stern, N. (2006) *The Economics of Climate Change: The Stern Review*. UK Treasury, London.

UK Sport (2005) *Staging Major Sports Events: The Guide*. UK Sport, London.

UNCSD (2007) *Sustainable Development: The Road towards the 2007 Session of the Commission on Sustainable Development (CSD-15)*. United Nations Commission on Sustainable Development, New York, New York.

Van der Ryn, S. and Calthorpe, P. (1991) *Sustainable Communities: A New Design Synthesis for Cities, Suburbs and Towns*. Sierra Club Books, San Francisco, California.

WBCSD (1998) *Exploring Sustainable Development, WBSCD Global Scenarios 2000–2005*. World Business Council for Sustainable Development, Geneva, Switzerland.

WCED (World Commission on Environment and Development) (1987) *Our Common Future: Report of the World Commission on Environment and Development (The Bruntland Commission)*. Oxford University Press, Oxford, UK.

WWF and SustainAbility (2007) *One Planet Business – Creating Value within Planetary Limits*. World Wide Fund for Nature–UK, Surrey, UK.

2 Policy, Politics and Sustainable Events

M. Foley, D. McGillivray and G. McPherson
Glasgow Caledonian University, Glasgow, UK

This chapter aims to give critical consideration to the emergence of events policy as a distinctive field of study within the wider events management literature. It examines the political, social and economic conditions within which an entrepreneurial events policy became prominent, before concentrating attention on the emergence of a more socially aware policy context in the early 21st century. The chapter concludes by challenging policy makers and politicians alike to more fully embed a concern with social utility into their events policy ambitions.

Chapter outline

- Introduction
- Events Policy and Politics: an Emerging Field of Study
- The Changing Function of Events
- The Emergence of the Social Policy Case for Events
- Community Cohesion and Identity
- From Social Impact to Social Leverage: the Policy Panacea?
- Summary
- Key Questions

Introduction

Urban events policy is being created and shaped to transform or restructure social space on the premise of attracting and winning major events to the urban environment. Local city policy makers and their central government counterparts are increasingly aware of the global 'neo-liberalized' order that is emerging (Brenner and Theodore, 2005). While still pre-eminent, the economic imperative to transform urban social spaces is now subject to some challenge. In recent years there has been a greater emphasis placed on the 'software' of people and places alongside the 'hardware' of infrastructure and economic return on investment. As we enter the 21st century, sustainable social, cultural and environmental benefits are likely to preoccupy policy makers, academics and citizens as the global argument of civic boosterism is challenged for overestimating benefits and underestimating costs (Whitson and Horne, 2006).

Events Policy and Politics: an Emerging Field of Study

The emergence of a distinct field of study that can be termed 'events policy' is a recent phenomenon. Getz (2007) allocates a chapter of his *Event Studies* text to the theme but, in the main, events policy has been an afterthought in the curriculum of higher education provision in events management and has been noticeable by its absence in the growing events research field. As a field of study, events management has broadly evolved three stages of complexity, depicted in Table 2.1.

First, we have the stage of events management. This stage works at a purely instrumental level. Reflecting on practical experience, it reaches general conclusions about what works organizationally and it essentially produces a 'how to' approach. There is little attempt to contextualize these general micro-level conclusions. This stage is replete with a veritable avalanche of published materials reflecting the need to underpin the academic study of a new field as demand for higher education courses grows at an exponential rate. In the second stage – what we call the events policy stage – some attempt is made to contextualize events within a macro-level context. Researchers formulate questions from a policy angle and inquiries are made into the socio-economic (and sociocultural) effects of an events-led policy. Attention is also paid to what constitutes an effective use of events and, occasionally, into what the goals of events policy might be (e.g. to develop civic pride). At the third level, events studies, events are located in a broader socio-historical context. This situates events from the perspective of social, cultural and economic reproduction.

Table 2.1. Events management stages of complexity.

Stage	Characteristics
Events management	Instrumental Practical experience Operational/logistical Micro-level concerns Abundant literature
Events policy	Macro-level contextualization Policy angle evident Social, cultural and economic effects of events considered Paucity of specialized literature
Events studies	Considers wider socio-historical context for events Macro-level concerns Informed by a range of academic disciplines Emerging literature

Here, we are concerned with debates about the significance of an events-led strategy for local and central governments approached with a theoretical preoccupation drawn from the third stage – events studies. In drawing from political economy and political science, we can analyse the role of events policy in the wider context of capitalist accumulation and reproduction, especially the role of events as a tool in inter-urban competition and the questions of power interests and decision making at local/central government level focusing specifically on public–private partnerships and coalitions of interest groups (Hall, 2006). Human geography, in particular, provides the analytical tools to question the role of events in the division of urban space, especially in the context of 'gentrification debates' (MacLeod, 2002) and the potential spatial injustices that are an outcome of events-led entrepreneurial governance. A sociological approach helps researchers to assess the importance of events in public culture debates, whereby they are used to generate and reinforce particular versions of public culture (Roche, 2000) and can legitimate existing or new discourses of national identity (Waitt, 2003).

The Changing Function of Events

Historically, the Roman emperors were well-versed in the use of welfare (bread) and festivities (circuses) as a means of retaining authority over their subjects. They believed that by providing sustenance and amusement the threat of discontent over their rule could be minimized. As Veyne (1990) suggests, the Romans' view was that 'it is good to provide recreation from time to time for the childlike people, in the interests of authority itself' (p. 418). Crucially, for our understanding of the historical role of state-supported patronage, in Roman times control was exercised over the nature and scope of the circuses offered for consumption.

Temporal confinement (select days and types of events were offered) focused the minds of the ruled and was convenient for the rulers as they could dictate the outcomes they sought from the gift of these amusements. In the present day, there are clear continuities with the past as spectacular events such as the Olympics are offered to the populace in return for their active consent and approval (Waitt, 2001).

What is certain is that hallmark, special or mega-events, along with associated culture-led regeneration processes, are part of the refashioning of urban governance in the context of the neoliberalized state and its roll-back of managerial welfare programmes. A key feature of this refashioning is that the principal risks are borne by a highly active entrepreneurial (local) state, with the involvement of the private sector being conditional upon the support of the public purse as a safety net. The underbelly of this is that, having abandoned welfare programmes in the midst of neoliberal roll-backs, local and central governments are now struggling to address the 'problem' of socially marginalized groups who have not shared equally in the (apparent) rewards emanating from the new consumerism. In fact, as Zukin (1995) argues, the socially marginalized are systematically excluded from the disciplined spaces of consuming cities. Cities have taken over the mantle from nations as the most important focus of regimes of accumulation and the outcome is inter-urban competition involving city branding and specialization as a means of attracting private investment and inward visits. The last decade has witnessed the emergence of an entrepreneurial event policy in the affluent West (particularly, though not exclusively) marked by a reliance on largely unaccountable public–private growth coalitions that enable publicly funded entrepreneurship to flourish. However, the presence of continuing spatial injustices (MacLeod, 2002), social polarities and disenfranchised groups has drawn attention to the (un)sustainability of an events policy based solely on economic logic.

Over recent years there has been an emergence of new policy-making bodies (e.g. Scotland's EventScotland), new festivities and the reinvention of traditional events as branded, lifestyle products. These changes have significant implications for nations, regions and neighbourhoods with respect to shifting the landscape of events from their original role as vehicles for collective identity to their centrality in global economic strategies – to the extent that they are subject to ever-greater controls and surveillance and thus become sites of social conflict over meaning and representation. The international competition for global events also influences national and local political action as the institutional foundations for 'winning' events are resourced to the detriment of other means of delivering on public policy objectives. The oft-cited touristic intention of events policy focuses on an entrepreneurial approach to urban politics within which cities (and nations) focus on territorial and urban competition through events-led specialization. However, it remains unclear as to whether, at the global/national level, greater integration is secured between the popular spectacular element of events and local community representation and empowerment – or alienation.

In bidding for the right to host hallmark or sporting mega-events, cities compete to secure the attention of global markets for investment and tourism. However, the governance structures formed to permit entrepreneurial activity to flourish can, at the same time, reduce levels of public participation and ownership of the policy-making process. Subsidized through the public purse, events and festivals have increasingly been invented or manufactured to satisfy the lifestyle aspirations of the sought-after tourist audiences. However, in so doing, the displacement outcomes of this sort of public policy are often stifled as positive, pro-growth messages emerge from political leaders. On a global scale there is no doubt that cities are trying to brand their identities and images through place and product association. The deliberate attempt to win the right to host large-scale sporting events allows them to develop a cultural infrastructure that accrues touristic advantage in showcasing the spectacle so that they can also win over people, investment and identity (Hall, 2006). Of course this is not a new strategy; the city planners of the 19th century did this too when hosting World Expos, which, although primarily about showcasing global trade and industry, were never without fanfare, entertainment and a demonstration of global public culture (Roche, 2000). It is the intensification of the process that is astounding and the extent to which local actors are peripheral to the power play and decision-making processes that legitimate the policy objectives. But perhaps this is too one-sided? Are there no intimations of the spectacle being opposed (Debord, 1967) as the emperor is shown to have no clothes? Perhaps the answer lies in the social and cultural milieu and in the focus of sustainability.

The Emergence of the Social Policy Case for Events

While the study of distinct events-related phenomena has grown significantly since the late 1980s, there remains a knowledge gap in understanding of the social impact of events and festivals on host communities and beyond. Over recent years much more academic attention has been paid to whether the needs of direct and indirect 'beneficiaries' (Whitson and Horne, 2006) are being adequately served by the furtherance of events-led urban strategies. The attraction and delivery of large-scale (often sporting) events is used by urban centres the world over to lever additional net economic benefits to their cities. However, the accompanying discourses of this neoliberalizing process – entrepreneurialism, managerialism and regeneration – reflect the instrumental economic ethos of government intervention in a significant number of post-industrial economies. What we need to ask ourselves is whether these intended outcomes are sustainable in the longer term when a circuit of cities adopts very similar events-led strategies. When they are competing with other equally spectacular global cultural forms, it is increasingly difficult for global event spectacles to impress and attract the targeted global investors and tourist tribes. Instead, events policy makers and city fathers seeking distinctiveness might be better served focusing on developing a social and cultural legacy that outlives the ephemeral economic boost of the 'mega-event'. This is certainly the suggestion of Chalip (2006), who argues that sport event production is too often about 'spectacle rather than festival' and 'economic impact rather than social value' (p. 111).

While spectacle might well attract the attention of global media conglomerates around the event core zone (Roche, 2000), as the road show moves on to its next destination, policy makers are invariably left with an anticlimactic fallout and a challenging set of internal political issues concerned with explaining how the 'legitimating rhetoric' (Chalip, 2006, p. 112) of economic return is to be turned into reality in the future. When the public gives its political leaders the consent to bid for events on the basis of securing transformations for professed beneficiaries – often the poor, the young and minority groups – then their failure to deliver takes on greater political significance. Policy makers are acutely aware that if the much-vaunted economic returns fail to transpire and the physical legacy depreciates thereafter, then the political fallout from citizens is likely to increase. It is here that the economic hegemony is in danger of breaking down, where the dualism of civic promotion and civic unity is challenged. If civic (place) promotion, with its economic imperative, continues to take precedence over investment in meaningful civic unity, then the fragile consensus that events represent good value for host communities will come under increased scrutiny.

It is in this context that the ubiquity of the events-as-economic-salvation discourse has attracted a fair amount of criticism. For example, Misener and Mason (2006) argue that, until recently, pro-growth urban renewal strategies have failed to give adequate cognizance to the wider community benefits accruable from investment in a sports event strategy. While the economic imperative had taken precedent, urban regeneration had been narrowly defined around the encouragement of public investment and infrastructural developments (the hardware). But in the sprint for city marketing gain, tourism inward visits and resources for development efforts, the diversity of host community beneficiaries has often been overlooked. Similarly, concern has been expressed at the way public resources are channelled to private beneficiaries, with the 'benefits' not always obvious to citizens – especially those in poorer communities. Until now, the economic imperative has tended to ensure that the social and cultural benefits of events have been downplayed. However, with the economic hegemony now being questioned due to the failure of some events to generate the professed returns, renewed focus has turned to the verification of the social impact of events on host communities and an accompanying critique of the actual beneficiaries of investment in events. This is a timely intervention, as the high-profile mega-event failures of Montreal (1976) and Athens (2004) have placed the issue of a sustainable people-focused legacy to the fore in the minds of policy makers, practitioners and academe alike (see Table 2.2).

No longer is it sufficient for potential host cities or nations to take for granted the support of their citizenry. In fact, securing the support of the local population has now been enshrined formally in the governance process with the creation of the term 'legacy' as a moniker for the planned, strategic and tactical leverage of social value to the relevant communities of interest (whether they be sports associations, local citizens or local government) (Chalip, 2006). The achievement of positive social externalities has, to some extent, become a prerequisite of a successful events-led policy imperative. Outside China, so-called 'white elephant' signature buildings are a thing of the past – physical legacies are only valuable if they facilitate wider social returns on investment and improvements in the host community's social and cultural capital. This is illustrative of a shift towards sport events, in particular, being used as a vehicle for regeneration and renewal (see the Olympics in Seoul, Barcelona and Sydney). What we are now experiencing is a step-change towards events having to transform and renew a city's cultural and social landscape rather than just its physical one. In policy terms, the events continue to act as a catalyst or a lever for economic growth but they are also now expected to invest in the development of the host city's social and cultural capital (Flinn and McPherson, 2007). Events policy in many UK cities is now inseparable from cultural policy and officials sit around the same table as social policy makers. We have seen shifts in social and urban policy from an (over)reliance on 'financial capital and infrastructural investment to a concentration on people and the development of social capital' (Coalter, 2001, p. v). Cities seek to develop a broad cultural tapestry not only as a tourist attraction but also as a tool in the sustainable development of communities.

Table 2.2. Event policy hardware and software.

Event legacy intention	Principal imperatives	Outcomes
Hardware (place)	Economic, physical	Physical infrastructure (e.g. stadia, transport) Inward investment Tourism Job creation Skill development
Software (people)	Social, cultural	Social capital Civic pride Quality of life Ownership and decision-making capacity Social cohesion Health Volunteerism

Community Cohesion and Identity

Historically, festivals and special events have played a significant role in defining a community's sense of place and identity. In the events policy field there is resurgence in interest in the role that collective celebrations might play in generating social cohesion through the building of linkages within and between communities and enabling these communities to communicate with each other in more productive ways. While the role of traditional festivities and fairs fixed in time and space in producing community identities is well covered in the literature, there remains some doubt as to the value of mobile and peripatetic sporting mega-events in generating the self-same 'benefits' to their host communities.

The theoretical basis for the social case for events is built on the view that they can work as the 'social glue' of communities by aiding capacity building and through cementing a sense of place identity (whether a nation, a city or a neighbourhood) (Waterman, 1998; Derrett, 2003). Proponents argue that events and festivals can assuage feelings of alienation and social isolation experienced in some of the most challenging community circumstances. Arai and Pedlar (2003, p. 199) suggest that festivals can 'reconnect leisure with the quality of community life, social engagement, and the achievement of the common good', a view mirrored by Foley and McPherson (2007). Other social benefits are linked to the feeling of pride in the host city engendered by the hosting of a large-scale event – but again, the evidence suggests that higher property prices, displacement, inconvenience and the financial legacy of revenue funding can be punitive for lower-income groups, in particular. Aligning with the renewed focus on social capital, McDonnell *et al.* (1999) define a series of positive social impacts emanating from the hosting of events. First, they argue for the benefits of generating shared experience, which can replace other forms of collective solidarity that have diminished in importance (e.g. trade unions, political parties). However, the critique of the depth of this solidarity is that it is unsustainable, more likely to be a fleeting and transitory coming together of people in proto-communities (Maffesoli, 1991). Second, critics ask whose version of 'experience' is being shared (Waitt, 2003). It is also proposed that the development of community pride – of subjective feelings of hope and a renewed achievement orientation – represents a positive social outcome of event hosting. Taken a step further, this renewed community pride can lever additional community participation, engagement and ownership. Yet, in her studies of Barcelona, Glasgow and Sydney, Garcia (2004) remains unconvinced of the linkages between urban sporting spectacles and the participation and representation of local populations. Others offer the opportunity for citizens to extend their cultural horizons and experiences as a positive externality accruing from hosting large-scale events. However, critical commentators suggest that this could also be seen as a means to exert social control to address the loss of identity associated with class, age, ethnicity and place brought about by the change in economic structures towards post-industrialism.

While the literature discussing the positive social impact of events is growing quickly, there is also a fairly significant body of work emerging on the negative social impacts of sporting mega-events, in particular. These include community alienation, whereby the host populations (or segments of it, at least) experience feelings of being ignored with respect to decisions about event bidding, planning and delivery. Hall (2006) documents the manner in which public–private pro-growth coalitions involved in running large sports events can increasingly operate in an autonomous fashion, even to the extent that they benefit from legislative fast-tracking to circumvent normal democratic processes. This creates a democratic deficit, which further distances community groups from active participation in decision-making processes. With respect to the ills generated during the delivery of a large-scale sporting event itself, McDonnell *et al.* (1999) suggest that a negative community image can be formed in the form of substance abuse, a (perhaps temporary) loss of amenities and the opportunity costs associated with expenditure on facilities and infrastructure to support large-scale events – the focus of the campaigns operated by Toronto's Bread Not Circuses protest group against the 2008 Olympics bid.

From Social Impact to Social Leverage: the Policy Panacea?

There is an ongoing debate within the events literature as to the most appropriate terminology to use to represent the social value of events. For example, Chalip (2006) decries over-use of the term 'impacts' in the literature, instead proposing use of the word 'leverage' to refer to the potential social value of sports events. Crucially, the focus on leverage represents a change in emphasis towards pre-event legacy planning instead of the *ad hoc* nature of many social impact (*post hoc*) studies. So, while economic and social impact studies can provide useful *post hoc* analyses of what outcomes were accrued, these studies do not tell us about '*why* those outcomes occurred' (Chalip, 2006, p. 112). This focus on the pre-event desired outcomes provides policy makers and politicians with a much more meaningful, action-based approach that can demonstrate the commitment of the host to securing social value from its events rather than merely acting to legitimate public sector investment after the event has ended. The host community is much more involved in deciding and owning strategies in a social leverage-based approach – thus lending itself to more interactive participation and engagement techniques. However, alongside a commitment to social leverage is the need for a longer-term commitment to empirical work designed to track social outcomes over an extended period of time, across levels of governance and through event phases (i.e. from bidding, through management, to legacy/impact evaluation). It is difficult to measure the value of events in strengthening the social fabric or as a tool for the exploration of identity (local, national and international), to explore social concerns of the time and to symbolically explore the existing social order. However, by adopting more innovative and creative methodological approaches it is possible to understand more about how events can enable greater cross-community sociability by providing opportunities for sharing time, space and activities at venues and in the wider cityscape and by facilitating informal social opportunities (e.g. by creating cultural festivities apart from the main venues). This task also requires us to look further into how lasting social networks are forged through events. While the burgeoning social capital (see Putnam, 1993, 2000) literature is clear on the benefits of social networks on health, community development and entrepreneurial success, there has been little detailed investigation of the role events can play in building sustainable community capacity. There is some evidence to suggest that events can permit dialogue and relationships to form across age, gender, social class and ethnic categories that are otherwise very difficult to bridge. If events policy and planning permits the social leverage to begin at the very earliest stage of the event production process (especially with respect to peripatetic sports events), then the foundations can be laid for community learning and well-being to be meaningfully practised around the vehicle of events. However, the challenge facing event policy makers is that, 'if events are mere entertainments, and audiences are crowds that need to be managed and controlled, then social leverage is not possible' (Chalip, 2006, p. 123). Instead, policy makers need to look beyond the economic imperative to plan in social legacy using a strategic approach – engaging its beneficiaries early on in the process and matching the city's overarching policy drivers to the intended outcomes associated with the event.

If, as the theory suggests, events can generate a sense of collective responsibility by encouraging participation in community initiatives, then their potential for long-lasting social value can be realized. The social capital literature in the fields of health, community development and volunteering indicates that social well-being, community learning and community safety are achievable outcomes from the creation of productive social capital – especially when decision making is decentralized and communities are empowered to improve their own lives. In the events field, Misener and Mason (2006) have shown that Manchester was successful in using its 2002 Commonwealth Games to generate social capital in its most disenfranchised communities. They suggest that in order to secure these benefits: community values should be central to all decision making; various stakeholders, particularly community interest groups, should be involved in strategic activities related to events (e.g. bid process, management, legacy); collaborative action should empower local communities to become agents of change; open communication and mutual learning throughout strategic activities related to events must be maintained to minimize power brokering; and events need to embrace the core values of residents, community groups and neighbourhood associations. This process also needs to involve respecting community definitions of place and space and not those only of private ventures. While there are dangers in attempting to institutionalize and impose social capital on communities, it is important that local governments play a significant role in the 'institutionalisation of group norms and values' and the 'formalisation of networks' (Misener and Mason, 2006, p. 45). The development of appropriate networks must, however, take cognizance of the complexities of social capital. This requires a rethink on behalf of stakeholders, including academe, to move from a concentration on hardware to the much more amorphous, people-oriented approach compatible with a commitment to software.

Summary

This chapter has argued for the more sustainable approach to events policy that has emerged since the late 1980s. Community groups need to participate more meaningfully in decision-making processes with their political leaders and local government structures. Rather than being the font of all knowledge, local governments must catalyse change, a model that chimes with the emerging focus in UK local government on Community and Cultural Planning, whereby subsidiarity is a key feature and services are delivered in partnership by a series of public, private and voluntary associations.

The vehicle of events must be used to engage and empower community groups to contribute to community building long after the 'signature' event itself has moved on. Creating appropriate structures is crucial here so that the usual suspects do not continue to feel marginalized as cities pursue events-led strategies. The challenge for local political leaders is to consider whether the existing networks and avenues to participation open to the city's citizens are effective. Policy makers must avoid destroying 'organic' social capital by over-planning and power brokering and by expecting all social networks to open up despite the power relations at work within these groups.

What is required is a much deeper commitment to ongoing legacy planning around a city's events, so that policy makers can maximize social utility not only during the celebratory phase of event delivery, but for the longer term. Only then can events secure the long-lasting effects about which their patrons proselytize on a regular basis. Perhaps the call to reconsider the social and cultural in events policy can temper the concerns of citizens and protestors alike. The spectacle need not be opposed, but rather diluted, so that the social outcomes of event policy are shared more equally across a range of beneficiaries in a move from entrepreneurialism to social entrepreneurialism.

Key Questions

1. As events management emerges as a distinct field of study, why is there a need for events policy to form a more important element of this field?
2. Until recently, policy makers have been concerned primarily with the hardware of events as opposed to the software. Why is this changing?
3. What are the main differences between the concept of social impact and social leverage, and why are these important for event policy makers?

References

Arai, S. and Pedlar, A. (2003) Moving beyond individualism in leisure theory: a critical analysis of concepts of community and social engagement. *Leisure Studies* 22(3), 185–202.

Brenner, N. and Theodore, N. (2005) Neoliberalism and the urban condition. *City* 9(1), 101–107.

Chalip, L. (2006) Towards social leverage of sport events. *Journal of Sport & Tourism* 11(2), 109–127.

Coalter, F. (2001) *Realising the Value of Cultural Services: The Case for Sport*. LGA, London.

Debord, G. (1967) *The Society of the Spectacle* (English translation, 1995). Zone Books, New York.

Derrett, R. (2003) Making sense of how festivals demonstrate a community sense of place. *Events Management* 8, 49–58.

Flinn, J. and McPherson, G. (2007) Culture matters? The role of art and culture in the development of social capital. In: Collins, M., Holmes, K. and Slater, A. (eds) *Sport, Leisure, Culture and Social Capital: Discourse and Practice*. Leisure Studies Association, Eastbourne, UK, pp. 119–138.

Foley, M. and McPherson, G. (2007) Glasgow's Winter Festival: culture leadership for the common good? *Managing Leisure* 12(3), 1–16.

Garcia, B. (2004) Urban regeneration, arts programming and major events. *International Journal of Cultural Policy* 10(1), 103–118.

Getz, D. (2007) *Event Studies: Theory, Research and Policy for Planned Events*. Elsevier, Oxford, UK.

Hall, C.M. (2006) Urban entrepreneurship, corporate interests, and sports mega-events: the thin policies of competitiveness within the hard outcomes of neo liberalism. *The Sociological Review* 54(Suppl. 2), 59–70.

MacLeod, G. (2002) From urban entrepreneurialism to a 'revanchist city'? On the spatial injustices of Glasgow's renaissance. *Antipode* 34(3), 602–624.

Maffesoli, M. (1991) *The Time of the Tribes: the Decline of Individualism in Mass Society*. Sage, London.

McDonnell, I., Allen, J. and O'Toole, W. (1999) *Festival and Special Event Management*. John Wiley and Sons, Brisbane, Australia.

Misener, L. and Mason, D.S. (2006) Creating community networks: can sporting events offer meaningful sources of social capital? *Managing Leisure* 11(1), 39–56.

Putnam, R. (1993) The prosperous community: social capital and public life. *The American Prospect* 13. Available at: http://xroads.virginia.edu/~HYPER/DETOC/assoc/13putn.html

Putnam, R. (2000) *Bowling Alone – The Collapse and Revival of American Community*. Simon & Schuster, New York.

Roche, M. (2000) *Mega-events and Modernity: Olympics and Expos in the Growth of Global Culture*. Routledge, London.

Veyne, P. (1990) *Bread and Circuses: Historical Sociology and Political Pluralism* (Brian Pearce, trans.). Penguin, London.

Waitt, G. (2001) The Olympic spirit and civic boosterism: the Sydney 2000 Olympics. *Tourism Geographies* 3(3), 249–278.

Waitt, G. (2003) Social impacts of the Sydney Olympics. *Annals of Tourism Research* 30(1), 194–215.

Waterman, S. (1998) Carnivals for elites: the cultural politics of arts festivals. *Progress in Human Geography* 22(1), 54–74.

Whitson, D. and Horne, J. (2006) Underestimated costs and overestimated benefits? Comparing the outcomes of sports mega-events in Canada and Japan. *The Sociological Review* 54(Suppl. 2), 71–89.

Zukin, S. (1995) *The Cultures of Cities*. Blackwell, Oxford, UK.

3 Sustainability as a Concept within Events

C. Smith-Christensen
Event Research International (ERi), Oslo, Norway

This chapter examines the concept of sustainability within the event industry, and specifically assesses the contribution of the events industry to sustainable development. The purpose is to improve stakeholders' ability to make informed decisions with regard to resource allocation, and to contribute to enhanced communication between stakeholders in fundraising and marketing.

Chapter outline

- Introduction
- The Concept of Sustainability within the Context of Events
- Responsible Events – Events for Sustainable Development
- Sustainable Responsible Events – Trend or Passing Fad?
- Externalities and Market Failures in the Event Industry
- Development Objectives – Considering Individual and Societal Needs
- Summary
- Question Introduction
- Key Questions

Introduction

The term 'sustainability' comes from the verb 'sustain', which derives from the old French verb 'sustenir', meaning to support, keep up or maintain something. In music, for instance, sustain is a parameter of musical sound in time, denoting the period of time during which the sound is sustained before it becomes inaudible. The adjective 'sustainable' follows as the ability to be sustained.

One of the first and most cited definitions of sustainability was created in 1987 by the Brundtland Commission, which defined sustainable development as development that 'meets the needs of the present without compromising the ability of future generations to meet their own needs' (UN, 1987).

While the concept of sustainable development represented a new approach to societal progress, it also introduced sustainability as a buzzword to become commonly used in managerial, technical, administrative and, sometimes, political forums. It was later attached to a number of terms including sustainable business, sustainable living, sustainable tourism and, now, sustainable events.

While buzzwords may be used to elaborate a text or to impress through a speech, buzzwords can also be ambiguous, making sentences difficult to dispute on account of their cloudy meaning. According to George Orwell's *Politics and the English Language* (1946), a critical essay on the English language, people use buzzwords because they are convenient. It is much easier to copy the words and phrases that someone else invented than it is to come up with one's own.

The Concept of Sustainability within the Context of Events

Sustainability is characterized as a process or state that can be maintained at a certain level indefinitely; thus 'sustainable events' would be events that can be maintained at a certain level indefinitely. If applying the strictest definition of sustainability, the term 'sustainable event' would primarily make sense from a management perspective, denoting an event organized as an autonomous cyclical process, which is the only process that can be maintained over time.

However, events are generally defined as transitory in nature, infrequent in occurrence and limited in time (Getz, 1991; Stiernstrand, 1996) – features opposing the general definition of sustainability. Thus in the context of events the term 'sustainability' is ambiguous. Consequently, if not specified, use of the term sustainability in the context of events may be flawed in its logic, hence representing a potential fallacy that can render an argument invalid. This should be of concern to all event stakeholders, who need an explicit vocabulary in order to make informed decisions and promote various agendas.

Sustainable events – a management concept

Events basically depend on three components: an organizing body; a place to host the event; and an audience. Each constituency is represented by stakeholders and custodians – the event management team, host community and event-goers, respectively – each essential for the event's existence (see Fig. 3.1).

> **Proposed Definition 1**
> Sustainable events: events managed as an autonomous cyclical process through the interaction between event management, host community and event-goers.

Events are not only a result of the interaction between event management, the host community and event-goers, but equally depend on the provision and allocation of resources, including human resources, infrastructure and funds.

- *Human resources*. Human resources are fundamental to the organization of events. Most events have a more or less formal event organization, with a management team including temporary employees, volunteers, etc. Second, human resources within the host community are also important. Events need the support of people directly or indirectly involved as product- and service-providers, people providing public services, local politicians and local residents, who not only represent a potential audience but whose acceptance and support are essential for the success of an event. Third, events depend on human resources in the form of event-goers, locals and/or international visitors actively taking part in the event.
- *Infrastructure*. Although the events industry confirms that people can achieve a lot with little or no remuneration (e.g. volunteers), there will always be the need for infrastructure. Besides the natural environment, necessary infrastructure includes sites or venues providing the physical platform for hosting the event, roads and airports

Fig. 3.1. Sustainable events (SE).

providing access, as well as services such as parking, electricity and waste management. Even events taking place in cyberspace depend on infrastructure, such as the World Wide Web and computers.

- *Funds*. While some events are more costly to pull off than others, most depend on a minimum amount of financial resources for marketing, licenses, insurance, tax, etc. Furthermore, few events are able to grow or maintain a momentum without financial resources. Funds are generally provided through the event owners, paying attendees, private sector sponsors and/or government allocating public resources.

The ultimate task of the event manager is therefore based on the following concept: through the mobilization and allocation of resources (human resources, infrastructure and funds), to produce a programme that maintains the support of the various stakeholders and custodians.

> **Proposed Definition 2**
> Sustainable events: events managed as an autonomous cyclical process through the interaction between event management, host community and event-goers, providing human resources, infrastructure and funds.

This definition of sustainable events should, however, not go unchallenged. For the concept to be meaningful it is, first of all, important to clarify how it applies to events organized one-off and events organized on a regular basis, respectively. Based on the aforementioned rationale, it makes little sense to talk about a sustainable one-off event. For regularly organized events, the life cycle discourse can provide certain insight, specifically into the challenge of maintaining momentum.

Only certain events could arguably be considered truly sustainable. Examples include events embedded in cultural and religious traditions (e.g. Christmas, Ramadan, Yom Kippur, Divali, New Year celebrations, etc.) and celebratory events based on historical dates such as constitution days, commemorations, etc. There are in addition a few other events that, due to broad international support, have managed to establish and maintain a hosting tradition. Such events include the Olympic Games and certain World Championships. These events are, despite immense cost, attractive to host owing to their prestige and the perception that they contribute to broader societal development objectives. This phenomenon leads us to the relevant question of whether an event that depends on public sector funding can be defined as sustainable. We will revert to this conundrum later in the chapter when addressing the case of externalities and market failures in the event sector.

Responsible Events – Events for Sustainable Development

Until now, the concept of sustainable events has been approached from a managerial stance. If, however, the intention is to address events in the context of sustainable development, it is relevant to consider the impacts that events have within a host community and on its ability to contribute to development goals.

Events produce impacts across the triple bottom line (TBL), which refers to the economy, socioculture and the environment. Impacts can be positive as well as negative, tangible in addition to intangible. While tangible impacts relate to material outcomes (e.g. venues, physical structures, etc.), intangible impacts entail non-material effects such as sociocultural benefits (e.g. community development, civic pride, etc.) and costs (e.g. disruption to lifestyles, noise, crowding, etc.), as well as socio-economic benefits (e.g. promotional benefits, induced development, etc.) and costs (e.g. resident exodus, under-utilized infrastructure, etc.) (Dwyer *et al.*, 2000).

Corporate social responsibility (CSR) is a concept whereby organizations and businesses consider the interests of society by taking responsibility for the impacts of their activities. Today most major corporate companies emphasize their developmental commitment by promoting non-economic and societal values through CSR charters, codes of conduct, statement of core values, etc. Recognizing that social responsibility can also be good for business and yield financial returns has led to an increased reference to corporate social investment (CSI). Considering its integrated nature, growth and professional evolution, it is reasonable to anticipate similar trends within the event industry, and expect an increased adoption of developmental strategies and arguing 'responsibility' accordingly.

Supplementing the proposed definitions of sustainable events, the concept of 'responsible events' is introduced to signify events that are locality-centric in nature and implement proactive measures (through resource allocation) to contribute to local sustainable development across the TBL (see Fig. 3.2).

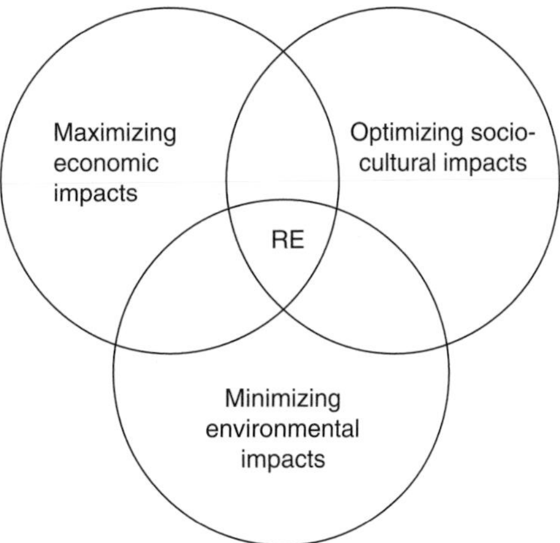

Fig. 3.2. Responsible events (RE).

> **Proposed Definition 3**
> Responsible events: events sensitive to the economic, sociocultural and environmental needs within the local host community, and organized in such a way as to optimize the net holistic (positive) output.

Measuring the responsibility of an event

The net holistic output measures the value of the gain across the TBL (i.e. economy, socioculture and environment) less the cost of enabling this extra output (adapted from Dwyer *et al.*, 2005, p. 71). While impacts of events is a popular research topic (Formica, 1998; Getz, 2000; Hede *et al.*, 2002), most researchers have, to date, applied a functional 'silo-based approach' to the evaluation of events, considering economic, sociocultural and environmental impacts separately rather than holistically (Fredline *et al.*, 2005; Sherwood *et al.*, 2005). Unfortunately, the net holistic output remains a theoretical measure until an all-inclusive approach denoting fiscal, or at least measurable, values to intangible outcomes is developed and generally accepted. This challenge is yet unsolved but increasingly addressed among academics.

For events to contribute to sustainable development there needs to be a balance between economic, sociocultural and environmental objectives, with strategies in place for optimizing positive and minimizing negative impacts. Instead of uncritically adopting CSR schemes applied in other industries, it is important to recognize the unique features of events and the events industry and develop operational strategies whereby event stakeholders act responsibly and thereby contribute to development. Ideally, programme development and resource allocation would be guided by local needs. Besides adopting responsible practices because it is 'the right thing to do', a responsibly organized event embedded within a destination through a programme addressing local needs is more likely to gain stakeholder support, which again can contribute to recurrence and thereby its sustainability.

Sustainable Responsible Events – Trend or Passing Fad?

There is a clear trend of events being promoted as 'sustainable', 'green' or 'carbon-neutral'. Up until now, sustainable events have primarily been used to flag environmental consciousness. Reasons for this are most likely that: the environment rates high on the public agenda; 'best practice' resources are available; and impacts have been relatively easy to monitor, estimate and communicate.

Still emerging, the events industry can benefit from looking to associated industries like tourism. While the tourism industry has promoted environmentally sensitive tourism for years, there is an increasing demand for products and services that are not only sensitive to but also proactively contribute to sustainable development. Sustainable, pro-poor and responsible tourism are some of the many classifications adopted. Despite this positive trend, the industry's movement towards sustainability and responsibility remains challenged by ambiguous semantics and lack of transparency and accountability relating to the implementation of these classifications.

As within the tourism industry, events are increasingly looking to certifications and brands to strategically establish and strengthen stakeholder partnerships. While certifications and brands may indicate responsibility, they do not necessarily guarantee an event's contribution to local sustainable development. A general problem is the lack of transparency, leaving event-goers as well as funding or sponsoring partners uncertain of whether the event in question actually should be considered responsible through its contribution to sustainable development.

A common challenge among event managers is to establish strategic partnerships with private sector sponsors and/or public sector funders. While many manage to secure sizeable sponsorships and maintain good and long-lasting relationships with their patrons, others struggle to secure the necessary funds. The latter generally represent smaller, community-based events, often including developmental objectives. Some event managers appoint professional fundraisers, while others depend on well-connected volunteers. In competing for funds and sponsorship, even the most professional event manager may find it challenging to argue the benefits, return on investment (ROI) and return on objectives (ROO) of supporting the event (see Box 3.1). A plausible explanation for these challenges may be that the fundraiser and potential funder/sponsor do not 'speak the same language'. The lack of an explicit vocabulary makes it difficult for those not familiar with the event industry to understand what is meant by sustainable and/or responsible events.

Thus, the intention of suggesting a stipulative definition of sustainable events, and introducing the concept of responsible events, is to improve communication among stakeholders and to enhance the capability for making informed decisions specifically relating to resource allocation.

Externalities and Market Failures in the Event Industry

Most event managers strive to organize if not an autonomous, then a financially viable event attractive to its target market. While attractiveness is a question of concept, programme and marketing, financial viability is a matter of resource allocation. The two following scenarios signify the importance of differentiating the concepts of sustainable events and responsible events.

Events depending on funds over and above what is generated through the market and event activities: The concept and programme of an event can be more or less commercially geared. While some events are autonomous and financed entirely through participation or entrance fees, other events may offer a programme providing free access to the public (Burgan and Mules, 2001). Examples include street parades, open-air markets and religious celebrations. In the case where free access is provided, the true cost of organizing the event

Box 3.1. Return on investment versus return on objectives.

Return on investment (ROI) is a performance measure used to evaluate the economic efficiency of an investment or to compare the efficiency of a number of different investments (Investopedia, 2008). Return on objectives (ROO), on the other hand, aims to gauge an investment's efficiency according to the achievement of more or less tangible goals, such as developmental goals across the TBL. While ROI is expressed as a percentage, measuring ROO is less straightforward, requiring the translation of intangible objectives into indicators that can be assigned a value (Burns *et al.*, 1986; Dwyer *et al.*, 2000; Fredline *et al.*, 2005; Sherwood and Jago, 2005).

exceeds consumers' provisions. Such events generally rely on a combination of private sector sponsorship, public sector funding, in-kind contributions and volunteering. Potential private sector sponsors primarily consider marketing synergies and ROI. Public sector funders, on the other hand, are generally interested in the event's ability to support political and developmental agendas, thereby optimizing ROO as well as maximizing the ROI of public funds. While recurring events may show previous impact studies, it is difficult for funders and sponsors to specifically gauge the likely ROO and ROI for first-time or one-off events. Contemplating involvement and support, both private and public sector stakeholders will be interested in the sustainability (i.e. resource allocation) as well as responsibility (i.e. contribution to development) of the event in question.

Events where externalities create market failures: In theory, market mechanisms regulate supply and demand. There are, however, circumstances where these mechanisms fail. In the events industry, market failures can occur when activities and economic transactions associated with the event cause externalities. An externality is an impact (positive or negative) from a given action causing costs or benefits to a third party. In other words, externalities cause market failures when the participants in an economic transaction do not bear all of the costs or reap all of the benefits of the transaction.

Externalities become problematic when private sector stakeholders are incapable or unwilling to provide the resources or activities required to produce an adequate demand for infrastructure or services needed to host an event (Bauer *et al.*, 2001, p. 71). Such unwillingness transpires when individuals or businesses are unable to capture all the benefits associated with their activities or investments (Burgan and Mules, 2000, p. 48). This is specifically an issue when impacts of an event fall into the category of public goods characterized by non-rivalling and non-excluding criteria (Solberg and Preuss, 2005, p. 139). Even if stakeholders collectively might want to invest in or fund an event, it is possible for the individual stakeholder to maximize his or her profit by opting out of the cooperative, allowing others to pay while enjoying the extra business the event generates. This is called the 'free rider problem' (Burgan and Mules, 2000, p. 48; Solberg and Preuss, 2005, p. 139).

While externalities caused by planning and staging events can occur across the TBL, the principal forms of market failures are discussed by Bauer *et al.* (2001, pp. 72–73) and include:

- *Market failure in destination marketing.* It is not uncommon that host communities need considerable marketing in order to compete for and attract non-local visitors to an event. Such marketing campaigns are generally costly. The market can fail when event industry stakeholders are unable to capture the full benefits of these marketing efforts and, instead of contributing to the cost, opt out and become free riders.
- *Market failure in the provision of infrastructure.* Some events, and specifically sports and business events, require huge investments in infrastructure such as stadia and conference and exhibition venues. Return on investment is often long-term, and the private sector, let alone the individual event manager, is seldom able to produce the funds required to build such facilities. Furthermore, these stakeholders are only some of the beneficiaries of the returns generated by these venues, and should therefore not carry the entire cost.
- *Market failure in the bid processes.* Certain events, generally major international events, entail a bid process involving high costs in addition to those of planning and staging the event. For many stakeholders wanting to bid, these costs, which may occur over long periods without any compensating income, can be too high and result in potential market failure.

Besides tangible developmental outcomes such as new public venues, improved roads, extended transport systems and so forth, the hosting of events can also produce less tangible societal externalities including improved destination awareness, social cohesion, cultural revitalization and empowerment opportunities.

Where an event produces externalities resulting in market failures, the event may be forced to rely on public sector funding unless rendered financially unsustainable. In some circumstances, where there is a conflict between individual and collective rationality, government might intervene to assist demand, supply and infrastructure, or otherwise reduce blockages (Bauer *et al.*, 2001, p. 71; Solberg and Preuss, 2005, p. 139). However, as pointed out by Solberg and Preuss (2005, p. 139), 'in an ideal (rational) world, however, the government would only be willing to support [an] activity as long as the aggregate socio-economic return exceeds the socio-economic costs'.

Yet, due to the difficulty in estimating the holistic impacts of events, and more specifically the challenge of applying meaningful measures to less tangible impacts, emphasis has been put on economic aspects such as an event's ability to attract non-local visitors who by their expenditures contribute to the local economy. This rather narrow-minded approach is not only due to inadequate evaluation methods and tools, but also could be attributed to inadequate terminology. While focus has been on economic impact and ROI, the sector is still challenged by the inability to make informed decisions based on TBL developmental considerations and measures of ROO.

Concerned with the above, it is necessary to reconsider the previously suggested definitions of sustainable events. If applying the strictest definition of sustainability, a truly sustainable event should generate sufficient funds through the market and not depend on subsidies from the public sector. However, considering the potential of events to contribute to sustainable development, rather than requiring autonomy (Proposed Definitions 1 and 2), sustainable events should denote events efficiently utilizing their available resources (human resources, infrastructure and funds), thereby being self-sustaining without (or with a minimum of) public sector support.

Proposed Definition 4

Sustainable events: events efficiently utilizing available resources (human resources, infrastructure and funds), thereby being self-sustaining without, or, in the case of externalities, with a minimum of, public sector support.

Development Objectives – Considering Individual and Societal Needs

Besides acknowledging the call for taking a holistic approach to development, it is just as important to take into account the local needs across the TBL. This is directly in line with the Brundtland Commission's definition of sustainable development (see earlier). Illustrating this, it is obvious that a wealthy suburb in a developed country has different development needs than a rural town in a developing country. However, needs may also vary vastly within a community and among stakeholders. In the context of events, both individual event-goers' needs as well as societal needs within the host community should be of concern. While individuals' needs are generally psychological, societal needs are both objective as well as psychological.

Psychological needs are described by Maslow (1943) through the hierarchy of needs, and include physiological needs, safety, belongingness, esteem and self-actualization. Besides individual variations within each stakeholder group, the psychological needs of event-goers and host community residents do not necessarily correspond. While event attendees may enjoy public spaces closed off from traffic, or outdoor concerts, residents may find it interfering with their daily wants and needs. Objective societal needs, on the other hand, generally concern the broader economy, socioculture and environment (i.e. the TBL), and could specifically entail development of a less seasonal tourism economy, improved social cohesion and resource management. While the programme of an event may demonstrate more or less sensitivity to local needs, such consideration should nevertheless be a parameter within the planning, design and marketing of an event, as well as within the actual implementation and follow-up of an event.

The ability to distinguish between the sustainability and responsibility of an event is specifically useful when negotiating individual and societal needs. While an event's contribution to sustainable development depends on its TBL responsibility and consideration of local societal needs, its sustainability depends on market support – in other words, the satisfaction of event-goers' needs. The ultimate challenge for an event manager could therefore be considered to be the planning and management of an event (i.e. resource allocation) according to the stakeholders' individual and societal needs.

Summary

This chapter has offered a critique of the sustainable event concept. Initially it was pointed out that the concept of sustainable events does not necessarily indicate a clear reference to the management of an event or its ability to contribute to sustainable development. Without a clear contextualization, the concept of sustainability is likely to be rendered a passing fad rather than a changing trend. The 'sustainable' concept is further critiqued by illustrating a scenario wherein an event produces externalities (Burgan and Mules, 2000; Solberg and Preuss, 2005) affecting the triple bottom line, resulting in market failures (Bauer *et al.*, 2001), and thus forcing the event to rely on public sector funds unless rendered unsustainable. Consequently it is suggested that, rather than applying the strictest definition, 'sustainable events' should denote events efficiently utilizing their available resources (financial, human, technical, etc.), thereby being self-sustaining without (or with a minimum of) public sector support.

The chapter put forward two main challenges: (i) to develop an unambiguous vocabulary concerning resource management as well as output; and (ii) to develop a transparent method enabling the measurement of the net holistic (positive) output of events, i.e. events' impact on local development across the TBL. Acting upon the first challenge, stipulative definitions of sustainable events were provided while the concept of responsible events was introduced.

The chapter concluded by emphasizing the importance of attaching a distinctive meaning to the term 'sustainable' when used within the context of events, and that stakeholders should be concerned with events' 'sustainability' as well as 'responsibility'. A key argument is that a 'sustainable event' would not necessarily contribute to sustainable development and thus be considered 'responsible', whereas a 'responsible event' would not necessarily have to be 'sustainable'. Consequently, for the 'sustainable' concept to be meaningful and promote informed decision making within the events sector, it needs to be used in consistence with broader and already established definitions. If not, the term will lend itself to misuse – risking 'sustainability' becoming a passing fad rather than a changing trend.

Question Introduction

You are the new manager of a local cultural festival in the small and diverse community of Summerville. The festival is the main event during the peak season and has been successfully running for more than 15 years. The festival programme has continuously developed and includes several music and theatre performances, a parade and a craft market. More than half of the attractions and performances are free to the general public. While the number of local individuals involved in the programme is higher than ever, the event management team is faced with a number of challenges.

Since the number of event-goers peaked 3 years ago, visitor numbers have dropped significantly. There are no estimates indicating the ratio of local to non-local event-goers. Recently, the event has been criticized in local newspapers for not considering local needs and catering mainly for tourists. Clearly, the event is struggling to retain local support. Furthermore, the event organization is struggling financially. For years the main sponsor has been the local car dealership. However, the agreement has expired. Furthermore, the new mayor of Summerville has aired her interest in bidding for a national sport event. The bid process is expensive and 'your' event will need to fight for funding over the same budget. In addition, there are false rumours that the event organization receives a significant amount of money in funding and sponsorship, but that most of it goes to running the executive committee.

Key Questions

1. How might you apply the concepts of sustainable and/or responsible event management towards securing private sector sponsorship and public sector funding?
2. Using the concepts of sustainable and/or responsible event management, suggest ways in which you can market the event and demonstrate the event's contribution towards sustainable development within the local community.
3. With the increasing number of event managers applying for funding, you have been requested to develop criteria ensuring that public funds are allocated to events, maximizing the return on local development objectives (ROO). Based on your personal experience from the event sector, draft a matrix of criteria across the TBL. (Base this task upon the local needs within a community that you know.)

References

Bauer, T., Lambert, J., and Hutchison, J. (2001) Government intervention in the Australasian Meetings, Incentives, Conventions and Exhibitions Industry (MICE). *Journal of Convention & Exhibition* 3(1), 65–87.

BSI (2006) *BS 8900:2006 Guidance for managing sustainable development*. British Standards Institution, London.

BSI (2007) *BS 8901:2007 Specification for a sustainable event management system with guidance for use developed*. British Standards Institution, London.

Burgan, B. and Mules, T. (2000) Event analysis – understanding the divide between cost benefit and economic impact assessment. In: Allen, J., Harris, R., Jago, L.K. and Veal, A.J. (eds) *Events Beyond 2000: Setting the Agenda, Proceedings of Conference on Event Evaluation, Research and Education, Sydney (July 2000)*. Australian Centre for Event Management, Lindfield, Australia, pp. 46–51.

Burgan, B. and Mules, T. (2001) Reconciling cost–benefit and economic impact assessment for event tourism. *Tourism Economics* 7(4), 321–330.

Burns, J., Hatch, J. and Mules, T. (eds) (1986) *The Adelaide Grand Prix: The Impact of a Special Event*. Centre for South Australian Economic Studies, Adelaide, Australia.

Dwyer, L., Mellor, R., Mistilis, N., and Mules, T. (2000) Forecasting the economic impacts of events and conventions. *Event Management* 6, 191–204.

Dwyer, L., Forsyth, P. and Spurr, R. (2005) Economic impacts and benefits of sport events: a CGE perspective. In: Allen, J. (ed.) *The Impacts of Events, Proceedings of International Event Research Conference held in Sydney July 2005*. Australian Centre for Event Management, Lindfield, Australia, pp. 67–77.

Formica, S. (1998) The development of festival and special events studies. *Event Management* 5(3), 131–138.

Fredline, L., Raybould, M., Jago, L. and Deery, M. (2005) Triple bottom line event evaluation: a proposed framework for holistic event evaluation. In: Allen, J. (ed.) *The Impacts of Events, Proceedings of International Event Research Conference held in Sydney July 2005*. Australian Centre for Event Management, Lindfield, Australia, pp. 2–15.

Getz, D. (1991) *Festivals, Special Events, and Tourism*. Van Nostrand Reinhold, New York/London.

Getz, D. (2000) Defining the field of event management. *Event Management* 6(1), 1–3.

Hede, A.-M., Jago, L. and Deery, M. (2002) Special event research 1990–2001: key trends and issues. In: Jago, L., Deery, M., Harris, R., Hede, A.-M. and Allen, J. (eds) *Events and Place Making, Proceedings of International Event Research Conference held in Sydney July 2002*. Australian Centre for Event Management, Lindfield, Australia, pp. 305–338.

Investopedia (2008) Return on Investment – ROI. Available at: http://www.investopedia.com/terms/r/returnoninvestment.asp (accessed 31 May 2008).

Maslow, A.H. (1943) A theory of human motivation. *Psychological Review* 50, 370–396.

Orwell, G. (1946) Politics and the English Language. Originally published in *Horizon*, April 1946 issue. See also http://blog.guykawasaki.com/2007/02/politics_and_th.html; Taylor, D.J. (2003) *Orwell: A Life*. Henry Holt and Company, New York, New York, p. 376.

Sherwood, P. and Jago, L. (2005) The economic performance of special events: a framework for comparison. In: Allen, J. (ed.) *The Impacts of Events, Proceedings of International Event Research Conference held in Sydney July 2005*. Australian Centre for Event Management, Lindfield, Australia, pp. 54–66.

Solberg, H.A. and Preuss, H. (2005) Major sporting events – are there any long-term tourism impacts? In: Allen, J. (ed.) *The Impacts of Events, Proceedings of International Event Research Conference held in Sydney July 2005*. Australian Centre for Event Management, Lindfield, Australia, pp. 125–142.

Stiernstrand, J.O. (1996) The Nordic model: a theoretical model for economic impact analysis of event tourism. *Festival Management & Event Tourism* 3, 165–174.

UN (1987) General Assembly 96th Plenary Meeting, 11 December 1987. 42/187. Report of the World Commission on Environment and Development. Available at: http://www.un.org/documents/ga/res/42/ares42-187.htm (accessed 12 April 2007).

4 Events and Sustainable Urban Regeneration

A. Smith
University of Westminster, London, UK

The purpose of this chapter is to evaluate if and how major events can deliver sustainable regeneration for host cities. The chapter begins by defining the key terms: regeneration, event regeneration and sustainable event regeneration. It then uses the recognized dimensions of sustainable urban regeneration as a framework in which to analyse a range of relevant international examples. This discussion helps to highlight the advantages and disadvantage of using major events as sustainable regeneration tools. The final section includes overall conclusions and recommendations for future practice.

Chapter outline

- Introduction
- Urban Regeneration and Sustainability
- Event Regeneration
- Sustainable Event Regeneration
- Events and the Environmental Integrity of Cities
- Events and the Economic Efficiency of Cities
- Events and Social Equity in Cities
- The Negative Social Effects of Events
- Summary
- Key Questions

Introduction

At first glance, events appear to be the antithesis of sustainability – they are short-lived, involve the mass movement of thousands of people and can disrupt existing plans for an area. It should be remembered that this applies to major events, and that smaller events will not exhibit the same unsustainable traits. But there is some hope that even major events can surmount these problems and deliver sustainable regeneration effects. By applying some of the lessons learned from 50 years of experience, cities can use them to achieve urban regeneration which adheres to the basic principles of sustainable development. Ultimately, this means following good practice in regeneration generally, while using the core advantages of events – their capacity to excite and inspire – to stimulate levels of support and participation that would be unattainable without event associations.

Urban regeneration is now one of the most commonly cited justifications for staging major events. It has moved from being a beneficial side-effect of new event venues to something that cities actively try to lever through event strategies. Indeed, many commentators assume that since about 1960 we have entered a new era, in which regeneration and city marketing are key objectives of major events. According to Liao and Petts (2006), the 1960 Rome Olympics was the first example of city-wide redevelopment resulting from an event. Barcelona now provides the most famous example of this type of strategy. Indeed, commentators now talk of a 'Barcelona model' of urban development, a distinctive characteristic of which is 'the use of major events as catalyst for city renewal' (Garcia, 2004, p. 321). This 'model' is an oversimplification of the innovative urban projects implemented around the time Barcelona staged the 1992 Olympic Games, which would be difficult to transfer to other contexts (Monclus, 2003; Smith, 2005). However, this has not stopped other cities trying to emulate Barcelona's success and now events are recognized as important tools by those responsible for urban regeneration policy.

Urban Regeneration and Sustainability

Regeneration is supposedly distinct from more general urban policy in that it involves attempts to reverse decline in cities. Initially the term was used to refer to housing renewal and other property-led initiatives (Oatley, 1998), but in recent years a more holistic conceptualization has emerged in which 'partnership, spatial targeting, integration, competition, empowerment and sustainability have assumed increasing importance' (Jones and Gripaios, 2000, pp. 218–219). The emergence of a more holistic approach to regeneration is reaffirmed by other contemporary definitions which describe regeneration as a 'comprehensive and integrated vision and action which leads to the resolution of urban problems and which seeks to bring about a lasting improvement in the economic, social and environmental conditions of an area that has been subject to change' (Roberts, 2000, p. 17). The emphasis placed on a 'lasting' or long-term approach and the new emphasis on social, economic and environmental conditions mean regeneration has strong parallels with the broader concept of sustainable development.

In some ways, the concepts of sustainability and regeneration are so similar that the term sustainable urban regeneration is a tautology. But there are some key differences, notably the continued focus of regeneration on the built fabric. Another inherent difference between conceptions of sustainable development and regeneration is that regeneration often involves the recovery of environments (and economies/societies) that have already been damaged, rather than efforts to restrict further environmental deterioration.

Event Regeneration

Although there is some consensus regarding what urban regeneration is, there is less written on what is meant by 'event regeneration'. In obvious cases, events are the fundamental cause of urban change; providing a reason to make interventions and a deadline for their completion, as well as a convenient source of funding, political will and civic support. But sometimes events act merely as a ways of gaining funding for, and participation in, wider regeneration projects. In some ways this can be understood as the difference between urban regeneration resulting from an event, and urban regeneration that includes an event (Carricere and Demaziere, 2002). To distinguish these approaches, Smith and Fox (2007) discriminate between 'event-led' regeneration and 'event-themed' regeneration. The former relies on projects fundamental to the staging of events to deliver change, whereas the latter uses an event as an opportunity to fund, promote and bolster wider regeneration projects. A slightly different approach is one that relies on 'leverage'. In an events context, the concept of 'leverage' involves 'those activities which need to be undertaken around the event itself which seek to maximise the long-term benefit from events' (Chalip, 2004, p. 228). It is the focus on the 'long term' that is important here, as this provides opportunities for sustainable regeneration.

Event projects have been established to lever a range of effects including increased tourism visitation, small business support, new housing provision, heritage restoration, employment creation, improved healthcare, increased participation levels in the arts/sports, new training opportunities and other forms of social development. These effects rely on parallel initiatives that are pursed in conjunction with an event, with event connections used to lever funding, participation and publicity (Smith and Fox, 2007).

Sustainable Event Regeneration

As well as defining event regeneration in general, it is important to establish criteria with which to assess its sustainability. O'Sullivan and Jackson (2002) assessed events against eight criteria for sustainable economic development summarized under the headings: capacity building and training; access to credit and capital; community enterprise; local business development; sustainable approaches to inward investment; responsible business practice; access to and distribution of work; and trading locally. These criteria are biased towards the dedicated focus on economic issues, but do illustrate that general criteria can be applied to analyse the sustainability of events. At a broader level, Bramwell (1997) makes a strong case for judging events by their economic efficiency, social equity and environmental integrity. Other authors have provided more detailed criteria. Like Bramwell, Hemphill *et al.* (2004) consider sustainable urban regeneration to be determined by an amalgam of a project's economic, social and environmental credentials. But their assessment criteria subdivide these generic traits into five subcategories: economy and work; resource use; buildings and land use; transport and mobility; and community benefits.

In Hemphill *et al.*'s (2004) study, overall sustainable regeneration performance is then calculated using a series of criteria associated with each of these headings. This detailed assessment tool is illustrated in Box 4.1. Its focus on the urban fabric means that it is a specific tool to measure sustainable urban regeneration, rather than merely generic sustainability criteria. Although it is not designed explicitly to assess the sustainability of event regeneration, most, if not all, event initiatives can be judged against it. This is emphasized by the fact that Hemphill *et al.* themselves use their criteria to judge the sustainability of the Olympic Village built for the 1992 Barcelona Olympic Games. Constraints of space mean that Bramwell's (1997) basic criteria are used to structure the discussion in the remainder of this chapter. However, Hemphill *et al.*'s criteria are also referred to where more detail is required.

Events and the Environmental Integrity of Cities

Perhaps the most obvious opportunity for environmental enhancement of cities using events is the associated investment in new venues. Building new facilities and associated infrastructures in dilapidated and redundant 'brown field' sites allows such areas to be reclaimed as integral urban zones. This fits with Hemphill *et al.*'s (2004) insistence that sustainable regeneration involves reclaiming contaminated land (point 22, Box 4.1). Chicago's World Expo in 1893 was arguably the first example of an event regeneration project that involved land reclamation. In the late 19th century, World Expos had become such large events that a central site was no longer deemed sufficiently spacious, so land was reclaimed (from the river) in order to stage the event (Gold and Gold, 2005). So began a tradition of using events to reclaim land that continues to the present day, with the most famous examples being the Sydney Olympic Games, held on the site of a former abattoir; and the Greenwich Millennium Festival, staged on a toxic industrial peninsula. As well as reclaiming damaged or unviable land, events have also been used to integrate isolated or peripheral sites on the urban fringe. This is notoriously difficult to achieve; something that Seville discovered when it staged the 1992 World Expo on an island in the middle of the Guadalquivir River. Despite new bridges and infrastructure, the site has remained 'little more than an offshore ghost town' since the event (Savage, 1997; cited in Gold and Gold, 2005, p. 135).

If sustainable regeneration is to be achieved, an important consideration is to plan for the effective post-event use of any new facilities. This helps to translate physical changes into wider social/economic

Box 4.1. Criteria for assessing sustainable urban regeneration performance. (Adapted from Hemphill *et al.*, 2004.)

Resource use performance

1. Reclamation of building materials
2. Retention of environmental features
3. Waste disposal
4. Waste minimization
5. Energy efficiency – building layout and design
6. Energy efficiency – building materials/ construction methods
7. Conservation of built heritage resources
8. Incorporation of environmental design
9. Performance of environmental management

Economy and work scoring performance

10. Number of jobs created per 1000 square metres
11. Net jobs created
12. Percentage of new enterprises still operating after 3 years
13. Quality of jobs created
14. Leverage ratios
15. Performance of incentive mechanisms
16. Partnership structure performance
17. Effectiveness of exit strategy
18. Incorporation of training programmes
19. End-user scheme satisfaction

Buildings and land use scoring performance

20. Ratio of open space to built form
21. Ratio of converted buildings to new build
22. Reclamation of contaminated land
23. Density levels in relation to plot size
24. Balance of uses
25. Occupancy levels
26. Office rental versus CBD rents
27. Quality of final product
28. Design quality
29. Quality of public space
30. Usage of public space
31. Quality of private space

Transport and mobility scoring performance

32. Land devoted to roads
33. Land devoted to pedestrians
34. Road improvements
35. Work travelling habits
36. Leisure travelling habits
37. Public transport links
38. Car parking provision – residential
39. Car parking provision – commercial
40. Integration of land use and public transport

Community benefits scoring performance

41. Access to open space
42. Access to leisure facilities
43. Access to retail facilities
44. Access to educational needs
45. Access to medical facilities
46. Access to entertainment facilities
47. Access to cultural facilities
48. Access to housing
49. On-site retail facilities
50. LA21 effectiveness
51. Community ownership
52. Community group involvement

regeneration. The physical legacy of the 1996 Atlanta Olympics was deliberately restricted by the large number of temporary constructions. These led to the event being labelled 'the disposable Games' (Rutheiser, 1996). Removing some venues after the close of the event may have minimized wasteful maintenance costs, but it meant opportunities to assist needy Atlanta neighbourhoods were missed. Atlanta's approach contrasted with that of Athens, where 95% of the projects for the 2004 Olympic Games were planned as permanent spatial structures (Beriatos and Gospodini, 2004). These cases highlight the dilemma faced by host cities: wanting to generate physical legacies, while ensuring that money is not wasted building and operating unnecessary new venues. Host cities that are risk-averse will attempt to restrict any negative financial legacy, whereas more ambitious cities will want to make a lasting physical impression. Those falling into the latter category have to manage the associated risk that new facilities will not be used after a major event.

Even if new venues are used in the post-event era, they are likely to render any existing facilities less popular or even redundant. A good example is the 1998 Commonwealth Games staged in Kuala Lumpur. Despite its relatively low level of economic development, Malaysia spent £94 million on stadia and infrastructure for this event (Silk, 2002). The existing stadium and swimming complex were perfectly adequate for staging these Games, but new facilities were built to impress an international audience and to symbolize the achievements of the incumbent government (Silk, 2002). This case demonstrates that sustainable regeneration considerations are often sidelined when the rationale for staging an event involves overriding political objectives. The use and refurbishment of existing facilities is perhaps a more sustainable strategy, as emphasized by its inclusion in the criteria developed by Hemphill *et al.* (2004) (point 21, Box 4.1). This approach was adopted by Los Angeles during preparations for the 1984 Olympic Games. Los Angeles converted its original Olympic stadium to provide the main venue for the 1984 Games, something also achieved by Barcelona in 1936/1992. In the contemporary era, it may even be possible to convert event venues constructed in different host cities. An innovative strategy is being planned by organizers of the 2012 London Games, who want parts of their Olympic stadium to be dismantled and used by future hosts. London representatives are currently negotiating with those cities bidding for the 2016 Games to try and introduce this more sustainable approach.

One problem with event regeneration is that the inevitable territorial concentration of events tends to privilege certain areas at the expense of others. This is true even though most events exhibit a degree of multiplicity – involving different events in different venues. A good example is the European Capital of Culture, where a series of shows, exhibitions and performances is staged over a whole year. Balsas (2004) cites Porto's staging of this event in 2004 as an example of the 'territorial inequity' of event regeneration. The event privileged the main streets and squares in the city, but neglected the urban fabric of residential neighbourhoods. More positive effects have been achieved when event venues have been deliberately sited in disadvantaged areas. The centrepiece of the 1998 FIFA World Cup – the Stade de France – was deliberately sited in St Denis, Paris, to improve local transport links and as a boost to a stagnating local economy (Dauncey, 1999). But even when events are deliberately staged in peripheral sites, this does not guarantee that adjacent neighbourhoods will feel the benefits. Using events to help a variety of geographically dispersed urban areas within a city does not seem to work as effectively as a spatially aggregated approach. The case of Athens, host of the 2004 Olympic Games, suggests that scattering event venues all over a city does not produce positive regeneration effects (Beriatos and Gospodini, 2004).

Events and the Economic Efficiency of Cities

It is insufficient to concentrate merely on the 'hard' physical legacy of events, as positive effects do not necessarily 'trickle down' to local people and small businesses. Economic and social considerations also need to be addressed if sustainable regeneration is to be achieved. One key theme within recent literature on event regeneration is that cities should aim to build upon existing economic resources. Although new economic activity is often needed to stimulate regeneration, there is a danger that 'existing forms of employment ... may be overlooked and undervalued' in event strategies (Raco, 2004, p. 35). It is important to ensure that local companies and disadvantaged individuals are able to benefit from the lucrative contracts usually associated with large events. Support for local businesses may be required, particularly as evidence shows that events can sometimes harm them. Although Barcelona's Olympic regeneration is widely applauded, it involved the eviction of hundreds of small businesses from areas that had traditionally offered low rents (Shapcott, 1998). Similarly, the organizers of London's Olympics had to negotiate the relocation of 284 businesses in preparation for the Games in 2012 (House of Commons Hansard, 2005).

One of the most recognized ways of leveraging regeneration from events is to use them to assist the long-term viability of local businesses. Unfortunately, research has highlighted that many businesses do not know about events in their local area, and therefore fail to capitalize on them properly. For example, Connell and Page's (2005) research into the effects of the World Medical and Health Games in Stirling, Scotland, revealed that 26.4% of local businesses were unaware it was being staged. Securing positive effects for businesses in urban areas relies on informing them of opportunities, gaining their participation for joint initiatives and generating new expenditure. Chalip (2004) suggests four main ways of maximizing trade and revenue from an event: (i) entice visitor spending; (ii) lengthen visitor stays; (iii) retain event expenditures; and (iv) use the event to enhance regional businesses relationships.

O'Brien (2007) argues that visitors can be encouraged to spend more and stay longer within a city if a major event is 'augmented' by other subsidiary events and attractions. In his Australian case study, this was achieved by including ceremonies, workshops, presentations, performances and other public occasions within the event programme. Chalip's (2004) third way of maximizing trade and revenue – retaining visitor expenditures in the local area – is a recognized principle of sustainable local economic development (O'Sullivan and Jackson, 2002). Retention is achieved by using local suppliers and local labour. This becomes more difficult as events grow in size; but it is possible, even for major events. For example, the Millennium Festival in Greenwich, UK, involved an innovative approach whereby an organization was established to link local labour and local companies to the event (Smith and Fox, 2007). Developing these local links, whether through the use of local sponsorship, labour or suppliers, also helps to retain ownership of the event within a community. This can advance social development goals (point 52, Box 4.1).

Some events are planned to encourage economic regeneration through the provision of new skills and support for local people. This matches Hemphill *et al.*'s (2004) insistence that sustainable regeneration involves both 'access to educational needs' and the 'incorporation of training programmes' (points 44 and 18, Box 4.1). Volunteer programmes are commonly employed to achieve such effects. As volunteers are needed to help stage events, by offering training and giving volunteers employment experience, new skills can be nurtured. In Lillehammer, Norwegian host of the 1994 Winter Olympic Games, 79% of the volunteers surveyed felt that they had enhanced their skills by being one of the 9100 volunteers involved (Kemp, 2002). The 2000 Sydney Olympic Games also employed an extensive scheme involving 62,000 volunteers. Accordingly, volunteer recruitment for such events usually focuses on how to obtain the numbers required. Sydney learned from Atlanta that it had to mobilize networks of private contactors to assist in the recruitment, training and management of voluntary staff (Webb, 2001). But even if such efforts are successful, it is unclear whether this actually contributes to social regeneration, particularly as few attempts have been made to ensure that those benefiting from volunteering were those most in need of assistance. People who volunteer are often enthusiasts who have volunteered before, and tend not to be marginalized members of local communities. A more targeted approach focused on the most disadvantaged (and least skilled) is more likely to contribute to sustainable regeneration.

To assist regeneration, some cities have also adopted vocational training programmes in conjunction with events. Such programmes may be particularly valuable if they allow disadvantaged local people to access temporary jobs that may give them the experience to work in that sector permanently in the future. As part of the construction industry training strategy implemented as part of the Sydney Olympic Games, 12,000 workers were trained, with special provision for workers from Aboriginal and non-English speaking communities (Webb, 2001). This inspired Toronto, where the Trades Council used the city's 2008 Olympic bid to pressure the government into developing skills training for their Aboriginal communities (Tufts, 2004). To ensure long-term effects, it is also important for host cities to pursue wider employment and educational initiatives. Greece adopted an Olympic Education Programme in conjunction with the 2004 Games staged in Athens. This project was based on school initiatives adopted by previous Olympic hosts. Grammatikopoulos *et al.* (2004, p. 67) note that these projects have tended to lack theoretical unity and subsequent evaluation; but state that 'they seemed to resonate with teachers as a source for integrated and imaginative pedagogical ideas and activities'. This emphasizes the power of major events as 'hooks' that can generate support for wider regeneration projects.

Events and Social Equity in Cities

Sustainable regeneration is that which encourages a fairer society. So event regeneration should be managed in a way that attempts to share any positive (and negative) impacts more equitably. Attempts may also be made to lever events to address key social problems. As Misener and Mason (2006, p. 40) argue: 'events may provide opportunities for community development over and above the justifications traditionally provided for hosting events'. Events have the reputation for being able to encourage a strong emotional response among host communities, meaning that needy communities and/or individuals could experience some form of social empowerment. Atkinson *et al.*'s (2008) research found that UK residents perceived 'inspiring children' and 'uniting people/feel-good factor/national pride' to be the most important intangible effects that could result from the London 2012 Olympic Games. But to achieve lasting regeneration, it is perhaps insufficient to rely merely on the 'feel-good factor' associated with events, particularly as it has a tendency to evaporate quickly. As Shipway (2008) suggests, events may encourage more long-term social effects if they initiate behaviour that may contribute towards social well-being. So perhaps we should be more concerned about encouraging the 'do-good' factor, rather than merely the 'feel-good' factor (Smith, 2008). This may allow events to alleviate social problems in cities such as crime, anti-social behaviour, obesity and stress.

In relation to the 2000 Olympic Games, Waitt (2003) indicates that community and national spirit was a powerful psychological reward for many residents of Sydney. Similarly, Ritchie (2000) states that the most profound legacy of the 1988 Calgary Winter Olympics was increased civic pride and social cohesion. For this to happen, Ritchie (2000) and Misener and Mason (2006) argue that the event must embrace the core values of residents, community groups and neighbourhood associations. Accordingly, communities need to be consulted about the event and subsequently be involved – both in staging the event and its benefits. Engagement such as this can create institutionalized and non-institutionalized networks between community members and between members and other stakeholders. The latter may allow positive change to accrue by building 'bridging' social capital between community members and elite decision makers. Indeed, events can be seen as methods for instigating 'multi-level governance', which encourages participation from disenfranchised groups and allows access to local, regional and national policy networks.

The need for community participation and local engagement is emphasized by the contents of Ritchie's (2000) and Smith's (2007) ten-point plans for effective regeneration legacies from events. These are detailed in Boxes 4.2 and 4.3.

Many of the principles cited in these criteria are associated with the processes involved, rather than the direction and content of policy. Following the principles of sustainable development, event regeneration is likely to be more sustainable if it involves those people it is trying to assist (points 1a, 2a, 4b and 10b, Boxes 4.2 and 4.3). Using this engagement, events can be shaped, supplemented and augmented to make them more relevant and accessible to local people (points 3a, 7a, 2b and 9b, Boxes 4.2 and 4.3). Augmentation can also be used to make sure there is some degree of territorial equity, so that events help needy populations

Box 4.2. Ten main principles of mega-event legacy enhancement. (Adapted from Ritchie, 2000.)

1a. Involve all stakeholders
2a. Build on the value of those stakeholders
3a. Supplement sports events with cultural, educational and commercial events
4a. Make events as regional as possible
5a. Undertake commitment to keep momentum going post-event
6a. Train residents to be good hosts
7a. Augment events with supporting events, e.g. conferences
8a. Capitalize on opportunities to enhance social understanding and community cohesion
9a. Publicize achievements well into the future to maintain effects
10a. Tap into another major characteristic of the host city/region

Box 4.3. Ten key principles for sustainable event regeneration. (Adapted from Smith, 2007.)

1b. Embed event strategies within wider urban regeneration programmes
2b. Use the event as a coherent theme and effective stimulus for parallel initiatives and more diverse regeneration projects
3b. Ensure that regeneration planning is fully incorporated into the initial stages of planning for an event
4b. Promote shared ownership and responsibility among all partners of the legacy and event programmes
5b. Design effective organizational and structural arrangements between event regeneration agencies and event management representatives to ensure joint working towards clearly defined and shared goals
6b. Allocate sufficient human and capital resources throughout the lifetime of event regeneration projects to achieve sustained effects
7b. Design event regeneration projects to prioritize the needs and engagement of the most disadvantaged members of the target community
8b. Try to ensure an even geographical dissemination of positive impacts among targeted areas
9b. Ensure that event-themed social and economic regeneration initiatives build upon, and connect with, any physical and infrastructural legacy
10b. Ensure community representation from the planning stage onwards to promote community ownership and engagement

even if they are geographically dispersed (points 4a and 8b, Boxes 4.2 and 4.3). This can be achieved by theming social/economic initiatives, rather than simply relying on the effects of event venues and associated physical enhancements. The criteria developed by Smith (2007) and Ritchie (2000) also highlight the temporal dimension of event regeneration (points 9a and 6b, Boxes 4.2 and 4.3). Initiatives need to be pursued that help cities maintain as much of the excitement, publicity and funding generated by events to ensure positive social effects are as prolonged as possible. This means planning envisaged effects well in advance and ensuring that momentum is not lost in the immediate post-event era.

The Negative Social Effects of Events

Overshadowing some of the positive effects identified above are reports of some negative consequences of major events that may compromise social regeneration. Olds (1998, p. 5) sees events as catalysts for long-term redevelopment planning, with existing communities paying the costs in terms of 'displacement, negative health effects, the breaking of social networks and the loss of affordable housing'. This can happen when events are designed to result in the regeneration of areas, rather than aiming for regeneration in areas (Raco, 2004). Although sustainable regeneration is meant to generate 'access to housing' (point 48, Box 4.1), events can also cause the opposite effect. Perhaps the most dramatic illustrations are provided by Asian Olympic Games. Approximately 750,000 people were forcibly relocated due to the requirements of the 1988 Seoul Olympics (Olds, 1998) and by 2004, 300,000 Beijing citizens had already been uprooted as part of the preparations for the 2008 Games (Wan, 2004; cited in Broudehoux, 2007).

It is hard to imagine initiatives as socially unsustainable as these. Many commentators (e.g. Waitt, 2003; Broudehoux, 2007) suggest that it is those most disadvantaged who usually bear these punitive costs. This is why some think major events are implicated in the revanchist city – playing a crucial role in the control of marginalized groups (Tufts, 2004). At the time of writing, the non-governmental organization Tourism Concern is running a campaign related to the negative social effects of the Olympic Games (see http://www.tourismconcern.org.uk). Such campaigns and related media stories seem to be increasing public awareness of the potential for negative effects from major events.

Even when marginalized groups are not further disadvantaged by events directly, there remains the possibility that a major event will distract attention from their plight. In this manner, events can act as smokescreens or 'carnival masks' (Harvey, 1989) behind which the inherent social unsustainability of some urban communities can be hidden. This is usually the position of those who theorize events as 'spectacles'. Therefore, although events may create and sustain a local and/or national collective identity, this may be part of a deliberate attempt to undermine existing identities, particularly those that threaten the interests of political and business elites (Waitt, 2003). Accordingly, Olds (1998) sees the social unity created by events as artificial, especially as it is used to push through urban redevelopment which would not normally be accepted.

As Hemphill *et al.*'s (2004) criteria emphasize, socially sustainable regeneration also means providing access to leisure and cultural facilities (points 41, 42, 46 and 47, Box 4.1). Obviously, flexible new event venues can provide such facilities for urban communities. New concert halls, sports stadia and urban parks are often the main legacy of major events staged in cities. But in practice, elite venues are rarely suited to community use. Even when community access is retained, it is often expensive. This is especially true when, as is often the case, these facilities are effectively privatized once a major event has been staged for the exclusive benefit of local elites and tourists. This is often necessary to recoup money to compensate for overspending by public authorities on major events. A related negative social outcome is the redistribution of funding from social programmes to allow event projects to be funded. For example, the development of Homebush Olympic Park for the Sydney Olympic Games meant that one local authority was required to transfer rateable land to an adjacent council in exchange for land comprising part of the Park. The budget shortfall this created meant that some local community and youth services were suspended (Owen, 2002). In this manner events can challenge the sustainability of surrounding communities, as they represent an opportunity cost. And rather than solving problems of social exclusion, according to Tranter and Keefe (2004, p. 182) an urban events strategy 'typically marginalises significant sections of society that are not interested in the events or lack the financial means to experience them'. This emphasizes that those managing events regeneration must seek to mitigate some of the negative effects of events, as well as maximizing positive impacts.

Summary

Overall, it is difficult to make general conclusions about the sustainability of event regeneration initiatives. Examples can be found of strategies that generally meet many of Hemphill *et al.*'s (2004) criteria, while others seem inherently unsustainable. Each strategy needs to be assessed on its own merits. The adoption of event-themed strategies by some cities means a very diverse range of envisaged effects is being pursued. This makes related strategies even more difficult to compare. Reassuringly, as regeneration gains prominence in the rationales provided for staging events, associated strategies seem to be getting more sophisticated. Correspondingly, major event strategies and the urban policy agenda are increasingly integrated. This may be a positive development as events seem to leave a more positive physical legacy when they are embedded within wider regeneration strategies. This matches the approach outlined by Carricere and Demaziere (2002), who advocate urban regeneration that includes an event, rather than using an event to encourage urban regeneration. As such, general criteria for assessing urban regeneration, such as those developed by Hemphill *et al.* (2004), are increasingly relevant tools for assessing the outcomes of event regeneration.

Key Questions

1. What are the specific qualities of major events that make them useful tools in urban regeneration?
2. How can venues for major events be designed to ensure that they will leave a sustainable legacy?
3. What additional projects can be employed by host cities to make sure the benefits of major events are felt by those most in need?

References

Atkinson, G., Mourato, S., Szymanski, S. and Ozdemiroglu, E. (2008) Are we willing to pay enough to 'back the bid': valuing the intangible impacts of London's bid to host the 2012 Summer Olympic Games. *Urban Studies* 45(2), 419–444.

Balsas, C. (2004) City centre regeneration in the context of the 2001 European Capital of Culture in Porto, Portugal. *Local Economy* 19(4), 396–410.

Beriatos, E. and Gospodini, A. (2004) Glocalising urban landscapes: Athens and the 2004 Olympics. *Cities* 21(3), 187–202.

Bramwell, B. (1997) A sport mega-event as a sustainable tourism development strategy. *Tourism Recreation Research* 22(2), 13–19.

Broudehoux, A. (2007) Spectacular Beijing: the conspicuous construction of an Olympic metropolis. *Journal of Urban Affairs* 29(4), 383–399.

Carricere, J. and Demaziere, C. (2002) Urban planning and flagship development projects: lessons from Expo 98, Lisbon. *Planning Practice and Research* 17(1), 69–79.

Chalip, L. (2004) Beyond impact: a generalised model for host community event leverage. In: Ritchie, B. and Adair, S. (eds) *Sports Tourism: Interrelationships, Impacts and Issues*. Channel View, Clevedon, UK, pp. 226–252.

Connell, J. and Page, S. (2005) Evaluating the economic and spatial effects of an event: the case of the World Medical and Health Games. *Tourism Geographies* 7(1), 63–85.

Dauncey, H. (1999) Building the finals: facilities and infrastructure. In: Dauncey, H. and Hare, G. (eds) *France and the 1998 World Cup*. Frank Cass, London, pp. 98–120.

Garcia, B. (2004) Cultural policy and urban regeneration in Western European cities: lessons from experience, prospects for the future. *Local Economy* 19(4), 312–326.

Gold, J. and Gold, M. (2005) *Cities of Culture: Staging International Festivals and the Urban Agenda, 1851–2000*. Ashgate, Aldershot, UK.

Grammatikopoulos, V., Papacharisis, V., Koustelios, A., Tsigilis, N. and Theodorakis, Y. (2004) Evaluation of the Training Program for Greek Olympic Education. *International Journal of Educational Management* 18(1), 66–73.

Harvey, D. (1989) *The Condition of Postmodernity*. Blackwell, Oxford, UK.

Hemphill, L., McGreal, S. and Berry, J. (2004) An indicator-based approach for evaluating sustainable urban regeneration performance Part 2, Empirical evaluation and case-study analysis. *Urban Studies* 41(4), 757–772.

House of Commons Hansard (2005) Series 5, Col. 157W, 7 November 2005.

Jones, P. and Gripaios, P. (2000) A review of the BURA awards for best practice in urban regeneration. *Property Management* 18(4), 218–229.

Kemp, S. (2002) The hidden workforce: volunteers' learning in the Olympics. *Journal of European Industrial Training* 26(2–4), 109–116.

Liao, H. and Pitts, A. (2006) A brief historical review of Olympic urbanism. *International Journal of the History of Sport* 23(7), 1232–1252.

Misener, L. and Mason, D. (2006) Creating community networks. Can sporting events offer meaningful sources of social capital? *Managing Leisure* 11(1), 39–56.

Monclus, F. (2003) The Barcelona model: an original formula? From 'reconstruction' to strategic urban projects (1979–2004). *Planning Perspectives* 18(4), 399–421.

Oatley, N. (1998) Restructuring urban policy: the single regeneration budget and the challenge fund. In: Oatley, N. (ed.) *Cities, Economic Competition and Urban Policy*. Paul Chapman, London, pp. 146–162.

O'Brien, D. (2007) Points of leverage: maximising host community benefit from a regional surfing festival. *European Sport Management Quarterly* 7(2), 141–165.

Olds, K. (1998) Urban mega-events, eviction and housing rights: the Canadian case. *Current Issues in Tourism* 1(1), 1–47.

O'Sullivan, D. and Jackson, M. (2002) Festival tourism: a contributor to sustainable local economic development? *Journal of Sustainable Tourism* 10(4), 325–342.

Owen, K. (2002) The Sydney Olympics and urban entrepreneurialism. *Australian Geographical Studies* 40(3), 323–336.

Raco, M. (2004) Whose gold rush? The social legacy of a London Olympics. In: Vigor, A., Mean, M. and Timms, C. (eds) *After the Gold Rush: A Sustainable Olympics for London*. IPPR/DEMOS, London, pp. 31–50.

Ritchie, J.R.B. (2000) Turning 16 days into 16 years through Olympic legacies. *Event Management* 6(3), 155–165.

Roberts, P. (2000) The evolution, definition and purpose of urban regeneration. In: Roberts, P. and Sykes, H. (eds) *Urban Regeneration: A Handbook*. Sage, London, pp. 9–36.

Rutheiser, C. (1996) *Imagineering Atlanta*. Verso, New York.

Shapcott, M. (1998) Commentary on 'Urban mega-events, evictions and housing rights: the Canadian CASE' by Kris Olds. *Current Issues in Tourism* 1(2), 195–196.

Shipway, R. (2008) Sustainable legacies for the 2012 Olympic Games. *Perspectives in Public Health* 127(3), 119–124.

Silk, M. (2002) 'Bangsa Malaysia': global sport, the city and the mediated refurbishment of local identities. *Media, Culture and Society* 24(6), 775–794.

Smith, A. (2005) Conceptualizing image change: the reimaging of Barcelona. *Tourism Geographies* 7(4), 398–423.

Smith, A. (2007) Large-scale events and sustainable urban regeneration: key principles for host cities. *Journal of Urban Regeneration and Renewal* 1(2), 178–190.

Smith, A. (2008) Community engagement, well-being and pride. Paper presented to the *ESRC Round Table on Leveraging Community Engagement, Well-Being and Pride from the London 2012 Olympic and Paralympic Games*, Canterbury Christ Church University, UK.

Smith, A. and Fox, T. (2007) From 'event-led' to 'event-themed' regeneration: the 2002 Commonwealth Games Legacy Scheme. *Urban Studies* 44(5/6), 1125–1143.

Tranter, P. and Keefe, T. (2004) Motor racing in Australia's Parliamentary Zone: successful event tourism or the emperor's new clothes? *Urban Policy and Research* 22(2), 169–187.

Tufts, S. (2004) Building the 'competitive city': labour and Toronto's bid to host the Olympic Games. *Geoforum* 35(1), 47–58.

Waitt, G. (2003) Social impacts of the Sydney Olympics. *Annals of Tourism Research* 30(1), 194–215.

Webb, T. (2001) *The Collaborative Games*. Pluto, Sydney.

5 Indicators and Tools for Sustainable Event Management

K.A. Griffin
Dublin Institute of Technology, Dublin, Republic of Ireland

This chapter outlines how, in theory, an environmentally integrated destination management model could be employed in an events context, thereby stretching the understanding of sustainability to include themes as diverse as Administration, Community, Heritage, Industry, Enterprise and Visitor. It is proposed that use of this integrated management approach, or model, could mitigate the negative and maximize the positive impacts of events.

Chapter outline

- Introduction
- Measuring Sustainability
- Indicator Models
- Towards Development of the DIT-ACHIEV Model
- Problems with the Development of Indicators
- The DIT-ACHIEV Model of Sustainable Tourism Indicators
- Observations on Application of the Model
- Challenges
- Summary
- Key Questions

Introduction

For many years it has been realized that the relationship between a conference/event and a destination is dominated by four essential realities: it is transitory, unequal and unbalanced, lacks spontaneity and is limited by spatial and temporal constraints (UNESCO, 1976). The challenge, therefore, is to manage events, which can be risky to the environment, society and economy, in as sustainable a fashion as possible. The problem, however, is that while an event organizer may be highly motivated, there are few methodologies available for the implementation of sustainable practices.

In theory, practitioners and supporters of sustainable practice are aware of the need to pay attention to the 'triple bottom line' of economy, society and environment, but in practice this is a difficult balancing act. For example, there is a solid literature on tourism/events and the natural environment, and also on economic impacts, and from these one can develop an understanding of the trade-offs and challenges that are faced by event managers. In the sphere of cultural impacts, however, the understanding is less well developed (Canziani, 2003), and overall there is a shortage of holistic tools which can be used to assess the impacts of an event.

Measuring Sustainability

The question that now arises is how we organize an event in a sustainable manner. In 1987, Redclift identified three major themes or issues pertaining to acting sustainably:

- the need to arrest environmental degradation and ecological imbalance;
- the need to avoid impoverishment of future generations; and
- the need for equity in the quality of life among present-day populations.

In other words, sustainable development encompasses not only environmental protection, but also economic development and social cohesion (Dooris, 1999). Agenda 21 (UNCED, 1992) represented a blueprint intended to set out an international programme of action for achieving sustainable development for the 21st century. It advocates action within the interconnected social, environmental and economic spheres.

Carrying capacity

With the increased interest in environmental concerns there comes an awareness of negative impacts, and the capacity of an area to absorb visitors is becoming more prominent. Beyond a certain point, the numbers arriving can have negative consequences for the evolution of an area (Beck, 1992). This is otherwise known as carrying capacity, which Theobald (1998) describes as important to understand in the limit and control of activities such as tourism or events which may threaten the sustained use of limited resources. Thus, the regulation and management of an area are important.

Carrying capacity is a relative management concept or framework, it is not a scientific theory, and because of this the preoccupation with finding techniques or methods that would allow us to determine when a destination is full has been plagued with problems. Given the diversity of factors that affect the nature of capacity, this calculation would seem to be exceedingly difficult, particularly when one considers the intangible qualities inherent in tourism carrying capacity (i.e. community perceptions, visitor satisfaction and attitude, political structures). Therefore carrying capacity needs to take account of many issues, as a means to an end and not, as it has been, as an end in itself.

The need for a broader framework

If sustainable events are to be achieved, all stakeholders must focus on alleviating the negative pressures and impacts generated. The sector needs to take a much more proactive role than it has done in the past if any lasting effect is to be achieved. The type of measures that need to be attended to include:

- All operators must handle energy, waste and water more efficiently.
- Credible environmental certification schemes linked to policies and practices are required.
- The sector needs to examine ways to reduce the environmental impact of travel.
- The industry must work with local authorities to manage increased numbers while avoiding further environmental damage.
- Practical, sustainable indicators are required.
- Events need to identify their impacts on biodiversity, cultural heritage and scenic landscapes and take action to reduce any negative impacts.
- The sector urgently needs to address problems such as litter in both urban and rural areas.
- The potential of marketing environmentally responsible events needs to be identified and developed.

Of these, one of the most complex areas to deal with is the development of sustainable indicators. The remainder of this chapter deals with this topic, in an effort to present a workable model of sustainability indicators that could be used by a local area, organization or event manager.

Implementation of sustainable development principles in the events industry will not only enhance the environmental quality of event destinations, but may also lead to sustainable competitive advantage and enhance the product and its positive impacts. Thus, it is important to inculcate the concepts of sustainability in the activities and practices of all the event's stakeholders – industry, local community, administration and event participants.

Indicator Models

While it is generally agreed that sustainability is the only long-term path for activities such as events, there remains an issue as to how it should be measured and implemented. As a preface to dealing with this issue, the nature of sustainable development and carrying capacity has been introduced above. The next stage is to introduce the DIT-ACHIEV Model of Sustainable Tourism Indicators and outline its potential application in an 'events' context as a tool for the measurement and implementation of sustainable action. Essentially this model utilizes a range of sustainability indicators; therefore it is important to undertake a review of indicators and their usefulness.

The development of indicators

Within the context of sustainability, indicators comprise 'time series information which is strategic to the sustainability of a destination, its assets and ultimately the fortunes of the... sector' (WTO, 2004).

A number of attempts have been made to develop indicator systems. One of the best known is based on the Organisation for Economic Co-operation and Development's (OECD) 'Pressure–State–Response' framework and was initially developed for environmental reporting, reflecting an emphasis on the environmental aspect of sustainability. This system proposes three kinds of indicators:

- *Pressure indicators*. These refer to the impact that activities have on the environment.
- *State indicators*. These describe the current situation of the impact (pressure) to be measured.
- *Response indicators*. These measure policies and actions taken due to changes in the state of sustainable development.

While this categorization does provide a framework for indicators, as does the DPSIR (Driving forces–Pressures–State–Impacts–Responses) framework that is widely used, it does not capture the totality of the visitor experience – which is the sum of the event product including people, economy, culture and customs, and not merely the interaction of events with the environment.

In response to the need for indicators that are applicable to a wide spectrum of settings, from virgin through emerging to mass event destinations, the World Tourism Organization's (WTO) 12-step framework for the development of indicators at the destination level is very useful (see Box 5.1).

Box 5.1. World Tourism Organization's suggested steps for indicator development. (Adapted from WTO, 2004.)

Research and organization
1. Definition/delineation of the destination
2. Use of participatory processes
3. Identification of tourism assets and risks
4. Long-term vision for a destination

Indicators development
5. Selection of priority issues
6. Identification of desired indicators
7. Inventory of data sources
8. Selection procedure

Implementation
9. Evaluation of feasibility/implementation
10. Data collection and analysis
11. Accountability, communication and reporting
12. Monitoring and evaluation of indicators application

Characteristics of selected indicators

A number of characteristics of indicators are central to the development of any such model. For example, consideration was given to a broad range of indicator types. Putnam (2002) suggests that consideration be given to four types of indicators:

- environmental condition indicators;
- environmental performance indicators;
- management performance indicators; and
- operational performance indicators.

In order to make the model as accessible as possible, consideration was given to the assertion by Morrissey *et al.* (2006, p. 49) that 'a degree of *simplification* is a prerequisite... to provide information in a form of practical use to decision-makers and understandable to the community'. Where possible, the selected indicators should also consider accuracy, bias, age, verifiability and completeness (Putnam, 2002). Finally, the following characteristics of indicators were taken into account (Flanagan *et al.*, 2007):

- Valuable indicators must consider long-term collecting of data.
- Indicators do not have to be specifically event-related once they can be used to indicate a healthy state of an event.
- Indicators must assist in indicating data that are *useful* and *consistent*.
- Indicators must indicate *change* over time.
- Indicators must assist in demonstrating trends and *movement* ('to' or 'from') relative to specified targets.

Towards Development of the DIT-ACHIEV Model

Mann (2000) argues that sustainability, and in particular, sustainable tourism development, needs to shift towards a greater emphasis on implementation, since many sustainable strategies have been devised but there are as yet few examples of successful initiatives. This assertion, that sustainable development needs to be interpreted in terms of what destinations and the industry can do to implement and operationalize sustainability, is central to the DIT-ACHIEV Model.

In any event destination a very broad range of interactions and activities occur. In the formulation of a model for the development of sustainability indicators, consideration of this spread of activities is required. At the outset, a list of 211 candidate indicators was developed, designed to capture the pressures on the sustainability of an area.

Following extensive analysis, this was reduced to the 33 indicators demonstrated in the DIT-ACHIEV Model of Sustainable Tourism Indicators (see Fig. 5.1). This refining process involved consultation with a broad range of experts including tourism and environmental managers at all levels, planners, enterprise development professionals, heritage and arts professionals, community-based practitioners, tourism and events industry personnel, scientific experts and expert academics, in addition to consideration of academic and professional literature.

Initially it was expected that the indicators would be derived directly from existing models; however, many models were found to be restrictive in the identification of robust indicators. Because of this, a new model was developed. This model (the DIT-ACHIEV Model) was initially designed around seven and subsequently six key 'fields of interest': Heritage, Infrastructure, Enterprise, Community, Visitor and Administration (Economics was initially considered but, as discussed in the following section, was later omitted); see Box 5.2.

Box 5.2. Key categories of indicators and their subcategories.

Heritage
- Flora and fauna
- Water
- Air
- Archaeology and history
- Culture
- Landscape
- Noise environment

Infrastructure
- Water supply and treatment
- Land supply/use
- Transport
- Visitor amenities
- Accommodation (location/quality/performance/seasonality)

Enterprise
- Cost of living
- Tourist spend
- Investment
- Labour
- Technology

Visitor
- Volume
- Behaviour
- Service levels
- Hospitality

Community
- Access
- Involvement
- Quality of life
- Beneficiaries

Administration
- Goals
- Capability
- Priorities
- Jurisdiction
- Policy

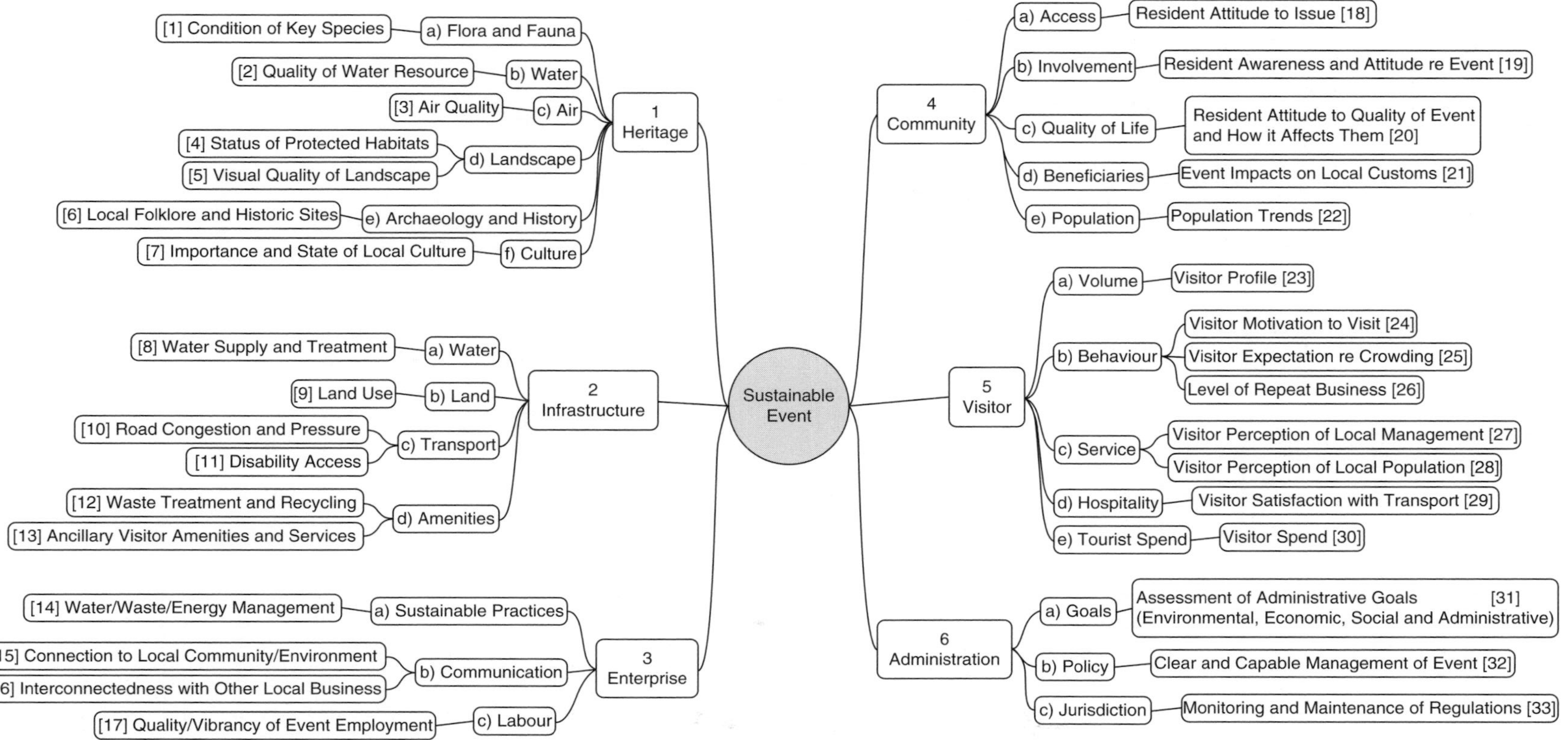

Fig. 5.1. The DIT-ACHIEV Model of Sustainable Tourism Indicators.

Problems with the Development of Indicators

As is apparent from an examination of indicators in any area, industry or activity, the major issue confronting the selection of indicators is the poor availability of many data sets. Across various leisure/tourism/event activities, the range of suitable indicators is often limited by availability of local or regional data. At a generic/national level there is much greater availability of information, but this must be extrapolated for use at a local level. In addition, many indicators address the sustainability of the local asset as a result of pressure arising from the local population rather than from any pressures that might be generated from a visiting population. General employment indicators, for example, may capture the phenomenon of income from an event, but in general its robustness as an indicator of a specific event is limited.

While data for several desirable indicators are not readily available at present, all are potentially available at a resource cost – which may be significant in some cases. The benefit of collecting information on an event or set of events has to be balanced against the costs involved. Because of this, the indicators included in the model which have a resource implication were considered very carefully, and included only where this cost was deemed to be unavoidable.

With regard to data collection, there are a number of methods by which a local area (authority, council, etc.) could do much to provide 'relevant', 'fresh' and 'sensitive' data without an excessive outlay of costs. For instance, it should be feasible to provide information on planning permissions, car registrations and unemployment updates at the smallest area for which census data are available and thus facilitate analysis at this important spatial scale. These constantly changing variables could provide important information to gauge inter-census changes. It should also be possible to capture information from the returns of commercial rates on accommodation, amenities and event service providers in an area. This would merely require the administrative records to include (and make available to researchers) geocoding as part of current information systems.

More frequent use of traffic-count technology at key 'hot spots' would appear to be a relatively inexpensive means of capturing rough trends in visitor throughput and would develop both a spatial and temporal profile of flows.

A more costly step in assembling the information needed to fill the indicator deficit involves the use of questionnaire-based surveys to examine both the visitor and the local populations. Such data are central to the management of sustainable events in an area. Apart from the expense involved however, the wisdom of pursuing this route is questionable for individual areas acting on their own. Issues of 'freshness', 'reliability' and especially 'comparability' immediately arise with the use of this methodology.

The DIT-ACHIEV Model of Sustainable Tourism Indicators

Reflective of the various issues just outlined and based on the complexity of data in the various indicators, it was decided that the emphasis of indicator selection should be on a small number of focused and straightforward indicators.

The subsequent model (Fig. 5.1) is divided into six fields of interest that are numbered from 1 to 6. Each of these fields of interest is composed of between three and six sub-fields, which are identified by letters (a–f). Where required, some of these sub-fields are subdivided into one or two indicators, resulting in the 33 indicators that are numbered using square brackets.

Assessable parameters

In order to evaluate each indicator there are from one to four assessable parameters. Samples of the indicators are outlined in Table 5.1, as are their assessable parameters, their availability and some general comments on their applicability. Thus road congestion, for example, is a good indicator of pressure and can reflect dissatisfaction and displeasure as well as potential environmental damage.

Application of the model

It is proposed that this model should be used to:

- establish a baseline for the state of an area in an objective and robust manner;
- develop a methodology for the identification of when carrying capacity is negatively impacted by an event; and
- assist in the development on an overall policy/plan for the management of sustainable events.

The application of the model would require a local administration or an organization which is willing to apply and test the model. Running the model would require detailed data collection of measurables to establish a baseline state of the parameters. Following this, indicators would be used to identify and examine temporal and spatial trends in each relevant parameter. Depending on the situation in which the model is applied, the positive or negative movement of certain indicators would indicate a move towards or away from sustainable goals.

Weighting of indicators

While emphasizing some indicators over others and prioritizing certain criteria is a relatively common practice, in the development of the DIT-ACHIEV Model no attempt has been made to apply weightings to the various indicators.

This was a deliberate decision so that the model can be applied universally. For example, in a rural marine location, lake and river water quality would be key indicators of sustainability, whereas in other environments such indicators could be of marginal importance. If, however, weighting or prioritization of indicators is desirable in a particular setting, a number of selection procedures must be followed:

- *Identification of locally significant indicators*. This must be undertaken through consultation with local key stakeholders and managers.
- *Identification of the most robust indicators*. A method such as the MEANS matrix could be used (Flanagan *et al*., 2007) to highlight the indicators which fulfil the greatest number of criteria – again the assessment criteria can vary according to the relative importance of factors such as budget, urgency of investigation or sensitivity of environment/economy/culture.
- *Identification of critical indicators*. In certain cases some indicators may identify crisis situations. These may be assigned priority status in such instances.

Ultimately the model is designed to be employed in a flexible manner, and adapted to the local situation according to sound environmental, economic and sociocultural principles.

Using indicators

The DIT-ACHIEV Model can be utilized to demonstrate different degrees of sustainability, depending on the location/situation in which it is adopted. Indicators such as those outlined in this model can be used for a number of purposes. Primarily in an events context, they can be used to identify the following:

- stresses on an area (e.g. traffic congestion, water shortages, visitor dissatisfaction);
- the impact of events (e.g. seasonality, habitat damage, local community employment);
- management effort (e.g. funding of pollution/litter cleanups); and
- the effect of management actions (e.g. changed water quality, number of repeat visitors to subsequent events).

Indicators can also provide an early warning of when a policy change or new action may be needed, as well as providing a basis for the

Table 5.1. Samples of indicators and assessable parameters.

Indicator	Assessable parameter(s)	Availability	Comments
[3] Air Quality	Overall air quality	Data for the study area – particulate matter, nitrogen dioxide levels, etc. – not usually available in enough detail	This is considered important by most measures of sustainability, but local level data are difficult to isolate – often linked to pollution from transport
[4] Status of Protected Habitats	Existence, maintenance and management of protected sites	Readily available	Easy to keep updated. Good to have especially as long-term indicator
[6] Local Folklore and Historic Sites	State of local folklore, local monuments and places of interest	Fragmented but generally available in the form of Sites and Monuments Record	Heritage is important for local identity and a vital attractive element for many locally embedded events
[7] Importance and State of Local Culture	(i) Local language/dialect	Generally well documented	Good – indicative of strength of local tradition and culture
	(ii) Local festivals	Usually tracked by local and regional tourism organizations	Festivals are easy to track and demonstrate local participation in organizations
[10] Road Congestion and Pressure	(i) Congestion	Not well recorded, but can be identified easily if seen to be important	Good indications of pressure, measures of seasonality and congestion – need data to be seasonal and represent different days and seasons. This is an issue for both visitors and locals. Congestion on busy event weekends versus quiet winter days
	(ii) Number of vehicles on various types of roads	Some 'counts' but generally unavailable	
	(iii) Parking	Number and distribution of parking spaces and cost of parking	Presence of parking is less important than use and pressure
	(iv) Accident data	Privacy issue – difficult to relate to event	Police and Road Safety Authorities in some areas record and disseminate this type of data
[11] Disability Access	Facilities with dedicated access for people with disability	Easy to identify, not usually centrally recorded	Capacity limitation for only a small number of tourists but may have serious impacts. Not just an 'event' issue but also important for local population
[16] Interconnectedness with Other Local Business	Participation in local cooperatives and partnerships	Not collected by any agency – availability would require survey	Indicates commitment to local community
[18] Resident Attitude to Issue	(i) Residents' attitudes to issues with access (ii) Residents' attitudes to traffic and congestion management	Needs survey or consultation with local population to assess their levels of satisfaction	Need to test awareness and feelings to see if actual problems exist. Disturbance by event could mean residents curtail their activities and feel problems

[20] Resident Attitude to Quality of Event and How it Affects Them	(i) Residents' attitudes to event employment (ii) Local perception of their relationship with visitors (iii) Issues raised regarding visitor behaviour (may vary according to event type)	Residents' perceptions/attitudes are more important than reality as seen by organizers – need to be assessed	Changes can trace positive aspects of events, indicative of more than just changes in an event. May indicate growth and long-term viability
[23] Visitor Profile	(i) Appropriate balance – peak and off-peak numbers (ii) Visitor numbers in various accommodations	Seasonality as a key element – easy to enumerate with cooperation from accommodation and other service providers	Indicative of seasonality, need commitment for gathering this. Important indicators for testing: contribution to local economies, overall impacts, where benefits are occurring, type of visitor, etc. – consistency important for assessing change over time
[27] Visitor Perception of Local Management	(i) Perceived management of issues (crowd control, noise, etc.) (ii) Perceived management of pollution/litter	Dependent on dedicated visitor survey. Needs to be gathered consistently	Visitor/participant perception – good indicator of likelihood to be repeat customer
[30] Visitor Spend	Characteristics of spend (seasonality, overseas and domestic, etc.)	Visitor survey required – can be derived (though not very accurately) from national data	Spend is a good indicator of seasonal fluctuation – would assist policy
[31] Assessment of Administrative Goals (Environmental, Economic, Social and Administrative)	The presence and attainment of SMART goals	Requires assessment of political administration	Goals are only useful if testable, i.e. SMART – Specific Measurable, Achievable, Realistic/Relevant, Targeted/Timely (long-term and short-term)
[32] Clear and Capable Management of Event	(i) Integrated planning (ii) Monitoring and evaluation to measure organizational performance	Difficult to 'measure' but evident in the planning of some sustainable events	Overarching (integrating) agency/body that serves as link between public and private sector organization on ground (e.g. strong legal structure – not voluntary or *ad hoc*), good feedback loop if put in a model
[33] Monitoring and Maintenance of Regulations	(i) Clarity in relation to regulatory role/power of organizations (ii) Clear strategies for enforcement of law/ regulations	Difficult to 'measure' but evident in some sustainable events destinations	If serious about sustainability needs enforcing, otherwise 'wishful' policies become irrelevant. But don't want a 'police state' either! Needs responsibility and infrastructure

long-term planning and review of events (UNEP/UNWTO, 2005).

Thus, in its simplest form the model sets benchmarks against which changes in the Administration, Community, Heritage, Infrastructure, Enterprise and Visitor, resulting from events, can be assessed. In a location where there is a perceived concern regarding visitor or local satisfaction, more resources would initially be spent on these aspects of the model, while these may not be of concern for other destinations. In fact, the only aspects of the model to be used in a particular setting may, for example, be those within the 'visitor' field of interest. The manner in which the model is adopted will result from the sustainable event strategy in which it is placed; however, to be seen as a true model of sustainable event management, all aspects of the model should at least be considered if not applied.

Implementing the model

What remains to be developed is a structure whereby the model can be applied in a real situation/scenario. The proposed methodology for implementation follows a structure similar to that suggested in the UNEP/UNWTO (2005) document *Making Tourism More Sustainable: A Guide for Policy Makers*, which is a management guide for governments around the world. This document is composed of three main themes that can be paraphrased in an events context (Denman, 2006):

- Define sustainable events and identify what needs to be addressed.
- Identify a working structure and strategies that are needed to be effective.
- Identify tools that can assist in the management of an event.

The first and last of these themes have been addressed within this chapter, and the second theme of identifying structures/strategies is now addressed. In operationalizing the model, the steps outlined in Box 5.3 are proposed for the formulation of a sustainable event strategy.

There are two key issues in this strategy formulation. First, it is important to establish the correct structures through which organizations can work with others towards more sustainable events, and thereby develop and drive policies and actions. Second, a process must be developed that embraces sustainability and identifies some of the strategic choices that need to be made – while considering the product, marketing, operation of the event and the behaviour of visitors. The tool that will be used to influence events development (in this case the DIT-ACHIEV Model) always needs to be considered.

Box 5.3. Methodology for the formulation of a sustainable event strategy. (Adapted from Denman, 2006.)

1. Create a multi-interest working group
2. Agree on initial issues to investigate
3. Undertake wide consultation
4. Prepare a situation analysis, including destination performance, needs and opportunities
5. Consult and agree on key issues and priorities
6. Determine strategic objectives
7. Develop an action programme
8. Establish or strengthen instruments to facilitate implementation
9. Implement actions
10. Monitor results

Observations on Application of the Model

Heritage

Based on an extensive assessment of impacts on ecological systems, it is evident that there are clearly observable impacts of events, but the causal relationship between events and local ecology is difficult to quantify. The overall status of ecology, however, requires continuing monitoring. Identifying the relationship of many of the dimensions is complicated by the influence of outside forces. For example, water quality is influenced by external factors such as sunlight and rainfall. Air quality is an even more difficult aspect to focus upon in a relatively small study area, as the spatial scale at which air quality varies makes this localized form of investigation difficult to monitor. However, such limitations cannot lead to complacency and continued monitoring is important to maintain or improve current standards.

An important aspect of ecological systems is the interrelationship between diverse aspects such as landscape, architecture, culture and the living environment. It is proposed that while landscapes and vistas are not straightforward to quantify and evaluate, themes such as landscape evaluation, visual landscapes and landscape quality could be explored in an attempt to bring together a number of these ecological dimensions.

Infrastructure

An examination of physical structures identifies a range of services upon which events are strongly dependent. However, services and facilities are widely dispersed and, despite the presence of 'honey-pots', event locations are diffused in nature. It would appear that the key event pressures on physical structures result from increased visitor demand during major events. However, other than infrequent high-intensity incidents of littering, traffic congestion and pressure on service providers such as restaurants and bars, outside these key periods, the physical structure is rarely pressurized by issues of capacity.

The main issue regarding physical structures is in areas where events are periodic. In these areas a shortage of supply, perhaps even lack of critical mass, of product raises issues of sustainability. Such event areas have small product bases, with poor supply of accommodation and are often poorly serviced by public transport. From the perspective of development and marketing, the sustainability of such a location causes difficulties for certain types of events. Conversely, this low level of service is seen by certain product providers, locals and even visitors as being desirable – but again, this depends on the scale of the event.

Economic structure

In the beginning 'Economic Structure' was identified as a separate field of interest in this model. However, as it evolved, it became apparent that the economic element should not be treated as a separate area/field of interest. Instead, it was used to develop a model which examines the utilization of event capital stock (ecology, physical and social) and the sustainability of its use. Therefore, the economic dimensions were integrated into the overall model. One of the reasons why this approach was adopted relates to the overall importance of economic sustainability for the survival of events. Linked to this was the difficulty of accessing accurate and usable data, at an appropriate scale.

Enterprise

The visible level of 'sustainability' achieved by local enterprises is one of the most evident measures of sustainability. Hence, adoption of eco-labels, awards and classifications is seen by many as proof of sustainable credentials. However, it is important that such sustainable practices in areas such as waste, water and energy management are embedded in the practice of the operators and suppliers, rather than merely representing 'green-washing' practices. A viable way of doing this is to ensure that open and clear channels of communication exist, in all directions, and are open to scrutiny at all times.

Community

In general, local communities appear to be tolerant of events. The economic, social and cultural benefits are well recognized. The negative issues identified include traffic problems and overcrowding, which are evaluated by the DIT-ACHIEV Model. Often, a local community feels that it is not consulted about any inconveniences arising from events. Going forward, there exists a need to monitor the level of communication between event stakeholders and the local community.

Visitor

A high percentage of visitors indicating that they would return to a repeat event signifies a high level of visitor satisfaction. However, visitor perceptions must be evaluated in greater depth. Issues such as access to and within an area, improved signposting and the need to monitor the natural environment all impact the overall perception of a visit and quality of service. In terms of this model, the importance of visitor satisfaction is recognized, but visitor satisfaction alone does not make a sustainable event. However, in order to regard visitor satisfaction in its broadest sense, the sub-fields outlined in the model allow for anticipated or unanticipated changes in visitor satisfaction.

Administration

Assessment of administrative goals (environmental, economic, social and administrative) requires the presence and attainment of SMART (Specific, Measurable, Achievable, Realistic/Relevant and Targeted/Timely) objectives. This format provides a transparent method for testing the process.

Clear and capable management of events looks at integrated planning, monitoring and evaluation and the measuring of performance. An overarching agency with 'legal' responsibility for an event that practises clear and capable management is a desirable goal. Monitoring and maintenance of regulations require clarity regarding the role of organizations in relation to regulation, and also clear strategies for enforcement of regulations. This involves monitoring and evaluating regulations to ensure they are being upheld.

Challenges

A challenge regarding the implementation of this model relates to the gathering and analysis of data. While there is very little events-specific data collection undertaken, there is a myriad of agencies involved in the collection of data which apply to the various aspects of this model. For example, numerous organizations collect information on the natural and physical environment, data related to employment and enterprise, general visitor numbers and income generated. In each of these examples, data are collected in a disjointed fashion and access to an individual data bank is often difficult and time-consuming. In addition, the plethora of data sets tends to be recorded at particular spatial scales that can be difficult to interpolate for a particular event or study area (i.e. national economic multipliers and cost of living formulae). This difficulty is magnified when one attempts to work across disciplinary boundaries and undertake broad-ranging research, as required in a truly holistic investigation of sustainability.

Therefore there is a need for local authorities, state agencies and voluntary groups to do more to provide data that are spatially coded. This would facilitate more accurate analysis of environmental, economic and social conditions at a local level. Interaction between the numerous public, private and voluntary organizations that gather data is also required so that agreement can be achieved regarding standardized formats, availability and quality of data. Cooperation between these agencies and event organizers would facilitate more accessible and more accurate investigation of many of the indicators.

Research into making an event more sustainable cannot be static; therefore, the data used in this model must consider change over time, once spatial and temporal benchmarks are set. Particular attention in this regard is required for the collection of locally specific data, focusing, for example, on the visitor, the local community and the local administration.

Finally, local authorities and event managers could begin by identifying 'hot spots' and begin to identify area-specific event-related pressures of importance. Once this is undertaken, weighting of indicators may be desirable in order to prioritize actions. However, weighting will vary from place to place, and must be based on local needs and demands.

Summary

This chapter has discussed a number of the challenges regarding how event managers and organizers could begin to act more sustainably. The chapter analysed the challenge of measuring sustainability and then introduced the concept of indicator models, leading to the DIT-ACHIEV Model of Sustainable Tourism Indicators. The challenges and difficulties of using indicators were discussed, as were possible future directions for such a methodology.

It is proposed here that the DIT-ACHIEV Model is a suitable tool for the management of sustainable events. An appropriate method of applying the model would be to follow the ten steps for the development of a sustainable event management structure as outlined in this chapter. In addition, the DIT-ACHIEV Model (DIT, 2007) demonstrates how an integrated management approach towards the mitigation of tourism impacts can be achieved. It is argued that this indicator model, which examines Administration, Community, Heritage, Industry, Enterprise and Visitor, can be employed in a variety of settings to mitigate the negative and maximize the positive impacts of an event.

To progress sustainability in an events context needs champions who are willing to adopt the model and test its applicability both spatially and temporally. Ideally this would be a local authority or event management organization that is interested in truly pursuing sustainability and is prepared to commit resources and time to the adoption and application of this model. Such commitment would highlight many challenges in the practicalities of employing this methodology, but would undoubtedly result in a deeper and more rewarding understanding of sustainable events.

Key Questions

1. Referring to literature you have consulted, discuss a number of different indicator types, identifying examples of each in an events context.

2. Referring specifically to the DIT-ACHIEV Model of Sustainable Tourism Indicators, identify how models can be used to make an event more sustainable.

3. What are the key data limitations that challenge the sustainable management of events?

References

Beck, U. (1992) *Risk Society: Towards a New Modernity*. Sage, London.

Canziani, B. (2003) A framework for managing the cultural impact of conferences and events. Paper presented at *BEST Education Network Think Tank III*, Alajuela, Costa Rica, 8–11 July 2003.

Denman, P. (2006) Tourism and sustainability: objectives, policies and tools for sustainable tourism. Paper presented to *UNWTO Seminar on Tourism Sustainability and Local Agenda 21 in Tourism Destinations*, Jeddah, Saudi Arabia, 18–19 February 2006.

Dooris, M. (1999) Healthy cities and Local Agenda 21: the UK experience – challenges for the new millennium. *Health Promotion International* 14(4), 365–375.

Flanagan, S., Griffin, K., O'Halloran, E., Phelan, J., Roe, P., Burke, E. and Tottle, A. (2007) *Sustainable Tourism Development: Toward the Mitigation of Tourism Destination Impacts*. Synthesis Report ERTDI-funded project 2004-SD-MS-21. Environmental Protection Agency, Wexford, Republic of Ireland.

Mann, M. (2000) *The Community Tourism Guide*. Earthscan Publications, London.

Morrissey, J., O'Regan, B. and Moles, R. (2006) Development of indicators and indices for the evaluation of the sustainability of Irish settlements and regional settlement patterns. In: *Proceedings of ENVIRON 2006, University College Dublin, January 2006*. Environmental Sciences Association of Ireland, Cork, pp. 17–22.

Putnam, D. (2002) ISO 14031: environmental performance evaluation. Confederation of Indian Industry.

Redclift, M.R. (1987) *Sustainable Development: Exploring the Contradictions*. Routledge, London.

Theobald, W.F. (1998) *Global Tourism*. Butterworth-Heinemann, Oxford, UK.

UNCED (1992) Report of the United Nations Conference on Environment and Development (Rio de Janeiro, 3–14 June 1992). Annex I. Rio Declaration on Environment and Development. Available at: http://www.un.org/documents/ga/conf151/aconf15126-1annex1.htm (accessed 16 March 2009).

UNEP/UNWTO (United Nations Environment Programme/United Nations World Tourism Organization) (2005) *Making Tourism More Sustainable: A Guide for Policy Makers*. UNEP Division of Technology, Industry and Economics, Madrid.

UNESCO (1976) The effects of tourism on socio-cultural values. *Annals of Tourism Research* 4(2), 74–105.

WTO (2004) *Indicators of Sustainable Development for Tourism Destinations: A Guidebook*. World Tourism Organization, Madrid.

6 The Economics of Sustainable Events

R. Raj and J. Musgrave
Leeds Metropolitan University, Leeds, UK

This chapter examines the relationship between economic impacts and potential benefits that events may bring to host communities. In addition, there is an exploration of measures of economic impacts and of ways in which host communities formulate their decisions. Finally, the chapter looks at contextualizing the catalytic effect that ensues when there is an increase in investment due to events taking place. The case study approach is used to support the arguments in the literature.

Chapter outline

- Introduction
- Economic Concept of Sustainability
- Economic Measures
- Economic Sustainability through Event Tourism
- Economic Impacts of Events on Host Communities
- Cost–Benefit Analysis of Sustainable Events
- Economic Legacy of Events
- Economic Development of Local Communities through Sustainable Events
- Summary
- Key Questions

Introduction

The act of balancing economic growth and social and environmental awareness is a complex and plural concept. The responsibility for this rests upon economies that have reaped the benefits of decades of industrialization. These economies are in a position to create the knowledge and skills set that will influence organizations to adopt more sustainable processes and practices. Evidently, the need for sustainable management is a direct consequence of worldwide industrialization and the consumption of natural resources. Moreover, the large expansion of developing countries over the last two decades has raised concerns about the environmental and social impacts of economic decisions made by the business community. Consequently, sustainable development has emerged as a high agenda item for future national and international economic strategies.

Clearly, the principles of economic sustainability refer to new approaches that will assist government and industry to implement efficient and effective economically responsible decisions, from which communities can benefit over longer periods without putting greater pressure on natural resources.

Within the boundaries of the events industry, sustainability is a relatively new concept. In events, economic impact studies are undertaken for a variety of purposes; frequently they consider elements of cost–benefit analysis concerning the cost of hosting the event in comparison to income generation and visitor expenditure. However, events often provide long-term economic benefits to host communities by means of an increase in community profile, increased employment, additional trade and regeneration. Further to this, it could be argued that a catalytic effect ensues whereby an increase in investment, coupled with additional monies, creates other tangible benefits such as improved tax revenues, increased property prices and a sense of personal wealth. This is evident with outdoor events such as the Notting Hill Carnival, which not only bring economic benefits to the host city, but also provide the city with the opportunity to market itself nationally and internationally.

Economic Concept of Sustainability

The economic concept developed and originated with the need to analyse and forecast the future activities of cities and countries. The British Government Panel on Sustainable Development (1994) states that economic sustainability means:

> Most societies want to achieve economic development to secure higher standards of living, now and for future generations. They also seek to protect and enhance their environment, now and for their children.

Present global economic systems overexploit natural resources and the world population is consuming greater quantities of these resources at an ever-increasing pace, beyond what nature can replenish. At the same time there is compelling evidence that the gap between rich and poor is fast becoming a chasm and the inertia of developing economies leaves behind a neglected society where health, famine, poverty and social injustices multiply. Consequently these issues have encouraged a shift in the zeitgeist.

Local economies depend on economic sustainability to make choices in a socially responsible environment. Economic sustainability is important for all nations, because the whole economy of a nation depends on strong economic and social sustainability. Economic sustainability helps organizations understand the importance and regenerative benefits of economic growth. Economic growth can only be achieved and sustained if companies improve their input and output cycle and increase the inflow of capital or revenues within the business environment. According to Hoexter (2006):

> Can the organization continue to survive in the current economic system? Does income exceed expense? Without economic sustainability any firm is not going to last unless it is massively subsidized by a larger or richer entity.

Figure 6.1 presents a model of the key fields of economic sustainability. The model illustrates that economic sustainability can broadly be defined as a consideration of: (i) production; (ii) the consumption of goods and services; (iii) the consumption of capital and resources; and (iv) people and institutions. Additionally, this model indicates the relationship and interactions of the mentioned elements that influence key decision makers, institutional policies and governmental strategies. Consequently, the concept of economic sustainability covers all areas of business in terms of generating input and output: costs, expenditure and income. Moreover, the theory of economic sustainability is linked with maintaining an effective business profit and utilizing varied capital items and resources within the business environment to counter any threats which may affect business productivity and economic stability.

It is important to emphasize that working towards economic sustainability is the responsibility of everyone, whether he/she is a user or a provider of information to business. Economic sustainability will not be achieved instantaneously but over generations, as many are businesses still couched in industrialized approaches to management and economics. There is a tendency to consider businesses as separate entities, whereas their true impact should be assessed holistically rather than based on the component parts.

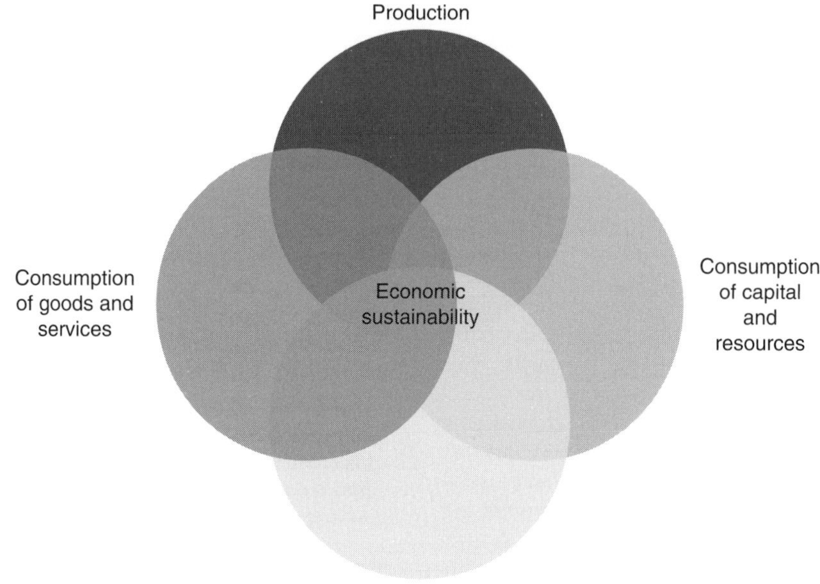

Fig. 6.1. The concept of economic sustainability.

Economic Measures

The economy is measured in a number of different ways to calculate the economic activity of a country and assess the maintenance of economic sustainability. Figure 6.2 provides a synthesis of tools that are currently being used by countries to measure their economic activity. Of these, GNP (gross national product) is an important tool for measuring the economy. GNP looks at products that are developed by a country for internal use and for distribution to international markets.

For example, in the UK, the Business Tourism Partnership proposes that the exhibition industry creates over £9 billion in the economy (Rogers, 2004). Key Note Ltd (2004) estimates that the corporate hospitality industry contributes over £900 million per annum and Mintel (2004) suggests that music festivals and concerts add in excess of £600 million.

Therefore festivals and events are now recognized by economists as key economic tools for local and national economies: they increase economic activities and inject new money into the economy and leave post-event impacts on the host community.

Economic Sustainability through Event Tourism

Event tourism can generate positive economic impacts, in addition to longer-term place marketing benefits and media exposure for destinations, along with sporting or cultural policy benefits. Indeed, Brown *et al.* (2004) assert that it is rare not to find a range of sport and cultural events vying for tourists' attention in most major cities.

Within the rural context, economic restructuring has had adverse effects on the economic opportunities for rural communities. The decline of farming as a significant economic power has boosted other entrepreneurial activities, such as tourism (Wilson *et al.*, 2001; Williams and Ferguson, 2005). Such rural development strategies may often be driven by bottom-up approaches to tourism development, which encourage local community participation, utilize social capital and limit dependency on external businesses. A grassroots approach to rural tourism development ensures that tourism becomes a community product. Community-based events are becoming increasingly popular, encompassing a

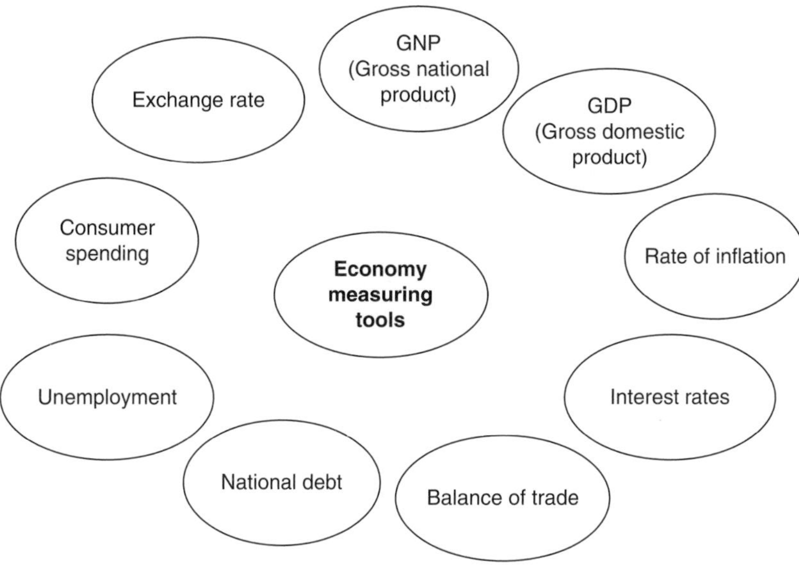

Fig. 6.2. Tools for measuring the economy.

diverse range of themes, and there appears to be a shift towards a more community-oriented events approach to regeneration. Ratcliffe and Flanagan (2004) assert that attributes such as value for money, service standards, unique experiences, information, authenticity and environmental quality are shared by tourism and destination regeneration and lead to competitive advantage for destinations.

Events that attract a wide inbound audience are recognized as having positive economic impacts on towns and cities as visitors spend money on accommodation, retail, food and drink and other activities – although there is a school of thought that suggests otherwise (Jones, 2001). Differentiating between different types of event visitors is crucial in terms of determining the true economic impact of an event. For example, UK Sport (2005) asserts that the potential economic impact of an event is determined by the nature of the sport, the location of the event, seasonal or geographic factors, and whether the event is competitor-intensive or spectator-intensive. Unsurprisingly, the economic impacts of the former are easier to forecast, as the number of competitors is generally known in advance.

Economic Impacts of Events on Host Communities

The decision to host most large-scale events is generally based on the impacts to the local economy (Dwyer *et al.*, 2000; Hoexter, 2006; Stern, 2006). This is also considered particularly important by local authorities, to justify the spending of public money (Getz, 1997). The economic benefits of events are one of the major aspects of holding mega outdoor events in a city – to boost financial assets for the local community. Events have the potential to generate a vast amount of tourism when they cater to out-of-region visitors, grants or sponsorships (Getz, 1997) of direct or indirect intent. Although definitive data concerning the impact of event tourism are not available owing to the complexity and diversity of the industry, Key Leisure Markets (2001) claimed that day trips in England are now worth more than domestic and inbound tourism combined.

Festivals and events have their bases in the long term and are seen in a very positive manner by event organizers, local and national government and the community at large, because of the economic sustainability they generate for the local community through event tourism. For example, events have an important role to play within both the national and local community in the context of destination planning, enhancing and linking tourism and commerce. Some aspects of this role include: events as image makers, economic benefit generators and tourist attractions; overcoming seasonality; contributing to the development of local communities and businesses; and supporting key industrial sectors. In general, events also have social impacts that are seen to strengthen community structures, enhance community cohesion and develop close ties between different ethnic groups. Figure 6.3 shows a number of benefits that events bring to a host community.

Events have both positive and negative impacts on their host communities, but emphasis is often focused on the economic analysis by event organizers and used for political initiatives. Environmental impacts on the host community are overseen by government and private industry to justify the perceived economic goals. Undoubtedly, in addition to creating community cohesion, festivals and events potentially give greater economic sustainability to host destinations by developing employment, additional trade and business development, investment in infrastructure, long-term promotional benefits and tax revenues.

However, the impact of events on host cities is changing in accordance with significant developments in the events market since the late 1990s. Consequently, the post-event evaluation is extremely important not only to review the situation, but also to identify and manage the impacts to assist in maximizing future benefits.

Cost–Benefit Analysis of Sustainable Events

Cost–benefit analysis (CBA) is a formal discipline used by event organizations to help assess or evaluate a project or business activity and make objective economic decisions. The technique was developed to gauge and enhance the quality and efficiency of any new business activity intervention and the cause and effect on the different stakeholders.

Within the feasibility stages of planning models, CBA can be used by event organizers

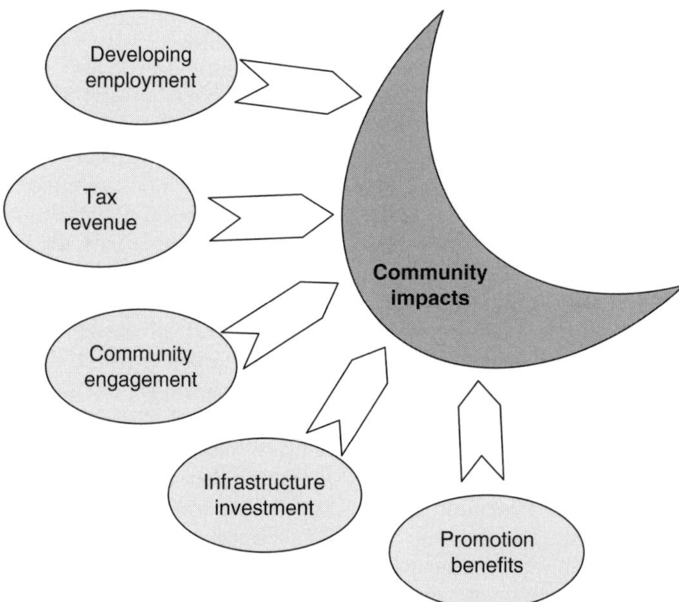

Fig. 6.3. Economic sustainability to host community.

to assess and evaluate the costs against benefits of any new activity, product or service, and provide a projected view of the economic impacts. For example, the economic analysis of large-scale events is based on the principles of providing economic benefits to the local community. Large-scale events and festivals are increasingly being used as a tool to assess and promote visitors to an area and boost the local economy for the host city. The CBA technique helps managers and organizations to identify the actual value of the economic impact being measured in a more standard format by assessing both the benefits and the costs incurred in the process of the event. Table 6.1 identifies a hypothetical community event and the economic costs/benefits of hosting such an event.

CBA measures the net benefits that will be generated from the event and the estimated number of tourists or visitors coming to the local area for the duration of the event. Events managers can use the CBA technique to assess the economic viability of large-scale festivals. A major study was carried out in Australia to assess the hosting of the Formula 1 Grand Prix (Burns *et al.*, 1986). CBA takes into account the opportunity cost that is directly related to the impacts of the event and helps the manager to make better decisions in relation to options available for hosting the event.

Table 6.1. Cost–benefit analysis of a hypothetical community event: local music sale and battle of local bands.

Costs	Benefits
Noise reduction strategies	Financial gain for local businesses
Cleaning up the area	International exposure through media and marketing
Pollution	Developing community cohesion and pride
Criminal damage	Creating jobs
Employment cost for workers and police	Cultural impact through increased tourism and visitors
Organization and development costs	New facilities for local area

The CBA approach has the following benefits:

- assesses the monetary value of the event;
- assesses the external effects of the event;
- proposes expenditure decisions;
- adds value to the promotion of cultural pride; and
- looks at positive and negative social effects of the event.

Limitations of CBA include:

- ignores the flow-on effects of the event;
- ignores the overall impact of the event on the economy; and
- very difficult to place a monetary value on the event.

The CBA method seeks to determine whether the benefits to the local community or region exceed the costs. The main advantage of using the CBA approach is to ensure a consistent evaluation process for analysing economic sustainability for the local economy and event organizers. Moreover, it is important that CBA should measure and analyse all of the economic impacts of an event. The sustainability of the event should be clear to offer long-term benefits for the host community.

Economic Legacy of Events

Economic legacy is seen by events organizers as a long-term critical success factor and is used as a catalyst for holding mega-events and festivals by key stakeholders. For example, the organizers of the London 2012 Olympic Games have taken the impact of economic legacy into account by learning lessons from previous Olympics venues. The bidding team for London's 2012 Games and the Greater London Council decided to utilize land that would otherwise not be used in order to leave a physical legacy in the host community for the future.

In their legacy vision, organizers of mega-events and festivals need to lay down clear goals at the planning stage to achieve legacy benefits. Legacy benefits can be achieved by adopting the rules shown in Fig. 6.4, which suggest that organizers of mega-events need to

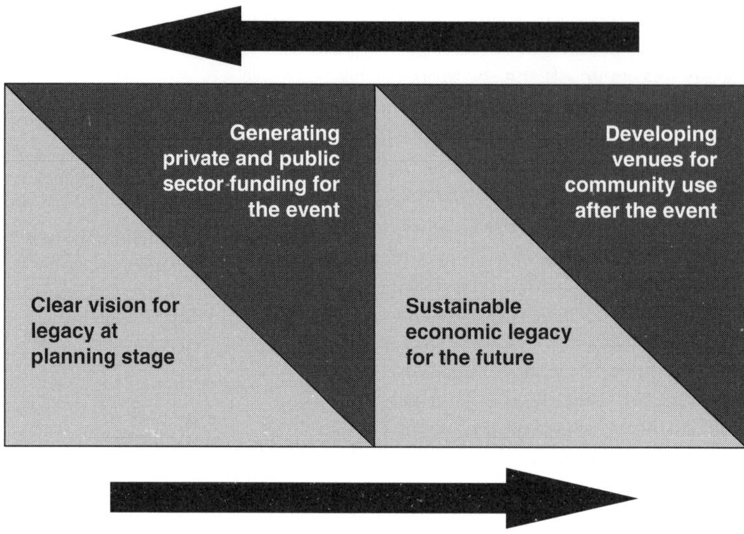

Fig. 6.4. Legacy rules.

take into consideration the full economic benefits and develop clear and efficient sustainable principles for the event well in advance.

Economic legacy is very difficult to analyse and characterize because, although several different models exist to measure the economic impacts of legacy in the events industry, there is no specific or authentic model available to measure the legacy impact on the host community.

The prime aim of the London Games is to leave a sustainable physical legacy that will generate economic sustainability for a number of decades. The London 2012 organizing committee has committed itself to working very closely with the host communities by addressing the following attributes (London 2012 Olympic Bid, 2003):

- creating jobs for local people in the area;
- creating affordable housing for local people;
- enhancing community cohesion;
- developing venues that will benefit local communities;
- creating open spaces for local communities;
- regenerating underdeveloped parts of the UK; and
- creating sustainability through the economic, social and environmental triple bottom line.

The basic idea of the London 2012 management committee is to create a sustainable economic legacy for local communities living around the Olympic site. As stated by Tom Russell, Group Director of Olympic Legacy at the London Development Agency:

> The most important legacy clients are the people that live and work around the Olympic site. If we are to create an area that will revitalize east London then it must be integrated with existing communities, and to do that local people must have a key role in the planning process. (LDA, 2008)

The development of legacy through major sporting events has been linked with sport for a long time. The idea of delivering long-lasting legacy through large-scale sporting events and community festivals is to ensure that local people play an important part in creating economic sustainability.

The economic legacy can be realized once the event has taken place and the new facilities are passed on to the local community to maximize the full potential benefits. Therefore, it is important for the organizers of large-scale special events to take into account the number of years it will take to develop actual facilities and generate long-term economic benefits. By the time the legacy has been passed on to the local community, the community may experience adverse effects and the actual benefits may have been squandered or lost in the process.

Large-scale events and festivals need to take into account urban generation and social impacts at the planning stage, as well as how the benefits will actually be passed on to the local community, before they can even consider discussing the economic legacy. A clear and open communication policy should be created, to discuss with and engage the local people in the continuous development and changes taking place in the area. In addition, the policy should promote the new facilities being developed in the area and describe how they will be passed on to the local community after the event, to make local residents feel part of the event. Moreover, consideration should be given the key issues that will help foster a better relationship and create a positive image.

Economic Development of Local Communities through Sustainable Events

The economic sustainability of events and festivals has brought about change in the development of local communities. Economic sustainable development is an inter-generational equity for local authorities, enabling them to use community-based festivals and events in strengthening communities, business districts, cultural, heritage and arts resources, and in attracting tourists and visitors. Events and festivals are an important economic sustainability concept for local authorities, to increase development in the local area by meeting the basic needs of local people and extending cultural opportunities to satisfy their aspirations for better community cohesion. Sustainable development of events and festivals has given greater impetus to local authorities and other key stakeholders to invest and develop cultural events within their own districts. Events and festivals yield greater economic returns for local councils because they attract people from around the globe to attend.

Economic sustainable development also represents leverage for local authorities. Local authorities are taking a coherent approach and adopting a practical delivery strategy to strengthen the impacts of events as part of economic sustainability. Large-scale community events can create a long-term strategic vision for an area by:

- developing holistic thinking;
- linking diverse communities through festivals;
- involving local community leadership and individuals;
- learning from local community groups;
- creating partnerships with local community groups; and
- making difficult decisions to enhance economic sustainability.

Local communities play a vital role when running large-scale events by providing appropriate support and sharing culture heritage. Such events and festivals can bring together local community people from different backgrounds to tackle issues that have been affecting them over a period of time. Events and festivals provide an opportunity for the community to share culture, individual values and social difficulties, build sustainability for the area and exchange information. Over the last few decades local and national governments have both participated in and increased investment in large-scale events to bring economic development to local areas.

In the context of these issues, the Notting Hill Carnival is used as a case study to analyse economic development in a host community.

Case study: Notting Hill Carnival

Rooted in the experiences of Caribbean people in England around a time of great change in the late 1950s and early 1960s, the Notting Hill Carnival was created by the local community in 1964 to share and develop West Indian cultural beliefs and celebrate their ancestors' freedom from slavery. The first event attracted over 200 people from the local community to celebrate their cultural values and was a search for identity, community and belonging. Over the years the carnival has had difficult times, because the indigenous community did not accept the cultural change being imposed on them by the immigrant community. However, with the passage of time the carnival has created a platform for Caribbean people to come together and share their social and cultural differences with the local community. Now it is about people coming together and having fun.

The Notting Hill Carnival has become an important part of the culture industry, accounting for the greater percentage of economic growth for local and national music and design artists. Carnivals are one of the major sources of employment for designers and artists all year round, by producing costumes for bands and carnival dancers. In addition, the Notting Hill Carnival creates thousands of jobs in the following industries:

- arts;
- clothing;
- car rental;
- hotels and catering;
- tour operations;
- marketing and advertising; and
- transportation.

The carnival has generated a significant economic impact on the local area since the late 1980s. In 2004 the Greater London Authority carried out detailed research looking at the overall economic impact of the carnival. The report (GLA, 2004) highlights that the Notting Hill Carnival is a key resource to the development of local businesses and the local community (see Table 6.2).

Table 6.2 indicates that the Notting Hill Carnival has generated a huge economic impact for the host community over the last decade. The Mayor of London has provided greater logistical support since 2004. Moreover, the carnival organizers believe that publicity and promotion of the event generate benefits for London in the form of improved image and repeat visitations. There is no doubt that the Notting Hill Carnival plays an important part in developing the economic benefits for the local community and local businesses. It is vital for event organizers and other agencies to develop a practical and cooperative approach to take this event to the next level of cultural, social and economic growth.

Table 6.2. Economic analysis of the Notting Hill Carnival. (Adapted from GLA, 2004.)

£93 million	London's economy
3000	Full-time jobs
1.2 million	People attended the carnival over 3 days
£45 million	Spent by carnival-goers in 3 days
£50 million	General financial boost to firms and individuals involved in the carnival

Summary

In the events industry economic impact studies are undertaken for a variety of purposes; frequently they consider elements of cost–benefit analysis concerning the cost of hosting the event in comparison to income generation and visitor expenditure. Festivals and events give greater economic sustainability to the host city and raise the city's profile by developing employment, additional trade and business development. It could be argued that a catalytic effect ensues whereby an increase in investment and additional monies are made available for local infrastructure and long-term promotional benefits are created. Further to this, other tangible benefits are improved tax revenues and increased property prices, with subsequent connections to the community. Significant economic benefits provided by outdoor events to a host city can create the potential for high-status profiles and increased tourism potential and awareness for the future.

Evidently, events have a major economic impact on and bring potential benefits to host cities, although these benefits have not been analysed in great depth. Moreover, festivals and events help to develop social and economic cohesion, confidence and pride that connect local community and local authorities together.

The case study within this chapter demonstrates how the Notting Hill Carnival has developed to become a centrepiece event for the local economy each year. It is now strongly viewed by the local community and small businesses as the significant attraction for tourism to the area, and both value the tourist market as a vital tool for the development of the local economy.

Key Questions

1. Discuss and evaluate the economic impacts of events on host communities.

2. Describe and evaluate the role of economic development for small businesses through sustainable events.

3. How does the economics of sustainable development provide economic sustainability to the host community?

References

British Government Panel on Sustainable Development (1994) *Sustainable Development: The UK Strategy*. HMSO, London.

Brown, G., Chalip, L., Jago, L. and Mules, T. (2004) Developing Brand Australia: examining the role of events. In: Morgan, N., Pritchard, A. and Pride, R. (eds) *Destination Branding: Creating the Unique Destination Proposition*, 2nd edn. Butterworth-Heinemann, Oxford, UK, pp. 279–305.

Burns, J.P.A., Hatch, J.H. and Mules, T.J. (eds) (1986) *The Adelaide Grand Prix: The Impact of a Special Event*. Centre for South Australian Economic Studies, Adelaide, Australia.

Dwyer, L., Mellor, R., Mistilis, N. and Mules, T. (2000) A framework for assessing 'tangible' and 'intangible' impacts of events and conventions. *Event Management* 6(3), 175–180.

Getz, D. (1997) *Event Management and Event Tourism*. Cognizant Communications Corporation, New York.

GLA (2004) *Notting Hill Carnival Review: A Strategic Review 2004*. Greater London Authority, Carnival Review Group, London.

Hoexter, M. (2006) The Concept of Sustainability: Internal Diversity and Points of Conflict. Available at: http://blog.futurelab.net/2006/10/the_concept_of_sustainability.html (accessed 30 May 2008).

Jones, C. (2001) Mega-events and host-region impacts: determining the true worth of the 1999 Rugby World Cup. *International Journal of Tourism Research* 3(3), 241–251.

Key Leisure Markets (2001) *Tourism in the UK*. MarketScape Ltd, London.

Key Note Ltd (2004) *Market Report 2004: Corporate Hospitality*, 4th edn. Key Note Ltd, Hampton, UK.

LDA (London Development Agency) (2008) LDA puts community at the heart of shaping London 2012 legacy. Available at: http://www.lda.gov.uk/server/show/ConWebDoc.2507 (accessed 15 June 2008).

London 2012 Olympic Bid (2003) Available at: http://www.london2012.com (accessed 14 July 2008).

Mintel (2004) Mintel Report August 2004: Music Concerts and Festivals. Available at: http://www.academic.mintel.com (accessed 30 June 2008).

Ratcliffe, J. and Flanagan, S. (2004) Enhancing the vitality and viability of town and city centres. The concept of the business improvement district in the context of tourism enterprise. *Property Management* 22(5), 377–395.

Rogers, T. (2004) Better Business Tourism in Britain, Business Tourism Partnership. Available at: http://www.business tourismpartnership.com (accessed 30 May 2008).

Stern, N. (2006) *The Economics of Climate Change: The Stern Review*. UK Treasury, London.

UK Sport (2005) *Staging Major Sports Events: The Guide*. UK Sport, London.

Williams, C. and Ferguson, M. (2005) Recovering from crisis: strategic alternatives for leisure and tourism providers based within a rural economy. *International Journal of Public Sector Management* 18(4), 350–366.

7 Environmental Impacts of Events

L. Dávid
Károly Róbert College, Gyöngyös, Hungary

This chapter considers the sustainable planning and developmental principles of events, mainly festivals. It examines the most important services of environment-conscious events. The environmental impacts caused by festivals are analysed through the example of Sziget Festival in Hungary. The aim is to provide a conceptual framework emergent from existing principles and guidance that will underpin the importance of sustainable event management.

Chapter outline

- Introduction
- Environmental Impacts
- Impacts of Festivals on the Environment
- Case Study – Sziget Festival of Budapest
- Summary
- Key Questions

Introduction

The events industry is fast becoming one of the most important sectors of the world economy, which can have both positive and negative effects on the surrounding environment and local communities. Controllable events can be a viable option only if the short- and long-term interests of the environment are taken into consideration. If conscious planning and development are not taken into account, sustainable event management development could take an undesirable turn (Puczkó and Rátz, 2002, 2005; Vargáné, 2005). Thus, during the planning and development phases, the application of an environment-conscious events planning and development attitude is required.

Events have direct and indirect connections with the environment. From the moment of decision making about travelling, people make some kind of impact on the environment. Natural resources, such as physical factors, can be grouped into two larger sets (Puczkó and Rátz, 2002, 2005):

- *The natural environment*, which contains traceable lifeless natural resources, the flora and fauna, as well as the landscape.
- *The man-made environment*, which contains everything that has been introduced or built in a given area by humans.

Environmental Impacts

When analysing the relationship between an event and its environment, the literature differentiates between the following groups of physical environmental factors from the point of view of the impacts made on them (Mathieson and Wall, 1982; Jenner and Smith, 1991; Boers and Bosch, 1994; Puczkó and Rátz, 2002, 2005):

- *Impacts on the natural environment*, i.e. air quality, geological factors, water quality, depletion of natural resources, flora and fauna.
- *Impacts on the man-made environment*, i.e. buildings and visual impacts, changes in land use, infrastructure.
- *Impacts on the ecosystem*.

The psychical impacts – like other impacts on the environment – are complex: there can be local and global impacts, direct and indirect impacts, reversible and irreversible, favourable (positive) and unfavourable (negative) impacts. The following sections summarize the most important environmental impacts of events (Puczkó and Rátz, 2002, 2005; Michalkó, 2007).

Air quality

Events involve a number of air-polluting exhaust gas- and steam-emitting activities such as road and air transport. Moreover, there are significant emissions at catering and accommodation establishments, as well as during events. Consequently CO_2, CO and NO_2 increase and different Freon derivatives are emitted, which swell the greenhouse effect. Noise pollution, which may result from transportation, the hospitality industry or the operation of entertainment facilities, also belongs to impacts that influence air quality. The greater the increase in facilities, participants and business in a given area, the more intense the air-polluting impacts become.

Geological condition

One of the impacts on the geological environment made by events is littering. Aesthetically, unremoved rubbish makes an unpleasant sight. Moreover, decomposition of litter may release toxic material into the soil. Unfavourable geological impacts may be caused by heavy metals that are released into the air by the ever-growing traffic and washed into the surrounding vegetation, flora and fauna. Additionally, untreated sewage leaks can affect not only the soil itself but also subsurface and underground waters.

Various outdoor, indoor, urban and rural events beyond designated areas can cause erosion; thus these activities contribute to the decrease of the vegetation cover, which is the habitat of plants and animals. The use of green field sites for festivals, and the continuous footfall of participants may cause compression, a process with an opposite outcome to erosion, which prevents the soil from maintaining normal water balance.

Water pollution

Water surfaces situated in and/or near event areas are usually exposed to significant environmental threats and pollution, which may be caused by the maintenance of additional facilities supporting events. Equally, there are indirect, unfavourable effects caused by suntan lotion, which forms a subtle surface film when it gets into water. This layer decreases the oxygen uptake and conveying ability of the water, which deteriorates the essential conditions of the water in local rivers, streams and coastal regions.

Another negative impact of tourism on water quality is in connection with the level of sewage treatment. Sewage treatment is a factor that provides basic life conditions for both local residents and the natural environment. Sewage originating from event tourism service providers should be treated and released back into living waters through multiple-stage technology; without this, adequate cleanliness cannot be maintained. The aforementioned leakages may penetrate and accumulate in subsurface waters. This accumulation of organic materials predominantly endangers standing waters (lakes, dead channels). The accumulation of organic material in water is called eutrophication. In the case of severe eutrophication waters should be declared unsuitable for bathing since their composition (high organic material and alga content, low level of oxygen) can negatively affect health.

Depletion of natural resources

The depletion of natural resources is accelerated by the use of fossil fuels in transportation, the heating of accommodation and the operation of catering facilities (which are usually non-renewable energy sources like coal, crude oil or natural gas). In more environment-friendly solutions, heating and energy consumption is based on hydro, solar or wind energy.

Wasteful and careless use of the drinking water supply significantly impairs the effectiveness of water management, and decreases available freshwater resources. The wasteful use of the water supply could be avoided by a more environmentally friendly attitude and modern technology.

Flora and fauna

Events can also have positive effects on the natural environment, since event tourism promotes valuable areas to receive protected status and to improve the natural environment. Although event attendees pose a less severe threat to the flora and fauna directly, it sometimes occurs as a result of event attendance that there is interference with the order of the natural habitat, which could negatively influence animals' breeding and feeding patterns. Agricultural activities and areas (meadows, woods) are on the decrease in many regions since these areas have other functions nowadays (for example, they are built on to improve event services). Thus animals' habitats and vegetation shrink. When ecological disturbance reaches a critical point animals will migrate. On the whole, events have negative effects on the natural environment; nevertheless, they may improve the following natural factors directly: changes in the landscape, protection and conservation of flora and fauna, introduction of new animal and plant species.

Impacts of Festivals on the Environment

During festivals there may be a number of environmental impacts affecting both the venue and local residents. Environmental impacts that emerge throughout the organization and actual performance of a festival can be felt during the activities in connection with festivals. These activities – such as the use of accommodation and catering facilities, travelling, participation in the festival itself – and the operation of the necessary infrastructure may result in significant impacts on the environment. By virtue of their characteristics, such as large number of visitors and longer stays, festivals have to a lesser extent positive, but mainly negative effects on their physical environment.

Negative impacts from tourism events occur when the level of visitor use is greater than the environment's ability to cope with this use within the acceptable limits of change. Uncontrolled conventional events pose potential threats to many natural and built areas around the world. This can put enormous pressure on an area and lead to impacts such as land degradation (erosion), increased pollution, discharges into the soil, natural habitat loss, increased pressure on endangered species and heightened vulnerability to forest fires. It often puts a strain on water resources, and it can force local populations to compete for the use of critical resources.

Festivals and events can create great pressure on local resources like energy, food and other raw materials that may already be in short supply. Greater extraction and transport of these resources exacerbates the physical impacts associated with their exploitation. Because of the seasonal character of the events industry, many destinations have ten times more visitors in the high season than in the low season. A high demand is placed upon these resources to meet the high expectations tourists often have (proper heating, hot water, etc.).

Environmental impacts caused by festivals are summarized below (Halmay *et al.*, 2006).

Festival transport

The different forms of travel used by event delegates, attendees, organizers and performers, and for the transportation of materials and refuse, have different impacts on the environment. While walking or cycling has a negligible effect, the air pollution, noise and the required

Table 7.1. Energy requirement for 1 passenger-kilometre. (Adapted from Halmay *et al.*, 2006.)

Means of transport	Energy consumption for 1 passenger-km (kJ)
Aircraft	6000
Train	2100
Coach	2100
Automobile with 1–4 passengers	7800–1900
Cyclist	120
Pedestrian	250

space for motor vehicles put significant loads on the environment. Passengers travelling by public transport, such as trains or coaches, have much less impact than those travelling by car or air. Table 7.1 shows the energy requirement for 1 passenger-kilometre.

Air pollution from event tourists' transportation has impacts at the global level, especially from CO_2 emissions related to transportation energy use. Additionally, it can contribute to severe local air pollution. Some of these impacts are quite specific to event tourists' activities. For example, especially in very hot or cold countries, tour buses often leave their motors running for hours while the tourists go out for an excursion because they want to return to a comfortably air-conditioned bus. Noise pollution from cars and buses as well as the events themselves (mass noise, music) is an ever-growing problem of modern life. In addition to causing annoyance, stress and even hearing loss for those in close proximity, it causes distress to wildlife, especially in sensitive areas. For instance, noise generated by outdoor community events can cause people to alter their natural activity patterns and subject many inhabitants to natural displacement.

Accommodation

The use of accommodation facilities does not pollute the environment to a great extent on its own. However, by their area use and interference with natural habitats, event attendees will directly disturb the environment. The heating, air-conditioning and lighting of accommodation facilities require effective energy use and the application of energy-saving devices and methods; for example, constructing buildings adhering to and going beyond European building regulations, using environmentally friendly materials, ensuring adequate insulation to avoid overheating and unnecessary air-conditioning, etc. Excessive water consumption is also a common problem, which may be caused by wasteful and uneducated event tourists, devices or appliances.

Meals

All participants and attendees have an influence on the environment when consuming meals – food products influence not only the quantity and composition of refuse, but also the method of production. Food production requires a large area, it may cause soil pollution and it poses environmental threats. Chemicals create a larger environmental load, while by demanding food originating from far-away countries event attendees contribute to the growth of fuel consumption and air pollution. Disposable packaging materials and multiple packaging result in excessive amounts of rubbish. Locally made, natural products are healthier and more environmentally friendly.

Energy

The energy consumption of tourism and festivals originates from the electricity and heating demand of accommodation facilities, the energy requirements for cooking and the fuel consumption of transport and travelling, as well as the operation of entertainment devices. The use of excess energy results in higher expenditure on the one hand, and on the other raises CO_2 and other greenhouse gas emissions.

Water consumption

During festivals water is used for food preparation, personal hygiene, cleaning and also for gardening around the venue of the event. Excess use of water will contribute to the ever-shrinking freshwater resources.

Waste

During festivals the waste resulting from beverage consumption is the most noticeable. Half of all refuse comes from the packaging of beverages. Recycling systems are not widely used within events, so the most often used bottles and glasses are the disposable ones. The other significant part of waste originates from leftover food and the cutlery used to consume it. In Hungary during a multiple-day festival that attracts 200,000 visitors, about 1000–1500 m^3 or 80–120 tons of solid rubbish is created, which amounts to 5–10 litres or 0.5–0.8 kilograms per person. This is twice the amount of domestic waste creation. Table 7.2 describes the main contents of festival waste.

It can be argued that most festivals often have the following environmental impacts:

- They contribute to the depletion of natural resources as well as to air, water and soil pollution.
- They decrease the numbers and varieties of plants and animals and ruin their habitats.

In order to have more favourable environmental impacts, the following sustainable planning and developmental principles should be taken into consideration throughout the organization of a festival:

- *Controlled use of resources*. The optimal and controlled management of natural, social and cultural resources.
- *Restriction of overconsumption and reducing the amount of waste*. By restricting overconsumption and reducing the amount of waste, long-lasting environmental damage that would be expensive to repair can be avoided; this in turn will effect the development and sustainability of tourism.
- *Conservation of diversity*. The assurance of natural, social and cultural diversity is a precondition for restrained and controllable events, which lays the foundation for the future development of sustainable event management.
- *Involving events in long-term developmental concepts*. Integrate events in higher-level (national, regional, local) strategies; carry out environmental impact analyses within event concepts.

Figure 7.1 presents the most important services of environment-conscious events.

Case Study – Sziget Festival of Budapest

August 2008 was the 16th time that Budapest and its green island Óbuda became the inevitable location of the cultural and music life of Europe. During a week in the most pleasant month of the year, Sziget Festival awaits students and young adults on vacation from Europe and other corners of the world with nearly 1000 programmes and 60 venues. Sziget is not

Table 7.2. The main contents of festival waste. (Source: http://fenntarthato.hu/fesztival/zftartalom; accessed 15 May 2008.)

Waste material	Description	Material	Weight (%)
Plastic bottles	0.2–2.5 litre soft drink, mineral water and beer bottles	PET	20–25
Plastic glasses	0.2–0.5 litre disposable plastic glasses	PP or PS	15–20
Tin cans	0.33 or 0.5 litre cans	(Metal alloy) aluminium or tin	5–10
Glass bottles	All sorts of glass, bottles	Clear and coloured glass	0–5
Paper	Paper wrapping, fliers, newspaper, periodicals, journals	White, coloured, cardboard cartons	10–15
Leftover food	All sorts of organic waste	All sorts of organic waste	15–20
Others	Plastic foils, contaminated waste	Absolutely mixed	5–35

PET, polyethylene terephthalate; PP, polypropylene; PS, polystyrene.

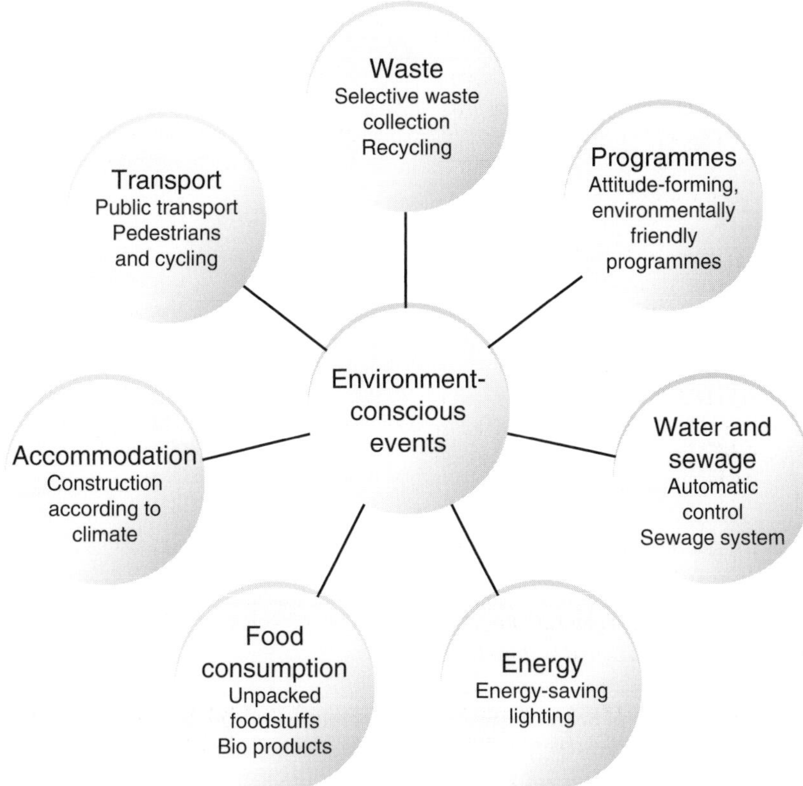

Fig. 7.1. The most important services of environment-conscious events.

only a festival, but also a week-long opportunity to camp out in the temporarily built festival city where, besides basic facilities, posting and banking services, restaurants, pubs, shops and a number of other amenities provide comfort and entertainment. Over the years the number of visitors has risen continuously. Back in 1993, 43,000 people visited the festival; this number had risen to 385,000 by 2008. Changes in the main indicators of Sziget Festival to 2008 are indicated in Table 7.3.

Forty-five per cent of the Hungarian visitors come from Budapest and 15% come from Central Hungary. Although 85% of visitors are under 30 years of age (they are fairly equally distributed in the range between 14 and 29 years), higher education graduates are heavily over-represented despite the comparatively low average age: they make up 43% of the festival visitors, while this number is only 13% of the total population of Hungary. Almost half of the 37,000 foreign visitors come from Germany and France. This group is also dominated by younger visitors: almost 90% of the foreign visitors are 30 years of age or younger. Two-thirds of the foreigners come by either air or car.

There is a significant difference between foreigners and Hungarians with respect to accommodation facilities used during the festival: slightly more than half of the domestic visitors (52.6%) slept outdoors on the island, 42.1% commuted from home, 5.8% stayed with friends and only 0.5% booked accommodation in a hotel, guesthouse or campsite. The vast majority (94%) of foreign visitors named the 'Island' as their accommodation during the festival. A mere 6% of the foreigners stayed at commercial accommodation (hotel, guesthouse or campsite).

Table 7.3. Changes in the main indicators of Sziget Festival. (Source: http://www.sziget.hu/fesztival and http://hu.wikipedia.org/wiki/Sziget_Fesztiv%C3%A1l; accessed 16 March 2009.)

Year	Total no. of visitors	Pre-purchased weekly tickets among foreigners (%)	Total budget (million HUF)	Price of pre-purchased weekly ticket (HUF)	Price of daily ticket (HUF)
1993	43,000	0	26	1,800	300
1994	143,000	15	120	1,800	300
1995	173,000	15	145	2,500	500
1996	206,000	30	180	2,800	700
1997	260,000	35	200	5,000	800
1998	266,000	50	290	6,000	800/1,200
1999	297,000	55	420	7,000	1,500
2000	324,000	60	580	8,000	2,000
2001	361,000	60	900	10,000	2,500
2002	355,000	60	1,005	12,000	3,000
2003	351,000	60	1,200	14,000	3,500
2004	369,000	60	1,450	16,000	4,000
2005	385,000	50	1,850	20,000	5,000
2006	385,000	40	2,250	20,000/24,000	6,000
2007	371,000	–	2,500	24,000	6,500
2008	385,000	–	2,700	25,000	8,000

HUF, Hungarian forint (€1 = HUF280, May 2009).

Environmental impacts of Sziget Festival

Almost all forms of environmental pollution can be measured during a festival of such scale. Taking a closer look at them thematically we can draw the following conclusions.

Littering, rubbish

During Sziget Festival in 2006 approximately 2200 m^3 of waste accumulated. This roughly equals the amount of rubbish that the residents of a ten-storey building mount up in 9–10 years. Due to selective rubbish collection, which has been going on since 2004, the amount of all types of waste has grown continuously (http://www.sulinet.hu/tart/fncikk/Kife/0/27217/fesztival_szemet.htm; accessed 15 May 2008), see Table 7.4.

Selectively collected waste is transported to selective rubbish dumps and recycling plants at the expense of the Ministry of Health and the sponsors (http://www.nol.hu/fesztivalia/cikk/459622/; accessed 3 May 2008).

Air pollution

The festival venue is situated near busy main roads and the concentration of pollutants is generally very high. In connection with the festival, local polluting sources must also be mentioned; for example, the extra emissions made by those who arrive by car, because CO_2 emissions can grow by as much as 30% during the festival (http://www.levego.hu; accessed 10 May 2008). Parking problems also deteriorate air quality in the area. The health-damaging effect of dust generated by visitors also increases during the entirety of the festival.

In order to improve the situation, visitors are encouraged to approach the festival venue by means of public transport. According to another strategy, a temporary car park could be made and used during the festival at the abandoned Óbuda Gas Works, owned by Budapest's municipal government. The Clean Air Action Group, which has had an opportunity to advertise itself on Civil Island, also emphasizes the problems caused by air pollution (http://www.obuda.blog.hu; accessed 13 May 2008).

Soil pollution

There are both physical and chemical manifestations of soil pollution at the festival. The former problem arises as soil compression because of the visitors' treading (it can reach 40% around

Table 7.4. The composition and changes in the amount of waste produced by Sziget Festival. (Source: http://www.sziget.hu/fesztival/info/kornyezetvedelem; accessed 14 May 2008.)

Year	Plastic goods (pieces)	Empty bottles (kg)	Batteries (kg)	Used cooking oil (kg)
2007	160,000	4,500	150	6,000
2006	150,000	2,500	110	2,500
2005	100,000	1,500	70	1,800
2004	80,000	900	45	1,100

the stages and catering facilities), while the latter results from the lack of sewage treatment and from the fact that the available toilets are not used (visitors do not use the installed lavatories). To overcome this problem the number of mobile toilets has been increased.

Noise pollution

The most critical aspect of the relationship between the festival and the local residents is the noise pollution. According to a local government decree, the threshold limit of noise generated by any free-time activity is maximized at 45 dB during the day between 07.00 and 20.00 hours, and at night between 20.00 and 07.00 hours this limit is 40 dB. During practice sessions and at the actual event, the limit was exceeded by well over 25 and 23 dB, respectively. It must be stated that because of the characteristics of the measured unit, a 3 dB increase will sound twice as loud. The very busy roads in the district (Váci road, Árpád road, Görgey road) generate over 70 dB during the day. Ironically, compared with the harmful effects of these roads, the noise from Sziget Festival is almost negligible.

To overcome these problems stages are erected and fitted with noise insulation material and there are automatic volume-control devices at problematic places. These appliances continuously measure the noise level and adjust the volume below the threshold limit without human interaction.

Sewage treatment

One of the greatest problems of the festival is sewage treatment. There are a growing number of bio-toilets on the island; nevertheless, the number of the more easily cleanable and illuminated container toilets really cannot grow owing to the lack of a sewage pipeline. In 2006, using a new technology, organizers were able to significantly improve the situation and created further toilet centres at the most frequented places of the island. This new technology does not require a pipeline system: sewage flows into a large tank from where it is transported away. Furthermore, there were newly installed hand-wash gears and the number of showers was also increased.

Light pollution

Although temporary and punctiform, at the same time the appearance of strong lights is dangerous for the environment because of the sudden, unexpected and short effects. As a result of the growing number of visitors and demand, public lighting was further improved on the island. In 2007 more than 4.5 km of road was illuminated during the festival. Nevertheless, the problem has not been solved.

Impact on local residents

The festival, which was first organized in 1993, witnessed no real problems with local residents until 1997. Since then, numerous signs of hostility appeared. However at the end of October 2007, Free Association Research, a public opinion research company, conducted a public opinion poll involving 300 respondents among residents of district IV in order to find out about what they thought of Sziget Festival. In answer to the first question, 'How much does the festival disturb you during the day?', 82% of the respondents said that it did not disturb them at all. On a scale from 1 to 10, 89% gave 1 or 2, while nobody gave 9 or 10. The average score given to this question was 1.5. Question 2, 'How much does the festival disturb you at night?', had similar results: 62% of the respondents were not disturbed at all and only 7% stated that they were disturbed significantly. The average score given to this question was 2.9 on a scale from 1 to 10. The final question was 'Do you believe that the authorities should prevent the organization of this festival in its present form or not?'; only a mere 6% thought that they should and 94% did not think that the organization of this festival should be prevented in its present form (http://www.sziget.hu/fesztival/hirek/107109.html; accessed 10 May 2008).

Environment protection at Sziget Festival

Selective waste collection has been implemented at the festival since 2004. Now, besides providing assistance for operation of the waste collecting system, the Ministry of Environment and Water, together with ÖKO-Pannon public benefit company, popularizes selection among the 'island dwellers' by means of a road show teaching environmentally conscious attitudes. One of the initiatives is that anyone handing over selectively collected waste can choose either a present from ÖKO-Pannon public benefit company (pass-holder, textile bag or writing pad) or one of the issues of the teaching material. In addition, festival-goers could get some soft drink, a cap, a T-shirt or other valuable presents in exchange for beer bottles, plastic bottles or cans, and there was even an apple-for-a-battery exchange option as well.

Summary

Events have direct and indirect connections with the environment. Events can have economic, social, cultural and physical impacts on the environment. It can be argued that most events often have common environmental impacts. First, they contribute to the depletion of natural resources as well as to air, water and soil pollution. Second, they decrease the numbers and varieties of plants and animals and ruin their habitats.

In order to have more favourable environmental impacts, sustainable planning and developmental principles should be taken into consideration throughout the organization of a festival. Sustainable events managers should consider the controlled use of resources, restriction of overconsumption and reduction of the amount of waste, conservation of diversity, and the involvement of events management in long-term developmental concepts.

Almost all forms of environmental pollution can be measured during Sziget Festival. It has been found that environmental protection plays a more and more important role. Examples of sustainable planning and development can be found at Sziget Festival, such as the activities of the Clean Air Action Group and ÖKO-Pannon public benefit company, the increase in the number of mobile toilets, the new waste collecting system and the automatic volume-control devices.

Key Questions

1. How can you analyse the impacts of events on the environment?
2. What are the main environmental problems of festivals?
3. Evaluate the impacts of Sziget Festival.

References

Boers, H. and Bosch, M. (1994) A Föld mint üdülőhely (The Earth as holiday resort). *Bevezetés a turizmus és a környezet kapcsolatrendszerébe* (*Introduction to the Connection between Tourism and the Environment*). KVIF, Budapest.

Jenner, P. and Smith, C. (1991) *The Tourism Industry and the Environment*. Special Report No. 2453. The Economic Intelligence Unit, London.

Halmay, R., Kovács, B., Nagy, T. and Újszászi, G. (2006) *Ajánlások zöld fesztiválok szervezéséhez* (*Recommendation to Organisation of Green Festivals*). Független Ökológiai Központ (Independent Ecological Centre), Budapest.

Mathieson, A. and Wall, G. (1982) *Tourism. Economic, Physical and Social Impacts*. Longman Scientific & Technical, Harlow, UK.

Michalkó, G. (2007) *A turizmuselmélet alapjai* (*Basis of Tourism Theory*). Kodolányi János Főiskola, Székesfehérvár, Hungary.

Puczkó, L. and Rátz, T. (2002) *The Impacts of Tourism. An Introduction*. Häme Polytechnic, Häme, Finland.

Puczkó, L. and Rátz, T. (2005) *A turizmus hatásai* (*The Impacts of Tourism*). Aula Kiadó, Budapest.

Vargáné, C.K. (2005) A turizmus fenntarthatóságának értékelése (Evaluation of tourism sustainability). *Agrártudományi Közlemények (Acta Agraria Debreceniensis), University of Debrecen, Hungary* 2005/16(Suppl.), 414–421.

8 Social Impacts of Events

D. Tassiopoulos[1] and D. Johnson[2]
[1]*Walter Sisulu University, Buffalo City, South Africa;* [2]*Cape Peninsula University of Technology, Cape Town, South Africa*

This chapter examines the social impact of events on host communities. The social impacts provided by events, according to Wood (2006, p. 165), are now widely recognized, as is the need to measure these impacts in non-economic terms. Olsen and Merwin (1977, p. 41) describe social impacts as 'changes in the structure and functioning of patterned social ordering that occur in conjunction with an environmental, technological or social innovation or alteration'.

Chapter outline

- Introduction
- The Event Offering as a Societal Impact Construct
- Social Impacts and Events
- Negative Social Impacts of Events
- Positive Social Impacts of Events
- Social Impact Theory and Events
- Social Impact Assessment and Events
- Approaches for Managing the Social Impacts of Large-scale Events
- Approaches for Managing the Social Impacts of Community (or Small-scale) Events
- Summary
- Key Questions

Introduction

Events are emerging globally as a significant and growing sector and are seen as having significant economic, sociocultural and political impacts. Concurrently, according to Arcodia and Whitfield (2006), Buch (2006), Chalip (2006) and Hughes (2007), there has been an increasing interest in devising ways to identify the various costs and benefits associated with events. It is, however, highlighted that although there are numerous studies associated with determining the economic impacts of events – and particularly, according to Wood (2006), the impacts of tourism – there is a relative lack of research which focuses on the social, cultural and political impacts of events.

The Event Offering as a Societal Impact Construct

Events play a significant role in the lives of communities: they are seen to provide important activities and spending outlets for locals and visitors, and they can also enhance the image of the local community (Tassiopoulos, 2005). Events are considered as having an integrating effect when introduced into a social system. In essence, events can become a vehicle for improving social relationships in surroundings, for attaining relationships between people, for strengthening people's abilities to understand one another, and for people's well-being (Kurtzman and Zauhar, 1997). The social function of events, particularity festivals, is closely related to the values that a community regards as essential to its ideology (such as social identity, historical continuity and physical survival) (Arcodia and Whitfield, 2006). The sociological basis of event development can be subdivided into the social phenomenon of events and the socio-economic basis underlying the development of events. The growth in event development, according to Cooper *et al.* (2005), can be ascribed as a social phenomenon, comprising:

- the desire to experience new attractions and to escape;
- the growth in communication and information technology, creating awareness and stimulating interest in various events;
- changes in mobility and accessibility, making travel to events accessible;
- increased leisure time and longer periods of vacation, together with rising real incomes, creating a desire to attend events; and
- the increase in world trade for business tourism, leading to various events such as conferences and conventions.

An event is an offering that is based upon simultaneous production and consumption. For the event output to occur, the event attendee must attend the event and consume the event product. An event is a personal service and, as such, can only be consumed by the event attendee attending the event. The implication of this for the host community where the event is taking place is that not only will the community be subject to the changes created by the stimulation and change in direction of the local economy, the community will also come into contact with a foreign population during the production process. Changes in economic growth and development will always be associated with changes in the sociocultural characteristics of a particular area or region. As events bring visitors into contact with the local host community, this adds further dimensions to the sociocultural change.

The contact between the event visitor and the host community can be beneficial or detrimental to the host community depending on their differences in culture and the nature of the actual contact. In reality, the social impacts of events can contain a mixture of both positive and negative strands that affect the host community and the event visitor (Cooper *et al.*, 2005, p. 225). Fredline *et al.* (2006) state that 'tourism destination managers are increasingly looking at events as an important mechanism for enhancing tourism development'. By evaluating these definitions it is clear that events can be regarded as a form of attraction for the event attendee, offering him/her something to do and to participate in, and that events now form part of tourism development. Thus it can also be regarded that events will have similar social impacts as tourism on a specific location or host community. Saayman (2001) identifies that, from a sociological perspective, there are certain social relations between people in the tourism context that can be adapted to the event context, namely:

- the confrontation of different cultures, ethnic groups, lifestyles, languages and levels of prosperity;
- the behaviour of people freed from many of the social and economic constraints of everyday life; and
- the behaviour of the host population, which has to reconcile economic gain and benefits with the costs of living with strangers.

Cooper *et al.* (2005) further advance that the following factors influence the attitude of people towards attending events: their age, education, income levels and socio-economic background. The age of the event attendee will within certain boundaries influence the type of event that will be attended. In terms of education, the selection of the type of event will also be a focus point. The income levels of the event attendee will influence the decision to travel, where to travel to and the nature of activities undertaken while attending the event. The socio-economic background relates to the previous experiences of the potential event attendee and will determine again the type of event he/she will select. Events can be regarded as social phenomena which involve social interaction between the event attendee and the host community. This interaction may cause social change. Events are influenced by social factors such as fashion, social status and the norms and values of a society. Events thus remind us that there is contact between two groups of people, the event attendee and the host community, and both may change because of the interaction. It is true to acknowledge that the interaction of people of different cultures and lifestyles will inevitably introduce change and will affect the perceptions and attitudes of each participant. Events can act as a powerful agent of change, although not all changes in societies can be linked to events. It is also evident from reviewing literature on the status of events that events are diverse and there has been a growth in staging events on a global scale, to the point that the prominence of event strategies can be identified in tourism plans that again are translated into direct visitation, flow-on visitation, catalysing urban development, branding a destination, legacies for a destination and, importantly, community enhancement (Getz, 1997). Saayman (2001) further points out that events are a major source of intercultural contact and the event–host and event–guest interaction can offer the opportunity for each to learn more about the other, which can lead to greater understanding between people. As with other elements of a destination, events may have positive or negative impacts on residents. For example, sound management of an event hinges on the capability of those responsible to avoid, or least to reduce, the negative impacts and emphasize the positive aspects (Fredline and Faulkner, 2000).

It is further proposed that these destination management objectives should be driven as much by ethical concerns, embracing equity and quality of life issues, as by more practical marketing destination issues. Social exchange theory, according to Oviedo-Garcia *et al.* (2007), implies that there is an increasing likelihood of the host population's involvement in tourism (including event) development if it is perceived that the potential benefits are greater than the costs. If the benefits are indeed perceived to be greater than the costs, then it is likely the host population will become directly involved in the exchange and this endorses future development in their destination. Economic, socio-political and environmental trade-offs, as perceived by the host population, all play an important part in determining their support for future development.

Social Impacts and Events

Although there has been significant research into the economic impact of events, there has been little discussion about measuring the social or 'intangible' effects of events (Chalip, 2006; Wood, 2006). There is a growing body of literature examining the social impacts of events on host communities. The necessity of measuring the impact of events for monitoring, control and evaluation purposes is recognized by a large number of studies, but a review of recent literature by Wood (2005) shows that the methods used and the aspects of the event being measured vary considerably. In the tourism context, according to Fredline and Faulkner (2000), resident reactions can be affected by factors such as stage of development, seasonality in patterns of activity and cultural differences between residents and tourists. It is proposed that the stage of tourism and event development may be relevant in two respects. First, the development stage of the host destination may have an underlying influence on the impact of the event as the perceptions of the residents will influence their reaction to tourists generated by the event. Second, the stage of an event's development needs to be considered, as resident reactions to recurring events become less negative over time largely because managers become experienced at minimizing the disruptive effects of the event on the local population (e.g. staging events during off-peak seasons to moderate fluctuations in demand on a destination). Cooper *et al.* (2005) refer to stage-based models, such as the Tourism Destination Life-Cycle Model of Butler (1980), which deals with how changes in the number and type of tourists over a period are associated with changes in tourism infrastructure, environmental assets and the competitive environment. In advanced stages of tourism development, however, event activity may reach a level that can aggravate the host community. Similarly, Doxey's (1975) Irridex Model deals with the host community's responses to the tourism (also read event) development taking place, which may pass through a series of stages including euphoria, apathy, irritation and antagonism as continued exposure to intensifying impacts is reflected by increasing annoyance. Such models are deemed too simplistic, as there are many other variables relating to the characteristics of the destination and the type of tourism activity that can affect the relationship between the stage of development and the host community reaction. Nevertheless, such models are invaluable in highlighting the negative social impacts that can be experienced unless preventive planning and management is undertaken. The need to measure the impacts of events for monitoring, control and evaluative purposes is emphasized according to Wood (2006).

Negative Social Impacts of Events

The following negative generic social impacts of tourism can also be ascribed to events.

- *Sex*. Some event attendees travel abroad to enjoy uninhibited casual sexual encounters, and sexual exploitation has grown as rapidly as tourism in many destinations. Major tourism markets and event destinations such as Thailand and Central European countries have actively marketed the sexual content of their products. The grave danger of this growth has led to the spreading of HIV/AIDS and other sexually transmitted diseases (Cooper *et al*., 2005, pp. 239–247).
- *Health*. The recent (since 2003) global outbreaks of avian influenza (called H5N1) and swine flu (known as the H1N1 infection) affecting humans pose a public health risk to event attendees and host populations. There are, however, also other less newsworthy diseases that have be noted when people from different countries interact, such as the recording of more than 8500 cases of malaria infections in the UK, which have been a result of tourist and visiting friends and relatives (VFR) traffic to malaria-infected destinations. Although these diseases are not fatal, they can cause social and economic stress to the host community who may have less immunity to the diseases than the visitor (Cooper *et al*., 2005, pp. 239–247).
- *Commodification, staged authenticity and standardization*. Commodification implies that the demands of tourism (inclusive of events) have led to the mutation and sometimes the destruction of the meaning of cultural performances and special events. Staged authenticity refers to simulated experiences that are developed to satisfy the needs of the visitor. Standardization refers to where the visitor attending an event searches for the familiar, leading to a loss of cultural diversity (Cooper *et al*., 2005, pp. 239–247).
- *Disruption of the lifestyle of residents*. Sherwood (2007) refers to increases in traffic and noise and the general disruption to normal daily routines caused by the hosting of an event in the destination. Furthermore, overcrowding, congestion and noise are ascribed to an influx of event visitors in the host destination.
- *Crime and vandalism*. Writers such as Mathieson and Wall (1982) have suggested that large numbers of visitors to an event carrying relatively large amounts of money and valuables with them will provide a source for illegal activities including drug trafficking, robbery, vandalism and violence. Influxes of visitors for events and tourism in general have been the catalyst for the growth of gaming activities, which has led to a number of destinations using casino developments as a means to attract visitor spending. Unless properly monitored and controlled, such developments can induce social behaviour that is detrimental to social cohesion.

Positive Social Impacts of Events

Cooper *et al*. (2005, pp. 246–247) have identified the following positive generic social impacts of tourism that can also be ascribed to events.

- *The fostering of community/civic pride*. Events can be used to put new life into ceremonies and rituals, making them come alive, combining them with skills and crafts. This can inspire and assist with fostering local pride of a host community and provides the best possible experience for the event attendee.

- *Creating sociocultural awareness and peace*. Events take people to new places and can broaden their understanding and knowledge of other cultures and environments. This can be regarded as an educational process and, if channelled properly, this education can lead to greater awareness of, and sympathy and admiration for, other societies. Cultural exchange that takes place between the event attendee and the host community can assist in fostering peace. The belief in the relationship between tourism and peace is so strong that in 1986 the International Institute for Peace through Tourism (IIPT) was set up.
- *Shared infrastructure*. When developments for events take place, for example the FIFA 2010 World Cup in South Africa, the local infrastructure is often enhanced to meet the needs of the developments. The host community can find that the quality of their life is enhanced through being able to enjoy this improved infrastructure. This type of infrastructure can include upgrading sporting venues, improvement of airports and general transportation.
- *Direct sociocultural support*. The funding generated from various events can provide funds to assist to restore heritage sites, conserve natural and cultural sites, or assist local charities. The proceeds earned from these events in terms of registration fees and goods sold are donated to various charities within the local community.

Social Impact Theory and Events

Social impacts can be defined in various ways. The following generic social impact definition is widely understood and used:

> By social impacts we mean the consequences to human populations of any public or private actions that alter the ways in which people live, work, play, relate to one another, organize to meet their needs and generally cope as members of society. The term also includes cultural impacts involving changes to the norms, values, and beliefs that guide and rationalize their cognition of themselves and their society.
>
> (Interorganizational Committee on Guidelines and Principles 1994, p. 1)

Social impacts can be felt in the following areas:

- *Culture*, i.e. shared beliefs, customs, values and language or dialect.
- *Community*, its cohesion, stability, character, services and facilities.
- *Political systems*, the extent to which people are able to participate in decisions that affect their lives, the level of democratization that is taking place, and the resources required for this purpose.
- *The environment*, the quality of the air and water that people use, the availability and quality of food that is eaten, the level of hazard or risk and noise to which people are exposed, the adequacy of sanitation, people's physical safety, and their access to and control over resources.
- *Health and well-being*, where health is understood in a manner similar to the World Organization's definition: 'a state of complete physical, mental and social well-being, not merely the absence of disease of infirmity'.
- *Personal and property rights*, particularly whether people are economically affected or experience personal disadvantage, which may include a violation of civil liberties.
- *Fears and aspirations*, i.e. people's perceptions about their safety, their fears about the future of their community, their aspirations for the future and the future of their children.

It is evident that the event visitor attending a particular event will bring with them a new culture that the host community of the staged event might not be aware of and both the host community and the event visitor are influenced, which can be positive and negative. However, according to Ohmann *et al.* (2006), consensus has yet to be reached in terms of defining social impacts with reference to events. It is evident from reviewing literature that evaluating the social impacts of events is not as prominent as is evaluating the economic impacts of events (Wood, 2006). Getz (1997) provides an in-depth look at the economic impact of events but stresses that the impact of events should also focus on the actual impact on the community and the environment, emphasizing the importance of evaluating the event's social and environmental impacts. Ohmann *et al.* (2006, p. 130) describe the social impacts of events as 'changes in the structures and functioning of patterned social ordering that occur in conjunction with an environmental, technological or social innovation or alteration'. Furthermore, the social impacts of events are considered the 'manner in which tourism and travel effect changes in the collective and individual value systems, behaviour patterns, community structures, lifestyle and quality of life'. Ohmann *et al.* (2006) furthermore note that there are a number of impacts, both negative and positive, that are potential consequences of hosting an event. However, it is not clear why certain impacts are more apparent at certain events and not at others. Empirical evidence is limited and thus it is difficult to identify any patterns in terms of developing an understanding of why certain impacts are more or less apparent at different events.

Impact assessment is broadly defined by Vanclay (2004, p. 268) as 'the prediction or estimation of the consequences of current or proposed action (project, policy, technology)'. Impact assessment is a generic term that can mean either an integrated approach or a composite of all forms of impact assessment such as environmental impact assessment, social impact assessment, health impact assessment, etc.

Social Impact Assessment and Events

Social Impact Assessment (SIA) is viewed as anticipatory research, according to Small *et al.* (2005), that gathers data on the likely impacts of a number of alternative options and uses the results to decide on the best alternative to implement. SIA is described (IAIA, 2003a, p. 2; IAIA, 2003b, p. 240; Vanclay, 2006, p. 10) as including:

> the processes of analysing, monitoring and managing the intended and unintended social consequences, both positive and negative, of planned interventions (policies, programmes, plans and projects) and any social change processes invoked by those interventions. Its primary purpose is to bring about a more sustainable and equitable biophysical and human environment.

SIA should be viewed as an overarching framework that embodies the evaluation of all impacts on humans of all the ways in which people and communities interact with their sociocultural, economic and biophysical surroundings (IAIA, 2003b). However Vanclay (2002, 2003) emphasizes that, in developing economies, SIA needs to be considered more as a framework of incorporating participation and social analysis into the design and delivery of development projects and/or as a process of research, planning and management of change arising from polices and projects. SIA thus needs to be process-oriented to ensure that social issues are included in project design, planning and implementation, as well as ensuring that development is acceptable, equitable and sustainable. The improvement of social well-being, with particular focus on poverty reduction, needs to be explicitly recognized as an objective of development projects and plans and, as such, should be a performance indicator considered in any form of impact assessment.

The SIA of events thus can bring about a more ecologically sound, socioculturally and economically sustainable and equitable environment.

Event SIA guiding principles

The following principles are specific to SIA practice and key elements in the SIA for events (IAIA, 2003a).

- Equity considerations should be a fundamental element of impact assessment and of development planning for events.
- Many of the social impacts of planned events can be predicted.
- Planned events can be modified by the event team to reduce their negative social impacts and enhance their positive impacts.

- SIA becomes an integral part of the event development process, involving all stages from inception to the follow-up audit, post-event.
- During event planning there should be a focus on socially sustainable development, using SIA to contribute to the determination of the best development alternatives.
- In all planned events and their assessments, avenues should be developed to build the social and human capital of the host community and to strengthen the democratic processes within the host community in terms of event participation and integration (the questions to ask are: what do they get out of it, and what is returned to them?).
- In all planned events, but in particular where there are unavoidable impacts, ways to turn impacted host communities into beneficiaries should be investigated by the event team.
- SIA should give due consideration to the alternatives of any planned event, and particularly in situations where there are likely to be unavoidable impacts.
- Full consideration should also be given to the potential mitigation measures of social and environmental impacts, even where the impacted host community may approve the planned event and where they are regarded as beneficiaries.
- The event team should incorporate local knowledge and experience as well as local cultural values into the event SIA.
- The event team should further ensure that at all times there will be no use of violence, harassment, intimidation or undue force in connection with the assessment or implementation of a planned event.
- Any developmental process that could infringe the human rights of any section of the host community should not be accepted and redeveloped.

Approaches for Managing the Social Impacts of Large-scale Events

Event SIA can therefore promote community development and empowerment, build capacity and develop social capital (social networks and trust). The event manager would need to practise SIA in a comprehensive manner and it would be advisable to conduct the process in a team approach. The event manager would need to ensure that the development of the event maximizes its benefits and minimizes its costs, especially those costs borne by people. A key issue for the event manager to remember is the differential distribution of impacts among different groups in society related to the event, and in particular the impact burden experienced by vulnerable groups in the host community should be a prime concern in the planning. The event manager can also identify impacts in advance, which can assist with the following (IAIA, 2003a):

- Better decisions can be made about the interventions that would be required for the particular event and how it should proceed; the event and scope of the event will determine this.
- Mitigation measures can be implemented to minimize the harm and maximize the benefits from a specific planned intervention or related activity.

When planning for the event the event manager needs to anticipate changes the event can bring about in terms of social change to the host community in one or more of the areas described in Table 8.1.

To manage the social impacts of events the event manager can focus the management process by having a set of SIA activities that will be concluded per event under specific SIA guiding principles. The SIA activities must be adapted per event and to the nature of the event (IAIA, 2003a).

The effectiveness of SIA, when applied to large-scale events, will depend as much on the effectiveness of its assessment process as it will on the quality of the data, assessment methods and analysis it uses. The specific features of the process need to vary according to the particular context in which it is to be applied. This requires consideration of the context's cultural, political and socio-economic characteristics, as well as of its existing legal and institutional arrangements.

The general structure of the SIA process is shown in Fig. 8.1, which also indicates the linear and cyclic relationships that may exist

Table 8.1. Conceptualizing social impacts associated with events. (Adapted from IAIA, 2003a, p. 4.)

Social impact on people	Description
Their way of life	How they live, work, play and interact with one another on a day-to-day basis
Their culture	Their shared beliefs, customs, values and language or dialect
Their community	Its cohesion, stability, character, services and facilities
Their political systems	The extent to which people are able to participate in decisions that affect their lives, the level of democratization that is taking place, and the resources provided for this purpose
Their environment	The quality of the air and water people use, the availability and quality of the food they eat, the level of hazard or risk, dust and noise they are exposed to, the adequacy of sanitation, their physical safety, and their access to and control over resources
Their health and well-being	Health is a state of complete physical, mental, social and spiritual well-being and not merely the absence of disease or infirmity
Their personal and property rights	Particularly whether people are economically affected, or experience personal disadvantage that may include a violation of their civil liberties
Their fears and aspirations	Their perceptions about their safety, their fears about the future of their community, and their aspirations for the future and the future of their children

between its main components. The main components can be summarized as follows.

Screening

Screening is undertaken to determine which measures require an assessment and which do not. It should be undertaken at as early a stage as possible. Where an assessment is shown to be needed, screening may also determine the general type and level of detail of the assessment which is required (e.g. by distinguishing where 'simplified' and 'full' assessments may be needed). Simple lists, which categorize proposed interventions according to whether they require a 'full', 'simplified' or 'no' SIA, may be used. Only those policy interventions with the potential for major and/or complex impacts will require a full assessment. In common with other stages in the assessment process, screening should assist in ensuring that assessment resources are used cost-effectively.

Scoping

Scoping is undertaken after screening, during the early stages of policy preparation, in all of those cases where an SIA is required. Its purpose is to determine the terms of reference for the impact assessment which is to be undertaken, taking into consideration, where relevant, whether a 'simplified' or 'full' assessment is required. In the case of a 'full' assessment, the scoping study might be expected to cover the following:

- the 'problem' the proposed policy intervention is addressing, the goals/targets it is expected to meet and the alternative forms it might take;
- the types of impacts to be assessed, the causal determinants to be investigated and the level of detail to which each may need to be examined;
- the types of additional mitigating and enhancing (M&E) measures that might be investigated to deal with any remaining potentially significant problems and/or to enhance its potential beneficial effects; and
- the types of data needed for the assessment, the types of assessment methods to be used and the consultations to be undertaken during the assessment process.

In the case of 'simplified' assessments, the scoping stage in the process will be brief and, in some instances, partly covered during the screening stage. In the case of 'full' assessments, although more substantial, they are still required to be cost-effective. Each assessment

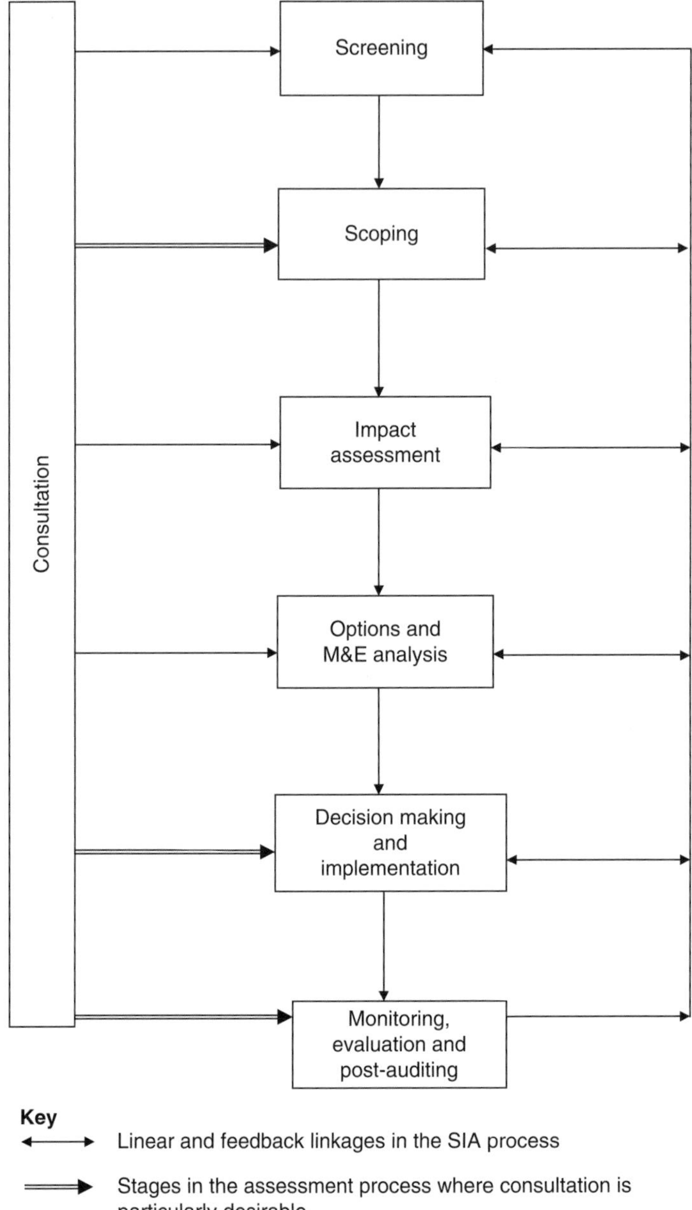

Fig. 8.1. Stages in the Social Impact Assessment (SIA) policy process for large-scale events (M&E, mitigating and enhancing). (Adapted from EDIAIS, 2007.)

should focus on those significant impacts that are relevant for decision-making purposes and use the most cost-effective data gathering and assessment methods. It should also alert, at an early stage, those responsible for the policy preparation to any potential problems which can then be taken into account in its subsequent planning, thereby avoiding possible delays and unnecessary costs later. The early identification and specification of alternative interventions is an important, creative exercise in the assessment process. It is undertaken at a stage in the process where new kinds of events development measures, and novel combinations of measures, might be identified for appraisal.

Impact assessment

Assuming all of the scoping tasks described above have been performed satisfactorily, the work plan for the impact assessment (whether 'simplified' or 'full') and how it is to be carried out should be well defined by the time this stage commences. It should also have been decided, in the case of a 'simplified' appraisal, whether this is to be undertaken entirely 'in house' and, in the case of a 'full' assessment, whether some external assistance is to be used. The main product of this stage in the assessment process should be an estimate (quantitative, or qualitative where the former is not feasible or appropriate) of the likely significant impacts for each alternative policy that has been investigated. It is important that equal consideration is given to the estimation of positive and negative impacts; otherwise the assessment will become unbalanced and promotional in character. The assessment should cover relevant economic, social and environmental impacts which relate to the goal of poverty reduction, and should be assessed according to different future scenarios and over different time periods (short term, intermediate and long term).

Options and M&E analysis

This stage in the assessment process partially overlaps the previous stage. Initially, at the impact assessment stage, all alternatives selected at the scoping stage will be submitted to a preliminary assessment. Then, on the basis of an options analysis, certain of these will be eliminated and only those that remain will be subject to a fuller assessment. Similarly, the specification of some of the remaining alternatives may be modified, by incorporating particular M&E measures, before the fuller assessments are carried out and a final options analysis is undertaken. This exemplifies the dynamic, rather than simple linear, nature of the assessment process (see Fig. 8.1).

Decision making and implementation

The findings of the options and mitigation analyses, and the supporting impact assessments from which these are derived, provide the information base (together with the findings of consultations based on these) for decision makers to determine which option, and its accompanying M&E measures, is to be selected for implementation. This decision should also incorporate any requirements relating to how:

- subsequent actions (e.g. lower-level programmes and projects) should be planned, appraised and implemented;
- the policy's implementation should be monitored and evaluated; and
- the SIA used in making this decision is to be post-audited.

Thus, when this decision is made, it provides a vital link between assessment at the approval and evaluation stages.

Monitoring, evaluation and post-auditing

A distinction is to be drawn between the monitoring and evaluation of individual event policy implementation and the monitoring, evaluation and post-auditing of the implementation of the strategic programme of policy initiatives for events development as a whole. In the former case, the purpose of monitoring and evaluation is to check whether individual policy measures are being implemented satisfactorily and are having their desired effects in achieving their short-term, intermediate and long-term goals. Where they are not, additional remedial measures should be identified, appraised, approved and implemented. In the latter case, the purpose of monitoring is to check whether the strategic impact assessment system itself, as applied to events development interventions, is working satisfactorily. It seeks answers to such questions as:

- Does the post-auditing of a sample of SIAs confirm or not that the types, size and significance of impacts predicted to occur have resulted or are there important discrepancies? If there are significant discrepancies, their causes should be identified and remedies proposed to strengthen future assessment practice.
- Is there clear evidence that the SIA appraisal and evaluation systems are having their intended influence on decision making and implementation? If not, proposals should be formulated to strengthen the integration of SIA into the planning, decision-making and implementation process.

In summary, the SIA system monitoring, evaluation and post-auditing provides an in-built mechanism to strengthen future SIA practice and to integrate it more fully in policy preparation, approval and implementation of large-scale events.

Consultation

Stakeholder consultation is an important component in any SIA system of the type that is being considered in this chapter. Its role is multi-functional and may contribute to different stages in the SIA process. This may include: (i) providing guidance when determining the scope of an assessment; (ii) providing information and expertise which assists in undertaking an assessment; (iii) reviewing and commenting upon an assessment; (iv) supporting the use of the assessment's findings in decision making and implementation; and (v) contributing to monitoring, evaluation and post-auditing.

The arrangements made for stakeholder consultation may vary considerably according to: the type and scale of the policy intervention being assessed; the cultural, political and institutional context in which this is taking place; and the stage(s) in the assessment process in which it is being used. At the strategic level of assessment, stakeholders mainly participate through organizational representatives rather than on an individual basis, though there are exceptions to this. Generalization is difficult but the following basic provisions are, in principle, desirable.

Some form of stakeholder consultation is desirable at a relatively early stage in the SIA process. Typically, this would be at the screening/scoping stage where consultees should have the opportunity to contribute to the determination of the scope of the assessment and to comment upon the content of the scoping report itself. Participants should preferably include representatives of relevant government departments, representatives of other donors also supporting enterprise development in the recipient country, and representatives of non-governmental organizations (including, in particular, small to medium-sized enterprise associations in the recipient country). For these consultations to be credible and effective, the scoping report should be publicly available, subject only to substantive confidentiality restrictions.

A second stage in the SIA process where consultation would be desirable and appropriate is when the full assessment, incorporating the options analysis and M&E analysis, has been completed but before any decisions on the approval of the proposed measure have been taken. The full assessment report should be publicly available, subject to the same confidentiality condition as mentioned above.

A third stage where consultation is desirable is where both specific and system evaluation reports are being completed and proposals for improvements, based on these, are being made. These reports should, in principle, also be made available. As in the two previously described stages, it is desirable that a written record is made of the consultation findings for submission to the decision-making authority prior to decisions being taken and for this record to be publicly available.

Approaches for Managing the Social Impacts of Community (or Small-scale) Events

In the case of community events (or small-scale events), however, most communities have neither the time nor the resources to conduct feasibility studies on a number of different event proposals. In reality, most ideas for events are generated by an individual, or a group within the community, who has identified the concept for an event that is suited to the community. SIA in such cases is considered 'resource intensive, time consuming and inappropriate' according to Small *et al.* (2005, p. 68). It is proposed that there should rather be 'a flexible but logical framework that incorporates practical tools for evaluating the sociocultural impacts of the event so that valuable feedback can be input into the organization of future events'. The alternative to pre-event impact projection is to 'learn from mistakes' and document the sociocultural impacts during and post the event. The retrospective approach can serve to clarify what has already happened and help impact projection for the future. Such studies combine hindsight (post-event analysis and conclusions), experience lessons learned and understanding (association of an event to specific impacts). This is achieved through identifying what has happened at the event and documenting how change had taken place, so that impact measurement and management can continue over time. This process is depicted in Fig. 8.2. Stages 1 to 3 of the framework contribute towards building a holistic picture of the event while stages 4 and 5 specifically measure the impacts that may arise from the staging of the event (Small *et al.*, 2005, p. 69).

Each stage of the framework depicted in Fig. 8.2 is detailed as follows:

- *Describe*. A description of the event characteristics including type, activities on offer, location and time, physical layout, geographical setting.
- *Profile*. A destination profile for the event host community that includes a profile of the destination as well as characterizes the subgroups of local residents most likely to be affected by the event.
- *Identify*. The range of sociocultural impacts most likely to occur because of the event being staged are identified, using any combination of research methods including brainstorming by a panel of experts, interviews and desktop research of literature.
- *Project*. The sociocultural impacts that are likely to occur from staging the event are projected; as with the SIA process, the projections are made before the event is staged and depict the pre-event perceptions of the host community.
- *Evaluate*. After the event is staged, the perceived sociocultural impacts of the event are evaluated. The aim is to determine the overall impact or acceptability of the event

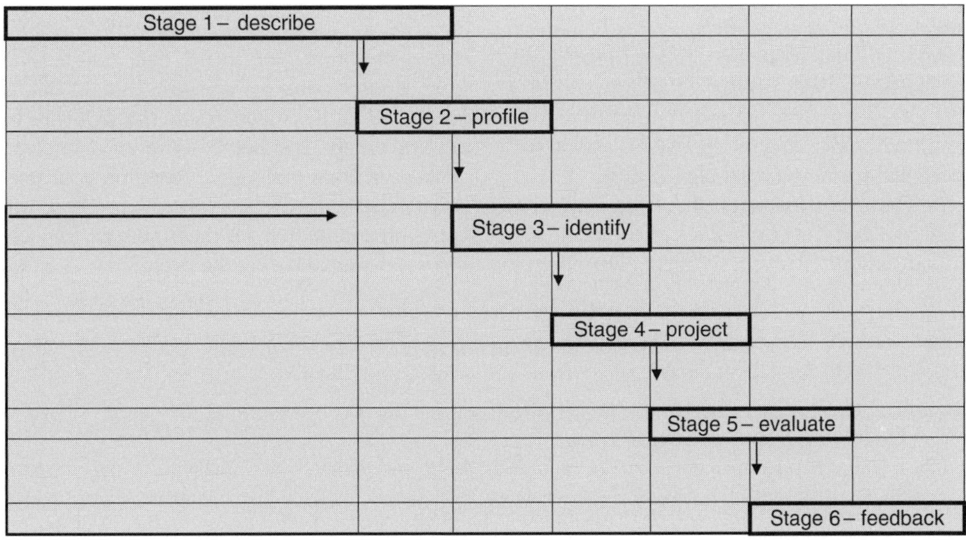

Fig. 8.2. Social impact evaluation framework. (Adapted from Small *et al.*, 2005, p. 69.)

in the eyes of the host community. Evaluation requires thorough data collection and analysis in order to make conclusions on the perceived negative and positive sociocultural impacts of the event.

- *Feedback*. The findings are communicated to the event managers and stakeholders. This is an opportunity to develop future strategies that can capitalize on positive impacts and minimize the negative impacts.

It is proposed by Delamere (2001, pp. 36–37) that events 'must be evaluated by their success in fostering community development, and the social and cultural impacts should be assessed continuously'. Increasing the awareness of these impacts and improving their measurement will enable constructive decisions to be made during the planning and management of community events.

Summary

Event managers and host communities have a stake in maximizing the social benefits and minimizing the social impact costs that are a result of staging an event. The social impact of events needs to be seriously considered by the host community and event managers if the legacies of hosting the event are to be viewed positively by the majority of residents. Consequently, this can result in events being considered on their total contribution to the quality of life of the host residents (Delamere, 2001, pp. 36–37). Events are much more than mere entertainments; they are social occasions with potential social value (Chalip, 2006).

The event manager should remember to first establish the core values of the host community where the event will take place, then to derive the important principles and then to develop the appropriate guidelines for the SIA of the event. The development of the SIA of the event is to be done in a participatory process including the host community, working with the event team. By inclusion of the host community a sense of 'ownership' in the development of the event is created, leading to positive support from the host community. It is advisable for event managers to invest in measuring the social impacts of their events on the host community. By taking such a step they will highlight the importance of their event to the broader tourism development process and identify what was positive and what was negative, which can lay the foundations for improvement for the future.

Key Questions

1. You are the new manager of a relatively small-scale community event company and you have a brief to establish the core values of the host community where the event will take place. How will you achieve this?

2. The brief from the organizers requires that you conduct an appropriate SIA of the said event. What is your plan of action and the factors you will have to consider in conducting the SIA of the event?

3. You are a member of the local organizing committee (LOC) of a mega-event that will be staged in your region in the near future. The LOC is responsible for ensuring that an SIA is conducted for this mega-event. The LOC has to develop criteria ensuring that the social impacts of the event are measured. Based on your personal experience of the events sector, how will you draft criteria that will measure such impacts before, during and after the event?

References

Arcodia, C. and Whitfield, M. (2006) Festival attendance and the development of social capital. *Journal of Convention & Event Tourism* 8(2), 1–18.

Buch, T. (2006) Resident perceptions of event impacts: Taupo and Ironman, New Zealand. Masters dissertation, AUT University, Auckland, New Zealand; available at http://aut.researchgateway.ac.nz/handle/10292/190

Butler, R.W. (1980) The concept of a tourist area cycle of evolution: implications for management of resources. *Canadian Geographer* 24(1), 5–12.

Chalip, L. (2006) Towards social leverage of sport events. *Journal of Sport & Tourism* 11(2), 109–127.

Cooper, C., Fletcher, J., Fyall, A., Gilbert, D. and Wanhill, S. (2005) *Tourism Principles and Practice*, 3rd edn. Prentice Hall, London.

Delamere, T.A. (2001) Development of a scale to measure resident attitudes toward the social impacts of community festivals, Part II: verification of the scale. *Event Management* 7(1), 25–38.

Doxey, G.V. (1975) When enough is enough: the natives are restless in Old Niagara. *Heritage Canada* 2(2), 26–27.

EDIAIS (Enterprise Development Impact Assessment Information Service) (2007) Practical Guide to Strategic Impact Assessment. Available at: http://www.sed.manchester.ac.uk/research/iarc/ediais/word-files/PracticalGuidetoStrategicImpactAssessmentSect.3.doc

Fredline, E. and Faulkner, B. (2000) Host community reactions: a cluster analysis. *Annals of Tourism Research* 27(3), 763–784.

Fredline, L., Deery, M. and Jago, L. (2006) *Host Community Perceptions of the Impact of Events, A Comparison of Different Event Themes in Urban and Regional Communities*. Sustainable Tourism CRC, Gold Coast, Australia.

Getz, D. (1997) *Event Management and Event Tourism*. Cognizant Communication Corporation, New York.

Hughes, S.M. (2007) Headline indicators for evaluating live events within the context of sustainability. Masters dissertation, University of East London, UK.

IAIA (2003a) *Social Impact Assessment – International Principles*. Special Publication Series No. 3. International Association for Impact Assessment, Fargo, North Dakota.

IAIA (2003b) US principles and guidelines for social impact assessment in the USA. *Impact Assessment and Project Appraisal* (September), 231–250.

Interorganizational Committee on Guidelines and Principles (1994) *Guidelines and Principles for Social Impact Assessment*. NOAA Technical Memo NMFS-F/SPO-16. US Department of Commerce, Washington, DC.

Kurtzman, J. and Zauhar, J. (1997) A wave in time: the sports tourism phenomena. *Journal of Sport Tourism* 4(2), 5–20.

Mathieson, A. and Wall, G. (1982) *Tourism: Economic, Physical and Social Impacts*. Longman, Harlow, UK.

Ohmann, S., Jones, I. and Wilkes, K. (2006) The perceived social impacts of the 2006 Football World Cup on Munich residents. *Journal of Sport & Tourism* 11(2), 129–152.

Olsen, M. and Merwin, D. (1977) Towards a methodology for conducting social impact assessments using quality of life indicators. In: Finsterbusch, K. and Wolf, C. (eds) *Methodology of Social Impact Assessment*. Dowden, Hutchinson & Ross, Stroudsburg, Pennsylvania.

Oviedo-Garcia, M.A., Castellanos-Verdugo, M. and Martin-Ruiz, D. (2007) Gaining residents' support for tourism and planning. *International Journal of Tourism Research* 10(2), 95–109.

Saayman, M. (2001) *An Introduction to Sports Tourism and Event Management*. Leisure Consultants and Publications, Potchefstroom, South Africa.

Sherwood, P. (2007) A triple bottom line (TBL) evaluation of the impact of special events. PhD dissertation, Victoria University, Melbourne, Australia; available at http://wallaby.vu.edu.au/adt-VVUT/uploads/approved/adt-VVUT20070917.123458/public/01front.pdf

Small, K., Edwards, D. and Sheridan, L. (2005) A flexible framework for evaluating the socio-cultural impacts of a (small) festival. *International Journal of Event Management Research* 1(1), 66–76.

Tassiopoulos, D. (2005) *Event Management, A Professional and Developmental Approach*. Juta, Cape Town, South Africa.

Vanclay, F. (2002) Conceptualising social impacts. *Environmental Impact Assessment Review* 22(3), 183–211.

Vanclay, F. (2003) International principles for social impact assessment. *Impact Assessment and Project Appraisal* (March), 5–12.

Vanclay, F. (2004) The triple bottom line and impact assessment: how do TBL, EIA, SIA, SEA and EMS relate to each other? *Journal of Environmental Assessment Policy and Management* 6(3), 265–288.

Vanclay, F. (2006) Principles of social impact assessment: a critical comparison between the international and US documents. *Environmental Impact Assessment Review* 26(1), 3–14.

Wood, E. (2005) Measuring the economic and social impacts of local authority events. *International Journal of Public Sector Management* 18(1), 37–53.

Wood, E. (2006) Measuring the social impacts of local authority events: a pilot study for a civic pride scale. *International Journal of Non-profit and Volunteer Sector Marketing* (August), 165–179.

9 Long-term Legacy Implications for Olympic Games

D. Sadd and I. Jones
Bournemouth University, Poole, UK

This chapter evaluates the lessons learned from the Olympic Games of Sydney and Barcelona in relation to legacy planning, especially the social consequences, and 'best-practice' lessons to be incorporated within the London 2012 planning in relation to future long-term legacies. London won the right to host the 2012 Games on the basis of its regeneration plans for an area of London containing socially deprived conditions.

Chapter outline

- Introduction
- Event Legacy
- Olympic Event Legacy
- Barcelona 1992
- Sydney 2000
- London Legacy
- Summary
- Key Questions

Introduction

All events have impacts and legacies. Large-scale events have major benefits, including destination image, urban developments and the legacy left behind after the event is held. In order to maximize the long-term potential for these benefits, legacy planning as early as possible is paramount. Case studies of the Sydney Games show that while they have been known as 'the best Games ever', the legacy planning for after the Games (beginning in 2000) was negligible and the consequences of this are ongoing (Cashman, 2006). For the organizers of the Barcelona 1992 Games, their built environment and the remodelling of the city were part of a larger-scale long-term redevelopment and their legacy planning was part of an overall vision for the city (Abad, 1995).

What appears to be a long-term strategic plan for London, especially in relation to the social impacts in the five boroughs involved in the staging of the 2012 Games, could become known as the 'London' model of urban rejuvenation for future mega-event planners, particularly with respect to long-term future legacy. All the 'paper' promises within the bid document discuss the major regeneration project with the associated large-scale spend on infrastructure; it is vital that the promises are turned into a long-term viable legacy.

> The task ahead for London is to embed the preparation for the hosting of the Games into a broader social policy agenda from the outset. Delivering social legacies are people based issues not facilities.
>
> (London Bid Document, 2005, p. xi)

Event Legacy

Event legacies are categorized into those that are economic, social, political, technological, environmental and legal. However, others include physical, psychological and cultural; and they can be further subdivided into those that are classified as hard legacies (generally those 'tangible' aspects) and those that are soft (generally 'intangible'). It is only economic and to some extent environmental, physical and technological legacies that can be objectively measured. Psychological, sociocultural and political legacies are more subjective and therefore more difficult to quantify and measure accurately, but do they need to be 'measured'? The sociocultural and psychological legacies are sometimes the most valuable, as stated by (Ritchie, 2000, p. 156), to 'enhance the long-term well-being or lifestyle of residents in a very substantial manner – preferably in a way that reflects the values of the local population'.

Event legacies may also have devastating consequences on the local population and local areas.

Olympic Event Legacy

An International Symposium on Legacy of the Olympic Games (1984–2000) was held in Lausanne in 2002 to discuss and explore the various aspects of Olympic Legacy. One of the key findings that emerged was that legacy, in Olympic terms, is crucial in the organization and ultimate evaluation of Games; yet, in attempting to define legacy, there can be several meanings of the concept. Volrath's (2005) definition suggests that legacy should include aims, motives, meanings and impacts in relation to the different translations of the term within the various languages and cultures of the Olympic family. Hiller (1998), however, prefers to use the word 'outcomes' instead of legacy, whereas Cashman (2006) refers to the term 'impacts'. The Symposium agreed that there had been insufficient attention given in the past to the concept of 'legacy' and identified a greater need for research on the subject; in particular, it recommended that legacy building should commence with the decision to bid for the Games (Ritchie, 1987; Cashman, 2006). Such a decision resulted in the appointment in 2008 of Tom Russell as the Legacy Director for London 2012, a decision which in itself was late as the bid was won in 2005, but at least the appointment has been made (London Development Agency, 2007). London's bid to host the 2012 Olympics was successful partly because of its legacy plans for the Games site area, which featured heavily in its bid documents.

Ritchie (2000) believes that legacy planning in respect of the Olympics can lead to the attainment of long-term benefits to host destination residents. However, Malfas *et al.* (2004) argue that while the Olympics may seem attractive through the positive economic benefits they accrue, the social impacts may be negative, particularly when residents are forced to move to make way for event infrastructure. They also highlight the Atlanta 1996 Olympic Games, when 9500 units of affordable housing were lost and US$350 million in public funds was diverted from low-income housing and social services to fund the Olympic preparation. In both Barcelona and Sydney, residents were forced to relocate (Beadnell, 2000; Mackay, 2000).

These examples illustrate how prior legacy planning is crucial and ideally that legacy planning should be instituted concurrently with the planning of the main Games. This is crucial from the outset of the planning, in order to identify and plan for any negative impacts that may arise. The clearance of the proposed Olympic site in London has already necessitated the forced removal of the Clays Lane, Peabody Estates residents and two traveller sites in Clays Lane and Waterden Road, and therefore it is already questionable as to where the positive social legacies from this lie. Hiller (1998, 2006), Olds (1998) and Lenskyj (2002) write about the negative impacts and legacies that hosting the Games have left on the communities in Sydney, Montreal and Calgary. Cashman (2006, p. 1) refers to the psychological impacts of the Sydney 2000 legacy on the population and how, after the Games had finished, the emotional legacy left many feeling like the 'carnival is over' and 'what happens next?'. There was little preparation for the immediate post-Games legacy planning in

Sydney and even now, some 9 years later, plans are still progressing for the development of the Olympic Park (Lochhead, 2005). While the disruption caused through the preparation stage will be inconvenient for some, there must be an outcome for the population, especially in the post-Games use of the Olympic facilities. In Sydney, the main stadium had to be reduced from a capacity of 120,000 to 80,000 to make it viable and even Jack Rogge, the International Olympic Committee (IOC) President, questioned why such a big capacity was required at the outset. Chalkley and Essex (1999) agree that while host cities can be transformed by the Games and have an enhanced international profile, some Games have negative legacies through stadia that become 'white elephants'.

While correctly considered post-Games use can result in positive outcomes, the IOC has recognized the possibilities of planning resulting in negative consequences. Since July 2003, the IOC has placed emphasis on maximizing the long-term legacy of the Games, and it is anticipated that from the 2012 London Games onwards the issues of infrastructure and the associated legacy developments will feature more prominently, achieving even greater significance. Well-planned infrastructure can lead to urban transformations of not just sporting venues, but also of transport (as seen in Athens), accommodation (Sydney and Barcelona), services, telecoms and the living environment. Chalkey and Essex (1993) and Essex and Chalkey (1998, 2003) further argue that the most successful Games to date (Barcelona) have been those that have taken the hosting of the Games as part of a wider regeneration development. In the case of London 2012, several venues will be dispersed around London; however, athletes and spectators are to be transported on high-speed transportation between venues. Chalkey and Essex (1993) further suggest that those events that have a mixture of public and private funding have produced 'substantial and impressive results'.

The main impacts and legacies from each particular Summer Games of the last 40 years can be divided as outlined in Table 9.1.

Table 9.1. Olympic impacts. (Adapted from Chalkley and Essex, 1999; Essex and Chalkley, 1998, 2003.)

Games	Main impacts observed
Mexico, Munich, Montreal	Political and social
Atlanta, Los Angeles	Economic and social
Barcelona	Social
Sydney	Environmental, technological and social
Athens	Environmental
Beijing	Social, political and environmental

However, the changing infrastructural impacts of each of the Games can be divided into themes, as seen in Table 9.2.

Smith and Fox (2007) write about the hosting of large events associated with physical regeneration of cities that stimulates 'softer' impacts of social and economic regeneration. In the case of Manchester 2002 and the hosting of the Commonwealth Games, all of the projects were games-themed and this has led to the phrase 'event-themed regeneration', as opposed to before when it was known as 'event-led regeneration'. Event-themed regeneration was a key strength of the legacy programme due to the organizational structures involved and the mix of projects linked to the Games. A greater range of benefits was gained by helping to avoid problems seen in other cities, such as post-Games use of facilities and local community engagement in the planning (Mace *et al.*, 2007). The organizers had a 'uniting' theme for regeneration and targeted approaches at the most needy beneficiaries. Programme managers said their programmes would not have been successful if not linked to the Games with social and economic initiatives. Hiller (2006) writes that the processes to transform urban spaces through regeneration receive little attention and that the Barcelona example of the extensive waterfront development is a prime example of such opportunities.

Barcelona 1992

The 1992 Olympic Games are a good example of what can be achieved through boosting the

Table 9.2. The changing infrastructural impacts of the Olympics. (Adapted from Chalkley and Essex, 1999; Essex and Chalkley, 1998, 2003.)

Summer Olympic Games		Winter Olympic Games		Distinct Olympic phase re: infrastructural development
PHASE ONE: 1896–1904 Small-scale, poorly organized and not necessarily involving any new infrastructure	**A**	PHASE ONE: 1924–1932 Minimal infrastructure transformation apart from sports facilities	**A**	
PHASE TWO: 1908–1932 Small-scale, better organized and involving construction of purpose-built facilities	**A**	PHASE TWO: 1936–1960 Emerging infrastructural demands, especially transportation	**A**	**A** = Prior to the 1960s, infrastructure transformations and expenditure were minimal
PHASE THREE: 1936–1956 Large-scale, well-organized and involving construction of purpose-built sport facilities with some impact on urban infrastructure	**A**	PHASE THREE: 1964–1980 Tool of regional development, especially transportation and Olympic Villages	**B**	
PHASE FOUR: 1960–1996 Large-scale, well-organized and involving construction of purpose-built sports facilities with significant impacts on urban infrastructure	**B**	PHASE FOUR: 1984–2002 Large-scale urban transformations, including multiple Olympic Villages	**B**	**B** = Cities that did improve their infrastructure but mainly focused on the sporting facilities
PHASE FIVE: 1996–2012 Urban regeneration projects have become recognized opportunities from the hosting of the games and the opportunities for enhanced place image. Scale of developments is in danger of imploding. Post-Games legacy planning beginning to gain momentum. Community involvement in planning gaining strength	**C**	PHASE FIVE: 2002–2010 Events being used to transform image in world's media and to enhance place image. Environmental concerns featuring heavily in planning, some community consultation	**C**	**C** = Cities that capitalized on the widespread opportunities for urban transformations and have recognized the role events can play within this process
PHASE SIX: 2012 onwards Less extravagance in Games to be replaced by collaborative planning and urban regeneration at the forefront of the rationale for hosting. Environmental issues of prominence and long-term legacy planning from outset	**D**	PHASE SIX; 2010 onwards Environmental issues of prominence, especially in fragile mountain regions. Collaborative planning essential	**D**	**D** = Games to return to celebrations of sport and culture with environmental issues being at the heart of a collaborative planning process. Less extravagance and opulence to be portrayed during Games

image of a city, increased tourism and urban regeneration. Barcelona's Olympic planning was focused on the long-term benefits to the city as a whole by having good transport links between the various sites, viable accommodation use post-Games, and an overall investment policy formulated in terms of social benefits, improved telecommunications (Botella, 1995) and the 'opening up of the sea to the city' (Mackay, 2000). All this took place within 6 years, as it was publicly acknowledged from the outset of the bid for the 1992 Games that they were to be an opportunity to re-launch the city of Barcelona. Waitt (2001) suggests that the actual hosting of a mega-event can also result in a phenomenon called 'civic boosterism', which has the capacity to unite polarized socio-economic sections of the community through the generation of feelings of community pride. The conclusion drawn from Waitt's study is that the local response to mega-events is complex, agreeing with other writers such as Ley and Olds (1988), Mihalik and Simonetta (1999) and Fredline and Faulkner (2000), in that the residents ranked intangible benefits higher than the economic ones. In Waitt's study, the level of citizen support diminished the closer the Games got, as they became more concerned about the negative benefits. The lesson for future Games is that is it imperative to garner, foster and maintain community support, especially if such communities perceive that they are not getting value for money from the infrastructure improvements. Therefore, organizing committees must ensure funding is secured at the earliest possible stage of capital improvement projects, so as to garner and foster community support.

Sydney 2000

Owen (2001, 2002) argues in the case of Sydney that, in the areas adjacent to the Olympic Park, the social and political impacts were overshadowed by the need to provide physical and symbolic legacies of the Games, i.e. the more tangible elements. Due to a lack of community participation in the planning processes, negative social impacts resulted, a situation not helped by restricting public access to community facilities and also by removing local authorities' planning powers. For Auburn Council, the Olympics provided an opportunity for urban governance to be approached with a more entrepreneurial style. This involved a more proactive stance, particularly in the development of facilities that could be marketed to attract investment into the area, but without losing the focus of the local residents' well-being. Such entrepreneurial governance included the centralization of planning powers including the streamlining of processes, a high level of private sector involvement and the subversion of the democratic principles of openness, accountability and community participation in planning (Owen, 2002). The important point is to ensure that local communities get the transparency and accountability they deserve in the planning of their future urban environment.

Sydney did, however, have world-class venues, the largest remediation project in Australia and the creation of the largest metropolitan parkland in Australia, alongside Newington being one of largest solar-powered suburbs in the world. The Sydney Olympic Park Act of 2001 wanted social, economic, environmental and financial returns from its investment in the park and to secure a lasting Olympic legacy. However, Lochhead (2005) writes that at time of the Games, as well as during the planning stages, the post-Games legacy was little considered. The Sydney Olympic Park Authority published their 7–10 year plan only in 2002, identifying eight main sites for development, including facilities for up to 10,000 workers and 3000 residents. They later decided to propose 'Vision 2025' envisaging a mix of uses within the urban area, resulting in a critical mass of residents and workers as well as transport infrastructure improvements. Under the longer-term programme, the precinct would retain its current amenity and major event capacity, but its viability would be significantly enhanced, particularly vital as both the main stadia have suffered such viability issues since the Games ended.

In several developments for the Sydney Games, the infrastructure was not approved at a local level but by the Minister for Urban Affairs, and the planning was from a regional and national perspective, with the result being sharp rent increases and ensuing homelessness in some areas. In Auburn, the Council retained control and ownership of many community facilities and services, enabling them to control costs and to offer employment to the local population. In conclusion, Owen (2002, p. 333) posits that 'entrepreneurialism is not the hegemonic ideology that many urban geographers believe'. He argues that this is because managerial and democratic practices can often function in the shadow of emerging entrepreneurial approaches, yet the strength of empowerment seen in some communities affords them the opportunity to resist this entrepreneurialism. Due to a lack of community participation in the planning processes, negative social impacts have resulted, not helped by restricting public access to community facilities and also by removing local authorities' planning powers (Lenskyj, 2002; Owen, 2002). Cashman (2006) also argues that the benefits of hosting the Games for the local population were very vague, especially in the case of Homebush, due to the envisaged benefits either being over-inflated or simply being too complex to measure in monetary terms. Additionally, often there is no post-Games monitoring in place to measure the long-term benefits, coupled with a lack of objectivity in terms of what is to be measured. Yet, the organizers of the Games disagreed with Cashman by arguing that these benefits can outweigh the negative ones, despite the overcrowding, increased costs, taxes and disruption. Often the local residents are not consulted about the development plans for their area, only being informed of the positive benefits that will accrue as result of the Games taking place; yet the developers/organizers often report that they have public support via opinion polls undertaken among the community and by asking potential detractors and community representatives to join the bid committees.

Owen (2002), writing about the 2000 Olympics, compared the urban governance policies of three local government areas in relation to the social and political legacies of their involvement in the Games. All three areas, Auburn, Ryde and Waverley, adopted quite different styles of entrepreneurial governance and also different styles of dealing with 'activist' elements in their neighbourhoods, resulting in some cases of communities securing considerable benefits accruing locally from the Games. In Auburn's case it is interesting to note that the former mayor, Patrick Curtin, was involved in most of the negotiations on behalf of the Council, yet in the intervening period before the Games took place an election had been held and Le Lam was elected to the position of mayor, thus displacing the one person who had been at the forefront of the negotiations on behalf of the community. Owen further writes of the shift in urban governments from a managerial approach towards urban politics, to one in which entrepreneurial attempts to improve economic and social welfare take precedence over managerial concerns. Old-style management involving the centralization of planning powers, privatization of government operations, relaxation of normal planning process and the assumption of risk by the public sector have 'resulted in reduced and ineffective community participation through the subversion of democratic principles' (Owen, 2002, p. 324). However, when considering the size of the planning involved in the staging of Olympic Games, special planning agencies have to be established to oversee the efficiency of the process, and it is the manner in which they exercise their powers that Owen investigated in her three case studies.

The case of Auburn Council was different from that of Ryde and Waverley, as there appeared to be little tension between the council and the Olympic organizing authorities. This was due mainly to the fact that much of the area was already owned by the state and federal governments, having received poor management for many years and had become degraded and desolate wasteland. The council involvement was mainly through providing supporting infrastructure, being very entrepreneurial and democratic in its dealings with the organizers. However, despite many of the perceived legacies being negative for the local communities, Auburn Council managed to keep the interests of their residents in the forefront of all their negotiations, and any local community opposition was carefully listened to and acted upon according to Cashman (2006). Unlike the other two areas, the Auburn residents were not losing the use of a facility while preparations for the Games took place, as the parkland was unusable anyway. The council and local community groups recognized through the consultation process that they would inherit the legacy of the Sydney Olympic Park, which for the council would generate income and be a place for the community to use. However, the council did suffer from a lack of openness, cooperation and information from the Sydney Organizing Committee for the Olympic Games.

London Legacy

By applying the key findings of the International Symposium of the Olympic Games 2002 to the London legacy planning so far, the following can be concluded.

1. The legacy-building starts with the decision to bid for the games. One of the key reasons for London winning the 2012 bid was on the basis that the legacy planning was recognized from the initial stage of deciding to bid for the Games.
2. There are several meanings of the concept of legacy, and in translation there are better words to include that express the historical roots and the Olympic Movement more comprehensively. London, while not explicitly conceptualizing legacy, has designed positive and long-lasting 'legacy' proposals.
3. Sustainable development is paramount within legacy planning in order to protect the environment, yet technological development is crucial for the Games. The infrastructure for the Games should be a beacon of environmentally friendly development. As proposed in the post-Games plans for the London Olympic Park, the main stadium will be reduced in capacity post-Games.
4. Intangible legacies are as important as tangible legacies, especially cultural legacies as the ultimate source of all other legacies such as the Games' rituals, torch relay, opening and closing ceremonies. The cultural Olympiad being rolled out nationwide and other intangible legacies will include skills training and a volunteer programme.
5. The IOC's role within legacy planning is one of ensuring the effective transfer of knowledge between organizing bodies and moreover to raise awareness of the importance of legacy planning. The IOC would like to ensure that genuine, lasting sporting legacies are created. Legacy, especially evidencing post-Games initiatives, will become a crucial component within the bid process. Knowledge transfer plays a crucial role within London planning.
6. More attention is required to research the legacy of the Games, especially longitudinal research and more comparative studies, as well as the creation of libraries of Olympic-related research and other documentation with all Olympic study centres interlinked. Several academic institutions are already involved in longitudinal research programmes.
7. Output from the conference can form part of the legacy of the Olympic Movement. This is already being used by the London Organizing Committee.

In the UK, the 2002 Commonwealth Games held in Manchester were an excellent example of legacy planning helping to demonstrate the positive impact mega sports events can have on the domestic population in terms of raising awareness, participation levels and volunteering in sport. In addition, the hosting of the Commonwealth Games played a noteworthy role in the regeneration of the area and gave a significant boost to the economy of the North-west of England. Given the magnitude of the Olympic Games in comparison to the Commonwealth Games and because they will be based in the South-east and beyond, the legacies have the potential to spread beyond London to other parts of the country, especially through the establishment of the Nations and Regions Group structure. The facilities, the volunteering programme, the infrastructure, the cultural integration and awareness must all be harnessed and focused towards the legacy goals being set. The timing of the Commonwealth Games was also important, as they showed the world that the UK can host major sports events successfully.

However, despite all the positive legacy plans that are in place and in order for the successful conclusion of well-organized Games in 2012, there are the inevitable negative legacy stories arising. Already in London, in order to make the site viable for development in the Lower Lea Valley, many different groups have been affected through forced relocation, including two traveller camps, the Manor Road allotment holders, the residents of the Clays Lane, Peabody Estate and many local businesses. Their respective legacies are all negative to date and while consultation took place, it was not equitable. Many sections of the bid documentation mention potential benefits for the local community to the Olympic Park, yet the evidence from previous Games points to these communities changing in social structure post-Games. It will be interesting to see the social structure of the new site's residents after 2012 and what the eventual long-term legacies for them become.

Summary

This chapter has evaluated the lessons learned from the past Games of Sydney and Barcelona in relation to legacy planning, especially the social consequences, and the 'best-practice' lessons to be incorporated within the London 2012 planning in relation to future long-term legacies. London won the right to host the 2012 Games on the basis of its regeneration plans for an area of London in socially deprived conditions.

All events have impacts and legacies; the larger the size of the event, the greater these 'consequences', with the Olympics having the greatest impacts and legacies. These large-scale events also have major benefits including destination image, urban developments and the legacy left behind after the event is held. In order for these benefits to maximize the long-term potential, legacy planning as early as possible is paramount. Case studies of the Sydney Games show that while they have been known as 'the best Games ever', their legacy planning for after the Games, beginning in 2000, was negligible and the consequences of this are ongoing. For the organizers of the Barcelona 1992 Games, their built environment and the remodelling of the city were part of a larger-scale long-term redevelopment, and their legacy planning was part of an overall vision for the city.

What appears to be a long-term strategic plan for London, especially in relation to the social impacts of the five boroughs involved in the staging of the 2012 Games, could become known as the 'London' model of urban rejuvenation for future mega-event planners, particularly with respect to long-term future legacy.

Key Questions

1. What lessons can London learn from the Sydney and Barcelona legacy planning, if any?
2. Evaluate how the Olympic event infrastructure requirements have developed since 1896.
3. How could Olympic event legacy differ from other event legacies?

References

Abad, J.M. (1995) A summary of the activities of the COOB'92. In: de Moragas, M. and Botella, M. (eds) *The Keys to Success – The Social, Sporting, Economic and Communications Impact of Barcelona '92*. CEO-UAB, Barcelona, Spain, pp. 11–17.

Beadnell, M. (2000) Sydney's homeless to be removed for Olympics. Available at: http://www.wsws.org/articles/2000/feb2000/olymp-f03.shtml (accessed 7 November 2006).

Botella, M. (1995) Organization of the Games. In: de Moragas, M. and Botella, M. (eds) *The Keys To Success – The Social, Sporting, Economic and Communications Impact of Barcelona '92*. CEO-UAB, Barcelona, pp. 18–43.

Cashman, R. (2006) *The Bitter Sweet Awakening – The Legacy of the Sydney 2000 Olympic Games*. Walla Walla Press, Sydney.

Chalkley, B. and Essex, S. (1999) Urban development through hosting international events: a history of the Olympic Games. *Planning Perspectives* 14(4), 369–394.

Essex, S. and Chalkley, B. (1998) Olympic Games: catalyst of urban change. *Leisure Studies* 17(3), 187–206.

Essex, S. and Chalkley, B. (2003) Urban Transformation from Hosting the Olympic Games. University Lecture on the Olympics. Available at: http://olympicstudies.uab.es/lectures/web/pdf/essex.pdf (accessed 16 March 2009).

Fredline, E. and Faulkner, B. (2000) Host community reactions: a cluster analysis. *Annals of Tourism Research* 27(3), 763–784.

Hiller, H. (1998) Assessing the impact of mega-events: a linkage model. *Current Issues in Tourism* 1(1), 47–57.

Hiller, H. (2000) Mega-events, urban boosterism and growth strategies: an analysis of the objectives and legitimations of the Cape Town 2004 Olympic bid. *International Journal of Urban and Regional Research* 24(2), 439–458.

Hiller, H. (2006) Post-event outcomes and the post-modern turn: the Olympics and urban transformations. *European Sport Management Quarterly* 6(4), 317–332.

Lenskyj, H.J. (2002) *The Best Olympics Ever? Social Impacts of Sydney 2000*. State University of New York Press, New York.

Ley, D. and Olds, K. (1988) Landscape as spectacle: world fairs and the culture of heroic consumption. *Environment and Planning D: Society and Space* 6(2), 191–212.

Lochhead, H. (2005) A new vision for Sydney Olympic Park. *Urban Design* 10(3/4), 215–222.

London Bid Document (2005) London 2012 Bid Team, London.

London Development Agency (2007) LDA appoints Tom Russell to head Olympic Legacy Directorate. Available at: http://www.lda.gov.uk/server/show/ConWebDoc.2308 (accessed 16 March 2009).

Mace, A., Hall, P. and Gallent, N. (2007) New East Manchester: urban renaissance or urban opportunism? *European Planning Studies* 15(1), 51–65.

Mackay, D. (2000) *The Recovery of the Seafront*. Aula Barcelona, Barcelona, Spain.

Malfas, M., Theodoraki, E. and Houlihan, B. (2004) Impacts of the Olympic Games as mega-events. *Municipal Engineer* 157(ME3), 209–220.

Mihalik, M.B. and Simonetta, L. (1999) A midterm assessment of the host population's perceptions of the 1996 summer Olympics: support, attendance, benefits and liabilities. *Journal of Travel Research* 37(3), 244–248.

Olds, K. (1998) Urban mega-events, evictions and housing rights: the Canadian case. *Current Issues in Tourism* 1(1), 2–46.

Owen, K.A. (2001) *The Local Politics of the Sydney 2000 Olympic Games: Processes, and Politics of the Venue Preparation*. University of New South Wales, Sydney.

Owen, K.A. (2002) The Sydney 2000 Olympics and urban entrepreneurialism: local variations in urban governance. *Australian Geographical Studies* 40(3), 323–336.

Ritchie, J.R.B. (1987) The impacts of the 1988 Winter Olympics on Calgary: a tourism perspective. Paper presented at *18th Annual Conference of the Travel and Tourism Research Association*, Seattle, Washington, 7–11 June 1987.

Ritchie, J.R.B. (2000) Turning 16 days into 16 years through Olympic legacies. *Event Management* 6(3), 155–165.

Smith, A. and Fox, T. (2007) From 'event-led' to 'event-themed' regeneration: the 2002 Commonwealth Games Legacy Programme. *Urban Studies* 44(5), 1125–1143.

Volrath, A. (2005) Eternity games – legacies and collective identity through sport events: studies on legacies of community building in the Sydney 2000 Olympic Games. In: Adair, D., Coe, B. and Gouth, N. (eds) *Beyond the Torch*. Australian Society for Sports History, Sydney.

Waitt, G. (2001) The Olympic spirit and civic boosterism: the Sydney 2000 Olympics. *Tourism Geographies* 3(3), 249–278.

10 Critical Success Factors in Sustainable Events

C. Haven-Tang and E. Jones
University of Wales Institute, Cardiff (UWIC), Cardiff, UK

This chapter examines critical success factors for events-led sustainable destination management strategies through the development of one rural and three urban case studies exploring the extent to which the seven success factors for business tourism are shared with events-led tourism strategies.

Chapter outline

- Introduction
- Events and Destination Development
- Community Participation and Events
- Critical Success Factors for Business and Event Tourism: the BESTBET Model
- Mapping Critical Success Factors
- Summary
- Key Questions

Introduction

Many UK regions and destinations are developing event strategies – often community-inspired – as events play an invaluable role in the cultural life of many towns and cities, providing a diverse range of entertainment and educational opportunities, adding to quality of life and income generation (SQW Ltd and TNS, 2005). The importance of major events is recognized by the North-west region of England, where the 2002 Commonwealth Games and Liverpool's successful European City of Culture bid helped improve the image of the North-west and the host cities (NWDA, 2004). Furthermore, the comparative advantage of many destinations is often similar (Ritchie and Crouch, 2003) and a vibrant portfolio of events can create distinctiveness and hence competitive advantage for destinations. Haven-Tang *et al.* (2007) propose a model identifying seven critical success factors for business tourism destinations: (i) leadership; (ii) networking; (iii) branding; (iv) skills; (v) ambassadors; (vi) infrastructure; and (vii) bidding.

Events and Destination Development

Many destinations around the world have undergone successful regeneration programmes; for example, Barcelona, Birmingham, Brighton, Glasgow, Manchester, Rotterdam and Sydney (BTP, 2004; Smith, 2005; Richards, 2007). Infrastructure developments, which are so important to successful event tourism destinations, often benefit host populations as well as tourists. Carefully designed event programmes can build on the infrastructure to reposition the destination and enhance destination image.

However, successful regeneration programmes can create homogenized destinations with similar comparative advantages in terms of physical resources, infrastructure, historical and cultural resources (Ritchie and Crouch, 2003). Events can combat homogeneity and build on the distinctive features within the destination, adding to the portfolio of tourist attractions to create sustainable competitive advantage through effective utilization of destination resources.

Event tourism has the advantage of being able to attract visitors in the off-season, when many suppliers have surplus capacity and can capitalize on the assets of the off-season, such as winter sports instead of summer sports and seasonal food and drink. As well as countering the negative economic impacts of seasonality, event tourism can act as a catalyst for urban regeneration. Many destinations that have hosted large events have been forced to upgrade existing facilities, services and transport infrastructures; thus creating legacies. For example, the 2002 Commonwealth Games was a significant driver in the regeneration of East Manchester and provided new facilities as lasting legacies (Robathan, 2008). Events can also provide key meeting grounds for international communities and can be developed alongside conferencing: for example, Derby Photography Festival and Burley Horse Trials. Hence, there is an intrinsic link between events and tourism.

As a result, many UK regions and destinations are pursuing event strategies and developing event facilities to ensure that events are a sustainable part of the destination strategy. For example, Capital Region Tourism includes events as a priority activity in its urban and regional propositions for South-east Wales (Locum Destination Consulting, 2003) and North-west England was reputedly the first region in England to develop a long-term strategic approach to major events, which emphasizes:

> The important role that major events have to play in the areas of tourism, image development and regeneration. Major events will attract more business and leisure visitors to the region, will help tackle negative perceptions and highlight the region's assets. (NWDA, 2004, p. 3)

Many large events receive substantial amounts of public funding, especially from organizations in the host destination (Burgan and Mules, 2001). Public expenditure is justified in terms of the economic impacts that events bring to host destinations, including cultural and international benefits, as well as being a catalyst for industrial and economic development. However, to have any real value for a destination, events must be part of a broader strategy, especially if events are to create lasting legacies.

Additionally, events should be anchored in the locality to create a bigger economic impact throughout the supply chain. Events that are parachuted-in represent only a short-term strategy for the destination and host community, and may leave few or no lasting legacies. Furthermore, Derrett (2004) suggests that local communities will be more accepting of an event if they believe it to have emerged from within the community, rather than it having been imposed on them.

Community Participation and Events

Staged displays of local culture enable communities to showcase their cultural and regional values and identities, as well as attracting and entertaining visitors. In particular, festivals create opportunities for community action, stimulate tourist demand, develop positive destination imagery, help position community identity (Chhabra *et al.*, 2003; McCabe, 2006) and offer the opportunity for environmental enhancement and income generation. However, while this can reinforce cultural identity and community cohesion, over-commercialization of community events may detract from the original principle of the event.

Changes in the economic structure of rural economies have implications for community identity and ultimately community survival. Local people and their lifestyles are fundamental to the success of rural tourism development, as they provide social capital, which needs to be utilized and developed to prevent rural community decline. Building social capital is a way of capacity building in terms of developing human capital and ensuring competitive advantage. Events which are developed by local communities as a source of celebration can aid rural communities through stakeholder community participation. Events that attract visitors also have the ability to draw additional financial resources into rural communities and their economies. The Wales Tourist Board (WTB, 2000, p. 75) asserts:

> Without the support of the local host community, the potential benefits arising from tourism are unlikely to be fully realized. This is particularly the case in smaller rural areas where the visitor experience is often more intimately linked with the people and the place.

As a result, events are just as important an element in the tourism product portfolio of rural destinations as they are in urban destinations. In response to the growing desire to celebrate unique identities, community-based festivals and events are becoming increasingly popular, encompassing a diverse range of themes 'from the specific, food and wine, through to multi-faceted celebrations, such as multi-cultural festivals' (Small *et al*., 2005, p. 66). Community festivals are often designed to celebrate and enhance group and place identity. Many community-based festivals and events are essentially small-scale, bottom-up events organized by volunteers for the benefit of the local community. Ultimately, such festivals and events are based on the celebration of community values, which contribute to community survival.

Critical Success Factors for Business and Event Tourism: the BESTBET Model

Drawing on research into best practice in business and event tourism destinations, Haven-Tang *et al*. (2007) proposed a model that identifies seven critical success factors for business tourism destinations: (i) leadership; (ii) networking; (iii) branding; (iv) skills; (v) ambassadors; (vi) infrastructure; and (vii) bidding. The model is based on case studies of three UK business tourism destinations: Glasgow (Box 10.1), Manchester (Box 10.2) and Newcastle Gateshead (Box 10.3). These three urban destinations had an explicit events strategy as discussed below. A rural case study of a fourth destination – Monmouthshire (Box 10.4) – is presented to explore how the success factors are shared across the typology of events.

Leadership

Manchester, Glasgow and Newcastle Gateshead have all benefited from local authorities with the political confidence and aspiration to develop the destination. Leadership includes: a clear vision and implementation strategy for

Box 10.1. Glasgow.

Glasgow is one of Europe's fastest growing conference destinations (McLardie, 2005). Glasgow is an urban destination with a rich industrial heritage and, like many UK destinations whose economies were based on heavy industry, Glasgow has undergone significant urban regeneration. As part of this regeneration, Glasgow City Council, Scottish Enterprise Glasgow, the then Greater Glasgow and Clyde Valley Tourist Board and relevant partners developed the Glasgow Tourism Action Plan 2002–2007. £100 million has been invested into the tourism infrastructure, including a new riverside museum and cultural quarter (Wild, 2003). The Glasgow City Marketing Bureau is a not-for-profit organization funded by Glasgow City Council with contributions from the private sector. Glasgow has a coherent destination brand that focuses on a strong cultural infrastructure.

Box 10.2. Manchester.

Manchester has an industrial past, often famed for its cotton-milling activities. However, the success of the 2002 Commonwealth Games, together with new venues, has rejuvenated the city. Marketing Manchester is publicly funded together with income from the private sector. The Northwest Conference Bidding Unit, launched in July 2004, is funded by the Northwest Development Agency and Marketing Manchester. The Unit is a key element of the North-west's tourism strategy and links into the major events strategy led by the Northwest Development Agency. The 2002 Commonwealth Games helped reinforce the brand identity of Manchester as a city with a vibrant popular culture and sporting history.

Box 10.3. Newcastle Gateshead.

Newcastle Gateshead is a destination traditionally famed for its industrial background, but has seen investment through regeneration projects that utilize culture, arts and sporting traditions. Gateshead Council and other voluntary, public and private partners formed the Gateshead Strategic Partnership, which facilitated the building of the Angel of the North, the Gateshead Millennium Bridge and Sage Gateshead, and transformed the Baltic Flour Mills into a public art space (Gateshead Council, 2005). The NewcastleGateshead Initiative is a destination marketing organization, established in 1999 (NGI, 2004). Culture[10] is a programme that aims to extend and consolidate the successes achieved through the 2008 European City of Culture bid. It is estimated that by 2010, Culture[10] will create £1.2 billion in new investment for the region and 24,000 new jobs in tourism, creative and cultural industries (Voluntary Arts England, 2003). Although their bid was unsuccessful, Newcastle Gateshead benefited from the 2008 European City of Culture bid, as it generated investment in the tourism infrastructure and transformed the image of Newcastle Gateshead (Gosling, 2004).

Box 10.4. Monmouthshire.

Monmouthshire is one of ten unitary authorities in South-east Wales, located on the Wales–England border. It includes parts of the Wye Valley Area of Outstanding Natural Beauty, famous for its role in the Picturesque movement of the 18th century, but less well known for its industrial heritage in the 16th century. Adventa, a local partnership of public, private and voluntary/community organizations, aims to develop Monmouthshire as a strong, vibrant, self-reliant and entrepreneurial rural county that sensitively capitalizes on its cultural, natural and social assets and delivers high-quality value-added products effectively, sustainably and profitably. There is little doubt that Monmouthshire is representative of a rural tourism destination, yet its location on one bank of the River Wye does little to differentiate Monmouthshire from similar rural tourism destinations in England, such as Herefordshire.

business tourism; appropriate funding; communication within the destination; strategic and operational coordination of the destination; and a destination team approach. For example, in Manchester, interviewees emphasized the vision and commitment of the Leader of the City Council. Manchester's strategy encourages bottom-up community events to support business tourism and build their *Original Modern City* brand, as they consider events to be a key strategic driver for tourism visits and economic investment. The events team helps community event organizers to develop long-term event sustainability, which enables the event to capitalize on additional tourism visits and ensure a sustainable events calendar.

In Glasgow, the Major Festivals and Events Unit (MFEU) adopts a similar approach by developing seven major festivals and events to encourage more visitors and generate larger economic impacts for the city. MFEU coordinates key stakeholders strategically and operationally. Event organizers in Monmouthshire can access a Promotion and Marketing Fund, designed to encourage strategic proactive marketing, especially in terms of attracting the 'out of county' market, to generate a wider events audience and create a more sustainable events portfolio.

Networking

Destination networks enhance market intelligence, as large international conferences and events rarely return to the same destination. Thus destinations can pass clients within destination networks. Glasgow, Manchester, and Newcastle Gateshead all belong to international trade associations which enable collaboration with colleagues in other destinations, promoting market awareness and understanding of client idiosyncrasies which are crucial to the decision-making processes. In Monmouthshire, while on a much smaller scale, networking is deemed critical so that event organizers can share knowledge and collaborate for the benefit of individual events and the wider destination.

An event organizers' forum exists at a local level to try and promote networking.

Branding

Branding provides a framework for destination coherence and brand image is a critical tool in a competitive and crowded tourism marketplace. Manchester's *Original Modern City* and Glasgow's *Scotland with Style* attractively represent the destination externally as well as resonating with internal stakeholders. Glasgow uses city branding to promote civic pride while the NewcastleGateshead Initiative has developed a destination brand toolkit to rationalize conflicting brands, create a sense of identity and secure adoption by the local business community and local residents. The city brands in these destinations have a clear approach, reasoned argument and collective aspiration. Glasgow, Manchester and Newcastle Gateshead also stressed the importance of promoting national and regional capital city status in external branding. They felt that it was a real attribute for a destination to have status as either a national or regional capital city.

Skills

The requirement for appropriate skills to underpin high-quality products and services is a priority for all destinations and can be the determining factor between comparative or competitive advantage. Most local community events are run by volunteers, illustrating one of the major differences between volunteer-run and commercially run events. The latter are far more business-oriented and recognize the need for professionalism and a holistic skills base. In Monmouthshire, training packages have been developed for event organizers to develop skills, increase professionalism and facilitate the transition from community-based events to more commercially aware events.

The use of volunteers can create human resource challenges, particularly in terms of ensuring a balanced skills base. However, Glasgow and Manchester both use large numbers of volunteers for their major events. The Events Unit in Manchester helps develop the professionalism of community event organizers to ensure sustainable events and one of the legacies of the 2002 Commonwealth Games was a volunteer database, listing a core of trained volunteers who continue to work on major sporting events. Similarly, following the Special Olympics, the MFEU in Glasgow created an events volunteer database. These examples illustrate how capacity building for events can be successfully achieved at a destination level and can be sustained beyond the initial catalyst event.

Ambassadors

The role, funding and proactivity of ambassadors can be crucial for a business tourism destination. Glasgow, Manchester and Newcastle Gateshead all run successful formalized ambassador programmes, which facilitate external promotion of the destination and help to provide market intelligence for business tourism events. However, the use of ambassadors may be variable, depending on the type, size and profile of the event.

Infrastructure

Compactness of the destination, accessibility and seamless integration of transport infrastructure are critical to business and event tourism, especially if trying to attract the European and international markets. Regional support for route development to improve and expand air access for international customers is important in this context. Glasgow, Manchester and Newcastle Gateshead offer direct air links to a vast array of national and international destinations, with route development funds to further enhance access. A range of suitable venues and accommodation capacity within the destination are obviously fundamental to attracting visitors to events. Rural destinations like Monmouthshire often suffer, as their product base is small-scale with few large-scale residential venues. However, the traditional supply of country house hotels and outdoor venues provides opportunities in the corporate, incentive travel and outdoor pursuits/management development markets.

Bidding

The process of bidding for an event or title can raise the profile of a destination, which demonstrates the importance of the bidding process. For example, bidding for the title of European Capital of Culture 2008 raised the profile of Newcastle Gateshead and created media attention, even though the bid was unsuccessful. Bidding involves the whole process of gathering market intelligence on appropriate markets for the destination and product knowledge about the destination. Although bidding strategies differed, the key message from all business and event tourism destinations was that 'you've got to be in it to win it!' Bidding propensity will depend on the type of event. For events such as international association conferences, mega-events and major or special events, competitive bidding is fundamental in the decision-making process.

A clear understanding of the fit between target markets and destination product is paramount to customer satisfaction. Events need to fit with the destination and build on a destination's comparative advantage to be successful. The next section maps the critical success factors from the BESTBET model (Haven-Tang *et al.*, 2007) on to event typologies, specifically mega-, special or major, hallmark and community events, while highlighting idiosyncrasies across the four typologies.

Mapping Critical Success Factors

Urban destinations, such as Glasgow, Manchester and Newcastle Gateshead, use events as a vehicle to create a unique destination proposition, building on their comparative advantages. Manchester, for example, uses its diverse calendar of community-inspired and community-led events to underpin its *Original Modern City* brand. The Manchester Pride festival helps to attract the North American gay market to Manchester, aided by the *Manchester Guide for Gay Visitors*, published by the destination-marketing organization Marketing Manchester. Hosting Euro-Pride and the annual convention for the International Gay Lesbian and Transgender Association has also showcased Manchester's vibrant gay scene.

As a rural destination, Monmouthshire has numerous examples of how community events demonstrate the role of events as visitor attractions, as well as for the benefit of the local communities. For example, the local community in the village of Llangattock Lingoed organized a Lammas Fair (a traditional August festival, focused around a hiring fair and religious observance) in August 2005, which attracted hundreds of visitors and was a combination of heritage and festival. 'The aim was to encourage local tourism, promote heritage and provide a social event for the community' (Village Alive Trust, 2005). The Monmouth Festival is also regarded as an asset for the area, as demonstrated by increased public funding for the festival. However, the voluntary organizing committee faced tensions between retaining the community element of the festival and using the festival to attract visitors to the area.

Table 10.1 maps the critical success factors for business and event tourism destinations on to event typologies, in order to identify critical success factors common to all event typologies and illustrate idiosyncrasies.

It is evident that all seven critical success factors are shared by mega- and special or major events. However, only five of the seven critical success factors are shared by hallmark and community events – leadership, networking, branding, skills and infrastructure – but to differing degrees. Leadership is critical to provide a vision for event tourism. Top-level political commitment coupled with funding to enable strategic and operational coordination is vital. This is even more critical for mega- and special or major events where the desire and determination to host the event is often 'based more on personal and political conviction than that of careful appraisal of merits' (Emery, 2002, p. 331).

Mixed-economy models of event funding may prove more sustainable in the long term for hallmark and community events, whereby events are viewed as a small to medium-sized enterprise (SME) and receive a mixture of public and private funding. This forces the true viability of the event, as well as how to differentiate and sell it. Ritchie and Crouch (2003) contend that in order to ensure competitive advantage for a destination, stakeholders must

Table 10.1. Mapping the critical success factors from BESTBET on to event typologies.

Critical success factor	Mega	Special or major	Hallmark	Community
Leadership	National and local government or regional development agency in partnership with key destination stakeholders with ministerial oversight. For example, Olympics Minister, London 2012 Organizing Committee and the Olympic Delivery Authority and the relationship with the International Olympic Committee	National or local government or regional development agency in partnership with key destination stakeholders. For example, Organizing Company of Glasgow 2014	Local government and/or regional development agency in partnership with key destination stakeholders. For example, National Eisteddfod of Wales	Community in partnership with local government and/ or support agencies. For example, Abergavenny Food Festival, Lammas Fair – Llangattock Lingoed
Networking	Inter-destination and intra-destination. As a result of the significance of the event, the destination cannot be insular	Inter-destination and intra-destination. As a result of the significance of the event, the destination cannot be insular	Intra-destination	Intra-destination
Branding	Strong event-led branding. Event ownership makes the event far more significant than the destination	Strong event-led branding. Event ownership makes the event far more significant than the destination	Strong destination-led branding	Variable destination-led branding
Skills	Delivery body at national level with professional management supported by professional and volunteer operatives. For example, London 2012 Organizing Committee and the Olympic Delivery Authority	Delivery body at national level with professional management supported by professional and volunteer operatives. For example, Organizing Company of Glasgow 2014	Professional management supported by professional and volunteer operatives	Professional, semi-professional or volunteer management supported by volunteers. For example, Abergavenny Food Festival
Ambassadors	High-profile/celebrity support pre- and post-bid	High-profile support pre- and post-bid	–	–
Infrastructure	International transport links critical plus purpose-built specialist venues and accommodation for peak capacity	International transport links plus some purpose-built specialist venues and accommodation for peak capacity	Good national and international transport links and appropriate event venues	Good regional transport links and appropriate event venues
Bidding	Competitive international bidding with long lead times and complex decision making by international committees	Competitive bidding with long lead times and complex decision making by external committees	–	–

share a common destination vision and an appreciation of how to effectively utilize destination resources.

Events can be very attractive to communities and destinations that are seeking to address issues of civic and local pride, identity, inward investment, economic development, employment creation and regeneration (Derrett, 2004). In the long term, developing events with an anchor in the locality will create a stronger tourism multiplier effect and promote cultural identity. However, for community events a balance has to be achieved between attracting visitors and retaining the community spirit of the events, as a successful community event needs passion, the local factor and active community groups.

Events can act as a catalyst for networks in the community and provide a model for cooperation, as organizing community events can extract expertise from within the community – enhancing human and social capital. The wider significance of mega- and special or major events produces far more complicated networks, both within and outside the destination. Networking promotes market awareness and can strategically harmonize event calendars. This strategic approach can counteract the detrimental impacts of seasonality in destinations, ensure a sustainable events-led destination management strategy and enhance benefits across the host community. Hallmark and community events that exploit their social capital to share their culture, which then becomes the product in the tourism experience for visitors, illustrates how cultural or community distinctiveness can shape events. Furthermore, organizing an event demands a mix of individual and collective effort.

Brown *et al.* (2004) suggest that while events play a significant tourism role in a destination, relatively little research exists on the use of events in destination branding. A strong destination brand, which is clearly understood and communicated internally and externally, is essential. Moreover, branding is critical as events can: observe a sense of place through inclusive activities; enable local communities to entertain visitors through their activities and sense of place; and externally portray the distinctive identity of the community and destination. Events based on indigenous cultural values and attitudes can provide authenticity and uniqueness, enabling thematic branding of the event and destination, although this may vary depending on whether it is a hallmark or community event. With regard to mega and special or major events, the politics of event ownership make the event more significant than the destination, e.g. Olympics, Ryder Cup, Rugby World Cup; hence the branding is event-led and destinations may find it difficult to leverage benefits for the destination.

Service quality is often the main determinant of competitive advantage, particularly when event providers adopt similar price and delivery mechanisms and destinations have similar comparative advantages. Hence, the need for high-quality skills to underpin event tourism products and services is crucial to ensure a sustainable events-led destination management strategy. As with the tourism and hospitality sectors, events have unique differentiating characteristics (Jones and Haven-Tang, 2005). However, events also pose other challenges for service quality and skills.

Many one-off or large events need short influxes of workers. For example, it is predicted that for the duration of the London 2012 Olympics, 70,000 volunteers, 27,000 temporary staff to stage the event and 6700 people to showcase London as a tourist destination will be required (Phillips, 2007). Therefore, pre-event growth and post-event contraction present a challenge. The use of volunteers is a critical but variable element in events, as the reliance on volunteers creates problems in terms of quality, skills, knowledge, attitude, training, motivation and supervision. The mix of skills that volunteers bring is vital but can be undermined by a lack of professionalism – especially with community events. An event is an experience and event staff and volunteers an inherent element in that experience. Furthermore, many events appeal to multiple markets, and therefore staff must understand diverse customer expectations.

Seamless integration of transport infrastructure to support event tourism and facilitate appropriate access to, and within, the destination is also essential. The importance of international air links is dependent on the type and size of the event. For example, international air links are crucial for mega- and special or major events, but less so for hallmark and community events. The significance of mega- and special or major events is such that they are often deemed to be an essential aspect of destination regeneration (Emery, 2002) and demand purpose-built, specialist venues.

The Northwest Development Agency has established a three-tiered approach (Global Giants, Organic Excellence, Attack Zone) to its events portfolio, which provides optimum utilization of extant venues (NWDA, 2004). Manchester also ensures that every major event has a resource for legacy building (Robathan, 2008). These approaches ensure a sustainable events portfolio, as events utilize existing venues rather than being a catalyst for regeneration projects. However, rural destinations like Monmouthshire often face capacity issues in relation to hallmark and community events. For example, the (predominantly voluntary) organizers of the Abergavenny Food Festival have to balance car parking, traffic management and public transport coordination with visitor experience, and while the supply of outdoor venues is plentiful, there is a limit on the number of agriculture-based events that the market can support.

Summary

The development and quality of an events-led sustainable destination management strategy is dependent upon a coherent, funded, well-researched and proactive event strategy, strategically and operationally coordinated, which addresses the key issues of leadership, networking, branding, skills and infrastructure. A holistic approach must be adopted to address these and ensure effective event delivery in the destination (Haven-Tang *et al.*, 2006). There are a number of ways in which events can be used to create a sustainable destination management strategy, within both rural and urban settings.

Destinations need to establish their events-led sustainable management strategies by identifying events that are growing, coupled with local or regional strategic conversations with event organizers/providers to agree investment, return on investment, willingness to work together and capacity. Clusters of event organizers/providers in a destination or region can enhance event development. Event clusters coordinated by the public sector and driven by the private sector can lead on event-specific agendas, tailored to their comparative advantages to ensure a competitive and sustainable events destination. In parallel to this, is consideration of the marketplace to establish the viability of the venture, i.e. viewing the event as an SME, and the feasibility of attracting new income streams into the local economy. A strategic and integrated approach will establish the portfolio of events within a destination, enabling strategic scheduling to extend the portfolio of events for the benefits of the local community, visitors and local businesses.

Many destinations like Glasgow, Manchester and Newcastle Gateshead have established successful events based on developing their existing customer bases, rather than creating new markets. These destinations are not creating new inroads, but are seeking to further develop their existing customer base through events. They are building on comparative advantage to create competitive advantage within an integrated sustainable destination management strategy.

Key Questions

1. Compare and contrast the role of the community in community-led events as opposed to mega-events.
2. Explain the role of events in destination development.
3. Identify the advantages and disadvantages of hosting mega-events in a destination.

References

Brown, G., Chalip, L., Jago, L. and Mules, T. (2004) Developing Brand Australia: examining the role of events. In: Morgan, N., Pritchard, A. and Pride, R. (eds) *Destination Branding: Creating the Unique Destination Proposition*, 2nd edn. Butterworth-Heinemann, Oxford, UK, pp. 279–305.

BTP (2004) *Better Business Tourism in Britain*. Business Tourism Partnership, London.

Burgan, B. and Mules, T. (2001) Reconciling cost–benefit and economic impact assessment for event tourism. *Tourism Economics* 7(4), 321–330.

Chhabra, D., Sills, E. and Cubbage, F.W. (2003) The significance of festivals to rural economies: estimating the economic impacts of Scottish Highland Games in North Carolina. *Journal of Travel Research* 41(4), 421–427.

Derrett, R. (2004) Festivals, events and the destination. In: Yeoman, I., Robertson, M., Ali-Knight, J., Drummond, S. and McMahon-Beattie, U. (eds) *Festival and Events Management: An International Arts and Culture Perspective*. Butterworth-Heinemann, Oxford, UK, pp. 32–50.

Emery, P.R. (2002) Bidding to host a major sports event – the local organising committee perspective. *International Journal of Public Sector Management* 15(4), 316–335.

Gateshead Council (2005) Main Attractions. Available at: http://www.gateshead.gov.uk/about.htm (accessed 2 August 2005).

Gosling, J. (2004) Capitalising on culture. *Conference & Incentive Travel* (June), 43–44.

Hall, C.M. (1992) *Hallmark Tourist Events*. Belhaven, London.

Haven-Tang, C., Jones, E. and Webb, C. (2006) *BESTBET: A Framework for Best Practice in Business and Event Tourism in Southeast Wales – Final Project Report*. UWIC, Cardiff, UK.

Haven-Tang, C., Jones, E. and Webb, C. (2007) Critical success factors for business tourism destinations: exploiting Cardiff's national capital city status and shaping its business tourism offer. *Journal of Travel and Tourism Marketing* 22(3/4), 109–120.

Jones, E. and Haven-Tang, C. (2005) Tourism SMEs, service quality and destination competitiveness. In: Jones, E. and Haven-Tang, C. (eds) *Tourism SMEs, Service Quality and Destination Competitiveness*. CAB International, Wallingford, UK, pp. 1–24.

Locum Destination Consulting (2003) *A Revised Tourism Strategy for Southeast Wales: Capital Region Tourism*. Locum Destination Consulting, Haywards Heath, UK.

McCabe, S. (2006) The making of community identity through historic festive practice: the case of Ashbourne Royal Shrovetide Football. In: Picard, D. and Robinson, M. (eds) *Festivals, Tourism and Social Change: Remaking Worlds*. Channel View, Clevedon, UK, pp. 99–118.

McLardie, N. (2005) City of Reinvention. Available at: http://www.seeglasgow.com/index.asp?pgid=1578&mtype=print (accessed 20 July 2005).

NGI (2004) Membership Guide. Available at: http://www.nrgplc.com/ngi/docs/ngi_membership_guide.pdf (accessed 2 August 2005).

NWDA (2004) *A Strategy for Major Events in England's Northwest*. Northwest Development Agency, Warrington, UK.

Phillips, L. (2007) Games of skill. *People Management* 13(11), 24–29.

Richards, G. (2007) The festivalisation of society or the socialisation of festivals? The case of Catalunya. In: Richards, G. (ed.) *Cultural Tourism: Global and Local Perspectives*. The Haworth Hospitality Press, New York, pp. 257–280.

Ritchie, B.R. and Crouch, G. (2003) *The Competitive Destination: A Sustainable Tourism Perspective*. CAB International, Wallingford, UK.

Robathan, M. (2008) Interview: Eamonn O'Rouke. *Leisure Management* 28(3), 28–31.

Small, K., Edwards, D. and Sheridan, L. (2005) A flexible framework for evaluating the socio-cultural impacts of a (small) festival. *International Journal of Event Management Research* 1(1), 66–76.

Smith, A. (2005) Conceptualizing city image change: the 're-imaging' of Barcelona. *Tourism Geographies* 7(4), 398–423.

SQW Ltd and TNS (2005) Edinburgh Festivals 2004–2005 Economic Impact Survey Stage 1 Results. Available at: http://www.lothianexchange.net/festivals_exec_summary_final_final.pdf (accessed 13 October 2006).

Village Alive Trust (2005) Lammas Fair proves a hit with one and all. Available at: http://www.villagealivetrust.org.uk/publications/lammassuccess.htm (accessed 17 March 2007).

Voluntary Arts England (2003) NewcastleGateshead Initiative–Culture[10]. Available at: http://www.voluntaryarts.org/cgi-bin/website.cgi?tier1=england&tier2=north%20east&tier3=special%20news (accessed 2 August 2005).

Wild, S. (2003) Brand identities. *Conference & Incentive Travel* (June), 41–44.

WTB (2000) *Achieving our Potential: A Tourism Strategy for Wales*. Wales Tourist Board, Cardiff, UK.

11 Critique of Consumer Marketing within Sustainable Events

N. Richardson
Leeds Metropolitan University, Leeds, UK

This chapter seeks to explore the lessons of other disciplines and provide a critique of sustainability. Service providers involved with events management, hospitality and tourism share many challenges. They are all service-based industries that seek to improve consumer attendance (often referred to as footfall); they are increasingly recognized as operating in fast-changing environments; and they cover an ever wider range of client scenarios and demands.

Chapter outline

- Introduction
- An Historical Sustainability Perspective
- The Sustainability Continuum
- Barriers to Sustainability Adoption
- Clarification of the Terminology
- Key Issues Surrounding Sustainability Positioning and Benchmarking
- Summary
- Key Questions

Introduction

If, for a moment, one considers the challenges facing, say, events organizers, a key question is: Why would consumers visit one 'event' rather than another? Answers to such questions are of crucial importance for events managers as well as hospitality managers and tourism developers. One answer is that all progressive companies should seek to align product offers with what customers want, hence ensuring that all investment and resources add customer value. However, a driver for this chapter is the large-scale absence of 'customers' in key sustainability studies, which tend to offer supply-side solutions. The events industry is worthy of consideration because other laudable service providers who carry out sustainable business practices are unlikely to have the complexity of hundreds of suppliers, a myriad of venues and large amounts of transactions and interactions all taking place simultaneously.

The notion of companies being motivated by more than economic profit is not new. Sustainability is not merely an altruistic stance, as consumers are more likely to prefer to acquaint themselves with events, venues and organizations that match their self-image (Baker *et al.*, 2007). It is critical that event managers understand the factors that consumers value when participating, attending or deciding to purchase, as in many cases the appeal is on both social and psychological levels. Companies need to be able to position themselves within their markets in order to make strategic, tactical and operational decisions. Hence they need to reflect on how they are perceived by different stakeholders in terms of sustainability.

An Historical Sustainability Perspective

The concepts of organizations and consumer transactions have developed since the 19th century (Howell, 2006), where both parties gained from their transactions. Organizations in other sectors, such as the UK Co-operative (Co-op), have been trading with identifiably sustainable principles since 1840. Among their guiding principles were education, training, information and concern for the community through sustainable development (Davies and Burt, 2007). Often they have been leaders in terms of product labelling, health education, fair trade and changing the attitudes of local workers towards taking responsibility for their own welfare. Indeed, cooperatives not only channelled funds (into the community) but existed to serve the community in which they traded.

However, the idea of mutual benefit was challenged when Milton Friedman famously argued 'the business of business is business': that is, a company's only moral responsibility is to promote the financial well-being of its shareholders. Despite his assertion, mainstream organizations have recently espoused their green credentials. This coincided with a widening range of 'sustainability' issues gaining importance with UK consumers such as ethical practices and increasing awareness of 'greenwashing', where simply stating green credentials is deemed insufficient (Ramus and Montiel, 2005). Why have contemporary organizations only relatively recently moved towards sustainability when it is argued that the Co-op has benefited from these practices since the 1840s? Simply put, there was a cultural step-change in the late 1990s that changed stakeholders' attitudes to sustainability.

Philip Kotler was central to the efforts of incorporating social and moral concerns into marketing 'science'. He proposed the notion of 'social marketing' for social ideas and causes in 1969, followed in 1972 by the 'societal marketing concept' based on a more ethical approach to marketing. Despite 35 years of extensive studies and academic debate on the efficacy of societal marketing, practitioners and academics are increasingly concerned that the social, ethical and environmental issues have not been redressed and if anything have deteriorated (Crane and Desmond, 2002).

In 1997 the Harvard Business Review published *Beyond Greening* (Hart, 1997), which brought the issue of sustainable development to the wider business community. The following year the term 'triple bottom line' (TBL) was coined in which the traditional economic focus was replaced with the new foci of social, environmental and economic responsibility (Elkington, 1998). The Hart and Elkington texts are considered two of the most important recent contributions on the subject of business sustainability development. The combined impact of these texts represented a step-change in how businesses would be expected to operate. This approach, often paraphrased as 'people–profit–planet', represents an emergent branch of social science (Starkey and Welford, 2001).

The TBL step-change brought about a process of 'creative destruction' where companies' capabilities and perceptions were challenged by the new paradigm of sustainability (Schumpeter, 1942, cited in McGee *et al.*, 2005). This in turn challenged and then changed companies' knowledge bases, leading to new opportunities and in turn market growth. Since 1997 the sustainable business development concept has gained credence, featuring in academic, consultancy and practitioner texts. However, customer-centric academic disciplines are still under-represented.

Event managers following the traditional profit-driven business model may find themselves reacting to emergent TBL factors (Fig. 11.1), ultimately leading to strategic drift (Mintzberg, 1990). Figure 11.1 illustrates how the best strategic intentions could be deflected by the failure to adopt or react to emergent elements of TBL and/or macro-environmental changes and/or changes in consumer values such as the growth in ethical or green goods. Part of the problem facing service providers lies in attributing responsibility, which in turn is hindered by the complex, interdisciplinary nature of sustainability.

The Sustainability Continuum

Consumers' thoughts, feelings and actions are subject to social and cultural factors. Hence socialized individuals take on attitudes, beliefs,

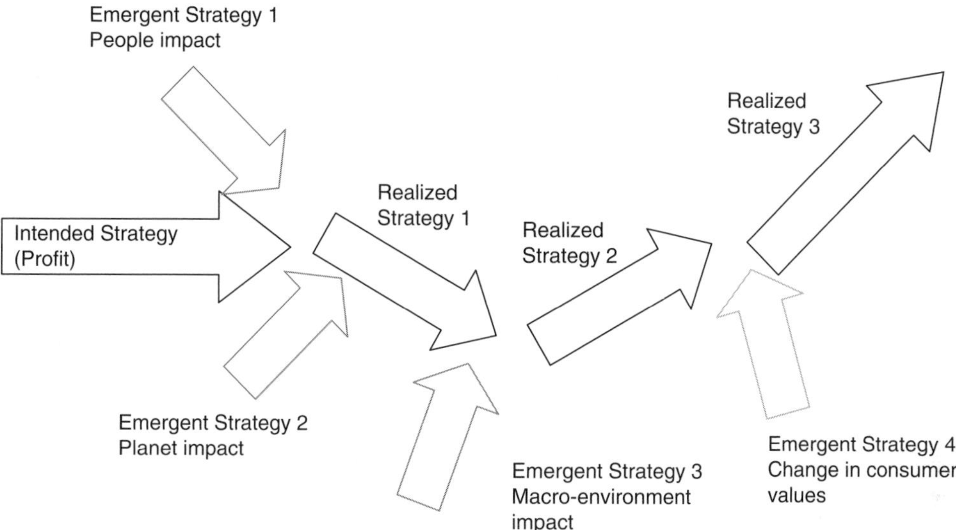

Fig. 11.1. Sustainability as an emergent strategy.

opinions and values of others (Petrick and Sheehan, 2007). Those service providers who are not aware of changes in society, such as the increasing awareness of sustainability, run the risk of alienating customers.

In practice, companies have many stakeholders with 'interests' such as employees, unions, suppliers, intermediaries, markets, government and, most importantly, customers. Each of these may have ulterior motives and may be motivated by self-interest. Undoubtedly all companies have 'sustainability' responsibilities; however, the question remains regarding who should take responsibility. Is it the company, consumer, community, regulator, legislator or politicians (Tilley, 2007)? This confusion has resulted in stakeholders ignoring and/or denying their sustainability responsibilities. Agency theory provides a framework that explains some of the internal tensions among corporate stakeholders, i.e. shareholders (deemed to be principals), directors and managers (deemed to be agents). Stakeholders' roles are changing, so bearing in mind Friedman's missive it is (arguably) appropriate to first consider sustainability from the principal's perspective.

Assuming Friedman's libertarian viewpoint to be one end of a sustainability continuum, it is sensible to consider what represents its polar opposite. This is deemed to be 'pure sustainability', which is philosophical and in some cases spiritual (Lorand, 2007). It is crucially important that companies are aware of their customers' perceptions of their position. Service providers need to be able to position themselves within their markets in order to make effective decisions; therefore, it is safe to assume that they (knowingly or otherwise) are located on the continuum (Fig. 11.2). Obviously such tools are limited in that companies are complex and dynamic, and hence the continuum can only be a snapshot. That said, it is the essential first step that progressive companies must take if they are interested in how their customers perceive their sustainability position.

Barriers to Sustainability Adoption

The events industry represents many differing types of businesses such as sole traders, partnerships, cooperatives, non-profit enterprises and other types of commercial endeavours. Each of these has differing aims and objectives which may facilitate or impede the adoption of sustainable practices. Friedman argued that corporations exist to advance the pursuit of shareholder value; however, they affect the lives and well-being of their (aforementioned)

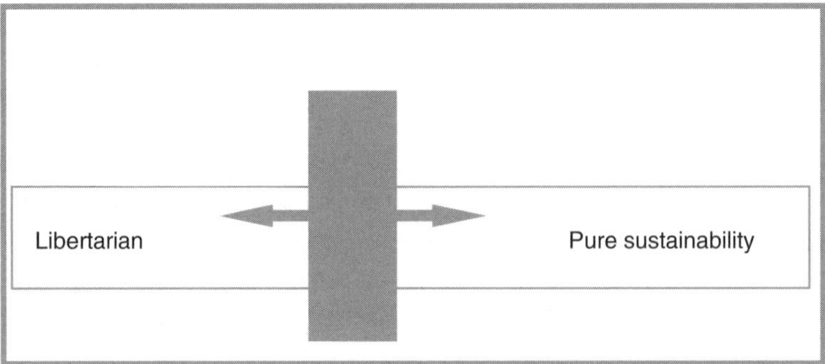

Fig. 11.2. Sustainability continuum.

stakeholders and hence service providers do not exist in isolation, which is the first flaw in Friedman's libertarian philosophy.

Libertarian attitudes may also contribute to the common assumption that modern business practices advocate 'selling more' while sustainability is about consuming less. Friedman's 'dominant' paradigm of free trade is increasingly criticized for being inherently unsustainable (Howell, 2006), and yet many companies fear turnover will be reduced if sustainability is adopted.

The irony of this is that businesses need to be at the forefront of the 'sustainability' debate, as trade takes place between and within business organizations and not governments. Business can promote sustainable trade patterns having the knowledge and potential for innovation, to make sure it is trading (whether locally, regionally or globally) within global sustainability constraints (Howell, 2006). That said, economists strive to measure sustainability by emphasizing an accounting approach focusing on the maintenance of capital stocks (ESI, 2005). Such supply-side approaches are valuable; however, at the core of any progressive company there must be a drive to align what the business produces to what customers want, hence ensuring that all investment of money, people and resources adds value for customers.

It is inarguable that customer attraction, retention and satisfaction are imperative to the survival and success of most businesses. Also, understanding customer needs and meeting and exceeding expectations have become part of the language of progressive companies (Pal and Byrom, 2003). The omission of customers (who increasingly want to buy from sustainable organizations) is nothing short of scandalous and is often an impediment to the adoption of sustainable practices.

Increasingly companies are seeking to adopt sustainable practices despite struggling with a wide range of definitions. Sustainability can, for example, refer to financial, administrative, technical, environmental and cultural sustainability. Also adoption and implementation can be impeded by the diversity of different situations, processes, impacts, relationships and related institutions (Willard and Creech, 2006). Further to this, sustainability is a characteristic of dynamic systems that change over time; it is not a fixed endpoint that can be easily defined (ESI, 2005) – however clarification of the terminology is necessary if progress is to be made.

Clarification of the Terminology

As there is no existing definition for sustainable services provision (SSP), this chapter now derives one by drawing on the different disciplines. In the 1960s Kotler proposed the extension of marketing approaches into non-business arenas when he defined social marketing as the approach for social ideas and causes. He currently defines it as 'the design, implementation, and control of programs seeking to increase the acceptability of a social idea, cause or practice among a target group' (Kotler and Armstrong, 2006, p. 239).

This suggests a range of approaches and different solutions to differing problems, which is not ideal from a sustainability perspective where global solutions are needed. Also it can be inferred that what matters is the supply-side selling of products and services through programmes. This chimes somewhat with Friedman's viewpoint; however, such sales orientations are considered to be contributory factors in consumers' awareness of green-washing (Ramus and Montiel, 2005).

Kotler subsequently introduced the 'societal' marketing concept which he now defines as:

> a principle of enlightened marketing that holds that a company should make good marketing decisions by considering consumers' wants, the company's requirements, consumers' long run interests and society's long run interests.
>
> (Kotler *et al.*, 2008 p. 19)

Although this includes community and consumer dimensions, it stops some way short of TBL. For instance, it offers no specifics regarding ethics or environmental sustainability but it does introduce the notion of long-term relationships. Dibb *et al.* (2006) discuss 'social responsibility and marketing ethics', which chimes with the ethical element of 'people' within TBL. Brassington and Pettitt (2007) take this further by linking 'societal' marketing with ethical marketing as elements of corporate social responsibility (CSR), which should inexorably lead to 'sustainable' marketing; however, they do not offer a definition of sustainability. Consider the following:

> Sustainable Services Provision (SSP) is predicated on the tenets of the Triple Bottom Line. Hence SSP decisions should be ethical and guided by sustainable business practices which ultimately are the only way to resolve the tensions between consumers' wants and long term interests, companies' requirements, society's long run interests and the need for environmental balance.
>
> (Adapted from Gosnay and Richardson, 2008)

Key Issues Surrounding Sustainability Positioning and Benchmarking

Having offered a definition of SSP, it is appropriate to consider the practicalities of service providers needing to know where they are positioned on the sustainability continuum (Fig. 11.2). Hence the next step is to reflect on some of the key issues affecting benchmarking within a sustainability framework (Fig. 11.3).

It is worth noting that TBL factors can impact on multiple elements; for example, adopting a CSR policy as part of SSP could impact on planet and profit. That said, the drive to boost profits is well covered elsewhere and hence this chapter considers only (some of) the issues regarding areas (subject to Schumpeterian change) that either exert influence or need to be benchmarked (Fig. 11.3).

Corporate social responsibility

A major driver for this chapter is the lack of references to TBL in customer-centric disciplines. This lack of coverage is not exclusively reserved for TBL, as McGoldrick (2002) only fleetingly refers to the issue of CSR twice in his 650-page tome, despite CSR having extensive coverage in other studies and texts. He alludes to 'some' organizations having CSR elements in their mission statements, which may include 'green' issues, ethical supply policies and charitable links. He is largely sceptical about the role and benefits of CSR; however, this contradicts the mainly positive thrust of many texts and studies that refer to social responsibility (Dibb *et al.*, 2006) or corporate social responsibility (Brassington and Pettitt, 2007; Jobber, 2007) and recent studies of CSR in UK retail (Jones *et al.*, 2007).

CSR needs to be viewed in terms of disparities of commitment within the wider context of stakeholder relationships. To improve relationship management requires understanding of both interpersonal (consumer) and person-to-firm (company) perspectives (Sparks and Wagner, 2003), both of which occur in modern event management networks.

Networks

Socially responsible event managers can build consumer trust that can be grown, say, through positive word of mouth. Trust can be shaped

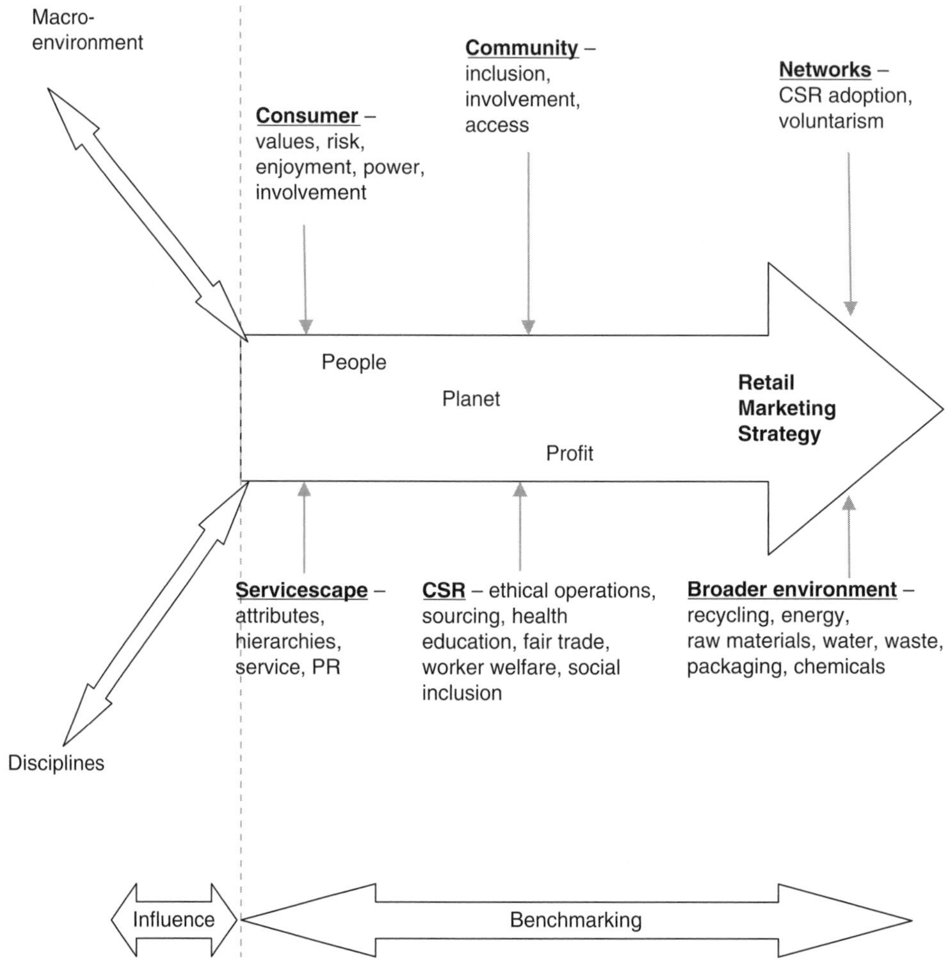

Fig. 11.3. A framework for sustainable services marketing (CSR, corporate social responsibility; PR, public relations). (Adapted from Gosnay and Richardson, 2008.)

by previous experiences and cooperative efforts and on the more general reputation an event organizer has built up through earlier behaviour. Event management businesses are undoubtedly networking organizations and interdependent stakeholders will need to develop trust in their partners such as suppliers. Hence there is a business case for measuring and developing trust within an SSP framework across a range of issues (Jones *et al.*, 2007).

Event organizers should be aware that often 'network' sustainability tends to be limited to the discussion to the network mechanism itself; that is, the formal or informal social arrangements that enable members to establish relationships and engage in joint activities (Willard and Creech, 2006). Often the degree of voluntarism impacts on the adoption of, say, CSR. Consider Fairtrade, which is founded on making a difference for producers and consumers and also respecting the environment. A necessity of Fairtrade is for the supply chains to be transparent (Howell, 2006); however, patterns exist in the adoption of CSR across differing organizations. Event managers who are highly motivated may adopt an idealistic stance or even one of enlightened self-interest, whereas stakeholders on whom they rely may only adopt CSR practices when coerced (Haberberg *et al.*, 2007). This potentially poses a risk for high-profile event management companies whose reputations may suffer from negative publicity.

Community

Successful events are often dependent on their location. McGoldrick (2002, p. 240) considers location at length and provides a detailed 'location checklist'; however, it features no references to the host community. This is remiss, despite being consistent with recent research that identified reticence on the part of larger UK companies to engage with the community (Jones *et al.*, 2007). This attitude simplistically reduces the site to 'a plot' and something apart from the community in which it is located. Links with the resident communities provided a key element of the Co-op's success as it defined the relationships in 'place' with local firms, consumers and regulations.

Social exclusion refers to diverse groups such as those with disabilities, the elderly, those on low incomes and homeless people, among others. Service providers need to recognize the potential benefit of an improved public relations role with the local community. Rather than simply complying with, say, disability law, companies need to be more sensitive to stakeholders' psychological needs and motivations if they are to gain and sustain a distinct differential advantage (Mitchell and Harris, 2005).

Charities are vehicles for countering social exclusion and enable 'trading up' on high streets and at events across the UK. An event manager, seeking a site, may benefit from an improved public relations role with the local community (Broadbridge and Parsons, 2003). Therefore, the adoption of sustainable practices, such as incorporating local charities into events, may improve prospects during planning processes not to mention underpinning any claimed green credentials. Further to this, affluent social groups comprise a substantial proportion of charity patrons (Williams, 2003) and would no doubt be a welcome part of an event manager's chosen demographic.

For service providers involved in events management, hospitality or tourism, many socially excluded groups may have access (to the event) impaired by lack of mobility (for both physical and financial reasons), which is an issue. Hence, another key element of social inclusion is accessibility and while progress has been made, studies indicate that only partial accessibility has been achieved (Baker *et al.*, 2007). Ultimately, accessibility is more than widening doors and building ramps.

Consumers

Event managers need to consider consumers' social and psychological variables and their potential impact on the effective management of long-term customer relationships (Wong and Sohal, 2003). While consumer decision-making research has been mainly cognitive in nature, increasing numbers of scholars acknowledge the importance of affective and emotional aspects (Da Silva and Alwi, 2006). Customers can develop many different types of involvement with activities, objects, ideas or even social issues such as sustainability. Customer involvement is increasingly important and there are five dimensions (Laurent and Kapferer, 1985, cited in Aldlaigan and Buttle, 2001, p. 233):

1. Interest in a product (its personal meaning or importance).
2. Pleasure in the form of emotional appeal.
3. Sign value, e.g. the degree to which the purchase expresses the consumer's self.
4. Importance of risk attached to negative consequences of a mis-purchase.
5. Risk probability relating to the exposure to such risks.

Also, in addition to the significance of consumer involvement is consumer power, which represents a consumer's power standing during service consumption. This may be a function of both individual factors (that reside in the consumer) and interpersonal factors (that arise in the social group). Consumers also attach varying degrees of symbolism and values to their purchases. Increasing numbers of consumers buy products that are identified as Fairtrade or other ethically produced goods (Richardson *et al.*, 2007). The risks for event managers are twofold: if their ethical or environmental profiles fail to align with consumers' values or alternatively reduce the enjoyment of the shopping experience, then increased customer attrition is likely.

Consumers experience involvement when events are connected to important goals or values such as sustainability. The importance of these issues becomes increasingly important to customers and correspondingly to event managers. Consumers struggle to evaluate often-contradictory claims. It is possible that the cognitive dissonance of claim and counterclaim has led to increasing perception of 'greenwashing' where simply stating green credentials is deemed insufficient (Ramus and Montiel, 2005).

Servicescape – there's more to service than being served

The term 'service' is taken to mean more than just serving customers. Indeed, the production, delivery and consumption of services revolve around the interpersonal interaction between service providers and consumers and are among the most significant determinants of consumer satisfaction (Menon and Bansal, 2007).

All interactions between the service provider and the customer provide an opportunity to portray the event organization, venue or attraction in a positive or negative light (Wong and Sohal, 2002). However, many managers focus on improving operational efficiency without a clear understanding of customer needs, so it may be impossible to make the necessary operational changes. Operations have to keep pace with customer change (Pal and Byrom, 2003) and the move to sustainability could be one such change. What is needed is not change for its own sake but the right change, and many examples now exist of companies that have moved towards TBL.

As previously discussed, a key challenge in discussing sustainability is the large number of variables – particularly as consumers immediately make judgements as to whether they belong or feel welcome (Baker *et al.*, 2007). Event managers who fail to align their sustainability profiles with consumers' values risk increased customer attrition.

Broader environment

It is prudent to consider environmental concerns since individuals have a connectedness with the broader environment in which they live. Their environmental interaction is extremely important, featuring intense emotional commitments (Petrick and Sheehan, 2007) that can affect their decisions. There is general agreement that consumers experience involvement when an event is connected to important goals such as centrally held values like sustainability (Mitchell and Harris, 2005).

Consumers are increasingly sophisticated, discerning and willing to change their spending habits if the experience does not meet their expectations. That said, they often struggle to evaluate (often) contradictory environmental claims, particularly when faced with an abundance of alternatives. Addressing such communications issues will become more commonplace as service providers' lives:

> will become more complicated. They must raise prices to cover environmental costs, knowing that the product will be harder to sell. Yet environmental issues have become so important in our society that there is no turning back.
>
> (Kotler *et al.*, 2005, p. 190)

Summary

Despite the sea-change in consumer opinion, academics in consumer-centric disciplines are trailing their peers in other disciplines as a result of having largely ignored TBL and sustainability (despite the Co-op having traded in a recognizably sustainable way since the 1840s). Growing recognition of green issues (mitigated somewhat by greater awareness of greenwashing) and CSR are not enough, and sustainability will increasingly be adopted by UK companies. Other disciplines (and practitioners) have responded to Hart and Elkington's

Schumpeterian effect; however, they often negligently ignore the single most important factor – consumers.

This chapter has considered the historical resistance to service providers adopting sustainability practices with particular reference to internal stakeholder dynamics. It is argued that all companies are positioned on the sustainability continuum and they need to face the positioning challenge of how to carry out sustainability benchmarking. Part of the problem is the challenge of defining sustainability, so the chapter has offered a working definition.

The subsequent framework (Fig. 11.3) may form the basis of practical considerations or further research into sustainability and the elements germane to the model have been critiqued. Events management, hospitality and tourism (sharing many challenges with retail) will continue to be complex, fast-moving industries and the influence of the macro-environment will continue. Also, the interdisciplinary nature of related academic research means that studies are dispersed across academic boundaries. That said, the proposed factors (Fig. 11.3) may form a basis for stakeholders wishing to adopt sustainability.

Key Questions

1. Sustainability is predicated on the triple bottom line, i.e. people–planet–profit. Using the framework provided, what existing practices can you identify in an organization of your choice that comply with a sustainable approach?
2. There are many barriers to the adoption of sustainability. Using an organization of your choice, what are the key barriers to the implementation of sustainable practices?
3. There are many roles/positions that could facilitate (or impede) sustainability adoption. Using an organization of your choice, who are the key actors and how may they impact adoption of sustainability?

References

Aldlaigan, A.H. and Buttle, F.A. (2001) Consumer involvement in financial services: an empirical test of two measures. *International Journal of Bank Marketing* 19(6), 232–245.

Baker, S.M., Holland, J. and Kaufman-Scarborough, C. (2007) How consumers with disabilities perceive 'welcome' in retail servicescapes: a critical incident study. *Journal of Services Marketing* 21(3), 160–173.

Brassington, F. and Pettitt, S. (2007) *Essentials of Marketing*, 2nd edn. Pearson Education, Harlow, UK.

Broadbridge, A. and Parsons, L. (2003) Still serving the community? The professionalisation of the UK charity retail sector. *International Journal of Retail & Distribution Management* 31(8), 418–427.

Crane, A. and Desmond, J. (2002) Societal marketing and morality. *European Journal of Marketing* 36(5/6), 548–569.

Da Silva, R.V. and Alwi, S.F.S. (2006) Cognitive, affective attributes and conative behavioural responses in retail corporate branding. *Journal of Product & Brand Management* 15(5), 293–305.

Davies, K. and Burt, S. (2007) Consumer co-operatives and retail internationalisation: problems and prospects. *International Journal of Retail & Distribution Management* 35(2), 156–177.

Dibb, S., Simkin, L., Pride, W.M. and Ferrell, O.C. (2006) *Marketing Concepts and Strategies*, 5th European edn. Houghton Mifflin, Boston, Massachusetts.

Elkington, J. (1998) *The 'Triple Bottom Line' for 21st Century Business*. Republished in Starkey, R. and Welford, R. (2001) *The Earthscan Reader in Business & Sustainable Development*. Earthscan Publishing, London.

ESI (2005) Environmental Sustainability Index – Benchmarking National Environmental Stewardship. Available at: http://www.yale.edu/esi/ (accessed 1 February 2008).

Gosnay, R.M. and Richardson, N. (2008) *Develop Your Marketing Skills*. Kogan Page, London.

Haberberg, A., Gander, J., Rieple, A., Martin-Castilla, J.-I. and Helm, C. (2007) Patterns in the adoption of corporate social responsibility. Paper presented at Corporate Responsibility Research Conference, Leeds University, Leeds, UK, July 2007. Available at: http://crrconference.org/programme/downloads/index.html#02bb5f99770e1281f (accessed 20 July 2007).

Hart, S.L. (1997) *Beyond Greening: Strategies for a Sustainable World*. Republished in Starkey, R. and Welford, R. (2001) *The Earthscan Reader in Business & Sustainable Development*. Earthscan Publishing, London.

Howell, R. (2006) Global trade and sustainable development: complementary or contradictory? Paper presented at Corporate Responsibility Research Conference, Dublin, July 2006. Available at: http://crr conference.org (accessed 20 February 2008).

Jobber, D. (2007) *Principles and Practice of Marketing*, 5th edn. McGraw-Hill, Maidenhead, UK.

Jones, P., Comfort, D. and Hillier, D. (2007) What's in store? Retail marketing and corporate social responsibility. *Marketing Intelligence & Planning* 25(1), 17–30.

Kotler, P. and Armstrong, G. (2006) *Marketing – An Introduction*, 8th edn. Prentice Hall, Harlow, UK.

Kotler, P., Wong, V., Saunders, J. and Armstrong, G. (2005) *Principles of Marketing*, 4th European edn. Prentice Hall, Harlow, UK.

Kotler, P., Wong, V., Saunders, J. and Armstrong, G. (2008) *Principles of Marketing*, 5th European edn. Prentice Hall, Harlow, UK.

Lorand, J. (2007) Business-as-usual and sustainability: which paradigm aligns with our beliefs? Paper presented at Corporate Responsibility Research Conference, Leeds University, Leeds, UK, July 2007. Available at: http://crrconference.org/programme/downloads/index.html#02bb5f99770e1281f (accessed 20 February 2008).

McGee, J., Thomas, H. and Wilson, D. (2005) *Strategy: Analysis and Practice*. McGraw Hill, London.

McGoldrick, P. (2002) *Retail Marketing*, 2nd edn. McGraw Hill, London.

Menon, K. and Bansal, H.S. (2007) Exploring consumer experience of social power during service consumption. *International Journal of Service Industry Management* 18(1), 89–104.

Mintzberg, H. (1990) The design school: reconsidering the basic premises of strategic management. *Strategic Management Journal* 11(3), 171–195.

Mitchell, V.W. and Harris, G. (2005) The importance of consumers' perceived risk in retail strategy. *European Journal of Marketing* 39(7/8), 821–837.

Pal, J.W. and Byrom, J.W. (2003) The five Ss of retail operations: a model and tool for improvement. *International Journal of Retail & Distribution Management* 31(10), 518–528.

Petrick, K. and Sheehan, B. (2007) Socialised consumption. Paper presented at *Social Science Seminar Series*, Leeds Metropolitan University, Leeds, UK, 28 February 2007.

Ramus, C.A. and Montiel, I. (2005) When are corporate environmental policies a form of greenwashing? *Business & Society* 44(4), 377–414.

Richardson, N., Eilertsen, C. and Kenyon, A. (2007) Does Fair-trade represent a marketing opportunity for the UK tourism industry? *International Journal of Management Cases* 9(3/4).

Sparks, L. and Wagner, B.A. (2003) Retail exchanges: a research agenda. *Supply Chain Management* 8(3), 201–208.

Starkey, R. and Welford, R. (2001) *The Earthscan Reader in Business & Sustainable Development*. Earthscan Publishing, London.

Tilley, F. (2007) Conceptualising sustainability entrepreneurship (summary of a talk delivered at the symposium). Paper presented at Corporate Responsibility Research Conference, Leeds University, Leeds, UK, July 2007. Available at: http://crrconference.org (accessed 20 February 2008).

Willard, T. and Creech, H. (2006) Sustainability of International Development Networks – Review of IDRC Experience (1995–2005). Available at: http://www.iisd.org/pdf/2007/networks_sus_int_dev.pdf (accessed 16 March 2009).

Williams, C.C. (2003) Participation in alternative retail channels: a choice or necessity? *International Journal of Retail & Distribution Management* 31(5), 235–243.

Wong, A. and Sohal, A.S. (2002) Customers' perspectives on service quality and relationship quality in retail encounters. *Managing Service Quality* 12(5), 424–433.

Wong, A. and Sohal, A.S. (2003) A critical incident approach to the examination of customer relationship management in a retail chain: an exploratory study. *Qualitative Market Research* 6(4), 248–262.

12 Assessing and Monitoring the Performances of a Sustainable Event

L. Lamberti, I. Fava and G. Noci
Politecnico di Milano, Milan, Italy

This chapter evaluates the principles and tools that event managers can use to monitor and estimate the sustainability performances of an event. The aim of the chapter is to show integrated event performance assessment with sustainability assessment in order to suggest a framework and a dashboard (named SED) for assessing the performances and managerial implications of sustainable events.

Chapter outline

- Introduction
- What Does It Mean to Assess Event Sustainability Performances?
- Sustainability Assessment
- The Characteristics of a Sustainable Event Performance Measurement System
- A Managerial Tool for Event Managers for Assessing Sustainable Event Performances: the Sustainable Event Dashboard (SED)
- Adopting and Using the SED
- Summary
- Key Questions

Introduction

The definition of a 'sustainable event', as detailed in Chapter 1 of this book, refers to a general event whose operation incorporates and is consistent with the principles of a sustainable development. Environmental sustainability-driven management of an event or destination may be implemented in different forms (Mihalic, 2000): (i) the adoption of environmental codes of conduct (e.g. the ISO 14000 certification testifies the attention paid to environmental safeguards); (ii) uncertified environmental practice and self-declared labels or brands; (iii) green branding on the basis of a competition prize for excellent practice or certified environmental good practice (e.g. the Italian Environmental-friendly Innovation award, annually assigned to the most relevant sustainable innovations in the country, attributes to the product/project awarded a brand that the winner can use as leverage to promote their offer); and (iv) green branding on the basis of accreditation schemes.

It therefore becomes crucial to measure the sustainability of the event considering its social, economic and environmental aspects before, during and after the event (life cycle analysis), as sustainability refers to a lasting condition. The possibility to properly assess sustainability has important effects not only on event organizers but also on the host area and the event stakeholders, since the organization of an event boosts negotiation processes that involve different stakeholders with different goals that impact on the performance of the event itself.

What Does It Mean to Assess Event Sustainability Performances?

An event may be seen as a process in which a series of inputs is processed to produce an immediate representation (the event itself), but also a varied set of impacts for the event stakeholders. The inputs are represented by the resources (e.g. financial, human, infrastructure) and the plans and policies for ensuring the carrying out and completion of the event. The outputs are conceptually all of the consequences of the event, both direct and indirect in nature. Direct outputs derive immediately (in terms of either time or space) from the event and they may differ in nature: financial outputs (e.g. tickets, sponsorships, media rights), infrastructural outputs (building and structures expressly developed for the event), intellectual outputs (know-how on the event, the visitors and the stakeholders useful for pursuing continuous improvement in following editions of the event) and other intangibles (e.g. visitor satisfaction, territorial marketing, return on location and organizer image, environmental impact of the event). Indirect outputs still derive from the event, but their level depends on other actors playing a role in the event; a classic example is represented by the indirect turnover generated for industries linked to the event (e.g. hotels/restaurants/cafés, transport, cultural heritage sites in the host area). These impacts are often even more significant than the direct incomes of the event (Lamberti and Noci, 2007). For instance, recent studies on trade shows and exhibitions show that each euro in direct revenues drives from 5 to 15 euros to linked industries according to the ability to attract international exhibitors and visitors (who spend more time in the host area than local visitors and can afford larger expenses in tourism structures). Macro-economists and tourism economists are still debating about the definition of proper multipliers for estimating the indirect economic impact of events, and the topic has immediate managerial and policy-making implications. Nevertheless, since the objective of this chapter is to understand how to support event management decisions through sustainability assessment, we focus mainly on the direct outputs of sustainable events.

When an organization organizes an event it sets the objectives to achieve, i.e. the expected values of the outputs to obtain after the event, so it is fundamental to be able to assess the event performances, i.e. the actual level of output accomplished. This is the way to understand if the event has been successful, thus to understand and prove the ability of the organizer. Assessing the performances, moreover, enhances the know-how on the event, supporting the planning of future editions under different viewpoints, and, if the performance measurement system is properly designed, makes it possible to understand the contribution of the actors involved in the project to the general performance. This is also useful from a motivational perspective, since properly assigning performance objectives is a good way to pursue global alignment of the resources to the macro-objectives of the organizer. To do that, organizers should clearly define:

- the relevant performances to assess;
- the target level of the performances;
- a set of (objectively measurable) indicators to assess the accomplishment of the objectives;
- the areas of responsibility for the resources involved (i.e. who is responsible for the accomplishment of a performance);
- the policies for calculating the indicators in terms of the way to calculate them and the frequency of measurement; and
- the incentives and the penalties according to the level of accomplishment of the target performances by the resources.

Finally, an important role of the performance measurement system is to communicate to the stakeholders the results of the event and their compliance to the objectives set during the planning of the event. This has deep implications also for fundraising activities: an event able to demonstrate its sustainability has more likelihood of being attractive to sponsors, public administration and also visitors and exhibitors particularly aware about sustainable development (Straughan and Roberts, 1999; Ginsberg and Bloom, 2004).

Sustainable event managers thus should be able to plan the event by setting triple bottom line (TBL) objectives, assessing TBL performances, and fairly and clearly communicating their results to the stakeholders. Moreover, they can also leverage on the performance measurement system in order to boost their efficiency and effectiveness. In the following we discuss this point in detail, starting from the basic question: how is it possible to assess sustainability performances?

Sustainability Assessment

The debate on sustainability assessment is very vivid. Authors agree that one of the main criticalities of the concept of 'sustainability' stands in its low measurability (Korhonen, 2003), due to:

- the multidimensionality of the concept (it involves environmental, social, financial and communication issues, and often the domain of impact of the action is hybrid);
- the low analysability of the concept (it is very difficult to forecast the impacts of the actions in time); and
- the time duration of the impacts of sustainable management.

The most conspicuous body of literature on sustainability assessment concerns the monitoring of environmental performances. Different theories about environmental accounting have been developed for the for-profit organizations, especially companies (e.g. Azzone and Noci, 1996; Barkin, 2006; Gray, 2006), as well as for non-governmental organizations (NGOs) and public bodies (e.g. Kobus, 2005). These theories aim mainly at adapting performance measurement systems to the emerging attention to environmental issues by introducing punctual key performance indicators (KPIs) able to monitor operations and organizational environmental performances. For example, the environmental costing framework (Bayou and Nachtman, 1992; Morhardt *et al.*, 2002) suggests integrating financial indicators (costs, revenues, etc.) with some financial and non-financial indicators of environmental outputs such as the waste generated, the costs and the savings related to recycling, etc. (Azzone and Noci, 1998). These approaches have been adopted quite widely by organizations, but are affected by the short-termism typical of the operational performance measurement (Azzone, 2000), making them poorly effective in strategic planning and management, especially as far as major projects and events are concerned.

As a result, more structured and long-term approaches to environmental planning were introduced. To this extent, since the 1970s, public bodies and NGOs have endorsed frameworks to support decision makers in identifying, between a set of solutions, the ones avoiding or reducing environmental damages. The most diffused approach is the so-called Environmental Impact Assessment (EIA), developed in 1970 in the USA as a part of the National Environmental Policy Act (NEPA). The EIA proposes a set of methods for the quantitative impact prediction of a project on water, air, soil, noise and landscape; moreover, it urges decision makers to assess the impact of current projects and to prevent environmental damage by implementing alternatives or mitigation measures, and it also introduces an enhancement in the planning process of the projects (Bass *et al.*, 1996). Over time, impact assessment has evolved to introduce also elements of corporate social responsibility (CSR), as in the case of the Child Impact Assessment (Muylaert, 1999), the Gender Impact Assessment and the Mobility Impact Assessment, which have been adopted in several countries (e.g. Canada, Belgium, The Netherlands and New Zealand) (Meier, 1997). The request for integration of CSR into impact assessment and the desire by the public sector to support not only the planning but also the ongoing management of projects, led to the definition of the Sustainability Assessment Framework (Devuyst, 1999) that has been deployed in a checklist of principles, named the Bellagio Principles for Assessment (Hardi and Zdan, 1997) developed by the International Institute for Sustainable Development (IISD). This checklist provides guidelines for planning and managing a sustainable project at a very strategic level, and it has been the founding stone of several applicative frameworks at national and local level. For instance, the ASSIPAC (Assessing the Sustainability of Societal Initiatives and Proposing Agendas for Change) framework, developed by the EIA Center of the Vrije Universiteit Brussels, presented in Table 12.1, is a good example of the

Table 12.1. The ASSIPAC Sustainability Assessment Checklist.

Letter code	Name	Content	Dimensions of analysis
A.	**Description of the event**	General description of the main characteristics of the event in terms of concept, goals, shareholders and investors, and governance	A.1. Name of the event A.2. Type of event A.3. General goals A.4. Specific goals A.5. Long-term goals A.6. Phases in the event A.7. Initiator definition and reputational analysis; fundraising policies and sponsor reputational analysis A.8. Host area description A.9. Decision-making policies A.10. Identification of sources of information
B.	**Description of alternatives for the event**	Overview of the possible sustainable alternatives for the event in order both to highlight possible strategic options in case of failure and to testify a sustainability 'superiority' of the concept undertaken	
C.	**Description of sustainable development policies, visions or strategies**	Overview of the sustainable development strategy in the host area and identification of existing sustainability standards	
D.	**Best available practice in an international context for the initiative and its alternatives**	Benchmarking of the international best-in-class practices in organizing and carrying out an initiative with a similar concept	
E.	**Discussion of the reactions to the initiative and its alternatives**	Analysis and discussion of the reactions of the stakeholders during the public consultation about the project	
F.	**Forces which obstruct a more advanced sustainable development of the initiative**	Analysis of the elements constraining an even more effective contribution to sustainable development by the event	
G.	**General characteristics of the initiative and its alternatives which could be favourable to sustainable development**	Analysis of the characteristics of the event and of the organizational policies	G.1. Integration of the event with sustainable development strategies of the area G.2. Integration and coordination with related initiatives G.3. Multidimensionality of the sustainability

			G.4. Partnerships with the host society G.5. Empowerment of and cooperation with the local community G.6. Impacts on future generations G.7. Budgetary and financial policies G.8. Other policies
H.	**Environmental characteristics of the initiative and its alternatives which could be favourable to sustainable development**	Analysis of the environmental impact of the event	H.1. Impact on mobility H.2. Environmental care system H.3. Natural resources use reduction H.4. Use of materials and waste reduction H.5. Protection of biodiversity H.6. Reduction of pollution H.7. Restoration and maintenance of ecological cycles H.8. Influence on climate change H.9. Influence on population growth H.10. Others
I.	**Social and cultural characteristics of the initiative and its alternatives which could be favourable to sustainable development**	Analysis of the social impact of the event	I.1. Contribution to empowerment and emancipation of groups within the community I.2. Contribution to equity in resource distribution I.3. Contribution to the reinforcement of local cultural identity and diversity I.4. Contribution to the protection and improvement of the health of the population I.5. Contribution to education and training of the local population I.6. Contribution to local employment I.7. Contribution to social, cultural and recreational exchanges between members of the host area I.8. Contribution to the affirmation of a sustainable lifestyle I.9. Contribution to the affirmation of strengthened democratic values I.10. Contribution to the independence of the local community I.11. Others

Continued

Table 12.1. Continued.

Letter code	Name	Content	Dimensions of analysis
J.	**Economic characteristics of the initiative and its alternatives which could be favourable to sustainable development**	Analysis of the economical impact of the event	J.1. Reinforcement of the local economy J.2. Support to private entrepreneurship J.3. Support to sustainable trade J.4. Others
K.	**Planning and design characteristics of the initiative and its alternatives which could be favourable to sustainable development**	Analysis of the patterns in the event project suitable to sustainable development	K.1. Development frameworks for transport reduction K.2. Development frameworks for the maintenance of the natural ecosystem K.3. Others
L.	**Assessment of the sustainable character of the initiative and its alternatives**	Comparative assessment of the event performances, with an in-depth discussion of the pros and cons of the alternatives. Comparative analysis of the event with the international best practices	
M.	**Proposal of an agenda for change**	Description of the plans for struggling unsustainable behaviour in the event and in the host area	
N.	**Conclusion**		
O.	**References**		
	Annexes	Description of the scientific methodology used in the different phases of the sustainability assessment	

kind of decision-making support provided by such frameworks. Aimed at bringing to bear an effective and responsible communication of the sustainability performances of the project, ASSIPAC is to be used as an indexed agenda for producing a sustainability report to communicate the essential characteristics of the project to investors, policy and decision makers and other stakeholders.

As such, the ASSIPAC or similar frameworks could represent a useful tool for drawing out a business plan for a generic sustainable initiative and, in particular, for a sustainable event. The most important part is represented by checklist point L ('Assessment of the sustainable character of the initiative and its alternatives'). The framework suggests a comparative approach to sustainability performance measurement, supporting business planning with a systematic comparison of the expected performances of the project with either its alternatives or past experiences similar in nature. ASSIPAC introduces two main levels of actions (or tiers): (i) the Sustainability Assessment Check (SAC); and (ii) the Sustainability Assessment Study (SAS). The SAC is an opening study aimed at exploring the possible conflict of the event with sustainable development policies. The SAS is a deeper evaluation of the sustainability consequences of the event. According to the nature and degree of development of the event, and the time and resources allocable to the assessment (in fact, SAS is far more time-consuming and expensive than SAC), the assessment team may decide to adopt either of the tiers. Hereby, the main steps of the assessment are briefly detailed.

Nevertheless, this kind of framework, although extremely useful in the planning and fundraising phases of event organization, is less likely to properly support ongoing event project management and ex-post evaluation because its application is requested in parallel with event planning, while poor indications are given about the following steps. As a result, sustainable event managers cannot yet lever on punctual tools to evaluate the sustainability performances *in itinere*, nor do they have at their disposal structured tools to comparatively evaluate the actual performances of different events, a key issue for pursuing continuous improvement. This issue is particularly relevant for periodic events hosted in the same location, since these events give the manager the opportunity to exploit past experience to improve the governance of the event, also from a TBL perspective.

Typically, during event project deployment, the control tool most commonly adopted by event managers is represented by the set of techniques related to project management, such as Gantt diagrams (graphical representation of the project activities – duration and priority – and their interdependence), PERT-CPM methods (programme evaluation and review technique–critical path method; aimed at highlighting critical activities, bottlenecks, etc.) and similar (for further details, see also Allen *et al.*, 2005). These techniques, together with the project leader's commitment and proper project planning, define precise targets, in terms of expected time, costs and quality, in the implementation of the event. A generally recognized limit of project management techniques is their lack of contribution to long-term strategic thinking, since their role is purely to assess and control, while their decision-making support to other projects is far more limited. This last point is the greater difference between project management and common accountability, which is based on the assumption of perpetual control of iterative activities aimed at assessing the performances to support organizational learning (Azzone, 2000).

Thus, it is very important to couple project management with some accountability principles to sustainable event management: generative learning derived from accountability can support continuous improvement, with beneficial effects on the TBL. A clear understatement of the positive effects of continuous improvement from a TBL perspective may be accomplished by observing the effect of a gradual shift to sustainability in the business models of many organizations.

The Characteristics of a Sustainable Event Performance Measurement System

A performance measurement system is a very complex object. In fact, as its role is to control the behaviour of an organization and to support management decision making and learning, it must satisfy a wide set of requisites (Watts and Zimmerman, 1986; Azzone, 2000):

- completeness;
- precision;
- long-term orientation;
- measurability;
- accountability; and
- timeliness.

Since the nature of the performances (e.g. operational performances versus strategic performances, financial performances versus non-financial performances) and their time effect (long-term effect versus short-term effect) are varied and concurrent in every economic activity, it is almost impossible that a single approach to performance assessment can satisfy all of the requisites mentioned above (Kaplan, 1988). For instance, completeness and precision are often in trade-off, since the adoption of a very complete performance measurement system makes it very difficult to reach the details with enough precision. Moreover, when completeness, precision and long-term orientation increase, it becomes very difficult to be timely in the assessment: the above-mentioned ASSIPAC framework is a good example of a complete and long-term oriented performance planning (that is conceptually not so different from assessment), but it is clear that if the manager wants to be particularly precise in its evaluation, the time for the elaboration becomes extremely long.

In order to overtake the trade-offs, organizations adopt different and complementary performance measurement systems (Kaplan, 1988; Simons, 1994) according to the needs of the managers who are going to use it. For instance, a project manager in an event is interested in the typical set of performances assessed by project management techniques, such as quality, cost absorption and compliance to the scheduling. In order to get proper control on the project, performance indicators must be punctual, assessable in real time and objectively measurable; so project managers need precision, timeliness and measurability in their performance measurement system. The long-term effects of the project and the social/environmental impact of the project, or its financial return, are in general less relevant for project management, since they have generally been considered in the planning phase. As a result, completeness and long-term orientation are less relevant and may be partially disregarded. Similarly, strategic managers or deciders are more interested in complete measures (such as the impacts, the expected and actual return on the investment and the global overview of the advances in the project), even if this implies a diminished precision.

A Managerial Tool for Event Managers for Assessing Sustainable Event Performances: the Sustainable Event Dashboard (SED)

In glancing back on what we have learned so far, we see it is extremely important for event managers to design a performance measurement system consistently to the organizational structure, i.e. the different roles and responsibilities in the project team. It is interesting to notice that a TBL perspective induces an enhanced focus on a wide set of (at least partially) non-financial performances (environmental and social impact, waste reduction, etc.), making the amount of potentially relevant performances extremely conspicuous. Nevertheless, a proliferation of the indicators adopted may lead to an excessive fragmentation of the as-is analysis, with a loss of effectiveness due to the difficulties in getting a global perspective on the event performances, especially as far as strategic decision making and continuous improvement are concerned.

Since the early 1990s authors and organizations have detected the need for synthetic tools able to support strategic decision making starting from the information gathered by the performance measurement system. Starting from a concept developed in France during the 1960s, the so-called 'tableau de bord' (Bourguignon *et al.*, 2004), i.e. a synthetic table for strategic reporting in which the most relevant performances were summarized, Kaplan and Norton (1992, 1996) developed the Balanced Scorecard (BSC) approach. The

BSC suggests that managers group the most relevant KPIs of a unit into four main perspectives: (i) financial performances; (ii) customer performances; (iii) internal performances; and (iv) innovation performances.

When the unit of analysis is a sustainable event, the set of variables to assess and strategically monitor increases noticeably. Therefore, it is necessary to enlarge the set of perspectives to be considered in order to deliberately encompass the TBL perspective into event management. As a result, a more complex dashboard can be useful, namely a Sustainable Event Dashboard (SED). In general terms, five main performance dimensions may be detected (Fig. 12.1):

- financial performances;
- environmental performances;
- social performances;
- visitors' and exhibitors' performances; and
- internal and innovation performances.

The SED differs from a standard BSC in two key aspects: (i) the output dimension (cf. BSC's financial performances) has been enriched with a clear focus on environmental and social performances, compliant to the TBL perspective of sustainable events; and (ii) internal and innovation performances have been merged in order to outline how sustainable internal performance management can highlight areas of improvement, and thus innovation opportunities.

The financial performances look at the behaviour of the event in terms of profit generation, return on investment (i.e. the profit-to-expenses ratio) of fundraising, etc. So it is a synthetic way to summarize the economic results of the event. When the organizer is a non-profit organization (e.g. the public government), the concept of 'profit' may be substituted by more complex metrics such as the sum of direct and indirect turnover generated or the increases in tax gathered.

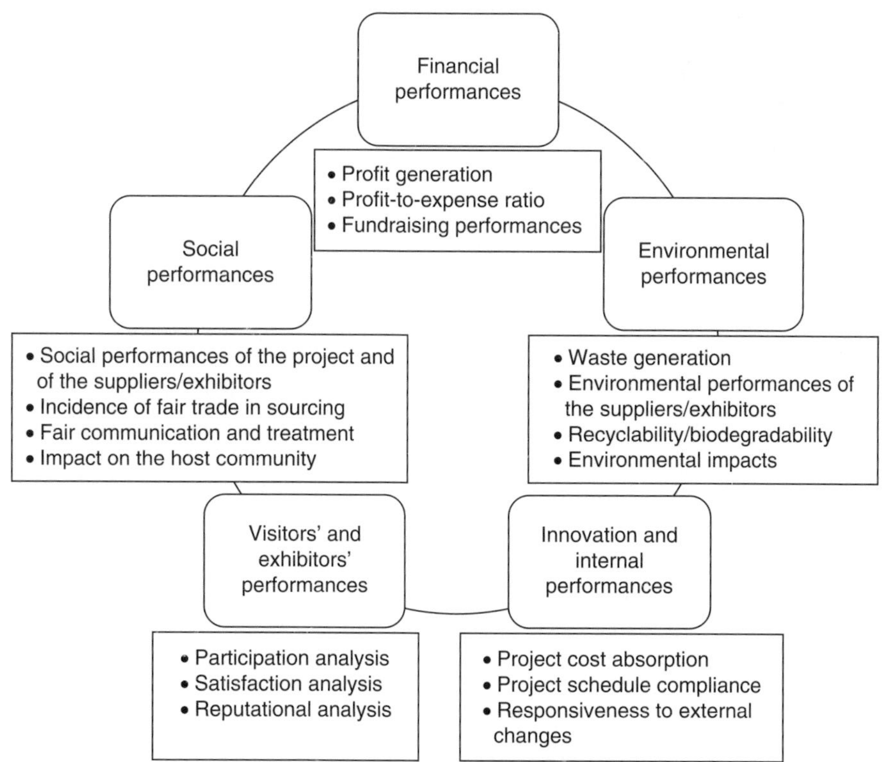

Fig. 12.1. The structure of the Sustainable Event Dashboard (SED) and possible dimensions of analysis.

The environmental performances look at the long-term impact on the environment of the event, as well as its current behaviour in terms of natural resource consumption and pollution. Two main categories of environmental performances may be detected:

- *Environmental performances of the event inputs and process*, such as the percentage of biodegradable or recyclable materials used for venue set-up, the waste generated during the project, the percentage of ISO 14000 (or similar environmental certification) certified suppliers/sponsors/exhibitors.
- *Environmental performances of the event outputs*, such as the amount of waste generated, its biodegradability/recyclability rate, the energy consumption.

The social performances look at the long-term impact on the social stakeholders of the event and its current behaviour in terms of event ethics, politeness in operations and other characteristics related to so-called 'event citizenship', i.e. the ability of the event to encompass the social expectations of the host area. Similarly to environmental performances, social performances may also be divided into two main categories:

- *Social performances of the event inputs and process*, such as the percentage of fair trade consumption material, the percentage of women employed, the percentage of SA 8000 (or similar) certified suppliers/sponsors/exhibitors.
- *Social performances of the event outputs*, such as the amount of donations gathered running the event, the reconversion rate of the structures after the event, the attitude towards the event by the host community.

Among all of the stakeholders interested in events, visitors and exhibitors have a more immediate pay-off by participation. In fact, visitors may pay for admission to the event, or at least they may have to move to reach the venue; they have direct and immediate expectations and enjoy the activities performed during the event. Sometimes events also host external exhibitors or performers with their own stands or pavilions (events like general or country fairs, exhibitions, etc.). Exhibitors are very relevant stakeholders since they too are customers (they generally pay a fee to the organizers to participate), and moreover their fairness and the attractiveness of their attendance is a critical factor for event success (in fact, it has been suggested to monitor their environmental and social performances in order to avoid dissonances in the event image). Thus, it is fundamental for the organizer to monitor the attractiveness for visitors and exhibitors by assessing the event's ability to meet their expectations. So important KPIs may cope with visitors' satisfaction (assessed through surveys during and after the event), the number and quality of exhibitors, event awareness (i.e. estimate of the percentage of the target market aware about the event's existence) and image, and the exhibitors' churn rate (i.e. percentage of exhibitors leaving the event after their first participation, a typical proxy of exhibitors' loyalty), among others.

These performances are extremely useful to understand whether the event concept is clear, attractive and univocally interpreted by the target audience; moreover, they give information about the effectiveness and the efficiency of the event's marketing and communication; and finally, a retrospective analysis could highlight the attendance response to the activities performed, with a beneficial effect on the planning of future editions.

Internal performances look at the efficiency accomplished in carrying out the project and the event itself; as a result, the classical project management KPIs (e.g. percentage of activities completed, percentage of delayed activities, percentage of the resources absorbed) are the most likely to be used. Moreover, internal performances may be used to understand the internal climate of the event team, such as the number of volunteers attracted and their rate of turnover, and the results of periodic internal satisfaction surveys may be beneficial for event managers to catch elements of dissatisfaction detrimental to the output of the event. Furthermore, internal satisfaction is one of the key performances under a sustainability perspective. In parallel, innovation performances in sustainable events deal with the ability of the event to efficiently (i.e. rapidly and cheaply) and effectively adapt and fine-tune its characteristics to changes in stakeholders' expectations, and to generate innovative ideas after the event (e.g. spin-offs, concept refinements in the next editions) (Ottman, 1998). These performances are of course generally more important when assessed with reference to a periodic event. Typical examples of KPIs for this category are represented by average time and costs for implementing major changes in the project, or the innovation rate of success (the number of successful innovations in the event concept divided by the total amount of innovations introduced).

Adopting and Using the SED

This model of dashboard is structurally very contingent in nature, so its main contribution is represented by the detection and the definition of the performance dimensions to assess in sustainable event management. The punctual choice of the relevant KPIs depends on several variables, such as:

- the event concept (e.g. the dashboard for a sustainable country fair will have a stronger focus on exhibitors than that for a film festival);
- its infrastructural characteristics (e.g. mega-events induce a more significant change in the host area than small events based on the host area's cultural heritage); and
- the organizations involved (e.g. an event organized by a for-profit company will probably have a greater focus on the immediate financial profitability than an event organized by the public sector).

Thus, it would be misleading and poorly rigorous to suggest a good-for-all list of KPIs for sustainable event management. Therefore the role of the event manager is very important in the choice of the KPIs: he/she should first of all clearly define the vision of the event, highlighting the most important objectives; these objectives should be translated into macro performances and then detailed into punctual performances and associated to correct KPIs in order to keep the project and the event under control.

Summary

In conclusion, some managerial issues in the adoption of the SED should be addressed. First of all, the SED must be considered just a 'glimpse' of the global event performance measurement system: it is a summarized extraction of the whole set of KPIs adopted at all the levels of the organization organizing the event. This means that the common project management tools, the operational control systems and the frameworks supporting sustainable event planning cannot be substituted by the SED, just accompanied and reinforced. The SED should be used and periodically assessed by event managers and planners, marketing and communication managers and project leaders to get a complete perspective on the key performances of the event during its implementation, its execution and in the after-event. Owing to its completeness and conciseness, the SED should be used to detect the potentially critical issues or the areas of improvement, but the exact determination of the causes of the problems and the levers to improve the performances can only be properly highlighted after a detailed analysis at a more operational level. So, the main function of the SED stands in being an alert control system about strengths and weaknesses, opportunities and threats, more than a tool for carrying on problem solving. Nevertheless, the performance measurement approaches presented so far in the literature either do not accomplish the same completeness (e.g. the project control tools) or have the problem of measurability and/or timeliness (e.g. the EIA frameworks), making them poorly effective as alert systems (Simons, 1991).

Finally, the main limitation of the SED can also represent a good lever for project leaders: by virtue of its simplicity and global overview on the event performances, the SED can communicate the global performances of the event very effectively. So it can also be used to promote the event, and in particular its sustainability, to potential sponsors, visitors or exhibitors and, more generally, the event stakeholders. As such, it can also be seen as a good basis for integrating the Environmental and Social Impact Assessment in the TBL accountability of the event.

Key Questions

1. What are the relevant performances of a sustainable event?
2. How does sustainability impact on event performance assessment?
3. How is it possible to assess the performances of a sustainable event?

References

Allen, J., McDonnell, I., O'Toole, W. and Harris, R. (2005) *Festival and Special Event Management*. Wiley and Sons, Sydney.

Azzone, G. (2000) *Innovare il sistema di controllo di gestione*. ETAS, Milan, Italy.

Azzone, G. and Noci, G. (1996) Measuring the environmental performance of new products: an integrated approach. *International Journal of Production Research* 34(11), 3055–3078.

Azzone, G. and Noci, G. (1998) Identifying effective PMSs for the deployment of 'green' manufacturing strategies. *International Journal of Operations & Production Management* 18(4), 308–335.

Barkin, S.B. (2006) Discounting the discount rate: ecocentrism and environmental economics. *Global Environmental Politics* 6(4), 56–72.

Bass, R.E., Herson, A.I. and Bogdan, K.M. (1996) CEQA Deskbook. A Step-by-Step Guide on How to Comply With the California Environmental Quality Act. Solano Press Books, Point Arena, California.

Bayou, M.E. and Nachtman, J.B (1992) Cost for manufacturing wastes. *Journal of Cost Management* 6(Summer), 53–62.

Bourguignon, A., Malleret, V. and Nørreklit, H. (2004) The American balanced scorecard versus the French tableau de bord: the ideological dimension. *Management Accounting Research* 15(2), 107–134.

Devuysy, D. (1999) Sustainability assessment: the application of a methodological framework. *Journal of Environmental Assessment Policy and Management* 1(4), 459–487.

Ginsberg, J.M. and Bloom, P.N. (2004) Choosing the right green marketing strategy. *MIT Sloan Management Review* 46(1), 79–84.

Gray, R. (2006) Social, environmental and sustainability reporting and organisational value creation? Whose value? Whose creation? *Accounting, Auditing & Accountability Journal* 19(6), 793–819.

Hardi, P. and Zdan, T. (1997) *Assessing Sustainable Development. Principles in Practice*. International Institute for Sustainable Development, Winnipeg, Canada.

Kaplan, R.S. (1988) One cost system isn't enough. *Harvard Business Review* 66(1), 61–66.

Kaplan, R.S. and Norton, D.P. (1992) The Balanced Scorecard – measures that drive performance. *Harvard Business Review* 70(1), 70–80.

Kaplan, R.S. and Norton, D.P. (1996) *The Balanced Scorecard: Translating Strategy into Action*. Harvard Business Press, Boston, Massachusetts.

Kobus, D. (2005) Development and testing a conceptual framework for assessment of progress towards achieving sustainable development in countries in transition. *Journal of Environmental Assessment Policy and Management* 7(3), 457–491.

Korhonen, J. (2003) Should we measure corporate social responsibility? *Corporate Social Responsibility and Environmental Management* 10(1), 25–39.

Lamberti, L. and Noci, G. (2007) *A Sino-European Comparison of the Exhibition and Convention Industry*. Polipress, Milan, Italy.

Meier, P. (1997) *Het Emancipatie-Effecten Rapport (EER). Eeninstrument voor een gelijkekansenbeleid*. Vrije Universiteit Brussels and Ministry of the Flemish Community, Brussels.

Mihalic, T. (2000) Environmental management of a tourist destination. A factor of tourism competitiveness. *Tourism Management* 21(1), 65–78.

Morhardt, J.E., Baird, S. and Freeman, K. (2002) Scoring corporate and environmental sustainability reports using GRI 2000, ISO 14031 and other criteria. *Corporate Social Responsibility and Environmental Management* 9, 215–233.

Muylaert, S. (1999) *Kindeffectrapportage in Vlaanderen: sitiatieschets en stand van zaken*. Vrije Universiteit Brussels, Brussels.

Ottman, J.A. (1998) *Green Marketing: Opportunities for Innovation*. NTC Business Books, Lincolnwood, Illinois.

Simons, R. (1991) Strategic orientation and top management attention to control systems. *Strategic Management Journal* 12(1), 49–62.

Simons, R. (1994) How new top managers use control systems as levers of strategic renewal. *Strategic Management Journal* 15(3) 169–189.

Straughan, R.D. and Roberts, J.A. (1999) Environmental segmentation alternatives: a look at green consumer behavior in the new millennium. *Journal of Consumer Marketing* 16, 558–575.

Watts, R.L. and Zimmerman, J.L. (1986) *Positive Accounting Theory*. Prentice Hall, Englewood Cliffs, New Jersey.

13 Changing Trends in the American Meetings Industry

M.C. Paxson
Washington State University, Pullman, Washington, USA

This chapter addresses trends in the conventions, expositions and meetings industry in the USA. It explores the areas of globalization/ international participation, the cloning of shows, competition and technology. The chapter also focuses on the diversity of approaches, often borrowed and adapted, that characterizes the US conventions and meetings industry. Finally, the chapter addresses relationships between sustainability and the trends.

Chapter outline

- Introduction
- Globalization
- The Cloning of Shows
- Competition
- Technology
- Sustainability and US Trends
- Summary
- Key Questions

Introduction

According to the American Society of Association Executives (ASAE), an organization with 23,000 members, approximately 6000 associations currently operate in the USA. About 100,000 more function at the regional, state and local levels (ASAE, 2008). Associations are big business in the USA, spending billions of dollars to hold thousands of meetings and conventions that attract millions of attendees.

The need to hold face-to-face meetings and attend conventions in a country as large and geographically dispersed as the USA has created a multibillion-dollar conventions and meetings industry. Major cities like New York and Las Vegas have the facilities to draw the largest events. Compared with a few years ago, however, large conventions are not as well attended as in the past. Regional events have taken prominence, so that smaller cities such as Seattle, Washington and Vancouver in the Pacific Northwest, and Tulsa, Oklahoma have developed competitive convention facilities. The major players in the conventions and meetings business in the USA are convention and visitors' bureaus (CVBs), destination management companies (DMCs), meeting planners and their clients, convention centres, specialized services and expositions.

Globalization

The conferences and meetings business is a very important sector of the tourism industry. In all its forms, it is purported to be the world's largest industry. In the USA the industry ranks 29th in terms of its contribution to the gross national product (CIC, 2004), above the pharmaceutical and medical manufacturing industries and just below the financial services industry. The USA has ranked first worldwide in the number of meetings held every year since 2003, according to the International Congress & Convention Association (ICCA, 2008). The US share of the 2005 world market for international meetings, 1039 events, was 11.6% (Table 13.1). At the same time, the relative US share of the market has been declining since 2002 in the wake of the September 11, 2001 terrorist attacks in New York City, rising energy costs and increased competition as countries including Croatia and Cuba have entered the market.

Historically, globalization in the USA was about outsourcing, capital movement and labour flows. Now it is about logistics, climate change, energy costs and the carbon footprint. Much of what is accomplished will be based on how the sunset of the fossil fuel era comes about. The conventions and meetings industry is on the front line, dealing as it does with logistics and getting people together in time and space.

The great economic revolutions in history occurred when the energy regime changed and with the birth of rapid means of communication. Coal- and steam-powered railways and printing for mass literacy were replaced by the internal combustion engine, electricity, the telegraph and telephone. Now, the third industrial revolution is at hand: hundreds of millions of people can distribute information to one another in an instant. This technology will be replaced by the next energy regime of distributed, renewable energies like non-polluting hydrogen-powered fuel cells.

One area of change in the conventions and meetings industry in recent years is the rise, consolidation and growing influence of global meeting planning companies. Four of the five top planning companies are based in the USA: Conferon, Helms Briscoe, Maritz and Smith Bucklin. At the same time, Maritz recently merged with the UK-based planning company Grass Roots resulting in arguably the largest provider of meetings and related services in the world. The fifth largest provider of convention and meeting services worldwide, MCI Group, based in Switzerland, widely viewed as Europe's pre-eminent association, communication and event management company, has partnered with Smith Bucklin to deliver seamless convention and meeting services worldwide.

Table 13.1. Top 25 international meeting countries in 2005. (Source: Union of International Associations, 2006.)

Country	Number of meetings	Percentage of all meetings
USA	1039	11.6
France	590	6.6
Germany	410	4.6
UK	386	4.3
Italy	382	4.3
Spain	368	4.1
The Netherlands	341	3.8
Austria	314	3.5
Switzerland	268	3.0
Belgium	242	2.7
China, Hong Kong & Macau	216	2.4
Canada	214	2.4
Australia	200	2.2
South Korea	185	2.1
Singapore	177	2.0
Sweden	170	1.9
Japan	168	1.9
Denmark	138	1.5
Greece	136	1.5
Portugal	125	1.4
Finland	119	1.3
Poland	118	1.3
Hungary	117	1.3
Turkey	109	1.2
Brazil	107	1.2
India	106	1.2
Czech Republic	103	1.2
South Africa	100	1.1
Norway	98	1.1
Russia	85	1.0
Argentina	74	0.8
Thailand	74	0.8
Mexico	73	0.8
Ireland	70	0.8
Malaysia	61	0.6
Egypt	48	0.5
Croatia	46	0.5
Chile	45	0.5
Total meetings (in list)	7622	85.0

What these organizations have in common is that their focus has shifted from supply to demand. Currently, convention and meeting management companies in the USA rely on municipal convention centres and visitors' bureaus to link with clients and suppliers. This reliance is likely to decline in future as clients displace suppliers as the focus of the work. Global planners and event management companies have established preferred vendor agreements with the blue-chip corporations at the national, regional or worldwide level. As these corporations have outsourced specialist services, such as conference and event management, smaller, more local organizations have stepped in to secure local conferences and meetings.

Two trends, the first for international associations to appoint a central convention and event management company and the second for outsourcing the management of associations to specialist association management companies, have also created opportunities for global management companies. Because of their enhanced buying power, large, global companies are able to secure competitive pricing and instant confirmation of arrangements.

The global reach of these companies poses a threat to the traditional role of municipal convention centres and visitors' bureaus, which represent only a single destination city. CVBs need to play to their strengths, if they are to survive. They might benefit by shifting their focus to destination coordination, promotion and leadership and by leveraging their role as the official and unbiased point of access for destinations. By focusing more on consumers to ensure high-quality visitor experiences, CVBs focus on demand and play to their strengths.

The Cloning of Shows

In the USA, many trade shows are adjuncts to association meetings and are owned by the associations. Others are sponsored by private entrepreneurial companies and operated on a for-profit basis. Ownership and management usually are accomplished by two companies working together for the success of the show. Other service companies, commonly referred to as DMCs in the USA, support the industry by supporting both the trade show management company and the exhibitors. The typical US model is not followed in other countries. Governments often plan and operate trade fairs in collaboration with organizing companies. For example, the government of China plays a major role in the sponsorship of most trade fairs produced in Beijing, Hong Kong and Shanghai. In the USA, organizers and sponsors of conventions and meetings typically work with a CVB and/or DMC. Outside the USA, the professional congress organizer (PCO) is the more typical meeting management partner. PCOs characteristically take on more supporting functions for the client than DMCs, representing the client in dealing with the CVB, DMCs, hotels, restaurants, transportation companies and other suppliers, often negotiating with vendors on behalf of the client. PCOs tend to be more familiar than their US counterparts with international issues such as local customs, taxation and government regulations. The PCO even may handle financial transactions, letters of credit and foreign banking accounts. DMCs usually bill the customer using a sliding scale based on volume or on a per-person basis rather than use the flat-fee arrangement typical of PCOs.

In addition to logistical concerns, cultural differences also pose challenges for the conventions and meetings industry. Some international shows do not travel well, such as exhibitions of agricultural machinery. Thus, companies with international expertise such as Blenheim or the Reed Exposition Group (Fig. 13.1) airlift components and create shows in venues outside the USA. According to Charles D. Yuska of the Packaging Machinery Manufacturers' Institute, a major challenge is finding ways to make the institute's big, complicated show user-friendly, i.e. enhance the experience for both the attendee and the exhibitor regardless of nationality or ethnic background and create a community (C.D. Yuska, Washington, 2008, personal communication).

Competition

Competitiveness among all destinations has increased. A Brookings Institution report in

Fig. 13.1. Reed Exposition Group at Cannes Conference.

2006 (The Brookings Institution, 2006) determined that the conventions and meetings industry in the USA is in a permanent state of decline owing to fundamental changes in the way business is done. Convention centres have not been able to deliver promised economic benefits, and convention centre headquarters hotels have exacerbated profitability problems. As a result, convention centre expansions currently outpace new centre development projects.

Branding is also an important issue. The loss of 'main street' or the town centre also has affected the industry, because it has changed how Americans travel. In the past, people enjoyed the unique differences of each city's restaurants, shops and sites. Trolley cars symbolized San Francisco, Disney represented Orlando, Macy's was synonymous with New York City and Starbucks 'said' Seattle. The globalization of the marketplace has made it more important than ever to redefine 'main street' as the place that makes an American city unique.

Many destinations claim to have superb venues and hotels, easy accessibility, diverse attractions and a unique cultural heritage. Future success in attracting visitors will depend on a city's ability to create a unique identity for itself that differentiates it from competitors. Branding must do more than create a clever brand identity on paper with slick slogans and videos. This is a critical role for CVBs.

Technology

The single most important technological development of recent times is the affordability of computing. It may take a generation to bring the world's untapped intelligence into the workforce, but the declining cost of computing will produce a tremendously well-equipped workforce. A second important technological innovation is the globalization of resources. We now have the ability to send work instantaneously to any resource that can complete the work. Businesses are 24-hour operations that can track and monitor products and projects through business process technology or performance metrics, a capability that was not available 5 years ago. These technological innovations likely will increase productivity, employment and economic prosperity.

Regarding the effects of technology on the conventions and meetings industry, the reality is that face-to-face meetings are a more expensive type of communication. The industry in the USA needs to become more technologically sophisticated. Fibre-optic solutions need to be developed and implemented industry-wide. A product currently under development by Microsoft for the conventions and meetings market features a common digital event marketing platform to provide a backpack of sorts containing common takeaways from meetings. The product includes applications for managing business cards, thus eliminating paper cards. It also contains video, audio and the slides from conference presentations in a single source, saving natural resources and attendees' time. In addition, the software provides a social interaction venue. People log in and connect with others having similar interests. The software was showcased at the 2008 Professional Convention Managers Association (PCMA) annual convention in Seattle, Washington. According to Jeff Singsaas, General Manager for Corporate Events and Microsoft Studios with Microsoft, for conferences of 2500 to 20,000 attendees, the cost of using the software is insignificant (J. Singsaas, Washington, 2008, personal communication).

Another innovation, RFID (radio frequency identification) badging, permits associations to monitor attendee choices from a menu of recorded video files and response systems in learning environments. The information can help association planners better understand attendees' preferences and make meetings more convenient for them. Steve Drew, Assistant Executive Director for Scientific Assembly and Informatics with the Radiological Society of North America, planned to pilot test RFID badging at the society's 2008 annual convention to customize exhibitor information for specific attendees as they visit vendors' booths (S. Drew, Washington, 2008, personal communication). Kent E. Allaway, Director of Meetings and Trade Shows with the Produce Marketing Association, points to onsite badge pick-up as the technology that is making the difference for his organization (K.E. Allaway, Washington, 2008, personal communication). Modelled on the airline kiosk, members who have pre-registered swipe a card that automatically generates a printed conference badge. The whole process takes about 2 minutes, avoiding long queues.

According to Susan Newman, Vice President of Conferences with the National Retail Association, the rapid technological advances of the past few years involving mobile phones and blogging have had the most significant impact on her organization (S. Newman, Washington, 2008, personal communication). Keeping customers' attention is much more challenging than in the past. Empowered consumers make the decisions, so that retailers have been forced to change the way they do business. The retail association electronically networks exhibitors and attendees both before and after a show, and can upload the show schedule instantaneously. The association also exhibits its store of the future, Exploration 08, which provides a cityscape of demos showing how people will shop 24 hours a day, 7 days a week, get global positioning (GPS) data, and view interactive billboards with their mobile phones. They also have developed a Dream Green Pavilion, which demonstrates how retailers can become socially responsible and profitable. While the National Retail Association has invested considerable resources in research and development related to environmental issues, Ms Newman has found that most convention centres in the USA have made little progress in environmental awareness. Few have taken any action in this important area. In fact, Ms Newman believes that some of the steps her organization takes, such as separating recyclables, may be reversed by naïve convention centre staff.

Much more needs to be done. The real challenge is matching the communication need to the appropriate tool. No one form of communication will be preferred. With five generations of communications technology working side-by-side, it might take a long time to determine which tools are best.

According to Esther Dyson, Chairperson of EDventure Holdings, investor, author of the book *Release 2.0* (1998) and a conference producer herself, conventions and meetings have always had great value and always will. First, effective conversations require the full attention of participants. That does not happen when people watch webcasts. Second, the best meetings occur when participants know they will be called on to contribute, not when they face a dark screen. The knowledge that someone has paid money and invested time to be part of a gathering matters a great deal. In the end, being physically present matters for the quality of learning and interaction. Even though the numerous technology options available, including videoconferencing, webcasting and podcasting, have changed whether and how conventions and meetings occur, people desire face-to-face personal contact. For these reasons, many knowledgeable industry insiders predict that the meetings industry will not contract, but flourish.

Sustainability and US Trends

Few newscasts today are completed without a reference to environmental issues such as global warming, carbon emissions and the sustainability of the planet. These issues now are the mainstream in the conventions and meetings industry in the USA. Craig T. Davis, Director of Convention Sales with the Greater Pittsburgh Convention and Visitor's Bureau, the first LEED-certified, environmentally friendly convention centre in the USA, has offered four reasons for taking action regarding the environment (Russell, 2008):

- Communities increasingly expect it of us. Our activities in the meetings industry are highly visible wherever we operate, attracting a lot of attention from the local community. We are expected to take leadership in implementing more programs where the good of the community is at stake. At the same time, because we often work in governmentally owned facilities, there is pressure to set a good example.
- The second reason is that our clients increasingly want us to be more ecologically considerate because their own members want it. Environmental concern has shifted from being a 'good cause' to an expectation. People today simply assume that environmental concerns are being addressed because they have become a fact of life in the United States. For this reason, the members of the organizations we host are applying pressure on meeting planners to address the role that environmental and sustainability considerations play in their conventions and meetings. In turn, this will make sustainability and the record of performance of convention centers and other meeting venues an important decision factor for clients.
- The third reason sustainability will become an important factor is that it will contribute to cost-effective operations, especially in areas such as energy usage. One of the key points of the sustainability concept is that industries must manage long term costs if they are to be successful in the long run, given that the costs of energy and waste disposal are among the greatest and least predictable for meeting planners, facility managers, and suppliers. As is often the case, action gets taken only when costs rise significantly.
- Finally, environmental and sustainability issues likely will become a matter of legal concern as communities and governments around the world strengthen regulation regarding how businesses will be required to manage their environmental and social impacts. Just as issues like smoking are firmly planted in the forefront of social issues in the United States, after decades in the shadows, we can expect best environmental practice in the meetings industry to be a legal requirement as public opinion evolves.

Consumers and citizens consider these problems to be beyond the capacity of government alone to solve. The public expects corporations to contribute significantly to solve these problems as well as resolve problems related to diversity, child labour and human rights. People want to know what is behind the brand and are beginning to vote with their wallets. They increasingly prefer to do business with companies that do the right thing.

Climate change and the price of energy will determine how people convene. For the first time, US companies are voluntarily asking how to decrease their carbon footprint and stay in line with their social responsibility mandate. The logistics of moving exhibits and people are enormous. So, the conventions and meetings industry must lead in energy efficiency and alternative energies with government providing incentives.

Charles D. Yuska, President and CEO of the Packaging Machinery Manufacturers' Institute, considers globalization to be one of the two most significant trends for his industry

(C.D. Yuska, Washington, 2008, personal communication). Technology is the other significant trend. The USA is the largest packaging market in the world, but Proctor & Gamble is building more manufacturing facilities outside the USA because of the shift of business overseas. The packaging machinery industry historically has purchased materials and supplies and done business locally as much as possible. Given the exodus of manufacturing from the USA, Yuska predicts that trade shows also will move from the USA to international venues.

There will still be face-to-face meetings because people are social animals. Virtual meetings will be part of the mix but not replace the intimacy of social engagement. One can go to an online university or participate in a video podcast, but lose the intangible benefits of learning from other participants and networking with peers after the event to develop the long-term relationships that interaction makes possible. Engagement and education will remain important, and people will continue to gather for meetings. Time-starved people will seek information and experiences of just the right type at the right time, making the peak experiences more meaningful.

Until recently, conferences in the USA were organized in the least sustainable ways in terms of the use of paper and plastic goods, fuel and food. Deirdre Irwin Ross, Director of Conference Services for the American Library Association, learned that the waste that was recycled at the association's most recent annual meetings was subtracted from the garbage that had to be removed (D. Irwin Ross, Washington, 2008, personal communication). If they recycled 1 ton of material, they had to pay for only 9 tons. They also are reviewing the conference schedule for future meetings. If the meeting day is organized with more attention to reducing the demand for bussing, the association can save fuel and help the environment. On the other hand, the Produce Marketing Association's Kent E. Allaway has found it difficult to recycle cardboard boxes, often damaged in transit, and the trash generated by 800 exhibitors and 16,000 attendees at their meetings (K.E. Allaway, Washington, 2008, personal communication). Many association members are changing to reusable packaging.

Charles Yuska of the Packaging Machinery Manufacturers' Institute believes that US companies often are not 'walking the walk' when it comes to sustainability (C.D. Yuska, Washington, 2008, personal communication). After a show, there are piles of trash and cardboard. Trade shows in Europe are ahead of US shows: exhibitors are required to sort the refuse they leave behind. Yuska believes that meetings professionals, facility staff and cleaning contractors must work in partnership, if real sustainability is to be realized in the meetings industry in the USA.

The five trends – globalization, technology, the empowered consumer, diversity and demographics and social responsibility and the environment – along with climate change, will affect people's ability to attend meetings. Curbs on travel, areas of the world inundated by water or facing drought, crumbling infrastructure, and the provision of power and water in cities in the USA and elsewhere will influence how and where meetings are held and change commerce drastically. Destination cities must change how they do business, but meeting planners and attendees will resist. It is important to consider worldwide conditions that may impact us and the industry 5 years into the future. An important resource about future thinking for every student of convention and meeting management is the Hospitality 2010 report (Deloitte Touche Tohmatsu & the Preston Robert Tisch Center for Hospitality, Tourism and Sports Management at New York University, 2005).

Summary

This chapter addresses a number of important issues, such as globalization, the translation of shows from one country and culture to another, the effects of consumer power, technology and the environment. Many more topics merit attention, including financial performance trends, competition, the importance of enhancing education and training programmes, and the need to attract and retain staff members with optimal personal qualities and skills, but space precludes addressing them.

The importance of face-to-face contact and personal networking will continue to sustain the industry. People are social, gregarious creatures by nature, and conventions and meetings are a wonderful way to bring people together for communicating and sharing experiences, for learning and memorable social encounters.

To those working in this dynamic industry, meeting planners of every sort and suppliers, the industry offers variety, excitement, opportunities for creativity, travel, fulfilment, enjoyment, challenges and changes, opportunities to build friendships around the world, and more. Few other industries can offer as much. Meetings industry strategist Joan L. Eisenstodt has written about 'the warmth and personality of the meetings phenomenon'. She refers to the 'skill and devotion, the generosity of sharing and the pride of service of those who produce meetings' as a strength of the industry (Hoyle, 2002). Meetings have even saved the world from disaster once or twice. Meetings conducted by the Kennedy presidential administration in the early 1960s headed off a confrontation between the USA and the Soviet Union. Conventions and meetings may not have the power to ensure world peace, but they do provide frameworks for discussion, uniting peoples worldwide, sharing ideas and information for the benefit of all. Whether the terms 'convention' and 'meeting' will be the most appropriate words to describe gatherings of the future is a topic for debate at a future meeting.

Key Questions

1. Discuss the impacts of globalization and international participation on the American hotel industry.
2. Identify the key relationships between sustainability and industry trends.
3. Why have organizations shifted their focus from supply to demand?

References

ASAE (American Society of Association Executives) (2008) Available at: http://www.asaecenter.org/PublicationsResources/modelslist.cfm?ItemNumber=12302 (accessed 6 May 2008).

The Brookings Institution (2006) Two Steps Back: City and Suburban Poverty Trends 1999–2005. Available at: http://www.brookings.edu/reports/2006/12poverty_berube.aspx (accessed 10 May 2008).

CIC (Convention Industry Council) (2004) Economic impact report. Available at: http://www.conventionindustry.org/aboutcic/pr/pr_091305.htm (accessed 2 April 2008).

Deloitte Touche Tohmatsu & the Preston Robert Tisch Center for Hospitality Tourism and Sports Management at New York University (2005) Hospitality 2010 report. Available at: http://www.Deloitte.com/dtt/cda/doc/content/be_hospitality_2010.pdf (accessed 6 May 2008).

Dyson, E. (1998) *Release 2.0*. Broadway Publishing, New York.

Hoyle, L.H. (2002) *Event Marketing: How to Successfully Promote Events, Festivals, Conventions, and Expositions*. Wiley Publishing, New York.

ICCA (International Congress & Convention Association) (2008) Available at: http://www.iccaworld.com/ (accessed 10 May 2008).

Russell, M. (2008) How would your meeting be ecolabeled? *Convene* 22(3), 72–74.

Union of International Associations (2006) *International Meeting Statistics for the Year 2005*. Union of International Associations, Ixelles, Belgium.

14 Planning Models for Creating Sustainable Events Management

S. Saeed-Khan and P. Clements
Leeds Metropolitan University, Leeds, UK

This chapter focuses on the planning and implementation of events and critically reviews and discusses whether current planning models explicitly or implicitly allow for the consideration and adoption of sustainable event management practices. It is within this context that generic and specific issues related to event sustainability can be discussed. Suggestions may be made as to how sustainable management and development may be more explicitly applied to current event planning models.

Chapter outline

- Introduction
- Current Sustainable Planning Models
- Event Planning Models – an Overview
- Effective Planning Models
- The Stages of Event Planning
- A New Sustainability Model
- Summary
- Key Questions

Introduction

Many events incur long planning and implementation time but also operate within changing and turbulent environments socially, economically and environmentally. As a consequence, planning takes on a critical role in ensuring that principles are adopted within a planning framework, and in recent years many of those principles have begun to include the concept of sustainable practice and environmental engagement. While event managers must maintain a certain level of flexibility within their planning, as each event is different, there must be a framework to assist in the achievement of key principles that can be applied to all or most events. Equally vital is long-term planning to ensure that changing market and world conditions – cultural, political, economic, lingual, meteorological and demographic – are not only taken into account to achieve successful event outcomes, but also that the event itself does not result in 'unsustainability' or indeed impact negatively on these factors (Torkildsen, 1999; Allen, 2002; Bowdin *et al.*, 2006). There is continuous debate as to whether these models incorporate, explicitly or implicitly, sustainable practices. Nevertheless, the proliferation of planning models proposed goes some way to reflect not just a *post hoc* summary of how events are planned and implemented but as frameworks to guide event practitioners, managers and academics as to the most effective and efficient way of producing events.

Current Sustainable Planning Models

There are many different planning models currently in existence that touch on varying aspects of sustainability, particularly in industries like construction and project management. However, they touch only on those aspects that are specific to their particular industry. The model developed for this chapter is intended to be all-encompassing, with the hope that it can be applied not only to every event, but also at every stage of the event planning process.

Event planning models have yet to explicitly embrace sustainability and it is suggested that by synthesizing or incorporating more generic sustainable development model elements, event planners may be better placed to ensure that sustainability is an integral part of event planning, implementation and evaluation. Sustainable development models have attempted to meet the challenge of not only defining and understanding the concepts of sustainability, but also offering insights into the relationships between the three 'Es' – economy, ecology and equality.

Grosskurth and Rotmans (2005) discuss how 'sustainability-related issues that touch a wide range of disciplines' can be developed into strategies for development. Although pertaining more to policy making, there are certain issues that can be applied to more specific planning contexts such as events. Principles of sustainability are plural and multidimensional, and as such any decisions are forged in complexity and subjectivity. Notwithstanding, there are planning models that provide a sense of objectivity. In essence, the models outlining the various dimensions of sustainability are numerous and slightly varied. The Triple Bottom Line Model (Fig. 14.1) describes aspects of social, environmental and economic care, while the Sustainability Ellipse (Fig. 14.2) illustrates the dependency, relationship and flows (stresses and benefits) between people and biosystem.

The Sustainability Pyramid (Fig. 14.3) identifies the process for sustainable development through five steps: determining a need; examining current practice; suggesting improvements based on the results of examination; implementing a plan; and proceeding.

All three of the above models represent varying approaches to sustainability; however, they aim to do this by focusing on different characteristics of the planning process – be it interactions between humans and their surroundings, different social, economic or environmental outputs, or indeed through legislation and policy. However, it is clear that with each of these models only one particular approach can be taken for the process to work.

In other models inter-linkages such as care, access, democracy and eco-efficiency show the

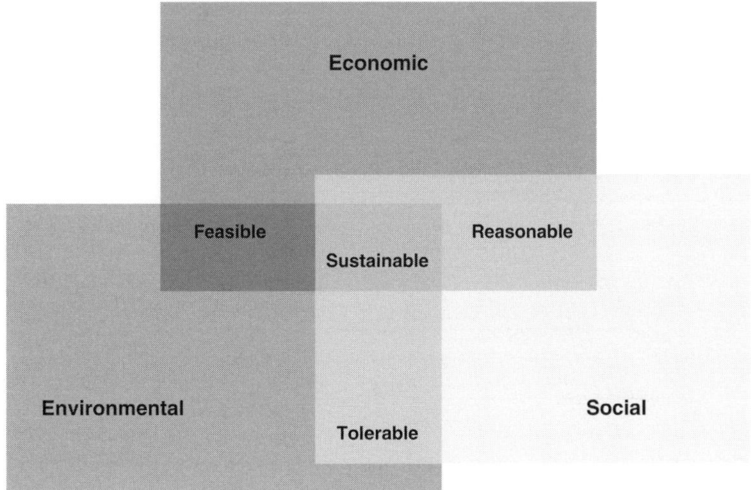

Fig. 14.1. Triple Bottom Line Model. (Adapted from Burkhardt, 2004.)

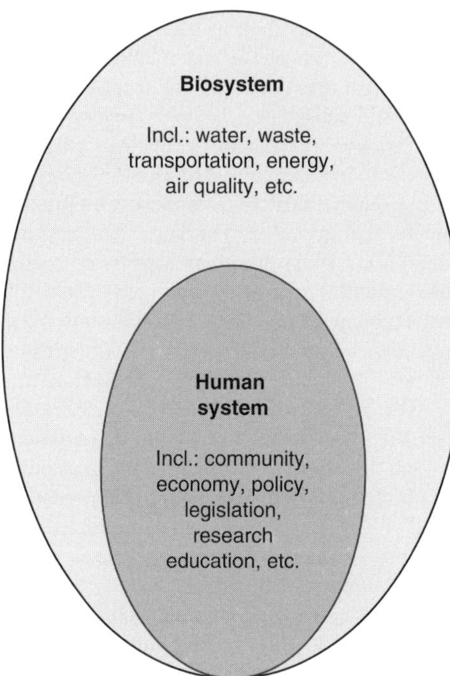

Fig. 14.2. Sustainability Ellipse. (Adapted from IUCN, 1994.)

relationship between dimensions that could translate into operational policy. Imperatives or priorities for each of the areas or domains require indicators to measure success. Further models visually assess a system's current condition compared with an optimal condition before making recommendations for improvement. However, in most models, the basics remain the same – the output one hopes to achieve is a more sustainable level of activity. It is how this is achieved that differs and, as stated previously, it can be difficult to find a model that is entirely inclusive. This is a necessity in events due to the wide impact that events have on the supply chain and its management, as well as the varied stakeholders involved in the production of each event, regardless of size or scope.

One particularly comprehensive model is the SCENE Model (Fig. 14.4). The SCENE (Social, Environmental and Economic) Model identifies three capital domains that contain a number of 'stocks' that can then be described or broken down into components or characteristics in quantitative, qualitative, functional and spatial terms. Indicators used to measure these stocks can be both quantitative and qualitative but must be communicable to all stakeholders in a simple yet effective manner. In an events context this may be income generated by a local music event but may also detail who received the income (distribution), for what purpose (food and beverage) and the spatial or geographic limits (local suppliers within a 5-mile radius of the event). The SCENE Model's examination of these stocks makes it one approach that is particularly relevant to events management, due in simple part to the wide-ranging impact that events have on the larger supply chain.

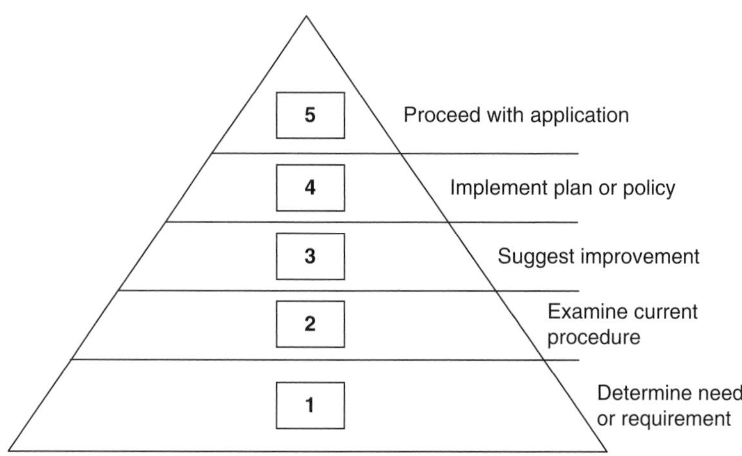

Fig. 14.3. Sustainability Pyramid. (Adapted from Atkisson, not dated.)

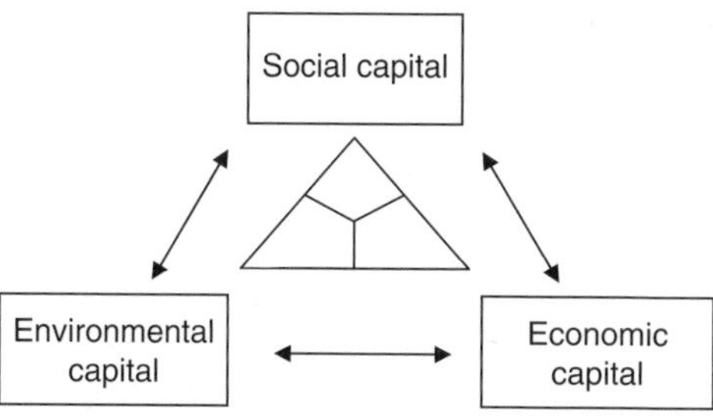

Fig. 14.4. The SCENE Model.

In an events context, an environmental stock such as waste disposal and recycling may be measured in terms of quantity as tonnage, quality as type of waste and recycling process, function in terms of what recycling provides, and spatial considerations in terms of geographic area affected or included. It is vital to lay equal emphasis and importance on each of the domains and to identify the relationship and flow between each stock. Flows within and between the stocks of the domains can be quite complex and can best be described as a continual process of input and output flow. Conversely, as an event grows, there may be a positive or negative growth in all three domains. Alternatively growth in one area (e.g. economic growth) may come at a price to one of the other domains (e.g. environmental). Equally, the cost of protecting the environment may show a strengthening in the environmental domain but a weakening in the economic domain.

Naturally, the issue of how information is gathered and used can be an issue in itself. It is recognized that an event may have many and varied stakeholders in terms of interest and power, where a commonly agreed indicator and measurement may be an issue in itself in terms of current relevance and importance. The issues of 'normativeness' and 'subjectiveness' are not for discussion here, but how and who sets the norms and performance indicators is a philosophical issue and one that may lead to a variety of planning strategies being offered. However, in order to establish any kind of comprehensive strategy, consideration of these indicators must be made when establishing a record of information, ideally early on in the process.

The monitoring and evaluation of indicators should take place throughout the whole planning process with equal emphasis placed on all domains. Trade-offs or flows must be mapped and made explicit, allowing open and transparent choices. However, the influences on an indicator may be numerous and complex. For example, the use of a water slide supplier impacts on all domains in terms of economic (cost of supplier), environmental (waste management practices) and social (local usage post-event). With specific respect to event planning, the following model suggests where and how these sustainable development models can be applied and/or adapted to the different generic stages outlined earlier.

Event Planning Models – an Overview

Accepting that events can be defined in a number of ways that reflect purpose, function, size, etc. (Jago and Shaw, 1998), it is understood that event management is a discipline that takes traditional management principles and places them in a context that holds a unique combination of characteristics. According to Silvers (2008), event management:

> encompasses the assessment, definition, acquisition, allocation, direction, control, and analysis of time, finances, people, products, services, and other resources to achieve objectives... including researching, planning, organising, implementing, controlling, and evaluating an event's design, activities, and production.

Clearly the size of the event and scope of management will affect the degree, level and influence an individual may have in terms of the adoption and practice of sustainable principles.

By definition, planning provides a roadmap to ensure that stated goals and objectives are achieved in the most effective and efficient manner. However, 'not all events are well planned and organised, including many of considerable stature and significance' (Torkildsen, 1999). Failure in planning, according to Catherwood and Van Rirk (1992), can detrimentally impinge on the organizers, consumers and stakeholders of major events and, without planning, the achievement of objectives through the creation of defined pathways may not occur. Watt suggested in 1998 that planning is 'determining what has to be done and how'; but more importantly, according to Pearce and Robinson (1989), in order to be considered effective, managers must have an understanding of what they plan to achieve – the overall goal. It is not only about whether the planning process acknowledges that it is responsible for the sustainable means to reach those ends, but also in the setting of the sustainable ends themselves. Accordingly, stages of planning and how and where sustainable practices are embodied within the goals and objectives of event planning are crucial.

Event planning models have been greatly influenced by project management authors, and Maylor (1999) suggests that there are a number of common stages embodied within them. Although it is recognized (Bowdin *et al.*, 2006) that without a plan team members have little or no idea of their objectives and no means by which to measure their success in achieving them, this does not mean a reduction in flexibility and 'good' planning should allow a speedy response to environmental changes – a positive impact from a sustainability point of view. However, Masterman (2004) is more critical and claims that planning models tend to be supported by research that is more reflective or appropriate to short-term benefits. These views may not be contradictory but instead may reflect differences in the appropriateness of planning models in embodying sustainability. By evaluating the stages that planning models go though, management can identify where sustainable practices may be incorporated and where there may be inadequacies not only in practical application but also in the process itself.

The Stages of Event Planning

A synthesis of existing planning models, including those of Betteridge (1997) and Veal (2002), to identify stages of the various planning models, is outlined below.

The following analysis identifies common themes at each stage and comments on any potential negative issues that arise regarding sustainable principles. It should be noted that these models tend to focus on mega-events, which implies in some instances processes that may not be as common or distinct for smaller events. By definition, mega-events have a potentially greater impact from economic, environmental and social points of view. It does not, however, assume that smaller events do not have any impact or that they do not consider sustainability issues. This is not to suggest that the planning models advocate non-sustainable practice but that, by providing a template for practice, they may to some extent allow for or encourage non-sustainable practices to become the preferred or easier option.

The table proposed as a model for sustainable events management attempts to take all of these stages into account. Because of the nature of events management, and the fact that there are very rarely compartmentalized sections within the planning process, some aspects will appear repetitive, yet the reality is that many of the aspects within that process do impact on more than one stage as outlined below.

Stage one: feasibility and research

In the initial stages, whether an event is to be bid for in response to a brief or whether it is an internally generated event, it is acknowledged that research, feasibility as a result of environmental scanning (competitor analysis, PESTEL and/or SWOT analysis) and the setting of aims, objectives and a vision within a concept that may or may not result in proceeding to the next stage, will take place.

This stage has a huge impact in terms of sustainability, given that decisions to proceed with an event are based on information search, evaluation and objectives that may shape the scale and type of event as well as the impacts the event may have. These can be seen in Table 14.1.

Cities bidding for the Olympic Games have often stressed the positive economic impacts of hosting the Games in terms of provision of new venues, infrastructure and increased tourism that, in hindsight, often reflect political agendas and the interests of lobbyists, rather than identifying the true cost in terms of taxpayer burden, displacement of local communities and ongoing use of facilities post-Games. These issues are often greatly overestimated, and the relatively low economic impact (investment and tourism) on regions outside the host city is often neglected.

Table 14.1. Stages and issues relating to sustainable principles.

Stage	Issues that relate to sustainable principles
One	Focus on or prioritizing of ROI objectives rather than wider societal and environmental objectives
	HR sourcing resulting in importation of labour rather than use of local labour market due to financial and skill limitations
	Suppliers used are based on criteria that relate to cost rather than sustainable business practice
	Emphasis on setting operational standards that meet minimum standards, rather than exceeding standards or benchmarks of sustainable practice
	Sourcing of external financing that reduces the amount of reinvestment in future events and local businesses
	Lack of clear and meaningful indicators that relate to/reflect sustainable objectives both in terms of final event and ongoing implementation, e.g. resource usage
	Recruitment of 'managers' who do not share or understand any sustainability remit
Two	Focus on or prioritizing of ROI objectives rather than wider societal and environmental objectives
	HR sourcing resulting in importation of labour rather than use of local labour market due to financial and skill limitations
	Suppliers used are based on criteria that relate to cost rather than sustainable business practice
	Emphasis on setting operational standards that meet minimum standards, rather than exceeding standards or benchmarks of sustainable practice
	Sourcing of external financing that reduces the amount of reinvestment in future events and local businesses
	Lack of clear and meaningful indicators that relate to/reflect sustainable objectives both in terms of final event and ongoing implementation, e.g. resource usage
	Recruitment of 'managers' who do not share or understand any sustainability remit
Three	Practices (e.g. marketing) that reflect over-use or dependence on non-renewable resources
	Appearance and image of the event result not only in minimal and hidden unsustainable practices, but also resources being diverted to non-core areas such as sponsor signage
	Focus on efficient use of part-time and temporary labour results in a focus on ROI activities rather than secondary sustainable activities, e.g. litter collection
	Branding as driven by major and influential stakeholders such as sponsors results in wastage and unnecessary packaging
	Demands of broadcasters and media divert focus away from local participation and involvement to that of celebrities and media-friendly schedules
Four	Event organizers are restricted on time and resources to undertake comprehensive evaluations, resulting in the continual replication of events regardless of practice and impact. Goldblatt (2002) admitted that many leading event management professionals disclosed that having to spend more time on the research and evaluation of events (often time that is unavailable) resulted in limited and meaningless evaluation
	Changes to events tend to take place as a result of either bottom-line changes or complaints (i.e. evaluation focuses on ROI and/or those who have the loudest voice)
	Changes to implementation practices as a result of ongoing process monitoring are ignored so long as the event is delivered on time and meets major stakeholder needs
	Process monitoring to ensure sustainable practice is often minimal and subject to emphasis on the meeting of financial goals rather than sustainable practice itself
	Long-term legacies, although stated, are hard to critically evaluate post-event and are subject to political interest and agendas
	Long-term legacies are poorly evaluated due to the lack of funding and resources necessary for the implementation of broader longitudinal studies
	Management of legacies is often ignored
	Difficulties in defining and measuring concepts such as community cohesion, health and well-being, inclusion

ROI, return on investment; HR, human resources.

Stage two: planning and coordination

Following the decision to proceed, preliminary plans are made, specifically in the areas of finance, marketing and human resources. Subsequent implementation requirements are then made in terms of organizational structure, personnel and budgets. It may be argued that there is a blurring of the latter points into the next stage – actual implementation and coordination of the event – where detailed planning, financial budgeting and control, policies, rules and regulations are discussed and monitored. Accepting that this stage can vary considerably in terms of complexity and timeframe, and can change in response to external and internal factors as well as the proximity to the event date, it is assumed that this stage only involves initial planning.

Stage three: implementation of event

This stage involves physical implementation, coordination and the event itself. With an increase in events and greater competition for the event consumer, there is ever-greater pressure for event organizers to be cost-effective and differentiate their event from the competition through marketing and image, rather than solely through functionality. Additionally, differing key indicators relating to sustainable impacts can be found, as shown in Table 14.1. For example, reliance on a major car sponsor to underwrite the costs at a hallmark food and wine festival that is traditionally held at a winery on the outskirts of the nearest town would mean that the event is focused on satisfying non-local corporate guests and the lack of public transport would encourage car use among attendees rather than more sustainable means of travel. Many sporting events are now built around media and broadcasting schedules to the extent that performance and spectator access have been compromised.

Stage four: breakdown, evaluation and legacy

This stage considers the wind up/shut down of an event, evaluation and feedback, and divestment and legacy of the event. The level and scale of legacy will naturally vary in respect of the event (e.g. the Olympics versus a community event). Mega sporting events such as the XVII Commonwealth Games in Manchester, large-scale events such as 'Street Athletics' and small-scale events such as the Sport England/ ASA project 'Everyday Swim' had the following respective key aims: 'inclusion', 'inspiration and motivation' and 'confidence-building leading to participation'. These aims raise the following questions: how is 'inspiration' defined and measured? What or which measurement tools could be most indicative of these: quantitative and/or qualitative? What timeframe should be set? What are the geographical parameters?

Clearly all of the aforementioned factors are not directly attributable to event planning models but may result due to the process that is recommended by event management theorists – a case of 'not what they say', rather more a case of what is not said or is ignored by event practitioners. Bearing this in mind, the next section looks at current sustainable development models and attempts to synthesize what is recommended as best practice, examining issues related to best practice in event planning and management.

A New Sustainability Model

All of the models recognize domains in varying degrees of complexity and relationship. However, there are a number of crucial issues that apply not just generically to sustainable development but specifically to events. First, event planning models have well-defined stages where issues of sustainability in terms of the distinct but interlinked economic, environmental and social domains may be considered. These may be subdivided into specific components with specific characteristics and indicators that may be used to measure or evaluate them relative to stated objectives. However, it is the implications of reaching or achieving these components and the impact that has on other domains or even within the domain that is the issue.

The Sustainable Event Planning Model (Table 14.2) notes in very broad terms in its final column the implications of certain components or issues on the other domains. It could be suggested that the difficulty lies in some of

Table 14.2. Sample Sustainable Event Planning Model.

	Primary domain					Characteristics					
Stage	Econ.	Enviro.	Social	Issue	Components	Quant.	Qual.	Func.	Spat.	Indicators	Domain implications
Feasibility and research	✔			Economic viability	Event profitability	✔		✔		Revenue/cost analysis	Environmental, social
					Cash flow	✔				Cash flow forecast	Environmental
					Stakeholder investment	✔			✔	Investment source?	Social, economic
			✔	Community involvement	Consultation process	✔	✔	✔	✔	Profile of decision makers	Economic
Planning and coordination			✔	Supply chain management	Local suppliers versus outside the region	✔			✔	Location/proximity	Economic
		✔		Supply chain management	Sustainability policy	✔	✔	✔		Record keeping, word of mouth	Social
Implementation of event		✔		Waste management	Recycling	✔	✔	✔	✔	Waste audit	Economic, social
	✔			Economic viability	Event profitability	✔	✔			Ticket receipts	Social
			✔	Labour force	Event employees	✔	✔	✔	✔	Employee profile	Economic
Breakdown, evaluation and legacy			✔	Legacy management	Community usage of facilities	✔	✔	✔	✔	Facility users by demographic/ geographic profile	Economic
	✔			Evaluation	Method of evaluation	✔	✔		✔	Evaluation method chosen	Environmental

the less quantifiable impacts where measurement is difficult and open to debate. Cost–benefit analysis has attempted to place a value on non-monetary variables, and more recently multidimensional indicators such as Gross National Happiness (GNH), the Human Development Index (HDI), Ecological Footprint (EF) and the Happy Planet Index (HPI) have gone some way to show or measure the interconnectedness between the domains. A critical discussion of these, and how they may be adapted at a more micro level and specifically adapted as holistic indicators and measurement tools for events, may be the way forward rather than taking each indicator in isolation.

The model illustrates how, at different stages of the event planning process, sustainability under the three main areas might be charted. It should be noted that the examples given do not represent a definitive list, but illustrate the relationship, flow and implications of each event element as it relates to a particular event. Naturally, as each event is different in size, scope, etc., the elements that will be taken into consideration at each stage will vary.

The model breaks down the event planning process into the four generic stages discussed previously. Primary domains (economic, environmental and social) are broken down into their relevant issues and then subdivided into their applicable components. Characteristics are then identified in terms of whether the component is, for example, a quantifiable commodity, such as revenue or attendance figures; qualitative characteristics may include type of waste collected as part of a recycling scheme or refer to the profile of members of decision-making committees. Functional characteristics might refer to a supplier's ability to supply staging that is fit for purpose, thereby impacting on an organization's decision to use them, while spatial characteristics may refer to attendees' geographic origin or the event's source of investment. Indicators are guides as to how and where these components can be measured.

The final column shows inter- and intra-domain implications. For example, under the primary domain 'economic', a component of the issue of economic viability may be stakeholder investment. The choice of investment source will have repercussions on the locality in that non-local investors may not reinvest profits within the local community. Alternatively, a decision to fund the event using local investors may impact positively on the local community but may have negative (intra-domain) implications if the cost of borrowing is higher than that offered by non-local investors. It is important to understand that certain primary domain implications may also result in additional implications to that domain (e.g. economic results in more economic, etc.) and not just across the other domains.

This model is by no means definitive or prescriptive but should encourage debate and offer at least a template by which event planners can explicitly consider issues of sustainability at each stage of the planning process, thereby taking a holistic approach to ensure true sustainability.

Summary

As discussed, sustainable planning is fast becoming a requirement in all industries, including event management. Due to the diverse nature of events it should not be considered appropriate or feasible to plan sustainability by looking at one area alone. The model proposed above (Table 14.2) will allow event practitioners to map areas they need to consider individually and per event, while simultaneously taking implications into account as holistically as possible. Every event has impacts that range far beyond simply the event ground and the event stakeholders. The waves of influence that ripple forth from each event run all along the supply chain and this, in turn, impacts not just the environment, but also the social capital and economic capital of the immediate region as well as further afield. This model attempts to take into account as many of these ripples as possible so that the event may be planned in a truly sustainable manner.

The model can also be utilized in conjunction with the new British Standard, BS 8901:2007 (BSI, 2007), which was launched publicly in November 2007 specifically for the events industry. It may assist event organizations in ensuring compliance with the Standard, as one can very easily draw parallels with the three-phase implementation of the Standard as it is currently set forth and the impacts outlined in the model above.

Increasingly, clients are demanding that more responsible, sustainable practice be a benchmark of the event planning process. As more and more industries incorporate their own environmental practice, they are demanding it of their partners. If sustainable practice is to become an inherent part of the event planning process, then the full impact of a particular event must be examined at every stage of development. It is only by examining each stage that good practice can truly be incorporated as the norm at every level of the business. It is hoped that practitioners will utilize the suggested model to plan events in the future and make sustainability an embedded part of their practice.

Key Questions

1. Identify ways in which impacts can be measured (key performance indicators) so that an objective evaluation can be made of events. How could you place a value on non-quantifiable variables?

2. Discuss how different stakeholders may have different perspectives on the costs, benefits and values related to an event. Give examples of different stakeholders and different events.

3. Using an event of your own choice as a case study, identify where and how negative impacts could or were minimized at each stage of the planning and implementation process with respect to the local community.

References

Allen, J., O'Toole, W., McDonnell, I. and Harris, R. (2002) *Festival and Special Event Management*, 2nd edn. John Wiley and Sons, Sydney.

Atkisson, A. (not dated) Natural Edge Project Pyramid of Sustainable Development. Available at: http://www.naturaledgeproject.net/ESSPCLP-Intro_to_SD-Lecture12.aspx (accessed 7 August 2008).

Betteridge, D. (1997) *Event Management in Leisure and Tourism*. Hodder & Stoughton Educational, London.

Bowdin, G., McDonnell, I., Allen, J., Harris, R. and O'Toole, W. (2006) Events Management. Butterworth-Heinemann, Oxford, UK.

BSI (2007) *BS 8901:2007 Specification for a sustainable event management system with guidance for use developed*. British Standards Institution, London.

Burkhardt, H. (2004) Universal Values and the Three Pillars of Sustainability: Foundations of Sustainability Education. Available at: http://www.cafeweltgeist.org/ihtec/Resources/UniversalValuesandtheThreePillarsofSustainability.doc (accessed 7 August 2008).

Catherwood, D.W. and Van Rirk, R.L. (1992) *The Complete Guide to Special Event Management: Business Insights, Financial Advice and Successful Strategies from Ernst and Young, Advisors to the Olympics, the Emmy Awards and the PGA Tour*. John Wiley and Sons, New York.

Goldblatt, J. (2002) *Special Events Best Practices in Modern Management*, 2nd ed. John Wiley and Sons, New York.

Grosskurth, J. and Rotmans, J. (2005) The SCENE model: getting a grip on sustainable development in policy making. *Environment, Development and Sustainability* 7(1), 135–151.

IUCN (1994) IDRC: Measuring Progress Toward Sustainability – New Tools and Methods. Available at: http://archive.idrc.ca/Nayudamma/progress_e.html (accessed 7 August 2008).

Jago, L.K. and Shaw, R.N. (1998) A conceptual and differential framework. *Festival Management and Event Tourism* 5(1/2), 21–32.

Masterman, G. (2004) *Strategic Sports Event Management: An International Approach*. Elsevier Butterworth-Heinemann, London.

Maylor, H. (1999) *Project Management*, 2nd edn. Financial Times Management, London.

Pearce, J.A. and Robinson, R.D. (1989) *Strategic Management: Formulation, Implementation and Control of Competitive Strategy*, 7th edn. Villanova University Press, Villanova, Pennsylvania.

Silvers, J. (2008) Event Management Body of Knowledge Project. Available at: http://www.juliasilvers.com/embok.htm (accessed 27 May 2008).

Torkildsen, G. (1999) *Leisure and Recreation Management*, 4th edn. E & F N Spon, London.

Veal, A.J. (2002) *Leisure and Tourism Policy and Planning*, 2nd edn. CAB International, Wallingford, UK.

Watt, D.C. (1998) *Event Management in Leisure and Tourism*. Addison Wesley Longman, New York.

15 Sustainable Planning for Community Venues

J. Mendes, M. Guerreiro and P. Valle
University of Algarve, Faro, Portugal

This chapter analyses various important issues concerning the implementation of a sustainable and strategic management process for community venues and proposes concrete approaches. The chapter focuses essentially on the issue of maximizing community venues for cultural purposes. The chapter also looks to find ways to optimize the satisfaction of those involved in the service and consumer process of cultural products, as well as the value placed on experience resulting from public events and organization.

Chapter outline

- Introduction
- Sustainability Development within Community Venues
- Modelling Sustainable and Strategic Stakeholder Management for Community Venues
- Strategic Planning Process
- Strategies for Achieving Customer Loyalty and New Customers
- Communication and Brand Positioning Strategies
- Sponsorship Management Strategies
- Summary
- Key Questions

Introduction

In an environment shaped by the phenomenon of globalization and increasing competition in the business field, the cultural sector has to meet new challenges that demand from the community new ways of thinking and being, both in terms of the management paradigm as well as the stakeholder relationship. The events industry is currently witnessing a generalized global trend in terms of strategic development and implementation, establishing a clear direction in satisfying public needs and expectations while ensuring a balanced management of diverse resources, objectives and interests.

The implementation of sustainable and strategic stakeholder management for community venues, based on the involvement and participation of various cultural agents in the decision process and recommendations of new approaches and methodologies, allows the definition of common objectives. These objectives include developing new forms of cooperation, knowledge networking on cultural needs and public segment expectations, integrated planning of cultural resources and rigorous monitoring of achieved results.

This chapter discusses some questions in the community venue field in terms of how to develop and implement a management approach in order to optimize the balance between managerial vision and artistic vision.

Sustainability Development within Community Venues

It is inevitable to face a 'dramatic change in the functions and functioning of arts organizations' (Kotler and Scheff, 1997, p. 23). Despite the general 'acknowledge[ment] that arts organizations are undergoing considerable changes in funding, governance and competition, only recently have basic concepts of management been applied to problems within the arts sector' (Cray *et al.*, 2007, p. 295). This is not a consensual or a specific field. 'The artistic vision for the organization usually conflicts with the requirements of other managerial functions' (Cray *et al.*, 2007, p. 297). However, the change is inevitable. In the last few years, cultural organizations have seen their governmental grants reduced. Thus they are more dependent on donations, the income from events and volunteers. Under this scenario it is essential to be different, to be unique and to develop creative cultural proposals. However, to be successful, it is important to go beyond this. It is vital to adopt management principles that ensure the success of cultural organizations and events. As Sicca and Zan (2005) have noted, marketing and fundraisers need to adopt greater professionalism.

To meet the needs, desires and expectations of all stakeholders is essential in any management process. In adopting basic marketing principles, companies must identify the market needs (and all stakeholders) and, once identified, look to satisfy these needs. However, it is important to note that cultural products are special products and must be managed in such a way as to preserve their characteristics. DiMaggio and Stenberg (1985) refer to the limitations in arts organization. Kotler and Scheff (1997, p. 17) argue 'this purely market-centred philosophy is inconsistent with what the concept of art is all about'. For Diggles (1986), the primary goal of marketing in the arts field is to attract an appropriate number of visitors and place at their disposal an array of cultural events, a key strategy in the management process. From this perspective, other strategic elements involve the cultural product itself. For Colbert (1994, p. 13), the goal is to invite consumers to appreciate a product that is special by its nature. Marketing 'does not tell an artist how to create a work of art. (...) the product leads to the public and not the inverse'. Colbert (1994, p. 14) regards cultural marketing as:

> the art of reaching those market segments likely to be interested in the product while adjusting to the product the variables of the mix to put the product in contact with a sufficient number of consumers and to reach the objectives consistent with the mission of the cultural enterprise.

This approach observes financial revenues as a critical factor for success. According to Colbert (1994), cultural products are specialty goods. It is a very complex product that, in the arts field, is performed in some place, i.e. the venue.

Aspects that represent the artistic product as special within the context of increasing competition and limited resources require 'the development of well-trained, experienced arts managers for top-level positions, as well as for specialists in audience development and fundraising' (Kotler and Scheff, 1997, p. 22). As noted by these authors:

> many arts managers and marketers have learned their skills on the job and lack the necessary education in modern management and marketing theory and techniques to effectively analyse, strategise, plan, implement, and evaluate.

This complex and new management paradigm for culture and the arts takes off from a systematic knowledge of the environment and takes into account all stakeholders. Under this scenario, the development of a process leading to sustainable and strategic stakeholder management for community venues requires the adoption of a new vision on the structure and operation of the cultural sector as well as the assimilation of new management paradigms.

Modelling Sustainable and Strategic Stakeholder Management for Community Venues

Stakeholder management has received considerable interest in both the general management literature and the project management literature (Billgreen and Holmén, 2008; Lund and Eskerod, 2008; Pomeroy and Douvere, 2008). A stakeholder is someone who can 'affect or is affected by the achievement of an organization's objectives' (Freeman, 1984) or represents 'persons or groups that have, or claim, ownership, rights, or interests in a corporation and its activities, past, present or future' (Clarkson, 1995, p. 106). According to Grimble and Wellard (1997, p. 175), a stakeholder is 'any group of people, organized or unorganized, who share a common interest or stake in a particular issue or system'. Varvasovzky and Brugha (2000, p. 341) state that they are:

> actors who can have an interest in the issue under consideration, who are affected by the issue, or who – because of their position – have or could have an active or passive influence on the decision making and implementation process.

Stakeholders may be 'persons, groups or institutions with interests in a project or program' (ODA, 1995). In the context of cultural organizations, the problem comes from the fact that 'the demands of arts or cultural stakeholders often conflict with a more business-like or management style' (Cray *et al.*, 2007, p. 295).

The concern with the involvement of stakeholders in the process of management of community venues is also related to the evolution of the management approach. Increasingly nowadays, the management process focuses on other factors besides economic goals. Social responsibility and the involvement of all stakeholders are part of the agenda and represent concerns of managers. This new approach requires the establishment of goals that include cooperation among stakeholders that take part in cultural organizations together with concerns of public needs and expectations. Achieving a market share and assessing results are also important issues that should be considered in the management approach of the arts field.

To carry out a cultural project successfully it is necessary to manage a strong alliance scheme with all stakeholders involved. It is the responsibility of a project manager to ensure that such partnerships are reached. When we put forward the concept of sustainable and strategic stakeholder management for community venues, we take into consideration all participating actors of a region. The challenge here is to consolidate common projects based on principles of excellence. Increased participation of stakeholders particularly in decision-making processes in terms of resource management has gained worldwide acceptance (Silva *et al.*, 2007). Reasons for involving stakeholders include:

- the need to understand the complexity of the cultural system;
- to ensure management systems, to identify potential conflicts inherent to proposed objectives; and
- to resolve areas of conflict and counterbalance existing patterns of interaction.

From this perspective, it is desirable to involve community venues on a management approach by taking into consideration marketing principles. However, it is important to understand that cultural products are speciality products. The complexity of sustainable and strategic stakeholder management for community venues comes from the need to identify and coordinate a large number of entities. It is particularly difficult to understand different target groups' expectations and measure the global performance of the cultural organizations.

From this management approach, it is important to take into account two factors: (i) the changes in terms of management techniques as well as the behaviour and attitude of involved actors; and (ii) the development and assimilation of a new culture of relations in order to incorporate a new system of values, together with the development and implementation of a vast net of processes of continuous improvement in the cultural scenario. These factors 'have important effects on structures, processes, and personnel' (Cray *et al.*, 2007, p. 296). Community venues must adopt flexible models of management, embedded in a systematic and dynamic relationship with stakeholders, oriented by excellence goals. Also, the management referential must be flexible and adaptable to the specific circumstances that characterize each cultural system and to the singularities that characterize the environmental context where the management process is set. The success of this approach depends on set principles and guidelines, described as good practices. The underlying principles and procedures of sustainable and strategic stakeholder management based on excellence constitute a good referential. From this perspective, one can put forward a management referential that looks to ensure a strategic and sustainable way of integrating all stakeholders involved in the management process of community venues.

In any case, the implementation of a strategic and sustainable management model in community venues must be supported around three critical areas for the success of the project: (i) leadership; (ii) focused on individuals; and (iii) the building of stakeholder partnerships. Implementing this approach successfully depends on the adoption of principles, procedures and guidelines described as good practice in organizations.

Leadership

According to Cray *et al.* (2007, p. 296), such changes 'impact most heavily on the leaders' of cultural organizations. They represent the organization to its external stakeholders and represent the link between the organization and its employees. The new context of cultural or arts organizations puts pressure on leaders to become more entrepreneurial (Mulcahy, 2003). 'One of the key functions of leaders is to set long-term goals for their organizations' (Cray *et al.*, 2007, p. 303).

The need for clear leadership in community venues is a crucial issue. Implementation of a process of sustainable and strategic management on the part of stakeholders is necessary to ensure that cultural or arts organizations adequately manage conflicts that may arise as a result of differentiated views. Cray *et al.* (2007, p. 298) also argue that, although the roles of leaders of cultural organizations are similar to those of non-profit organizations, there are specific aspects involved. Of important consideration are the artistic vision and the strong influence of the artistic director. Often, the strategic decision-making process encounters forces that conflict with the more rationalist orientation. According to these authors, 'leadership and leaders in arts organization are relatively unexplored topics'. Evrard and Colbert (2000) note that the artistic director and the managing director lead the organization taking into account the different perspectives. This situation may be difficult to manage. While managers look to ensure the financial security of the organization and its long-term survival, artistic directors want short-term artistic recognition (Cray *et al.*, 2007).

Personal engagement and enthusiasm in management are basic requirements for the success of cultural programmes. Clear leadership is essential to clarify and create the direction of the unit and the coherence of intentions, both inside and outside the organization (EFQM, 1999). For the specific case of community venues, leadership of the management team is expressed through a capacity to involve the actors, to adjust strategies and to project an image of differentiation of the cultural performance (Silva *et al.*, 2007). It is also crucial that the leader balances this process, taking into account the visions and interests of management directors and artistic directors. Leadership comprehends the balancing of conflicts that come from the hybrid nature of the players that make up the value chain.

The implementation of sustainable and strategic stakeholder management for community venues requires from leaders some tenacity and commitment in order to achieve the desired goals and motivation. This approach requires medium- and long-term planning in line with the immediate returns expected from artists.

Individuals

Individuals represent customers (actual and potential visitors) and employees. These are two important actors in the management referential for the community venues considered. Also, the value chain of artistic or cultural productions involves suppliers, businesses and the community itself. In this process towards change in arts organizations, it is important to invest in qualified staff (Cray *et al.*, 1997, p. 297). Cray *et al.* (1997) note 'both administrators and those who study arts organizations are limited in their ability to deal with the problems induced by change due to a lack of empirical research in the area of arts management'.

As such, it becomes even more difficult to engage all elements that make up the arts organization team in terms of management. However, the success of this management approach is deeply connected with the way employees understand the management model and are engaged with the goals of the organization. It is important to ensure training programmes to employees. As Pine and Gilmore (1999) note, the success of each performance depends on how well each employee understands his/her role. In order to provide quality cultural experiences, it is essential to meet the expectations and maximize the degree of satisfaction of employees at community venues (Mendes *et al.*, 2007).

By individuals we refer to both employees and customers. Customers are the main actors in the value chain of cultural or arts organizations. Cultural products are of special nature and need to be directed towards target individuals and groups to enhance participation levels, in this way meeting expectations and satisfying needs. To secure loyal visitors is just as important as securing new ones. As such, it is vital to monitor customer satisfaction after each performance in order to develop new cultural proposals (Valle *et al.*, 2006). Satisfied visitors are an important consideration for a sustainable and strategic management organization without affecting the artistic quality of the products.

Potential of partnerships

Integrating cultural programmes within community venues not only provides national and international notoriety but also enhances the overall corporate image, of which other well-established organizations are well aware. Organizations work more efficiently when there are mutual benefits and interaction between its stakeholders, based on confidence, expertise and knowledge (Vink *et al.*, 2008). The building of partnerships with entities and/or producers can be a strategic approach and can serve to dynamically stimulate cultural events within community venues. A cooperative climate understands that actors are cognizant and are part of a value chain, where all events are complementary and contribute to the success of the cultural experience. Joint development of programmes and projects, a common vision on the role of community venues and the establishment of cooperation agreements between public and private entities represent important goals in the cultural sector (Guerreiro *et al.*, 2007).

A close and continuous relationship between all actors and public and private organizations, at the regional, national and international scale, is required in order to support cultural projects. By creating synergies for all partners involved, new management paradigms can be developed.

Since strategic and sustainable management is essentially an interactive process, a key question is how to identify the main stakeholders culturally and the best way to involve them effectively.

According to Bourne and Walker (2005, cited in Lund and Eskerod, 2008, p. 2):

> Effective project managers require keen analytical and intuitive skills to identify stakeholders and work with them to understand their expectations and influence upon project success. This facilitates managing a process that maximises stakeholder positive input and minimises any potential detrimental impact.

One of the most popular approaches used to handle this issue is through stakeholder analysis. Pomeroy and Douvere (2008) describe the concept as a range of tools for the identification and description of stakeholders, their interrelationships and current and (potential) future interests and objectives, and examine the question of how and to what extent they represent various segments of society. More specifically, stakeholder analysis can be defined as 'an approach and procedure for gaining understanding of a system by means of identifying the key actors and stakeholders in the system and assessing their respective interests in that system' (Grimble and Chan, 1995). In general, stakeholder analysis requires the identification and characterization of stakeholders as well as forms to influence them. It is up to stakeholders to influence an organization or a system, to develop an understanding of why changes occur, to establish who can make changes happen and to discern how to best manage them (Grimble and Wellard, 1997; Mitchell *et al.*, 1997).

Under sustainable and strategic management, all actors share a responsibility in the cultural scenario. It is essential that community venues and their leaders involve all interested parties in an effort to integrate a common vision resulting in a social contract. As such, the development and implementation of holistic approaches in terms of consumption and cultural products, within the wider and multidimensional contexts, are aspects that should be considered, especially concerning the social responsibility of all those involved in the process.

Strategic Planning Process

Strategic planning, total quality management and benchmarking are managerial processes that have been introduced and developed to improve cultural organizational performance. When all interrelated activities are understood and managed systematically and decisions taken on the basis of reliable information in terms of stakeholder expectations, performance of such organizations is more efficient (EFQM, 1999). Community venues engaged in the implementation of these methodologies are generally compared with two types of management processes: internal and external. The former is often similar to other organizations, while the latter creates synergies across the cultural sector based on the involvement and commitment by stakeholders in developing and implementing cultural projects.

A sustainable and strategic stakeholder management implies the following considerations:

- establishment of cultural objectives for the area/region;
- development and implementation of a plan based on concrete objectives; and
- development of a monitoring system.

The concerns of managers must therefore focus on a set of key processes so as to prevent waste of resources and fragmented images of culture. Achieving results as well as performing well is one of the central questions of the approach. Management based on processes and facts creates a reliable environment between the stakeholders involved, which represents an important aspect for greater consolidation (Mendes *et al.*, 2007). Participation may range from communication, where there is no actual participation, to negotiation, where decision-making power is shared among the various stakeholders (Pomeroy and Douvere, 2008). The objectivity of facts and management development allows for a more realistic assessment of stakeholder participation and involvement, thus contributing to the rationalization of decision-making processes for community venues.

Most key processes for community venues should:

1. Ensure a regular programming of quality.
2. Develop and consolidate cultural habits in residents.
3. Develop partnerships with stakeholders.
4. Integrate in national and international networks.
5. Create a privileged space of debate and discussion about culture.

In pursuing these aims, the planning process of community venues must lead to the development of a range of strategies through the support of stakeholders, in this way establishing concrete cultural policies for a specific region. In observing possible scenarios, the following represent essential considerations.

Strategies for Achieving Customer Loyalty and New Customers

Customer loyalty programmes are essential tools. However, programme diversity is generally a shared desire by visitors participating in cultural events. In order to satisfy this expectation, community venues should adopt this line of approach. The profile of visitors seeking cultural activities (whether at the national or international level) is ultimately made up of individuals of middle and upper academic backgrounds, representing a segment that should be given priority in order to attract new visitors.

Acquiring new customers is an important challenge since this represents an investment which in the long term will have visible effects. Given that target groups also include children and youth, it is important to adopt a compatible approach in terms of cultural consumption. As such, customer relationship marketing will need to be diversified in order to encompass different age groups and education levels. Close involvement with schools and educators who teach culture-related subjects such as theatre, dance and music is an influential approach (Guerreiro *et al.*, 2007).

Communication and Brand Positioning Strategies

Effective communication and brand positioning must support the management process of community venues. This can be done through specific objectives and the implementation of a media plan. Continuous assessment is equally important in determining the effectiveness of the communication strategies implemented. Considering that brand positioning is a long-term strategy, communication and coherence are recommended in terms of name and logo. The objective is to increase notoriety through events and community venues of different market segments. In any organization, brand positioning represents a central strategic element. Besides constituting an internal cohesive vehicle, it represents coherent brand positioning – elements that strongly contribute to the building of a corporate image.

Sponsorship Management Strategies

Relying on scarce public funding may represent an obstacle when looking to provide quality, attraction and innovation. Especially when we think about the cultural or artistic sector, 'because of the increasing difficulty in obtaining funding, cultural organizations no longer just look to the government' (Kolb, 2005, p. 192). Colbert (1994) noted that this kind of organization 'turn[s] to the private sector for financial support'. Identifying alternative sources of funding is of strategic importance and should be obtained from private businesses as well. This is due to two main reasons: (i) because nowadays sponsorship management is one of the most efficient and popular fundraising techniques; and (ii) because it is an effective way of involving community actors in cultural and event projects. It is a sign of marketing vision when the cultural organization 'treats its current and potential donors not as targets but as potential partners' (Kotler and Scheff, 1997, p. 478).

For Colbert (1994, p. 191) sponsorship is, above all, a promotional tool. And from this point of view, sponsorship 'involves interaction between two distinct parties: the sponsor, which provides funds, goods, or services, and the sponsored group, which receives them'. For Kolb (2005), sponsorship is something that makes part of the 'pricing and funding as revenue sources' and, from this point of view, it is 'a broad term that covers many kinds of business/non profit relationships from financial to in-kind operational support' (Independent Sector, 2003, cited in Kolb, 2005, p. 193). Sponsorship consists of the negotiation of an agreement that benefits both the cultural organization and the sponsor.

Artists are usually very sceptical about this relationship because they fear that the business vision could contaminate, in a negative way, arts. However, sponsorship is a very important fundraising and promotion tool. As Field (1999, cited in Kolb, 2005, p. 193) noted, 'sponsorship has now become the fastest growing form of marketing for cultural organisations'. Further, this is a very interesting way to involve community members in the community venues. As a sponsor, each organization usually benefits from the visibility of the event and it provides 'entertainment options for the corporation's employees and guests' (Kolb, 2005, p. 192). On the other hand, it is very usual that the organization uses the sponsor as a promotional vehicle (Colbert, 1994). Kolb (2005) has summarized the main benefits of sponsorship for corporations and cultural organizations (see Table 15.1).

The plan of action in this area should start with the definition of the cultural or artistic event, the identification of primary target segments and the selection of potential business sponsors. One important task is to analyse the market in order to identify all the potential partners. Between them, it is of critical interest to look for organizations that have a positioning

Table 15.1. Sponsorship strategies. (Adapted from Kolb, 2005, p. 195.)

Benefits for corporations	Benefits for cultural organizations
Access to the organization's audience	Funds for special projects
Use of venue/performances or events	In-kind donations
Tickets for employees	Enhanced image
Marquee/programme advertising	Positioning of product
Seats on the board	Access to employees
Visiting artists or exhibits at worksite	Access to client/ customer
Brand differentiation	Sharing of expertise in marketing and strategy

strategy compatible with the positioning of the event and the same target segments.

Summary

Ideally, cultural products should be conceived and offered in order to fulfil the needs and expectations of different market segments and also be cost-effective. New cultural products, increased customer demands and competition stimulate the development of other management paradigms and supply solutions. Sustainable and strategic stakeholder management for community venues should be structured to nurture the dynamic development of a set of relations with stakeholders, in this way maintaining or stimulating change in terms of habits and cultural practices. At the same time, it is important to consider the involvement of stakeholders in the decision process of community venues. Greater stakeholder involvement represents a cultural change towards a more active role in the planning, organization, implementation and control stages.

Such an involvement has its implications and should be understood as a dynamic and coherent process, in terms of both habit and cultural practices change and collaboration forms and stakeholders' participation.

It is commonly accepted that the majority of stakeholders, claiming social co-responsibility within regional cultural development, are fully aware of cost/benefit issues, which are usually considered and managed as an investment on image and positioning of organizations they represent.

Hence, sponsoring is taken as a strategy aiming at specific purposes and whose rationale, within a management perspective, is to provide to organizations adopting it more benefits than costs. The inclination to acknowledge sponsoring merely as an altruistic gesture of organizations that, while being ignorant of what to do with their profits, decide to invest part of the sum in charity institutions, is no longer sustainable.

Every possible form of involvement and inter-organizational interaction and relationship should be preceded by an impact evaluation report and benefits to participants. Since collaboration between parts should take place in a long-term perspective, this specific issue has even greater importance.

This process of change should be viewed as a method of developing and adopting new forms of cultural management and articulating this process with all those taking part. The final objective is to reinforce competitiveness and attractiveness of cultural products through close collaboration with stakeholders, as well as to establish collective motivation and responsibility in the development of cultural practices and habits in a region. Partnerships, collaboration agreements and other forms of institutional cooperation between stakeholders are as important as the pursuit of common objectives. The scheduling of a joint agenda enables stakeholders to take further steps towards a more sustainable and strategic management, thus representing a symbol for greater understanding and convergence in the cultural development of a region.

Key Questions

1. Cultural products are speciality products traditionally managed by artists. Nowadays, it is important to find a balance between management principles and the artistic vision.

Should cultural products be managed by an artist with management knowledge or should they be managed by a manager with an artistic vision?

2. The adoption of a new vision on the structure and operation of the cultural sector and the assimilation of new management paradigms may clash with the artistic vision. How should these forces be balanced?

3. How can sponsoring effectiveness and other forms of cooperation between stakeholders and community venues be assessed within a sustainability and medium-/long-term relationships framework?

References

Billgreen, C. and Holmén, H. (2008) Approaching reality: comparing stakeholder analysis and cultural theory in the context of natural resource management. *Land Use Policy* 25(4), 550–562.

Clarkson, M.B.E. (1995) A stakeholder framework for analysing and evaluating corporate social performance. *Academy of Management Review* 20(1), 92–117.

Colbert, F. (1994) *Marketing Culture and The Arts*. Morin, Montreal, Canada.

Cray, D., Inglis, L. and Freeman, S. (2007) Managing the arts: leadership and decision making under dual rationalities. *Journal of Arts Management, Law, and Society* 36(4), 295–313.

Diggles, D. (1986) *Guide to Arts Marketing: The Principles and Practice of Marketing as They Apply to The Arts*. Rhinegold Publishing Limited, London.

DiMaggio, P. and Stenberg, K. (1985) Why do some theatres innovate more than others? An empirical analysis. *Poetics* 14(1–2), 107–122.

EFQM (1999) *Eight Essentials of Excellence*. European Foundation for Quality Management, Brussels.

Evrard, Y. and Colbert, F. (2000) Arts management: a new discipline entering the millennium? *International Journal of Arts Management* 2(2), 4–13.

Freeman, R.E. (1984) *Strategic Management: A Stakeholder Approach*. Pitman, Boston, Massachusetts.

Grimble, R. and Chan, M.K. (1995) Stakeholder analysis for natural resource management in developing countries. *Natural Resources Forum* 19(2), 113–124.

Grimble, R. and Wellard, K. (1997) Stakeholder methodologies in natural resource management: a review of principles, contexts, experiences and opportunities. *Agricultural Systems* 55(2), 173–193.

Guerreiro, M., Mendes, J. and Valle, P. (2007) *Teatro das Figuras – Plano Estratégico 2007–2010*. Teatro das Figuras, Faro, Portugal.

Kolb, B.M. (2005) *Marketing for Cultural Organisations – New Strategies for Attracting Audiences to Classical Music, Dance, Museums, Theatre and Opera*, 2nd edn. Thomson, Cork, Ireland.

Kotler, P. and Scheff, J. (1997) *Standing Room Only – Strategies for Marketing the Performing Arts*. Harvard Business School Press, Boston, Massachusetts.

Mendes, J., Silva, J.A., Guerreiro, M. and Flores, A. (2007) Integrated quality management in tourism destinations. A proposed model for fostering competitiveness. Presented at *Destinations Revisited. Perspectives on Development and Managing Tourist Areas, ATLAS Annual Conference*, Viana do Castelo, Portugal, 5–8 September 2007.

Mitchell, R.K., Agle, B.R. and Wood, D.L. (1997) Towards a theory of stakeholder identification and salience: defining the principle of who and what really counts. *Academy of Management Review* 22(4), 853–886.

Mulcahy, K.V. (2003) Entrepreneurship or social Darwinism? Privatization and American cultural patronage. *Journal of Arts Management, Law, and Society* 33(3), 165–184.

ODA (1995) *Guidance Note on How To Do Stakeholder Analysis of Aid Projects and Programmes*. Overseas Development Administration, Social Development Department, London.

Pine, J. and Gilmore, J. (1999) *The Experience Economy*. Harvard Business School Press, Boston, Massachusetts.

Pomeroy, R. and Douvere, F. (2008) The engagement of stakeholders in the marine spatial planning process. *Marine Policy* 32(15), 816–822.

Sicca, L.M. and Zan, L. (2005) Much ado about management: managerial rhetoric in the transformation of Italian opera houses. *International Journal of Arts Management* 7(3), 46–64.

Silva, J.A., Guerreiro, M., Mendes, J. and Valle, P. (2007) *Hábitos e Práticas Culturais dos Residentes no Algarve*. Delegação Regional da Cultura do Algarve, Faro, Portugal.

Valle, P., Guerreiro, M., Mendes, J., Silva, J.A. and Fortuna, C. (2006) Públicos de grandes espectáculos culturais: uma análize categórica de segmentos de mercado. Presented at *XIII Jornadas Anuais de Classificação e Análize de Dados*, Universidade Lusíada, Lisbon, 6–8 April 2006.

Varvasovzky, Z. and Brugha, R. (2000) 'How to (or not to do)... a stakeholder analysis. *Health Policy and Planning* 15(3), 338–345.

Vink P., Imada, A.S. and Zink, K.J. (2008) Defining stakeholder involvement in participatory design processes. *Applied Ergonomics* 39(4), 519–526.

16 Analysis of a Supply Chain in the Events Context: Where Does the Food Come From?

S. Beer
Bournemouth University, Poole, UK

This chapter examines some of the broader issues relating to the consumption of food and drink at an event that might form part of the planning process informally or within a process such as BS 8901:2007, the British Standard for sustainable event management (BSI, 2007). These ideas are explored using a range of examples and a number of more specific case studies.

Chapter outline

- Introduction
- A Model of Sustainability
- Politics
- Economics
- Social Factors
- Technology
- Environment
- Measurement
- What is Sustainable Food and Drink?
- Summary
- Key Questions
- Revision

Introduction

Food production, sourcing and consumption represent one of the most important issues relating to the concept of sustainability in its broadest sense, as well as within the specific area of events management. This chapter outlines a model of sustainability based on PESTE analysis, which focuses on its political, economic, social, technological and environmental dimensions. The model is applied to food production and consumption in general, but more specifically with regard to consumption in the context of a range of events management scenarios.

A Model of Sustainability

PESTE is a way of thinking about the broader environment that looks at its political, economic, social, technological and environmental dimensions. This would seem to provide a very good model for examining any aspect of sustainability – in this particular case, the sustainability of food at events. Many authors have addressed these broader dimensions to food and for an introduction to this area the reader is referred to works by Mepham (1996), Germov and Williams (1999), Atkins and Bowler (2001) and Eastham *et al.* (2001).

Within the political dimension various small 'p' and large 'P' political issues are examined. The key factor in any decision often relates to price, and the whole economic context is crucial. Social factors are critical to explaining the demand for more sustainable options with regard to food consumption, but the whole concept of sustainability is, in fact, a social construct that is ever evolving and also closely linked to concepts of authenticity.

Before we go on to look in detail at the model, there are two other factors to be borne in mind. We may well have decided that sustainability has political, economic, social, technological and environmental dimensions, but in each case what does this actually mean? This is discussed further in the text that follows and is also illustrated with respect to food and drink in Fig. 16.1.

At the same time, in some way we need to try to measure sustainability, or at least give it some sort of value in different situations. If we are unable to do this how are we going to be able to measure where we are now, set targets and monitor progress? Also how can we say that one system is potentially more sustainable than another? Again this is discussed further below.

Politics

One of the problems of this form of analysis of a concept such as sustainability is that it very soon becomes apparent that many of the different sections overlap. The first area that is examined is the political dimension; because of this overlap, slightly more space is given to it than to some of the other sections.

As mentioned before, we can view the political dimension with a large 'P' or a small 'p'. Large 'P' politics refers to the politics of government and associated laws. With regard to concepts of sustainability and food and drink, this can be extremely important. On one level government sets policy that will influence the whole operation of the food supply chain. For example, there is a whole series of regulations relating to the Common Agricultural Policy that may have effects with regard to the supply of products in terms of quantity and also place of origin. Certain countries could have import bans imposed on them because of problems with their animal health status – they may have foot-and-mouth disease, for example. Other countries may have import quotas imposed upon them with associated tariffs. There is always a temptation to try to get round these barriers to enhance profits, but this could be extremely dangerous in terms of the environment and the law. For example, what would be the consequences of reintroducing foot-and-mouth disease into the UK or introducing some non-native species of plant or animal that may well go on to cause environmental damage?

It must also be remembered that governments set our laws. This has particular relevance for the sustainability of food supply chains, in that many of the products that are considered to have some sort of added value in terms of their sustainability credentials are covered by laws relating to trademarks or

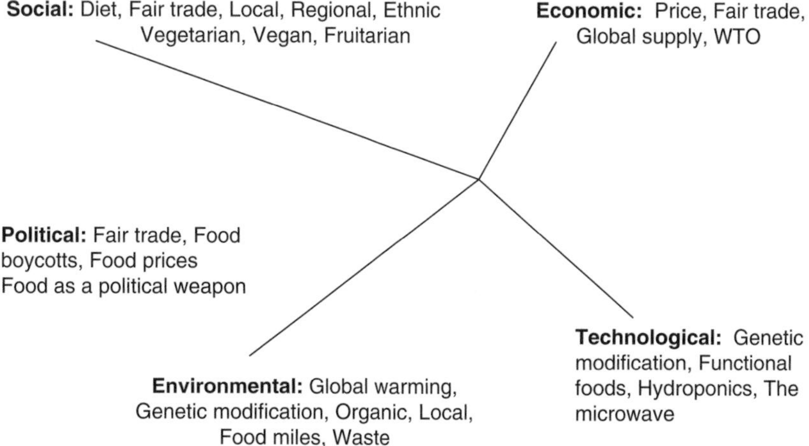

Fig. 16.1. The multiple dimensions of sustainability in terms of food and drink. (Adapted from Beer, 2008a.)

authenticity. Therefore, if you are selling food at an event and claim that it is local, organic or free range when it is not, you are breaking the law and would be subject to prosecution, as shown in Box 16.1.

Given this, one would imagine that terms such as 'organic', 'free range' and 'local' have some sort of legal definition. 'Organic' is well-defined. In 1993, EC Council Regulation 2092/91 (European Commission, 2007) came into effect and became the basis for the regulation of organic food production. This sets out the systems used in organic farming and growing. All foods sold as organic must originate from certified growers, processors and importers. This regulation is implemented in the UK under the Organic Product Regulations 2004. In the UK the Advisory Committee on Organic Standards (DEFRA, 2007a) advises the UK government on organic standards, approval of organic certifying bodies, and research and development. In the UK organic supply is overseen by one of nine certification bodies: Organic Farmers and Growers Ltd (UK2), Scottish Organic Producers Association (UK3), Organic Food Federation (UK4), Soil Association Certification Ltd (UK5), Bio-Dynamic Agricultural Association (UK6), Irish Organic Farmers and Growers Association (UK7), Organic Trust Limited (UK9), CMi Certification (UK10) and Ascisco Ltd (UK15) (DEFRA, 2007b).

'Free range' is also defined with specific reference to eggs or poultry meat. It is considered to be a Special Marketing Term (SMT) and, as such, products must be produced according to the criteria set out in the appropriate marketing regulations (DEFRA, 2008a).

'Local' is a term slightly more difficult to define. *The Sunday Times* (Timesonline, 2007) recently reported a Trading Standards investigation that puts this debate in an interesting light, as shown in Box 16.2.

A report commissioned by the Food Standards Agency (COI, 2007) tried to gain some consensus. In a survey, 40% of respondents said that local food was food produced within a 10-mile radius of their home. Having said that, 20% defined it is being produced within their county, 15% in a neighbouring county and 20% as having been produced within their region! It is possible to extend this debate by looking into the nature of specific foods that are produced in specific ways, in specific areas and also protected by legal definitions. Thus some products have certificates of Protected Designation of Origin (PDO), Protected Geographical Indication (PGI) or

Box 16.1. Wiltshire pub fined for misleading menu. (Porter, 2008.)

'A Wiltshire pub has been fined £3600 after admitting misdescribing food on its menu as "organic" and "free range". The Beckford Arms in Fonthill Gifford, near Salisbury, pleaded guilty to four offences. The pub, operated by Ding Dong Inns, has replaced the head chef and manager who were in charge when officers from Wiltshire Trading Standards visited the pub in September and October last year.

'New manager Feargal Powell said the pub had apologised to customers and explained the circumstances, and is confident the business will continue to trade successfully. Magistrates were told that that the menu had incorrectly described sausages, steak and mince as "organic" and ham and eggs as "local" and "free range".'

Box 16.2. Waitrose sticks knife into rival. (Timesonline, 2007.)

'Whole Foods Market, the American organic food chain that opened a London store in Kensington last month, is being investigated by trading standards officials after a complaint from Waitrose.

'It is thought that the complaint relates to the way that Whole Foods defines local produce as food sourced from anywhere in Britain.

'The response from the organic retailer was: "we don't have a strict definition of local – that is up to our customers. We give them the name of the product and where it is from so they can make their own decisions."'

Traditional Speciality Guaranteed (Certificate of Specific Character, CSC). These designations are for iconic products such as West Country Farmhouse Cheddar and the Arbroath Smokey. For further discussion of these types of products, see DEFRA (2008b), ElAmin (2006a,b) and Beer (2008b). For the event organizer or anyone involved in running the food and drink aspect of an event, this means that there is a legal framework in terms of the nature of products and their character that must be adhered to. You cannot claim that an item is something it is not. Moreover, these regulations come in addition to all the regulations relating to food safety that must also be adhered to (FSA, 2008).

Small 'p' politics refers to the internal political dynamics of a situation or event. Within an events context, there may be pressures from sponsors, both from the public and private sector, to source and present food in particular ways. For example, a local authority may be very keen to be seen to be promoting local food. This can be at variance to the actual clients' and event-goers' requirements. For example, at one particular outdoor sports event, the participants and spectators were much more enthusiastic about stealing food from a demonstration kitchen than watching the demonstrations using local food, as the commercial onsite catering was so poor. Also, if decisions are made about the nature of the food supply for a specific event, is that decision made with the potential customers in mind or some other political agenda? Many events regardless of size have an internal political structure/agenda that can be overriding in terms of decisions in subjects such as food supply.

Economics

Many consider that sustainable food, whatever this means, will often be expensive food, although this is not necessarily the case. At the same time, the dynamics of catering supply at an event can be complex; so much so that often event organizers will simply outsource the catering to a contractor who may not be prepared, or able, to supply a 'sustainable' package.

Customer focus

Any organization that seeks to supply a product must focus on its consumers; this is the very nature of the marketing process. Having said this, there is often a lot of cynicism with regard to how customer-focused companies/organizations really are. Are they customer-driven or do they drive the customer? In terms of food there are many examples that stoke this cynicism. You are sitting at home watching one of the numerous cookery programmes on television and there is the celebrity chef expounding recipes and ideas to you. You open up the book that accompanies the series and he/she is ingrained. You open your magazine and there he/she is again; and finally you go to the supermarket and there is the happy, smiling face of the chef beckoning to you from the shelves to buy new products and lines.

Price premium if a different option

There is no doubt that food preferences have changed. Given the decline in the real cost of food over time, theoretically consumers in the UK have some surplus income to spend on food. Of course other things have come along to compete for this money, such as the growth of interest in information technology and larger mortgages, but to a certain extent this surplus cash has fuelled changes in consumers' demands of food. It tends to be in wealthy countries that consumers start to spend more money on food because of its social, environmental or animal welfare credentials. There is a tendency for such food to be more expensive. Part of this may well be down to supply and demand as products of a more sustainable nature are often in shorter supply; this is part of the kudos of buying the product in the first place. These products may also cost more to produce.

Costings – a case study

Bearing in mind that there are infinite combinations of costs, the following case study puts some of these ideas into perspective. Consider a mobile catering unit that is working 100 days per year. Overheads, including transport, insurance and a part-time member of staff, amount to £56,500 per year. An industry standard method of calculating prices is to take 'three times the ingredients costs'. If the caterer uses 'standard' food supply chains she/he will need to sell some £84,750 worth of food to break even. The same principles applied to 'local food' (here given a premium of 30%) and organic food (here given a premium of 100%) would result in profits on food sales of £16,950 and £56,500, respectively. If the increased costs are not passed on, losses of £8475 and £28,250 result. Simply passing on the premium results in the status quo. These figures are summarized in Table 16.1.

In the final account the operator must make a decision: do customers want the product, will customers pay a premium and how much will they pay?

Such deliberations may be complicated by the ways in which some events operate. As previously indicated, the catering for an event may be organized by a contractor who may not be prepared or able to supply a 'sustainable' package. Sometimes these arrangements represent a closed shop that is difficult and costly to break into. In bidding, the contractor will invariably offer a high tender to get the work. This means that they have to hit their subcontractors and customers with higher prices to cover the costs. More enlightened event managers will look at tenders with more than just price in mind; this is all part of the sustainability equation.

Social Factors

The food consumer is complex, often self-contradictory and difficult to understand, particularly with regard to what they say and then subsequently do. The world has changed and will continue to change. In effect, what we have been and are still going through is a process of cultural shift (Beer and Redman, 1996). Food culture has changed, with consumers supposedly demanding more sustainable products.

Table 16.1. Example of a theoretical event catering operation and the financial effects of using different sources of supply.

			Ingredients		
Event days per year	100		Basic	Local (30% premium)	Organic (100% premium)
Overheads			28,250	36,725	56,500
Trailer	45,000	Food sales based on 300% mark-up including premium passed on to customer			
Depreciation	4,500				
Insurance	2,000		84,750	110,175	169,500
		Profit	0	16,950	56,500
Labour (£/day)	80	Food sales based on 300% mark-up premium not passed on to customer			
Total	8,000				
			56,700	56,700	56,700
		Profit	0	–8,475	–28,250
Mileage (£/mile)	1.2				
Average daily mileage	100	Food sales based on 300% mark-up premium added on and passed on to customer			
Total	12,000				
			84,750	93,225	113,000
		Profit	0	0	0
Pitch hire (£/day)	300				
Total	30,000				
Total	56,500				

Thus, although still small, the organic market is growing rapidly. The Soil Association (2007) indicated that year-on-year sales were increasing by 32% and that in 2006 retail and catering sales stood at £1937 million. Not all of these sales are to higher-income groups; over 50% of families in lower-income groups are buying some organic food. Obviously, dimensions of sustainability are not the only factor people consider when purchasing food (Soil Association, 2005). The British food consumer has become, theoretically, a very complex person. The multiple traits of this complexity in terms of food purchasing decisions are illustrated in Fig. 16.2.

Fair trade

As well as environmental concerns associated with food, social concerns are also to the fore. There is a great disparity between the amount of money that farmers or primary producers earn and the returns for those further up the supply chain, such as processors and retailers. As a result of this, the Fair Trade movement developed and ultimately this has evolved into a number of brands, including the Fairtrade mark. The Fairtrade mark is essentially a consumer label that appears on products as an independent guarantee that the primary food producer is getting a better return for his/her crop.

Many organizations have achieved Fairtrade status whereby they have expressed a commitment to developing systems that support the fair trade ethos – with regard to their catering, for example. Of course, if the coffee is purchased from an ethical source that supports overseas farmers but the milk that goes into the coffee comes from standard sources that may well exploit farmers closer to home, the true reality of 'fair trade' may be a little tarnished.

Authenticity

This brings us to the question of authenticity; after all, if the consumer is buying a product for specific reasons, surely he/she wants that product actually to be what it is supposed to be. Trendwatching.com (2008), one of the world's leading trend identification companies, recently highlighted the importance of authenticity.

Commentators such as Reisinger and Steiner (2006) have suggested that the nature of authenticity should be determined by every individual on his/her own terms. They have also suggested that the term authenticity is in fact meaningless and should be dropped. Unfortunately, this seems to ignore the fact that human beings are social animals. Beer (2008a) has suggested an alternative view that takes society into account. Couched in the terms of philosophy, Beer maintains that:

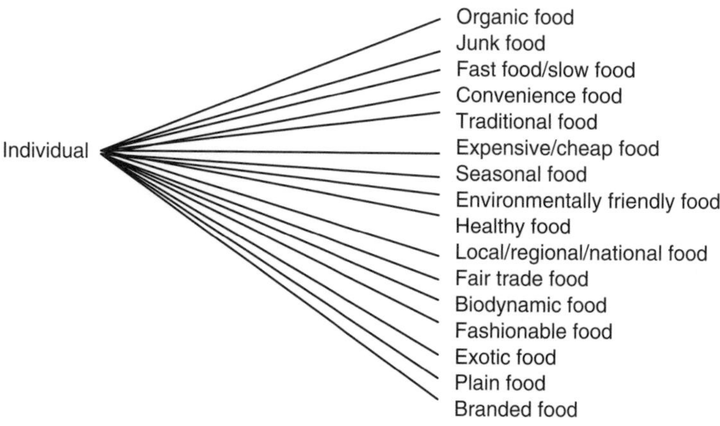

Fig. 16.2. An impression of the range of complexity with regard to the food that consumers choose to purchase. (Adapted from Beer, 2008a.)

> In effect individuals (the self) have a view of reality and authenticity that potentially varies with time and context, but is also dependent on their relationship with society (others) and the thing about which we are asking questions of reality (the thing).

The key problem is that individuals may have a view of what is authentic and it may have been developed as a result of a whole series of experiences, but 'society' also has a view and has enshrined these views in terms of food and drink in laws and trademarks. The question still remains: what is authenticity?

Technology

The fourth element of the model relates to technology. Within the context of food and drink and the sustainability of events, this may be viewed primarily from two perspectives. First, the whole process of food and drink preparation and distribution is a technological process and it is up to the event organizer to ensure that everything is deployed to make certain this is done effectively in terms of food quality and safety. Quality assurance has spawned an industry and subject in its own right, but there persists a problem of definition. Many people believe that quality assurance involves producing high-quality products. This is not the case. Quality assurance is about delivering a given specification at a given price and being able to do this consistently. Modern catering technology enables us to do this and, if used correctly, to exceed customer expectations even in the most difficult of situations.

The second area that we need to look at is the nature of the food and drink products themselves. Modern food production systems produce food that is far from natural. The use of pesticides, fertilizers and other agrochemicals has revolutionized world agriculture. At the same time it has meant that food and drink often contain residues of these chemicals, as do the environment and the fauna and flora that live there; this includes us. Here lies one of the major objections that many individuals have to modern food and farming methods.

It is not only to plants that these methods are extended; many animals are produced in very highly automated systems. Certainly animals have provided cheap protein for several generations, but the potential objections to intensive systems are clear. Therefore how sustainable are these systems and how sustainable are the events that utilize food produced from them?

The ultimate use of this technology has to be in genetic engineering. Here the issues can become highly focused. In the production of genetically modified organisms scientists are literally transferring the genes from one organism to another. The image is that of 'cut and paste'; but this is not how inheritance works. The reality is far more complicated. The possible benefits are considerable, the downsides likewise. Environmental campaigners have likened it to opening Pandora's box. Again these are issues that need far more discussion than is available here and the reader is directed towards extensive discourse on the Internet starting at some of the web sites listed at the end of this chapter.

Environment

In the section on political factors it was indicated that many of these different dimensions overlap. Given this, much of the discussion that has taken place already contributes to the environmental dimension of the model in terms of the different types of sustainable designation for food, such as organic, biodynamic and genetically modified, and the changing attitudes of the consumer in becoming more environmentally aware. There are, however, a number of outstanding issues, principally food miles and food waste.

In its simplest sense, 'food miles' is a measurement of the distance that your food has travelled from the place of production to the place of consumption. The idea behind it is that transporting food has an environmental impact in terms of energy use and congestion and that, ideally, it is better to consume food that is produced closer to home. Although used for a long time it has been suggested that the concept was originally developed by Tim Lang (2006), who maintained that: 'The point was to highlight the hidden ecological, social and economic consequences of food production to consumers in a simple way, one which had objective reality but also connotations'. Studies have indicated that the direct environmental, social and economic costs of food transport in the UK are over £9 billion each year (AEA Technology, 2005).

However, the very simplicity and accessibility of the concept is a primary flaw: simply looking at distance is, in effect, meaningless. For example, a leg of lamb may be transported from New Zealand with thousands of other legs of lamb in a large ship and the energy expenditure per leg may be minimal. Locally produced lamb may be transported in small lots on lorries and thus have a higher energy burden per kilogram. Also, production methods used in a country like the UK are very energy-intensive and this may well offset any transport cost, in terms of energy, when the product is compared with one produced in a country that does not need to use glasshouses or artificial fertilizers to promote plant growth. The food miles concept is often discussed in more popular circles because of its simplicity, but can give rise to false perspectives. Having said that, many of the studies that have examined the energy cost of transport versus that of production do not seem to compare like with like, and what is the point of consuming organic produce that is then being air-freighted or shipped halfway around the world? Further discussion of the different sides of the food miles debate can be found in Stacey (2008) and McKie (2008).

In relation to food miles there are also other considerations such as: the spread of disease (foot-and-mouth disease was imported into the UK following an absence of many decades); the erosion of food culture (what about the indigenous food culture of the UK?; Beer 2008b); and the effect of food production in developing countries that is targeted at overseas exports rather than feeding the local population.

Food wastage has recently received considerable coverage in the UK (BBC, 2008). A report from the waste and resources action programme indicated that 6.7 million tonnes of food is thrown away each year in the UK; this is worth over £11 billion and accounts for almost one-fifth (19%) of domestic waste (WRAP, 2008). In terms of event management, the issue of waste is a poignant one. Waste represents a cost to the business in terms of the opportunity cost of the food – it could have been consumed by the customers at the event or alternatively consumed by other fee-paying customers at a different event. It costs money to dispose of waste food; it also represents damage to the environment in terms of its disposal and the waste of environmental resources in terms of its production. The same can be said about other types of waste associated with an event, specifically with regard to catering this includes disposable cutlery and plates. Simply put, it represents throwing money into the waste bin!

There are many waste minimization strategies that can be employed by the event caterer. These include careful portion control and careful stock management, particularly with regard to sell-by dates. What the caterer has to be very careful about is recycling of food, either in terms of ingredients or cooked food, as there are very severe implications in terms of food poisoning if this is not undertaken in a very disciplined and careful manner. See the specific references for food service operation management at the end of the chapter for further guidance in terms of operation management.

Measurement

It was indicated initially that it is important not only to recognize the various components that may or may not contribute to the sustainability of event catering, but also to be able to measure them. Once something can be measured, targets can be set and performance monitored. In many ways this is not an easy thing to do. Some of the areas within the model do not lend themselves to measurement, such as the various political and social factors for example. These dimensions of sustainability are notoriously difficult to measure. Criteria can be adopted, but the selection of these criteria is often very subjective and far from definitive. Economic factors are much easier to quantify, as illustrated in this chapter and also in texts such as Dittmer (2003) and Pavesic and Magnant (2005). Similarly, there will be various aspects of the technological – food service and food wastage, for example – that can be measured.

This whole area of benchmarking is something that is becoming a fundamental principle of operations management. In terms of sustainable events management it is an area that needs further development, and with the introduction of BS 8901:2007 this may gain some additional focus. With the difficulty in actually demonstrating sustainability, it is important that event managers understand their customers and their expectations. Success can be demonstrated when these can be met and, if possible, exceeded, although in many cases the management of this process will be 'qualitative' rather than 'quantitative'.

What is Sustainable Food and Drink?

In the final analysis, we need to try to understand what sustainable food and drink in an events context actually means. Sustain (2008) has developed seven principles of sustainable food that are outlined in Box 16.3.

When looking at these criteria many individuals might consider them to be somewhat extreme. Sustain is an organization whose primary purpose is to campaign on food sustainability issues, so this may well be the perspective that one would expect. For an events manager, again, it comes back to understanding your customers. Specific individuals may consider themselves early adopters or leaders within the whole area of sustainable event management, and believe that adopting standards that may lead the consumer in a particular direction is appropriate. This must be left up to the individual to decide, bearing in mind the principles of the triple bottom line. Ultimately the individual event managers must decide where they will position themselves and specific events with regard to these and other criteria.

Summary

This chapter has attempted to unpick some of the multiple dimensions of sustainability. The first problem we have is actually to define what sustainability means, and then what this means for food and drink consumption at events that themselves want to be sustainable. It is possible that many people will consider this irrelevant or an opportunity for tokenism. That is wrong for a whole series of different reasons. The chapter proposes a model of sustainability that looks at the multiple dimensions of politics, economics, society, technology and the environment. Each of these dimensions has an effect on sustainability in that, for something to be truly sustainable, each of the five must be stable. Within each dimension there are important considerations to be reflected upon, but they need to be looked at as a whole. Thus we cannot have environmental sustainability, for example, if the solution is not economically viable. There may be a need for political will, and society may force this or hold it back. Finally, technology may be able to provide us

Box 16.3. Seven principles of sustainable food. (Sustain, 2008.)

In our opinion, people and businesses adopting a sustainable approach to food should:

1. Use local, seasonally available ingredients as standard, to minimize energy used in food production, transport and storage.
2. Specify food from farming systems that minimize harm to the environment, such as certified organic produce.
3. Limit foods of animal origin (meat, dairy products and eggs) served, as livestock farming is one of the most significant contributors to climate change, and promote meals rich in fruit, vegetables, pulses, whole grains and nuts. Ensure that meat, dairy products and eggs are produced to high environmental and animal welfare standards.
4. Exclude fish species identified as most 'at risk' by the Marine Conservation Society, and choose fish only from sustainable sources – such as those accredited by the Marine Stewardship Council.
5. Choose Fairtrade-certified products for foods and drinks imported from poorer countries, to ensure a fair deal for disadvantaged producers.
6. Avoid bottled water and instead serve plain or filtered tap water in reusable jugs or bottles, to minimize transport and packaging waste.
7. Promote health and well-being by cooking with generous portions of vegetables, fruit and starchy staples like whole-grains, cutting down on salt, fats and oils, and cutting out artificial additives.

with solutions, but we should ensure that we are not looking to bad technology for them.

In many ways, the key to the whole process for the event manager is to know yourself and your customers. What do you actually want from the event industry and what role do you think sustainability should have in events that you are involved with? How well do you know your customers? Can you actually stand in their shoes? Can you develop products that will help your customers realize their aspirations? Once you have this knowledge, the second important principle is to ensure that what you say you will do actually is what you do. Managing consumer expectations is all-important, and when you make claims for a product in terms of its sustainability these claims should be justifiable and should be seen to be justifiable.

Key Questions

1. What do we mean by a sustainable event and what role does food and drink play in this?
2. Prepare a costed proposal for the catering manager of an in-house restaurant at an events complex on how she/he might move to an organic menu.
3. How could sustainability, in terms of food and drink, be used to develop a unique selling point for an event? Should not all events be sustainable in this way?

Revision

Revision for this chapter is summarized in Fig. 16.3.

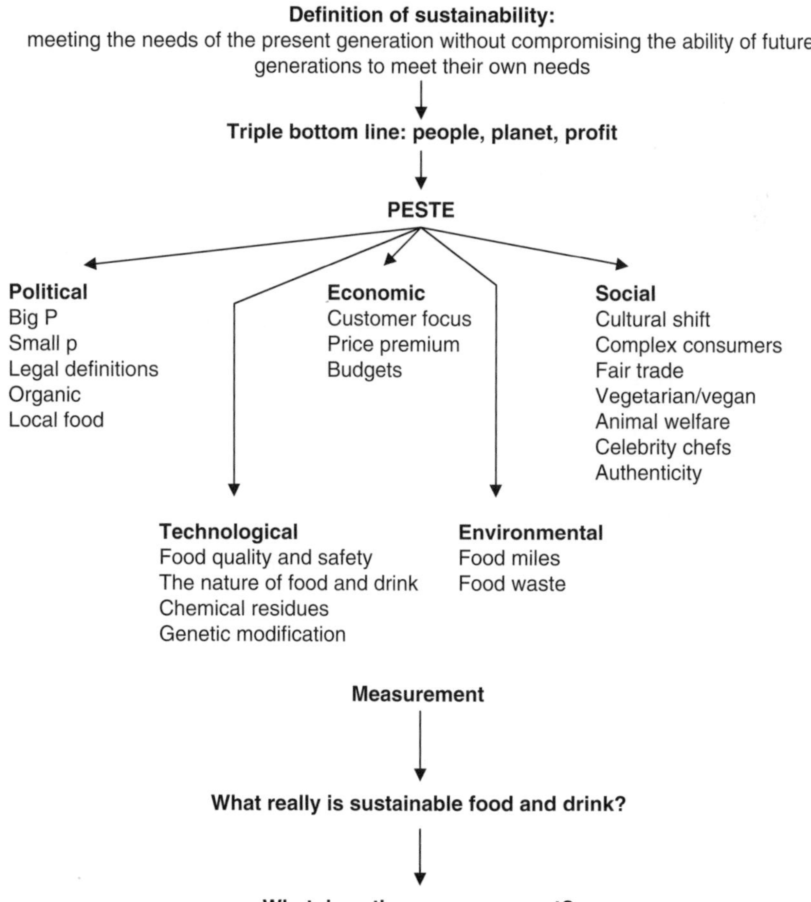

Fig. 16.3. Revision.

References

AEA Technology (2005) The Validity of Food Miles as an Indicator of Sustainable Development. Available at: https://statistics.defra.gov.uk/esg/reports/foodmiles/execsumm.pdf (accessed September 2007).

Atkins, P. and Bowler, I. (2001) *Food in Society. Economy, Culture, Geography*. Arnold, London.

BBC (2008) Food waste on a staggering scale. Available at: http://news.bbc.co.uk/1/hi/uk/7389351.stm (accessed 2 September 2008).

Beer, S.C. (2008a) Authenticity and food experience-commercial and academic perspectives. *Journal of Food Service* 19, 153–163.

Beer, S.C. (2008b) What is ethnic? Reappraising ethnic food and multiculturalism in Great Britain – the white British. Opportunities from ethnic diversity. In: Lindgreen, A. and Hingley, M. (eds) *Food Marketing in the Age of Fusion and Fragmentation*. Gower, Aldershot (in press).

Beer, S.C. and Redman, M. (1996) The relationship between post war cultural shift, consumer perspectives and farming policy. In: Edwards, J.S.A. (ed.) *Culinary Arts and Sciences: Global and National Perspectives*. Research Machines, Southampton, UK, pp. 351–362.

BSI (2007) *BS 8901:2007 Specification for a sustainable event management system with guidance for use developed*. British Standards Institution, London.

COI (2007) *Local Food. Omnibus Research Report*. Food Standards Agency, Southampton, UK.

DEFRA (2007a) Advisory Committee on Organic Standards (ACOS). Available at: http://www.defra.gov.uk/farm/organic/standards/acos/index.htm (accessed 27 September 2007).

DEFRA (2007b) Approved UK (organic) certification bodies. Available at: http://www.defra.gov.uk/farm/organic/standards/certbodies/approved.htm (accessed 27 September 2007).

DEFRA (2008a) Eggs and poultry – frequently asked questions. Available at: http://www.defra.gov.uk/foodrin/poultry/faq/marketing.htm#freerang (accessed 20 May 2008).

DEFRA (2008b) EU Protected Food Names Scheme – UK registered names. Available at: http://www.defra.gov.uk/foodrin/foodname/pfn/products/registered.htm (accessed May 2008).

Dittmer, P.R. (2003) *Principles of Food, Beverage, and Labor Cost Control*, 7th edn. John Wiley and Sons, New York.

Eastham, J., Sharples, L. and Ball, S. (2001) *Food Supply Chain Management. Issues for the Hospitality and Retail Sectors*. Butterworth-Heinemann, Oxford, UK.

ElAmin, A. (2006a) Northern foods appeals Melton Mowbray pork pie decision. Available at: http://www.meatprocess.com/news/ng.asp?n=64826-northern-foods-melton-mowbray-geographical-indications (accessed 24 September 2007).

ElAmin, A. (2006b) Northern foods reaches deal on Melton Mowbray pork pies. Available at: http://www.meatprocess.com/news/ng.asp?n=71868-northern-foods-melton-mowbray-geographical-indications (accessed 24 September 2007).

European Commission (2007) Agricultural and rural development: organic farming. Available at: http://ec.europa.eu/agriculture/qual/organic/reg/index_en.htm (accessed 27 September 2007).

FSA (2008) Food Standards Agency web site. Available at: http://www.food.gov.uk/ (accessed 20 May 2008).

Germov, J. and Williams, L. (1999) *A Sociology of Food and Nutrition. The Social Appetite*. Oxford University Press, Melbourne, Australia.

Lang, T. (2006) Locale/global (food miles). *Slow Food (Bra, Cuneo, Italy)* 19(May), 94–97.

McKie, R. (2008) How the myth of food miles hurts the planet. *The Observer* (Sunday 23 March), p. 30.

Mepham, B. (1996) *Food Ethics*. Routledge, London.

Pavesic, D. and Magnant, P. (2005) *Fundamental Principles of Restaurant Cost Control*, 2nd edn. Prentice Hall, Upper Saddle River, New Jersey.

Porter, J. (2008) Wiltshire pub fined for misleading menu. Available at: http://www.thepublican.com/story.asp?sectioncode=7&storycode=59214&c=1 (accessed 20 May 2008).

Reisinger, Y. and Steiner, C.J. (2006) Reconceptualizing object authenticity. *Annals of Tourism Research* 33(1), 65–86.

Soil Association (2005) *Market Report*. Soil Association, Bristol, UK.

Soil Association (2007) *Market Report*. Soil Association, Bristol, UK.

Stacey, C. (2008) Food miles. Available at: http://www.bbc.co.uk/food/food_matters/foodmiles.shtml (accessed 17 June 2008).

Sustain (2008) 7 Principles of sustainable food. Available at: http://www.sustainweb.org/sustainablefood/ (accessed 6 June 2008).

Timesonline (2007) Waitrose Sticks Knife into Rival. *The Sunday Times* (29 July), p. 3. Available at: http://business.timesonline.co.uk/tol/business/industry_sectors/retailing/article2157877.ece (accessed 16 March 2009).

Trendwatching.com (2008) Local and Authenticity still Rule. Available at: http://www.trendwatching.com/trends/statusstories.htm (accessed 6 June 2008).

WRAP (2008) New WRAP Research Reveals Extent of Food Waste in the UK. Available at: http://www.wrap.org.uk/wrap_corporate/news/new_wrap_2.html (accessed 17 June 2008). Full report available at http://news.bbc.co.uk/1/shared/bsp/hi/pdfs/foodwewaste_fullreport08_05_08.pdf (accessed 17 June 2008).

Specific references for food service operation management

Ball, S., Jones, P., Kirk, D. and Lockwood, A. (2003) *Hospitality Operations: A Systems Approach*. Continuum, London.

Cracknell, H.L., Kaufmann, R. and Nobis, G. (2000) *Practical Professional Catering Management*, 2nd edn. Macmillan Press, London.

Dittmer, P.R. (2003) *Principles of Food, Beverage, and Labor Cost Control*, 7th edn. John Wiley and Sons, New York.

Heizer, J. and Render, B. (2006) *Operations Management*, 8th edn. Prentice Hall, Upper Saddle River, New Jersey.

Johnston, R. and Clark, G. (2001) *Service Operations Management*. Prentice Hall, Harlow, UK.

Lillicrap, D.R., Cousins, J. and Smith, R. (2002) *Food and Beverage Service*, 6th edn. Hodder and Stoughton, London.

Pavesic, D. and Magnant, P. (2005) *Fundamental Principles of Restaurant Cost Control*, 2nd edn. Prentice Hall, Upper Saddle River, New Jersey.

Payne-Palacino, J. and Theis, M. (2005) *Introduction to Foodservice*, 10th edn. Prentice Hall, Upper Saddle River, New Jersey.

Reid, R. and Sanders, N. (2007) *Operations Management*, 3rd edn. John Wiley and Sons, Danvers, Massachusetts.

Slack, N., Chambers, S. and Johnston, R. (2007) *Operations Management*, 5th edn. Prentice Hall, Upper Saddle River, New Jersey.

Spears, M. and Gregoire, M. (2007) *Foodservice Organizations*, 6th edn. Prentice Hall, Upper Saddle River, New Jersey.

Van Looy, B., Gemmel, P. and Van Dierdonck, R. (2003) *Services Management*, 2nd edn. Prentice Hall, Harlow, UK.

Useful web sites

BBC Food: http://www.bbc.co.uk/food/
Biodynamic Agriculture Association: http://www.biodynamic.org.uk/
DEFRA: http://www.defra.gov.uk
Food Manufacture: http://www.foodmanufacture.co.uk/
FSA: http://www.food.gov.uk/
Heritage Prime, Biodynamic Food Producer: http://www.heritageprime.co.uk
National Farmers' Retail & Markets Association (FARMA): http://www.farma.org.uk/
Pampered Pigs, organic pork producer and farm shop: http://www.pampered-pigs.co.uk
Soil Association: http://www.soilassociation.org
RSPCA: http://www.rspca.org.uk
RSPCA Freedom Foods: http://www.rspca.org.uk/servlet/Satellite?pagename=RSPCA/FreedomFood/FreedomFoodHomepage
Sustain: http://www.sustainweb.org
The meaning of food: http://www.pbs.org/opb/meaningoffood/
Vegan Society: http://www.vegansociety.com/home.php
Vegetarian Society: http://www.vegsoc.org/
World Food Habits: http://www.lilt.ilstu.edu/rtdirks/

17 Networking Processes and Stakeholders' Power Relationships: Impact on Event Activities in a Rural Region of Italy

A. Capriello[1] and I.D. Rotherham[2]
[1]*University of Eastern Piedmont, Novara, Italy;*
[2]*Sheffield Hallam University, Sheffield, UK*

This chapter presents a case study focused on a rural area between Lakes Orta and Maggiore in Italy. The study analyses the roles of networking processes and stakeholders' power relations in promoting a vibrant rural community through leisure and tourism events. The chapter reviews literature on stakeholders' power relationships and sustainable development planning models.

Chapter outline

- Introduction
- Sustainable Development and Stakeholders
- Networking Processes and Sustainable Development Planning
- Stakeholders, Networking Processes and Events
- Event Organization and Networking Processes
- Networking Processes, Regional Development and Event Innovation
- Case Study – the Rural Area between the Two Lakes
- Summary
- Key Questions

Introduction

Events are frequently identified in plans for destination development and promoted as an attractor for leisure activity visitors. Benefits from hosting events include fostering the place image and marketing activities, invigorating remote areas, reducing environmental pressure on honey-pot attractions, increasing and improving local infrastructure, and attracting off-peak tourists (Getz, 2005, 2007).

Festivals and events might be considered a means to achieve sustainable development aims whenever social, economic and environmental objectives are included in the policy makers' agenda and translated into factual measures. In the described context, the aims should be oriented to foster participation and community ownership of initiatives through an equitable distribution of the benefits and costs of growth (Warburton, 1998; Richards and Hall, 2000).

Festival and event tourism potentially contributes positively to a locality, but does not automatically secure local economic development (O'Sullivan and Jackson, 2002). Also, the triangular equilibrium balancing the interests of local people, visitors and the festival activities and celebrations is difficult to achieve (Quinn, 2006). It is worth noting that while smaller events, perhaps relating to literature, flowers, music or other forms of leisure consumption, might be considered less ambitious as policy actions, they can have significant local economic impacts (Hughes, 1999). Some consider that enhancing the experience of the local community is important and may help strengthen community involvement and residents' pride in the area (Thomas and Wood, 2003). Additionally, in the current climate of risky and expensive tourism development projects, most rural festivals need little assistance from state or federal governments (Janiskee and Drews, 1998). Yet, smaller events may have low demand and low value, and from a tourism perspective are depicted as problematic. Getz (2008, p. 407) indicates that some do require investment and also that others are disinterested in tourism as they are primarily community or culturally oriented. Tourism professionals and event organizers are also sometimes unaware of the benefits associated with events (Tomljenovic and Weber, 2004).

Sustainable Development and Stakeholders

Sustainable development is a contested concept with many potential interpretations. This is particularly so in connection with the relationship between sustainability and development (Bramwell and Lane 2000, p. 3). Sustainable tourism development requires: (i) holistic planning and strategy formulation; (ii) preservation of ecological processes; (iii) protection of human and natural heritage; and (iv) development in which productivity can be sustained over the long term for future generations (Bramwell and Lane, 1993, p. 2). Sustainable forms of local economic development imply the consideration of 'longer term' and 'intergenerational equity'. The potential of tourism-based activities to help achieve environmental preservation and conservation has been widely recognized (Mathieson and Wall, 1982; Bramwell and Lane, 1993; Stewart, 1998). With the creation and promotion of leisure products, the attainment of these aims depends on multiple stakeholders actively involved in policy development (Bramwell, 1998).

Freeman (1984, p. 46) defines a stakeholder as 'any group or individual who can affect or is affected by the achievement of the organizations' objectives'. Stakeholders are sometimes newcomers to a rural area and they act as leaders, innovators and catalysts (Getz and Carlsen, 2000). The application of sustainability concepts to tourism development planning implies a consideration of all stakeholder groups (Sautter and Leisen, 1999). Accordingly, Byrd (2007) identifies four distinct groups represented by the present visitors, the future visitors, the present host community and the future host community. Although each stakeholder controls resources and capital, it does not possess all the resources to achieve the target objectives (Bramwell and Lane, 2000). In addition, resource dependency and stakeholder interdependency generate different forms of collaboration. Thus, network relationships are a major focal point for contemporary discussion on regional development.

Networking Processes and Sustainable Development Planning

Encouraging collaboration between stakeholders is relevant to the promotion and management of leisure products (Kotler *et al.*, 1993; Gunn, 1995). The approach connects with the complex organization of recreation activities and the functional interdependence between markets (Haywood, 1992; Murphy, 1997). The creation and promotion of holiday experiences require the management of comprehensive inventories of products and services. These link key brand values and assets (natural and landscape features, climate, culture, food and wine, amenities and communities) with the aspirations and needs of key customers (King, 2002).

For destination development, the best way to build a network is to intertwine the key attractors with appropriate social actors and institutions (Johns and Mattsson, 2005). Moreover, the proliferation of relationships connected with destination transformation contributes to increase information exchange that assists knowledge creation (Pavlovich, 2003). The establishment of networks is also associated with social and environmental objectives. This aligns with the growing importance of, for example, EU funds for development projects and programmes (Long, 1996; Hall, 1999) and cross-sectoral initiatives that bring together different stakeholders into sustainable development projects (Selin, 1999). Networks and partnerships help ensure ongoing development, preservation and nurturing of culture as a resource for rural tourism (MacDonald and Jollife, 2003).

It is suggested that a sustainable tourism product was generated by social networks and relationships in the Peak District National Park in England (Saxena, 2005). Saxena identifies four different actor attitudes (enthusiasts, activists, pragmatists and opponents) towards partnership building and in their perceptions of cross-sector networks. Dredge (2006) emphasizes the characteristics of pivotal members in terms of expertise, professionalism and networking ability. These were important for network cohesiveness and the development of shared views and understanding. She also notes the imbalance between active network participants and dormant members of the wider community. This may be an obstacle to cohesion and development of a common platform of interests. The efficacy of networking processes also depends on the density of social networks, the area involved and the motivation of entrepreneurs (Wilson *et al*., 2001; von Friedrichs Grängsjö, 2003; von Friedrichs Grängsjö and Gummesson, 2006; Ross and Lynch, 2007). An assessment of the stakeholders' position and relationships also identified the following limitations to networking processes:

- a low involvement of the private sector, as stakeholders are often public sector actors (Medeiros de Araujo and Bramwell, 2002);
- the effectiveness and efficiency of local community participation are threatened by lack of both financial resources and experience in tourism, and potentially by the cultural remoteness of host communities (Tosun, 2000);
- the stakeholders with the resources have considerable power to influence destination planning processes (Bramwell and Sharman, 1999); and
- business considerations and technical rationality dominate over environmental concerns (Bramwell, 2006).

Stakeholders, Networking Processes and Events

The importance of networking processes is related to complex relationships generated through production and promotion of events. In the light of this context, Getz *et al*. (2007) identify the following stakeholders:

- The festival organizations represented by employees, volunteers and directors, which might be legally or contractually bound together.
- The co-producers represented by performers, associations, restaurant and food sales, and interested organizations. They are tangibly involved in creating the event experience.
- The facilitators active in providing cash grants and sponsorship and in-kind support.
- The allies and collaborators, which are professional organizations involved in other festivals. They might also support the event producer through lobbying and marketing partnerships.
- The regulators identified by local authorities and agencies, as approval is frequently required to host a festival.
- The suppliers and venues, which might also be festival sponsors.
- The audience, which is particularly important to assess in terms of the potential popularity of the festival.
- The impacted as represented by charities, the community at large and special interest groups. They might experience negative impacts as well benefits from the cultural entertainment and other activities.

To understand the main features of the collaborative relationships in events it is important to identify the role of networking processes in their organization. It is also pertinent to evaluate events and their contributions to innovation and regional development in a host area.

Event Organization and Networking Processes

According to Long (2000, p. 58), festival and event management is based on resource interdependencies between partners in terms of finance, staffing and expertise. This interaction is related to the need to ensure economic efficiencies in multilateral relationships. Thus private and public sector partnerships are vital to the provision of quality events and help them develop a more focused customer orientation. They are also considered to be a new source of finance in a context of limited and uncertain budgets. This orientation generates a change of the private sector's position from event provider to event facilitator (Pugh and Wood, 2004). The event organizers must interact with local businesses and the general public to plan the event. This interaction over the period of the event's organization may raise awareness of community resources and also of deficiencies. It produces social links between previously unrelated groups and individuals, and identifies possibilities for the development of the community's resources; generally encouraging a stronger interaction between existing community organizations (Pugh and Wood, 2004). The social networks that can develop through the organization of festivals have the potential to be maintained beyond the short life of the event (Arcodia and Whitford, 2005). Festivals and events that involve volunteers may provide opportunities for training and development in a variety of skills, and encourage more effective use of local educational, business and community spaces.

To maximize success event managers may engage in network building to obtain resources and grow the activities. Some festival organizations work with stakeholders through personal informal relationships or natural allies in the professional community (Getz *et al.*, 2007). Networks may encourage diversification of existing weak ties with people not yet involved and they may generate novel connections to local industry, and this may create innovative festival programmes (McCarthy *et al.*, 2007).

Networking Processes, Regional Development and Event Innovation

Relationships between stakeholders help explain the role of event programmes in regional development. Networks in regional communities are fundamental not only to leverage opportunities for promoting and marketing of local industry, but also in creating the prerequisites for regional product innovation. The case study of Lismore in Australia demonstrates that festival activities such as recipe competitions and celebrity chef demonstrations allowed local growers and interstate visitors to discover new interconnections between gastronomy and other economic industries (Mackellar, 2006). The importance of knowledge sharing is also considered an incentive for participation in event networks (Stokes, 2004a). Network membership allows access to complementary expertise and increased professional skills from shared knowledge and experience of others. In this way regional development is supported by the events innovation process and enhancement of stakeholders' strategies. In particular, strategies for events tourism were mostly influenced by 'soft' networks or sets of informal relationships that helped shape the directions of events tourism (Stokes, 2004b).

However, developing new events and stimulating tourism demand for existing events require enhanced collaboration. In a study of six Australian states, Stokes (2008) reveals the importance of collaborative strategy in making rural or small communities distinct from larger towns and cities. Collaborative processes can be created through round tables and other participatory mechanisms. Additionally, decision-making criteria are normally coherent with those of sustainable tourism development models, to include economic, social, cultural and environmental impacts.

Interactions between actors are collaborative, although often characterized by conflicts resolved by power games. Thus, there is a need to reconcile partners' strategic objectives with the nature and influence of political relationships (Long, 2000). Larson (2002) introduces a metaphor of a project network, the political square market (PSQ), to analyse the networking processes among the actors involved in marketing the Storsjöyran Festival in Sweden. Those actors remain in a wider network, as they have a potential interest to enter the PSQ and wait for the right opportunity. The open access to the PSQ 'led to flexibility relating [to] participants and the opportunistic interaction resulted in turbulence within the PSQ' (Larson 2002, p. 138). Turbulence caused by interactions between actors might produce such benefits as product development and innovation.

Case Study – the Rural Area between the Two Lakes

The rural communities between Lakes Orta and Maggiore are located in a region with strong natural distinctiveness (Fig. 17.1). The uniqueness of the places is also represented by the rich and significant heritage possessed by local municipalities and religious institutions. However, it seems that the maintenance and restoration of key aspects of this resource are not yet sustainable. This is due to current financial constraints among those responsible for their conservation.

The Piedmont Region has always been actively engaged in the preservation of its heritage, with restoration actions directed to safeguard or recover key individual assets. Furthermore, it also has current policies oriented to support integrated plans directed to preserve the historical and architectural wealth in homogeneous geographical areas. A bottom-up approach is adopted that is directed at creating leisure and tourism products through collaborations of cooperative operators, local public institutions and voluntary associations. This principle supports the idea of improving quality of life in the region and also marketing it for its leisure potential. In 2007, three projects were approved concerning the Piedmontese areas of Pinerolo, Langhe and Susa Valley.

In the geographical context of this study, local institutions identified an opportunity to develop a shared project linking to local markets for leisure and tourism activities. The project aims to coordinate the actions of locally active professional and voluntary bodies in promotional and management work. A partnership was constituted involving local administrations, schools and universities, religious bodies and associations. Table 17.1 shows the details related to the partnership members.

Ameno, Armeno, Colazza, Gozzano, Invorio, Massino Visconti and Miasino are all municipalities particularly committed to the initiatives. Since the project was agreed, the geographical area represented by these municipalities was branded under the name 'Cuore Verde tra i due Laghi' ('Green Heart between the two Lakes').

An Agreement Protocol was signed on 16 July 2007 by those promoting the project. This identifies the promotion of events and festivals as a priority. It was also decided that these should combine ideas such as the role of contemporary arts in engaging people with their historical and natural assets. Additionally, a sustainable development model was proposed that reflects the needs of residents and helps empower local actions. This approach was in order to promote both traditional activities, through agricultural and craft work, and the regional folk culture expressed by festivals and ethnographic museums. Through community round tables, the municipalities' mayors expressed their interest in improving the quality of life for residents. This objective was to be attained through the active participation of local people. The proposed initiatives are directed at reinvigorating the towns' squares for these rural communities.

Financial support from the Piedmont Region is limited and is focused on sustaining initiatives proposed by the communities in accordance with their key priorities. Thus, the partners declared their future intention to involve banking foundations and to access European funds. This was in relation to their financial requirements in order to recover heritage that was either damaged or under threat. At the start of 2008, the 'Cuore Verde tra i due Laghi' project was approved by the Piedmont Region. Thus, translating the aims of the project into actions has required coordination and the presence of cooperative working groups. The first preliminary meetings were directed at building the partnership, and three working groups were identified. These concerned the following topics:

- Contemporary Arts, coordinated by Asilo Bianco, Poetry on the Lake and Ameno Blues Group;
- Heritage and Religious, managed by the Parish Priest of Ameno; and
- Gastronomy, supervised by the Province of Novara and the Mountain Community between the two Lakes (an administrative body).

The interaction between the three working groups is important in terms of generating an

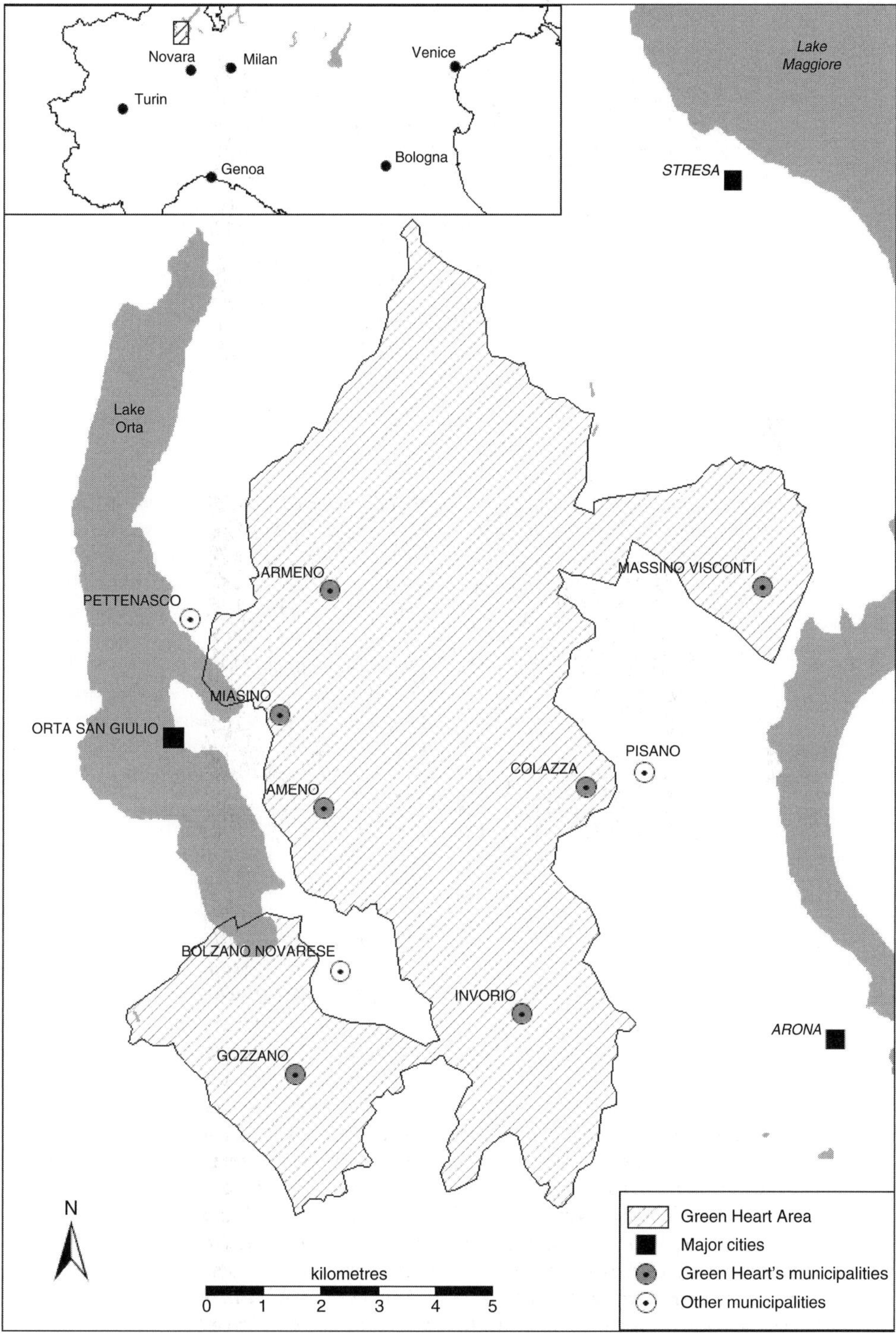

Fig. 17.1. The geographical context.

Table 17.1. Members of the partnership.

Public operators	Local administrations	Province of Novara Mountain Community between the Two Lakes Municipalities of Ameno, Armeno, Colazza, Gozzano, Invorio, Massino Visconti, Miasino
	Schools and universities	University of Eastern Piedmont Istituto Comprensorio of Orta (primary and secondary schools)
Non-profit operators	Religious institutions	Parishes of Ameno and Lortallo, Invorio Inferiore and Superiore, Bolzano Novarese and Vacciago, Armeno, Sovazza, Miasino, Carcegna and Pisogno, Colazza
	Associations	Asilo Bianco (project coordinator) Poetry on the Lake Ilbox Motore per l'Arte Associazione Storica Cusius Slow Food

events programme in the area. Before considering the events activities and networking processes of stakeholders, the socio-economic context and the role played by leaders are described.

The socio-economic context

The economy in these rural communities is based mainly on farm and craft sectors and they suffer from significant depopulation. The regional hospitality sector has traditionally concentrated investment on the shore of Lake Maggiore in tourist areas such as Stresa.

Important architectural assets are related to the history of the territory. After Saint Julius and Julian's evangelization in the 4th century, clerical power in terms of local landholdings increased progressively throughout the Middle Ages. The heritage associated with this influence is seen in local parish churches such as in Armeno and Carcegna near Miasino.

During the 16th and 17th centuries the diffusion of religious practices and the edification of numerous parish churches were influenced by enigmatic personalities such as Saint Carlo Borromeo and Carlo Bescapè. With the Catholic Counter-Reformation, the Sacro Monte (Sacred Mountains) of Orta was built and the devotional complex has become a religious destination today included in the UNESCO World Heritage list. Furthermore, with faith perceived as a unique tool to alleviate diseases and epidemics, devotional trails were developed in the area by local residents.

In the 19th and 20th centuries increasing interest in the area was generated by the introduction of cruise excursions on Lake Maggiore, the advent of the railway and the development of international communications. Luxury hotels were built in Stresa and managed by family-owned businesses. Private country residences were constructed by European noblemen and an entrepreneurial middle class living in Lombardy or Piedmont Region. Nowadays, some of them belong to the municipalities, such as Palazzo Tornielli in Ameno and Villa Nigra in Miasino. After World War II, Lake Maggiore was transformed into a mass leisure destination with large numbers of day visitors from Milan and Novara. On the other hand, Lake Orta became an industrial area, where household goods and kitchenware were produced. With pollution and associated damage to vegetation in and around the Lake, there was little interest in the area's tourism potential. This is now reflected in only limited hospitality presence, but also in the maintenance of traditional rural communities rather than the development of new housing. In the 1980s, actions to begin the recovery of the damaged ecology of Lake Orta were undertaken.

Today, with the economic world populated by tourist products, Lake Maggiore's hospitality industry has been struggling to either keep or strengthen its market niche. To enhance its competitiveness it has also developed locally based events. This event programme includes international initiatives such as 'Le Settimane Musicale di Stresa e del Lago Maggiore' ('The Musical Weeks of Stresa and Lake Maggiore'). In addition, with crises in the local manufacturing sector, a re-launch of Lake Orta as a tourist destination has been proposed by stakeholders. The strategic marketing plan also includes steps to more fully involve the rural communities between the two Lakes in the initiatives.

Leaders and co-shared interests

Since 2004, local municipality administrators in the rural area have targeted their policies towards actions to preserve the historical and natural assets in their territories. These aims are coherent with the objectives of the 2005 Tourist Strategic Plan of the Province of Novara. These objectives are directed to launch the area for leisure and tourism, sustain the local economy and preserve the fragile environment.

There are other influences too. The presence of artists and writers, who have chosen to reside in the hills around Lake Orta, has helped trigger several cultural initiatives. In July 2005, a Blues Festival organized in Ameno was attended by 400 people and sponsored by the Province of Novara. The initiative drew on local politicians' musical interests, and strengthened relationships with local facilitators. The event also represented a first attempt to market the 'place' and image of the area and reduce the anonymity of the town. In the light of its success, the Province of Novara supported the further events in 2006 and 2007.

There is a formal group active in promoting the area, called 'Asilo Bianco'. It is located in Ameno and aims to promote contemporary arts in the area. Its activity is focused on topical issues such the environment, sustainable development and recycling. The objectives of the institution are also to develop an interest in the arts through the discovery of local heritage. Since June 2006, the association has been the promoter of a culture project involving the Province of Novara, the municipalities of Ameno and Miasino, and the Nature Reserve of the Sacred Mountains of Orta. The project is directed to host three artists and three writers between September and October and they receive an annual grant from a banking foundation. At the end of the period the artists translate their impressions of the experience into a work. Some of their outputs enrich the historical heritage, as in the case of the contemporary art installation in Villa Nigra in Miasino in October 2006. Writers have the opportunity to find ideas for their novels, and sources include interrogation of the state archives. A key aspect of the project has been the creation of an international social network between artists and writers. The described collaboration has also helped generate an events programme in the area.

The further aim of this initiative is to help repopulate the area during the summertime. In particular, workshops organized by artists and writers also function to establish relationships between residents and tourists. Thus, the future restoration of Villa Nigra is directed to hosting these cultural activities with the creation of an International Centre for Contemporary Arts. However, it is still difficult sometimes for local people to understand the artists' behaviour, and there may be conflicts in terms of land use during the event and traffic restrictions.

Discovering the ancient origins of the rural communities is another objective of other local organizations. Since the recent arrival of a new religious community, they have reintroduced Catholic ritual practices such as the procession as a means to networking with residents. Additionally, the restoration of the parish church in Ameno presented the opportunity to host children's activities during the summer. The planned activities included a dialect school for the younger generation in the area. This initiative was a tool to build a special link to the local older people and to facilitate the learning of folk stories and re-discovering this rural community's ancient traditions.

Events and networking processes

Between June 2007 and July 2008, four events took place in the Green Heart that were connected with the preliminary stage of the Green Heart's project. Table 17.2 presents the title, purposes, period and places of interest of each event.

Table 17.2. Description of events.

Event 1	
Title	Opening artists' studios and artistic packages of the local products
Purposes	Networking with the public through the explanation of artists' works
	Enhancing the value of three local products through artistic packages
Actors	Event organizer: Asilo Bianco
	Facilitators: Province of Novara, Municipality of Ameno
	Suppliers: Local producers
	Co-producers: Italian artists living in the area and/or linked with Asilo Bianco
Period	30 June–1 July 2007
Places of interest	Ameno
Event 2	
Title	Papers/Leaves and Writing Event
Purposes	Promotion of a tourist guide realized by artists
	Marketing new food from local farm production
Actors	Event organizers: Asilo Bianco
	Facilitators: Province of Novara, Municipality of Miasino, banking foundation[a]
	Suppliers: Local producers, publisher[a] and local hotel[b]
	Co-producers: National artists hosted by Asilo Bianco
Period	6 October 2007 – Third National Day on Contemporary Arts
Place of interest	Miasino (Villa Nigra)
Event 3	
Title	Contemporary Art Exhibition
Purposes	Promotion of the area through contemporary art and local heritage
	Marketing the local cuisine
Actors	Event organizers: Asilo Bianco
	Facilitators: Piedmont Region, Province of Novara, Swedish Minister of Culture, Swedish Embassy, municipalities of Ameno and Miasino
	Suppliers: Local hotel[b]
	Co-producers: International artists from Sweden
Period	30 March–6 July 2008
Places of interest	Miasino, Orta (Sacro Monte) and Armeno
Event 4	
Title	Picnic on the Grass
Purposes	Promotion of the area through local heritage
	Marketing local food products
Actors	Event organizers: Asilo Bianco
	Facilitators: Province of Novara, local municipalities and parish churches
	Suppliers: Local producers and local retailers
	Co-producers: Volunteer associations
Period	15 June–6 July 2008 (on Saturdays and Sundays)
Places of interest	Ameno (church, contemporary exhibition), Armeno (church), Bolzano Novarese (church), Colazza (church), Gozzano (church), Invorio (church), Massino Visconti (church), Miasino (Villa Nigra), Orta S. Giulio (Sacro Monte), Pettenasco (Museum of Wood Craftworks), Pisano (church)

[a]These institutions cooperated to realize the tourist guide.
[b]The hotel was involved to promote the local cuisine.

As noted earlier, the events are intended to help market the area as a Contemporary Art Centre through the support of local stakeholders. This aim is achieved through measures directed at embedding interest in the conservation of natural and historical resources with potential benefits for the local economy. Analysis of these initiatives reveals the strategic role played by Asilo Bianco as event organizer. In particular, its personal network was central to identifying the event co-producers as represented by artists. At first, the main involvement was oriented to Italian artists living in the area. The following event generated cooperation with international artists from Sweden, previously hosted by the association. This cooperation has been oriented to create collaboration between the Gothenburg area and the Green Heart territory with an initial focus on contemporary art exhibitions. The future evolution of this alliance will be addressed by a co-joint marketing activity through interactions between the local producers of the two territories.

In terms of generating economic benefits, specific measures were designed by the working groups. In particular, as the interest of the Province of Novara has been to protect farm production through the development of entrepreneurial activities, there was a specific focus on marketing gastronomy during the events programme. With the first event, three local products were marketed by means of packages created by artists (Fig. 17.2). This marketing measure was adopted as a tool to reinforce the products' image, reducing their anonymity among the event audience.

At end of the second event, the involvement of local actors such as farmers and pastry cooks was fundamental in inventing new recipes for the area. At the third event, one restaurant proposed a local menu, also through the discovery of ancient recipes. Finally, during the fourth event, retailers promoted a selection of products sold in a picnic basket together with a tour guide book produced by the artists.

Moreover, to address the sustainable development objectives shared by municipalities, the events were directed at networking with the audience. In particular, local artists opened their studios and explained their works at the first event. Additionally, contemporary art installations were used to enhance local heritage such as the parish church and the Public Garden in Ameno (Fig. 17.3).

In order to increase community ownership of the event, wood carvings of birds by a local sculptor were commissioned to enrich the gazebo in the Public Garden in Ameno. They were also included as a point of interest for the contemporary art exhibition (Fig. 17.4).

To support social inclusion and the environmental aims of local municipalities, a bus

Fig. 17.2. Packages created by artists to promote local farm products.

Fig. 17.3. A contemporary art installation in Ameno parish church.

Fig. 17.4. Gazebo with sculptor's carved wood birds in Ameno Public Garden.

Fig. 17.5. A didactic laboratory in Ameno.

service from Orta was organized to reduce traffic problems and allow participation of disadvantaged groups. The events programme also included didactic laboratories organized in collaboration with local schools. The initiatives were undertaken to show the manual activity of artists with a specific focus on environmental issues (Fig. 17.5). This is a part of a wider project coordinated by the Primary Schools' Directors in Invorio and Colazza. It was directed at increasing the awareness by children of local heritage, as they will be the 'future host community'. In particular, the planned activities intend to enhance the knowledge related to the woodland areas between the two Lakes.

Summary

Local events and festivals are often described as having low demand and low value (Getz, 2008), but are less risky in comparison with mega-events. In the case study presented, the development and operation of events was generated through a mix of public investments relating to proposals for specific initiatives by local communities. Moreover, given a relatively lower participation level, local events and festivals have less adverse environmental impact and so achieved the aims of preserving natural resources. Yet despite their limitations in terms of scale, and maybe because of this, local events are coherent with a sustainable development model. The initiative leaders are motivated to invigorate the locale in terms of heritage, culture and economy.

In order to achieve social inclusion objectives and enhance quality of life in the rural communities, specific actions were developed by the working groups. The priority of the working groups was to promote the architectural and natural resources and allow innovation through the actor networks. The intention was to overcome the barriers represented by the territories of Green Heart's municipalities. In particular, in the case of the fourth event, the network was a strategic tool in generating product development and stimulating creativity, coherent with the metaphor proposed earlier by Larson (2002).

In terms of sustainable event management, these findings suggest the need to focus the marketing strategy on networking processes. These relationships were shown to be important in identifying clear objectives shared by all the main stakeholders, encouraging entrepreneurship, promoting product differentiation and protecting the uniqueness of the destination.

However, in the case study there was still a high degree of dependence on both public funds and inputs of volunteer activity. Furthermore, the nature of the partnership is imbalanced in terms of the interests represented. There is an over-representation of public institutions and non-profit associations, and so a limited input by local businesses. Informal networks still remain important in developing and innovation of the leisure and tourism product in the rural communities' case study area.

This aspect is also fostered by the continuing lack of an events policy for the whole Lakes area. This limits the potential mutual benefits from any integrated action to promote events tourism in the geographical area. Furthermore, there are still outstanding environmental issues and conflicts. For example, reduction of the environmental pressures on honey-pot attractions on the lakeside is not included in the current destination planning processes. Here, business considerations and technical rationality dominate over environmental concerns. Another issue is whether or not the emerging cultural activities might be integrated into the current provision of leisure and tourist products in the area.

Key Questions

1. Discuss and analyse the roles of networking processes and stakeholders' power relations in promoting a vibrant rural community through leisure and tourism events.
2. Describe how events are identified in plans for destination development and promoted as an attractor for leisure activity visitors.
3. Discuss the strengths and weaknesses of the Green Heart Area's policies in terms of sustainable events management.

References

Arcodia, C. and Whitford, M. (2006) Festival attendance and the development of social capital. *Journal of Convention and Event Tourism* 8(2), 1–18.

Bramwell, B. (1998) Selecting policy instruments for sustainable tourism. In: Theobald, W.F. (ed.) *Global Tourism*, 2nd edn. Butterworth-Heinemann, Oxford, UK, pp. 361–379.

Bramwell, B. (2006) Actors, power and discourses of growth limits. *Annals of Tourism Research* 33(4), 957–978.

Bramwell, B. and Lane, B. (1993) Sustainable tourism: an evolving global approach. *Journal of Sustainable Tourism* 1(1), 1–5.

Bramwell, B. and Lane, B. (2000) Collaboration and partnerships in tourism planning. In: Bramwell, B. and Lane, B. (eds) *Tourism Collaboration and Partnerships. Politics, Practise and Sustainability*. Channel View Publications, Buffalo, New York, pp. 1–19.

Bramwell, B. and Sharman, A. (1999) Collaboration in local tourism policymaking. *Annals of Tourism Research* 26(2), 392–415.

Byrd, T.E. (2007) Stakeholders in sustainable tourism development and their roles: applying stakeholder theory to sustainable tourism development. *Tourism Review* 62(2), 6–13.

Dredge, D. (2006) Policy networks and the local organisation of tourism. *Tourism Management* 27(2), 269–280.

Freeman, R.E. (1984) *Strategic Management: A Stakeholder Approach*. Pitman, Boston, Massachusetts.

Getz, D. (2005) *Event Management and Event Tourism*, 2nd edn. Cognizant, New York.

Getz, D. (2007) *Event Studies: Theory, Research and Policy Planned Events*. Elsevier, Amsterdam.

Getz, D. (2008) Event tourism: definition, evolution and research. *Tourism Management* 29(3), 403–428.

Getz, D. and Carlsen, J. (2000) Characteristics and goals of family and owner-operated business in the rural tourism and hospitality sectors. *Tourism Management* 21(6), 547–560.

Getz, D., Andersson, T. and Larson, M. (2007) Festival stakeholder roles: concept and case studies. *Event Management* 10(2/3), 103–122.

Gunn, C. (1993) *Tourism Planning: Basics, Concepts, Cases*. Taylor and Francis, Washington, DC.

Hall, C.M.J. (1999) Rethinking collaboration and partnership. A public policy perspective. *Journal of Sustainable Tourism* 7(3/4), 274–289.

Haywood, K.M. (1992) Identifying and responding to the challenges posed by urban tourism. *Tourism Recreation Research* 17(2), 9–23.

Hughes, G. (1999) Urban revitalisation: the use of festive time strategies. *Leisure Studies* 18(2), 119–135.

Janiskee, R.L. and Drews, P.L. (1998) Rural festivals and community reimaging. In: Butler, R., Hall, C.M. and Jenkins, J. (eds) *Tourism and Recreation in Rural Areas*. John Wiley and Sons Ltd, Chichester, UK, pp. 157–175.

Johns, N. and Mattsson, J. (2005) Destination development through entrepreneurship: a comparison of two cases. *Tourism Management* 26(4), 605–616.

King, J. (2002) Destination marketing organisations. Connecting the experience rather than promoting the place. *Journal of Vacation Marketing* 8(2), 105–108.

Kotler, P., Haider, D.H. and Rein, I. (1993) *Marketing Places: Attracting Investment, Industry, and Tourism to Cities, States and Nations*. Free Press, New York.

Larson, M. (2002) A political approach to relationship marketing: case study of Storsjöyran Festival. *International Journal of Tourism Research* 4(2), 119–143.

Long, P. (1996) Inter-organisational collaboration in the development of tourism and the arts. In: Robinson, M., Evans, N. and Callaghan, P. (eds) *Culture as the Tourist Product*. Business Education Publishers, Sunderland, UK, pp. 255–278.

Long, P. (2000) After the event: perspectives on organizational partnerships in the management of a themed festival year. *Event Management* 6(1), 45–59.

McCarthy, B., Moscardo, G., Murphy, L. and Pearce, P. (2007) Mining and chamber music: terra nova, exploring new territory in the development of music-tourism networks. In: Andreu, L., Gnoth J. and Kozak, M. (eds) *Proceedings of the 2007 Advances in Tourism Marketing Conference* (CD ROM). Publications de la Universitat de Valencia, Sueca, Spain.

MacDonald, R. and Jollife, L. (2002) Cultural rural tourism: evidence from Canada. *Annals of Tourism Research* 29(3), 720–742.

MacKellar, J. (2006) Conventions, festivals, and tourism: exploring the network that binds. *Journal of Convention and Event Tourism* 8(2), 45–56.

Mathieson, A. and Wall, G. (1982) *Tourism: Economic, Physical and Social Impacts*. Longman, London.

Medeiros de Araujo, L. and Bramwell, B. (2002) Partnership and regional tourism in Brazil. *Annals of Tourism Research* 29(4), 1138–1164.

Murphy, P. (1997) *Quality Management in Urban Tourism*. John Wiley and Sons Ltd, Chichester, UK.

O'Sullivan, D. and Jackson, M.J. (2002) Festival tourism: a contributor to sustainable local economic development, *Journal of Sustainable Tourism* 10(4), 325–342.

Pavlovich, K. (2003) The evolution and transformation of a tourism destination network: the Waitomo Caves, New Zealand. *Tourism Management* 24(2), 203–216.

Pugh, C. and Wood, E.H. (2004) The strategic use of events within local government: a study of London Borough Councils. *Event Management* 9(1/2), 61–71.

Quinn, B. (2006) Problematising 'festival tourism': arts festivals and sustainable development in Ireland. *Journal of Sustainable Tourism* 14(3), 288–306.

Richards, G. and Hall, D.R. (2000) *Tourism and Sustainable Community Development*. Routledge, London.

Ross, T. and Lynch, P.A. (2007) Small business networking and tourism destination development: a comparative perspective. *International Journal of Entrepreneurship and Innovation* 8(1), 15–27.

Thomas, R. and Wood, E. (2003) Events-based tourism: a survey of local authority strategies in the UK. *Local Governance* 29(2), 127–136.

Sautter, E.T. and Leisen, B. (1999) Managing stakeholders: a tourism planning model. *Annals of Tourism Research* 26(2), 312–328.

Saxena, G. (2005) Relationships, networks and the learning regions: case evidence from the Peak District National Park. *Tourism Management* 26(2), 277–289.

Selin, S. (1999) Developing a typology of sustainable tourism partnership. *Journal of Sustainable Tourism* 7(3/4), 260–273.

Stewart, E.J. (1998) The place of interpretation. *Tourism Management* 6 (1), 44–52.

Stokes, R. (2004a) A framework for the analysis of events – tourism knowledge networks. *Journal of Hospitality and Tourism Management* 11(2), 108–122.

Stokes, R. (2004b) Relationships and networks for shaping events tourism: an Australian study. *Event Management* 10(2/3), 145–158.

Stokes, R. (2008) Tourism strategy making: insights to the events tourism domain. *Tourism Management* 29(2), 252–262.

Tomljenovic, R. and Weber, S. (2004) Funding cultural events in Croatia: tourism-related policy issues. *Event Management* 9(1/2), 51–59.

Tosun, C. (2000) Challenges of sustainable tourism development in the developing world: the case of Turkey. *Tourism Management* 22(3), 289–304.

von Friedrichs Grängsjö, Y. (2003) Destination networking: co-opetition in peripheral surroundings. *International Journal of Physical Distribution and Logistics Management* 33(5), 427–448.

von Friedrichs Grängsjö, Y. and Gummesson, E. (2006) Hotel networks and social capital in destination marketing. *International Journal of Service Industry Management* 17(1), 58–75.

Warburton, D. (1998) *Community and Sustainable Development: Participation in the Future*. Earthscan, London.

Wilson, S., Fesenmaier, D.R., Fesenmaier, J. and van Es, J.C. (2001) Factors for success in rural tourism development. *Journal of Travel Research* 40(2), 132–138.

18 Local Markets and Sustainable Development

P. Jones,[1] D. Comfort[1] and D. Hillier[2]
[1]University of Gloucestershire, Cheltenham, UK;
[2]University of Glamorgan, Pontypridd, UK

This chapter explores the revival in the fortune of local markets within recent years. The chapter focuses on how this revival can contribute to sustainable development. It includes a description of the origin and development of markets, an examination of the general causes of their decline, an outline of the recent revival of local markets and a discussion of the environmental, economic and social benefits associated with these markets.

Chapter outline

- Introduction
- Origins and Development of Markets
- General Causes of Decline
- Market Revival
- Contributions to Sustainable Development
- Summary
- Key Questions

Introduction

Looking back to times long past, occasional and periodic markets in many ways epitomized the modern concept of sustainable development. Traditionally such events attracted people from all walks of life drawn from the surrounding areas to buy and sell the essentials of everyday life. The food on sale was produced locally using traditional farming methods, and clothing and basic household goods were made using natural local materials. While farmers drove their cattle over land to the market and some traders would use horse-drawn carts to carry their produce, the majority of people simply walked. The accent was very much on local self-sufficiency and markets provided important social meeting places where people could share information and exchange ideas. Initially these markets took place in the open air, but gradually partially or fully covered markets became increasingly common. By the 19th century, market halls and covered markets were both the central and the dominant element in the urban retail environment and they still had a local flavour, although over time a growing number of non-food goods were sourced from further afield.

From the 1960s onwards within the UK, changes in living and working conditions, and little short of a retail revolution, saw the growth of supermarkets and superstores and the increasing dominance of a small number of large national retailers, fuelling increasingly unsustainable consumption, posing a threat to many traditional local markets. A national survey report (Rhodes, 2005) has suggested that 'markets across the UK... are in decline' and that 'the valuable economic contribution of markets is under threat'. That said, the

Government's 'Planning Policy Statement 6; Planning for Town Centres' (Office of the Deputy Prime Minister, 2005) stresses that 'markets can make a valuable contribution to local choice and diversity in shopping as well as the vitality of town centres'. The Statement recommends that local authorities should not only 'seek to retain and enhance existing markets and, where appropriate, re-introduce or create new ones', but also 'ensure that their markets remain attractive and competitive by investing in their improvement'.

Origins and Development of Markets

Within the UK markets have long been a defining feature, in some ways the *raison d'être*, of urban and economic life. Many towns claim to be able to trace the origins of their markets back for 1000 years, but the 13th century witnessed a major expansion in the number and size of markets. Within Cheshire, for example, markets have existed in Chester, Middlewich and Nantwich from before the Norman Conquest, but many more began in the following two centuries. Aldford and Alderley, for example, were granted market rights in 1253, Macclesfield in 1261 and Congleton in 1272, and some 23 official markets are recorded in medieval Cheshire. More generally, Letters *et al.* (2005) report that 'the network of legally established markets and fairs in Medieval England, almost all of them authorised by royal grant, was dense, highly developed and apparently organised much earlier than that in most of Europe'.

For centuries these markets took place in the open air – initially often around churchyards and later, as towns grew in size, in town squares – and many of these open-air markets are still functional today. However, by the second half of the 18th century, there were moves to provide a more permanent and sheltered setting for both market traders and their customers. Schmiechen and Carls (1999) argue that the impetus for this move came because of:

> The extraordinary growth in the urban population that took place after about 1750... [that] taxed the existing food-distribution system beyond its capacity. Local governments sought to increase the food supply by inventing a new public market system, and as a result, urban dwellers, learned to be consumers in the modern sense – that is they mastered the rituals by which buying and selling became the central feature of modern life.

Furthermore, Schmiechen and Carls (1999) trace the 'birth of the market hall' to the separation of the market 'from dirty and wind swept streets and marketplaces into an enclosed and modern building that boasted a number of amenities' and to 'a widespread shift in market ownership from private to public hands'. They cite Bristol (1776), Halifax (1790), Plymouth (1804–1807) and Glasgow (1817) as illustrations of the rise of this new genre.

St John's Market in Liverpool, designed by John Foster, the city's architect, and opened in 1822, is widely recognized as being the first of a new and much larger generation of market halls. It consisted of a simple parallelogram design covering almost two acres and had 136 stone-trimmed arched bay windows, supported by 116 interior cast-iron pillars. The hall had a five-division wooden roof, two divisions of which were raised above the others to form a windowed clerestory that illuminated and ventilated the market below. The interior of the market was divided into five shopping avenues, each largely devoted to a particular range of foods, and each avenue was lined with stalls. This model was replicated, albeit with variations in size, layout and building materials, in a large number of provincial towns and cities throughout much of the 19th century. More generally, Schmiechen and Carls (1999) describe the period 1830–1890 as 'The Grand Age of the Market Hall' (p. 160), and, in as much as it paved the way for 'the modern environmentally controlled retail spaces: the department store, the supermarket and the shopping mall', so it was partly sowing the seeds of its own decline.

While the 19th century was the 'grand age' of market halls and covered markets, many new markets were also built during the following century. In some cases small and increasingly obsolete and congested markets were replaced by larger and better appointed facilities; in other towns new markets were built to replace those destroyed either by air raids during World War II – as in the case of

Coventry and Plymouth, for example – or by fire as at Birkenhead in 1969 and 1974 and at Leeds' Kirkgate Market in 1976. In many towns and cities new markets were built as part of town and city centre redevelopment programmes and traffic management schemes from the 1960s onwards. In many towns, as in Birkenhead and Leeds, open-air markets are still held, often 1 or 2 days a week, immediately outside the market hall. By the end of the 20th century markets were still part of the urban retail environment, but in all too many towns they seemed to have become a declining, neglected and often threatened element within that environment.

General Causes of Decline

While all markets have their own distinctive characteristics and mix of traders, a number of general factors appear to be combining to pose not necessarily a new, but certainly a growing, threat to their commercial well-being and in some cases their continued existence. Changes in living and working behaviour have been affecting markets for some time. The process of residential decentralization, which has seen relentless suburban expansion in most towns and cities during recent decades, the personal mobility afforded by mass motor car ownership and the growth in the number of households where both adults are in full-time employment have all contributed to the increasing popularity of one-stop weekly shopping trips to large and easily accessible stores on out-of-town and edge-of-town sites. More and more customers are accustomed to being able to park their vehicles close to retail outlets, usually without charge, where they shop. Where markets are not conveniently close to accessible and free car parking, this has increasingly become a deterrent to market patronage.

As retailing has become characterized by increasingly marked concentration, so a relatively small number of retailers have increased their market share. This has made them the dominant players in the supply chain with increasing power over suppliers and manufacturers, which allows them to compete fiercely on choice, price and quality with all other retailers. It also gives them much greater knowledge about their customers, which allows them to customize their offers much more closely to meet customer needs and expectations. The well-chronicled growth in both retail concentration and out-of-town retail provision has been accompanied by the decline and closure of many thousands of small traditional retailers and by widespread expressions of concern about the viability and vitality of many town centres. As small retailers within town and city centres, market traders have been, and continue to be, vulnerable. They are finding it difficult to maintain their customer base and while many older customers have remained loyal to 'the market', it is becoming increasingly difficult to attract new, younger, more sophisticated customers with higher levels of disposable income.

While the early Town and Country Planning legislation sought to encourage and concentrate retail investment and development within existing urban centres, the spirit of this legislation was often honoured more in the breach than in the observance for much of the 1970s, 1980s and into the 1990s. As such, planning has contributed to the creation of a new retail landscape which appears to offer traditional markets at best a peripheral role and at worst no role at all. During the last decade, the Government's 'rediscovery' of the virtues of town and city centres, the commitment to 'put town centres first' and the focus on 'sustainability' have been accompanied by a general presumption against further out-of-town retail development. As such this might be seen to favour traditional markets and the traders who operate within them. However, the planning restrictions on new retail development in edge-of-town and out-of-town sites has placed a massive premium on medium and large sites within town and city centres. Market sites, which often occupy such prime sites, are vulnerable to development pressures; and where markets are perceived to be 'financially underperforming', they are all the more vulnerable.

Large numbers of market halls and covered markets are now well over a hundred years old; they are clearly showing their age and are in need of renovation, refurbishment and revitalization. However, many of these markets have suffered from a sustained lack of investment from either the local authorities or the private companies that own and/or operate them, or from the market traders themselves. On the one hand, local authorities have clearly felt that investment in other public goods and services would yield more obvious economic, social and political returns and while private owners/operators have taken a narrower economic perspective on costs and benefits, there has been a similar reluctance to commit capital resources to market improvements. On the other hand, the market traders themselves are overwhelmingly small, single individual or family businesses, and in what they perceive to be a harsh trading environment, their first priority is to survive from week to week rather than to set aside scarce financial resources for general market improvements.

The need to meet increasingly stringent regulations relating for example to health and safety, food hygiene and access for disabled customers has also posed a series of challenges to both those owning/operating markets and those trading within them. At worst many markets look careworn and physically unattractive and may flout current legislation, and even at their current best they do not offer the sophistication of modern shopping environments. The majority of shops and stores run by the major multiple retailers, and the large shopping centres and malls to which consumers have now become accustomed, offer a vastly different retail experience. Many local authorities and private operators have also been increasing stall rental rates over and above the general level of inflation, in an attempt to make good overall reductions in rental income caused by declining occupancy levels and to reduce the gap between retail rental levels in general and those currently generated within markets.

Market Revival

Despite all the challenges outlined above, the last decade has seen a fledgling revival of the market traditions in many parts of the UK. This revival reflects a range of factors including: the growth in demand for fresh, local and naturally grown foodstuffs; public concern about food scares and the environment; reaction to the increasing homogenization of town and city centres that are dominated by the same corporate retailers; and central and local government policies designed to enhance the variety and vitality of town centres. It is manifest in a variety of ways. A number of traditional market halls are being renovated and refurbished. Newcastle City Council, for example, started work to revitalize the Grainger Market, a 19th-century Grade I Listed Building, in 1998 in the belief that it represented an important opportunity for city centre regeneration. The focus has been on: re-establishing the market as a vibrant centre of activity; encouraging a wider variety of stalls, services, catering and entertainment within the market; creating a dedicated new fresh food hall; and developing a specific identity for the market that would establish it as one of the premier locations in the city centre. The initial £2 million phase was completed in 2004 and embraced a number of environmental improvements, including the restoration of many of the market's traditional features, the creation of an events space that is available for showcasing local art and for craft exhibitions, new seating areas, some lighting improvements, the installation of CCTV, refurbishment of the toilet facilities, and the introduction of a more rigorous local authority management programme designed to facilitate the maintenance of a modern and tidy retail trading environment. The second phase includes further refurbishment of a number of stalls, improvements in lighting and building works designed to enhance and highlight the market's original iconic entrances.

In Chester, where the history of market trading stretches back almost 1000 years, a new market is planned to replace the latest market hall opened in 1967, and is part of a wider urban regeneration scheme. The new market will have a high-profile location fronting on to the city's central square, it will be more spacious than its current counterpart and it will offer a much improved environment for trading 7 days a week. The front entrance will feature a three-arched façade to provide a striking entrance to the market and its two floors will provide 75 permanent and an additional 14 casual stalls. The lower floor is to be primarily devoted to food while the upper floor will be predominantly for dry goods, but some space has been designated as either for additional retail use or as a restaurant facility depending on the level of demand.

The past decade has witnessed continuous growth in the number of farmers' markets. A farmers' market is defined as one in which farmers, growers or producers from a defined local geographical area sell their own produce direct to the public. The first farmers' market in the UK was established in 1997 and their numbers have grown rapidly since then, rising to 200 in 2001 and to over 400 by 2007. These markets offer a low-cost entry point for farmers and producers who have not traditionally sold directly to consumers before and the market atmosphere emphasizes the links between producers and consumers. A farmers' market in Cheltenham, for example, started in 2001 and is held every second and last Friday of the month along the Promenade in the heart of the town's fashionable shopping centre. The market is a venue for local farmers and local producers to sell their produce to local people, offering a range of meats, a wide variety of fruit, vegetables and seasonal salad produce, fish, dairy produce, bread, wines and ciders and preserves. This market operates an accreditation scheme that seeks to guarantee that all produce has been grown, reared or processed on the stallholder's premises and that all stallholders come from within 45 miles of the town. In Cardiff there has been an interesting initiative designed to integrate a farmers' market into the local community. Here, the city's Riverside Community Market Association was established in 1998 and operates from 10.00 to 14.00 hours every Sunday.

Some of the UK's most well-known street markets are in the East End of London and serve both local residents and a large tourist industry. Brick Lane Market developed in the 18th century when farmers sold livestock and produce outside the city boundary, but it now serves as a general market for the local community. Petticoat Lane, arguably the oldest and most famous of these street markets, was established over 400 years ago by Huguenot lace makers. The market is open Monday to Friday from 09.00 to 14.00 hours in Wentworth Street, while on Sundays it spreads to encompass ten separate streets. On Sundays the market has as many as 1000 stalls selling clothing, shoes, leather goods, jewellery, china and glass, electrical goods, toys, tourist souvenirs, cooking utensils and a wide range of household goods. Some traders always operate at the same location whereas others vary their pitches; some trade all year round, while others are either occasional or seasonal. While regular weekly street markets have a long history, many have been enjoying a recent revival and in some places new occasional and/or seasonal street markets are being established. The Garston Casual Market on the south side of Liverpool was established in 1921, but following European Commission-funded improvements the number of traders and patrons has increased markedly. The market now has some 50 outdoor stalls and the product range includes fresh food and vegetables, flowers, freshly baked bread and pastries and a range of meats.

A growing number of more specialist occasional street markets are also being held in many towns and cities, and a few illustrative examples serve to give something of the character and content of these events. In Wolverhampton and Bilston, for example, an International Market was held over 4 days in October 2007. Traders were drawn from France, Germany, Italy, Spain, China and Cuba as well as from various parts of the UK, and the products on offer included fruit, vegetables, a range of breads and 'takeaway' foodstuffs and craft products. In November 2007, what was billed as an Eco-Friendly/Ethically Trading/Homemade/Original World Goods/Organic Food 2-day market was held in the central square of the small market town of Nantwich in Cheshire. Here some 16 stall holders offered a variety of clothing, toys, jewellery and some foodstuffs. Many towns also have Christmas 'gift' markets, typically selling wooden handmade toys, children's books, leather goods, hand-made jewellery and hand-decorated glassware, foodstuffs and wine, for as long as a week in early to mid-December.

Car boot sales became an increasingly popular form of local market from the 1980s onwards. Essentially a car boot sale is a market in which private individuals, who pay a small fee to the organizers, offer a wide variety of personal and household goods and occasionally plants and foodstuffs for sale from simple stalls, from the floor, from vans or literally from the boot of their car. The vast majority of the goods on sale are usually second-hand, principally personal possessions that are no longer required, but new goods and seconds are sometimes sold by more professional traders. Car boot sales are often held in car parks and grassland fields and Sunday is the most popular trading day. While the advent of e-Bay has reduced their number and frequency, many car boot sales are still held every week in various parts of the country.

Contributions to Sustainable Development

The concept of sustainable development can be traced back to the 13th century, but in more modern times it reappeared in the environmental literature in the 1970s (Kamara *et al.*, 2006) and since then it has gained increasing prominence. However, the concept has a number of sets of meanings. On the one hand there are definitions that recognize that human beings live on a planet with finite natural resources and fragile ecosystems on which human life ultimately depends, while on the other there are much wider definitions that look to embrace ambitious social and economic, as well as environmental, goals and to meet human needs in an equitable manner. Typical of the first set, for example, is ecological sustainability defined by Callicot and Mumford (1997) as 'meeting human needs without compromising the health of ecosystems'; while the definition favoured by the UK Government – namely, to 'enable all people throughout the world to satisfy their basic needs and enjoy a better quality of life without compromising the quality of life of future generations' (HM Government, 2005) – typifies the latter.

In adopting this wider view, the UK Government's Sustainable Development Strategy identified four priority areas: 'sustainable production and consumption'; 'climate change and energy'; 'natural resource protection and environmental enhancement'; and 'sustainable communities'. At the same time the strategy identifies 'well being as being at the heart of sustainable development' and recognizes the importance of 'changing behaviour' in moving to a more sustainable future. The range of markets described earlier are very small players in the UK's overall retail marketplace, but they can be seen to be making important contributions to the UK Government's sustainable development goals. While there are considerable variations in the contributions individual markets and types of markets are making to sustainable development, a number of general environmental, economic and social benefits can be identified.

Environmental benefits associated with markets include reductions in CO_2 emissions and waste, greater reuse and recycling, and potentially the encouragement of greater biodiversity. Where local farmers and producers are taking their produce to farmers' markets and regularly supplying market halls and street markets, for example, this reduces the food miles required to deliver food to consumers. As such, markets stand in marked contrast to many of the internationally sourced food products on supermarket shelves. At the same time, many markets draw the vast majority of their customers from within surrounding neighbourhoods. Where this encourages customers to walk or cycle or to take public transport to do their market shopping, this too reduces carbon emissions and the pollution and congestion associated with motor car journeys.

The majority of the foodstuffs sold in markets have much less packaging than much of the food on sale in the major supermarkets; in turn, this leads to much less waste materials being generated for disposal by landfill. In some ways car boot sales can be seen as the ultimate in recycling. For example, Toys to You, a registered charity, suggests that some 40 million children's toys were thrown away last year and that 13 million of them ended up in household dustbins and landfill sites. Where parents and children can sell these unwanted toys at car boot sales, it offers another child the opportunity to enjoy such toys and can promote environmental and economic awareness among the next generation of adult consumers. More generally, where farmers are looking to market their produce more locally, this can encourage more diverse agricultural practices and this in turn can enhance biodiversity.

Markets also generate a number of direct and indirect benefits for the local economy. The level of income generated by the traders and, in the case of farmers' markets, the food producers who are also traders, within a market represents the largest single benefit to the local economy, although the level of income clearly varies depending on the number of traders and the popularity of the market. Research undertaken in London by the New Economics Foundation (2005) suggests, for example, that the farmers' market at Marylebone with 35 food stalls and that at Ealing with 15 food stalls generated annual turnovers of £1.3 million and £304,000 respectively, while the street markets at Lewisham (21 food stalls) and Walthamstow (15 food stalls) generated £5.06 million and £3.8 million, respectively. There are also direct local employment benefits in that many street market and market hall employees are local residents.

The existence of a market also has an impact on surrounding retailers, but at times this impact is contested. On the one hand, there are arguments that markets attract shoppers into a district and that local retailers benefit from the increased numbers of shoppers. Retailers surveyed in the New Economics Foundation's (2005) research in London, for example, indicated that markets were good for their business. In a similar vein the research suggested that over 50% of market customers had shopped, or intended to shop, at local conventional retailers that day. On the other hand, retailers trading from shops and stores around markets may object particularly to street traders on the grounds that they may compete unfairly with them and take away some of their business, that they may obscure shop windows and displays, and that they may change the ambience of the general shopping environment. In Chester, for example, proposals to locate a number of casual market stalls outside the new market hall were abandoned after opposition from surrounding retailers. More generally, the income generated by markets will have a multiplier effect within local economies. By encouraging customers to support local businesses, they are seen to be important in stimulating local economic development and aiding regeneration by bringing both customers and commercial vitality back into town and district centres. In addition, as in the case of the Grainger Market in Newcastle, the refurbishment of traditional market halls in town and city centres can be important in bringing traditional buildings back into mainstream use and thus in contributing to urban regeneration.

A range of social benefits is also associated with markets. Markets can play a central role in raising awareness of the origins and nature of food, of the importance of healthy eating, of the links between production and consumption, and more widely of sustainability. Farmers' markets and food stalls within street markets and market halls, for example, provide direct contact between producers and consumers, and customers are able to obtain first-hand information on how food is produced, processed or should be prepared. Customers are often given the opportunity to sample foods they have not previously eaten. At the same time, customers often have the opportunity to learn more about the environmental and economic impact of intensive agriculture *vis-à-vis* more traditional methods of production. More generally, this can help to build awareness of the relationship between consumption and production and to draw on everyday issues to develop an understanding that current levels of production and consumption are the source of many of the environmental challenges facing society. In addition, it can emphasize the need to develop products and services that use fewer natural resources and generate less waste, to encourage people to seek to meet their needs in more sustainable ways and ultimately to rethink current business models.

Markets can also enhance social capital and as such they make a number of important contributions to sustainable development. Markets can play a valuable role in improving access to fresh and nutritious food, for example, and so can be instrumental in improving the local population's diet and health. At the same time many markets provide a valuable meeting place, thus facilitating social contact in the community. Markets therefore offer increased opportunities for local people to learn about, and often to become involved in, community initiatives and projects, while they can also facilitate closer working cooperation between local businesses. Specialist Christmas markets hold a unique visual attraction for some people and in general street markets can bring colour and vitality to otherwise drab urban landscapes. Such positive images are often retained in people's minds and as such contribute to social capital. More generally, markets can be seen to be important in supporting sustainable communities. In this context, the Institute for Sustainable Development in Business (Nottingham Trent University, 2007), for example, argues that there is a growing emphasis: on the need to balance and integrate the social, environmental and economic components of the community; on localization, with local food being seen as a key component; and on ways in which markets are able to cater for the needs of diverse cultural traditions within multicultural societies.

Summary

Local markets have long been important events within society, and they have provided a diverse and changing array of economic and social activities. Major market halls, once the retail focus of towns and cities, have become marginal and careworn, and many have closed and fallen into decline. The recent revival of local markets has produced a range of environmental, economic and social benefits. As such, they are making a small but significant contribution to sustainable development and they also provide valuable opportunities for a growing number of people to engage with sustainable thinking. The environmental benefits include reductions in greenhouse gas emissions, packaging and food miles, and in the car mileage associated with conventional supermarket shopping. The local economy also benefits from the presence of markets in that they generate income and employment opportunities. That said, while there are arguments that local markets attract shoppers who will also then patronize existing High Street retailers, many such retailers have expressed concerns that market stalls actually have a detrimental impact on their business. The social gains associated with local markets should not be undervalued. On the one hand, for example, market traders are often prepared to discuss the characteristics and origins of their produce with customers, thus giving them a deeper understanding of the environmental and economic impact of different methods of food production. On the other hand, local markets also often enhance the social capital within communities by facilitating social contact and by bringing colour and vitality to urban landscapes. It would be foolish to suggest that local markets can challenge the power and dominance of the corporate retail giants; but as more and more people visit and shop at local markets, this may help disseminate greater awareness of the imperatives of sustainable development and of the importance of encouraging sustainable consumption.

Key Questions

1. Conduct a survey of the local markets in an area with which you are familiar and evaluate their contribution to retail and leisure provision.
2. Discuss the ways in which local markets can promote sustainable development *and* sustainable thinking.
3. Assess how local markets currently contribute to postmodern societies.

References

Callicott, J.B. and Mumford, K. (1997) Ecological Sustainability as a conservation concept. *Conservation Biology* 11(1), 32–40.

HM Government (2005) Securing the Future, Cm. 6467. Available at: http://www.sustainable-development.gov.uk/publications/uk-strategy/index.htm (accessed 26 July 2005).

Kamara, M., Coff, C. and Wynne, B. (2006) GMOs and Sustainability. Available at: http://www.cesagen.lancs.ac.uk/resources/docs/GMOs_and_Sustainability_August_2006.pdf (accessed 3 November 2006).

Letters, S., Keene, D. and Jamroziak, E. (2005) Markets and Fairs in Thirteenth-Century England Data Collection 900–1516. Available at: http://www.data-archive.ac.uk/findingData/snDescription.asp?sn=4969 (accessed 12 May 2006).

New Economics Foundation (2005) Trading Places: The local economic impact of street produce and farmers' markets. Available at: http://www.neweconomics.org/gen/uploads/w2rrxbb4htuk3t55fbvmhh 5514122005114341.pdf (accessed 12 May 2006).

Nottingham Trent University (2007) What has the retail sector got to do with sustainable communities? Available at: http://www.susdev.co.uk/sustainable_communities_2.htm (accessed 7 January 2008).

Office of the Deputy Prime Minister (2005) Planning Policy Statement 6; Planning for Town Centres. Available at: http://www.odpm.gov.uk/stellent/groups/odpm_planning/documents/page/odpm_plan_036805.pdf (accessed 20 May 2005).

Rhodes, N. (2005) *National Retail Market Survey*. Retail Enterprise Network, Manchester Metropolitan University Business School, Manchester, UK.

Schmiechen, J. and Carls, K. (1999) *The British Market Hall; A Social and Architectural History*. Yale University Press, New Haven, Connecticut.

19 Greening Live Earth UK

E. Harvey
SaltaSustainable and Leeds Metropolitan University, Leeds, UK

The main objectives of this chapter are to: (i) present a practical case study of managing the process of 'greening' the Live Earth (LE) concert at Wembley Stadium and highlight the key issues around 'greening up' a major UK event with many different stakeholders; and (ii) use the experience of LE to offer practical guidance to other events organizers on improving the environmental profile of their events.

Chapter outline

- Introduction
- Live Earth – Environmental Strategy and Objectives
- Greening Live Earth at Wembley Stadium
- Main Greening Activities
- Legacy
- Overcoming Barriers to Greening
- Key Challenges
- The Principles of 'Greening' – Best Practice
- Summary
- Key Questions

Introduction

'Live Earth: The Concerts for a Climate in Crisis' was a series of eight global concerts held on 7 July 2007, spearheaded by Al Gore (former US Vice President) and Kevin Wall (Worldwide Executive Producer of Live 8). The aim of the Live Earth (LE) concerts was to use the immense global reach of music to engage people on a mass scale to combat climate change, whether at home, through work or politics. The concerts also launched an ongoing, worldwide climate campaign called 'SOS' (Save Our Selves). The overarching aim of SOS is to increase awareness of global warming, its causes and risks, and to help motivate people around the world to take action (see http://www.liveearth.org for more details).

Concerts were held across six continents, at Giants Stadium in New York, Aussie Stadium in Sydney, Copacabana Beach in Rio de Janeiro, Coca Cola Dome in Johannesburg, Kakuhari Messe in Tokyo, Oriental Pearl Tower in Shanghai, HSH Nordbank Arena in Hamburg, and Wembley Stadium in London. Concurrent with the lead-up to the concerts, a major web site was also launched, providing information about the challenges of global warming and inviting people, corporations and governments to take action. The 'Live Earth Pledge' invited visitors to the site to commit to changes in their own lives.

Worldwide, almost one million people attended the concerts in person, and almost two billion people saw and heard the broadcasts over television, radio and the Internet. LE was carried across 100 television channels,

20 of the world's leading networks, radio in 130 countries, and in a major Internet-based campaign.

Live Earth – Environmental Strategy and Objectives

From the moment the events were planned, the LE team aimed to make the events 'green' by bringing them as close as possible to the ideal of 'zero net impact'. To do this they appointed an International Green Team Manager and a number of national Green Team project managers around the world – collectively called the LE Green Team. The main Green Team objectives were to:

- reduce CO_2 emissions associated with the events first and foremost;
- measure and offset remaining emissions through independently verified, reputable schemes; and
- encourage the events industry to become more sustainable by collaborating with and securing sustainability legacy pledges from partners along the way (venues, production companies, audience, artists, merchandising teams, etc.).

The results of the worldwide LE greening activities are available in the *Live Earth Carbon Assessment and Footprint Report* (Live Earth, 2007a).

Greening Live Earth at Wembley Stadium

Wembley National Stadium Limited

Wembley Stadium is the new national venue run by Wembley National Stadium Limited (WNSL), a subsidiary of The Football Association. The doors of the new stadium opened in March 2007 to a full programme of music and sporting events throughout that spring and summer (Figs 19.1 to 19.3).

Although a new build, few sustainable measures were built into the design of the stadium, which occurred 8 years prior to its opening. The exceptions to this were: (i) sustainable transport planning, with the focus on the delivery of major upgrades to the public transport links servicing the stadium, the delivery of a charter train service for corporate clients, as well as the support and part-funding of the local authority's design and implementation

Fig. 19.1. Inside Wembley Stadium.

Fig. 19.2. Aerial view of Wembley Stadium.

Fig. 19.3. Wembley Stadium logo.

of an Event Day Parking Control Scheme – in place for an approximately 1.5 mile radius of the stadium; (ii) the installation of sensor taps in the washrooms, to switch taps off automatically; and (iii) the pitch watering system, regulated by moisture sensors in the pitch, which shuts down the water system after the pitch has had what it needs.

The methods

The LE Green Team worked closely to develop methods for 'greening up' the LE events around the world, described in its document *Live Earth Green Event Guidelines*™ (Live Earth, 2007b). These guidelines provided a global basis for the practical implementation strategy to improve the environmental profile of each national event. The manual includes an introduction to the main issues and is divided into sections, including an introduction to the main issues and sections for different partners such as venues, promoters, production teams, key suppliers (e.g. food and drink), artists and communications teams.

The manual targeted opportunities for 'big wins', such as energy, waste, transport, water and supplies. More specifically, it focused on raising awareness and encouraging more environmentally sound choices among collaborators, such as: reducing power usage and choosing renewable options; reducing waste and recycling more; reducing air and car miles and increasing the use of more sustainable transport options; sourcing sustainable materials (e.g. set design and construction, merchandising, signage, disposables); encouraging better food and drink choices; and reducing water usage. The manual was devised to be adapted to the unique requirements of each country venue by each national greening project manager, working with key stakeholders. The manual was used as the basis for undertaking initial site reviews at Wembley.

'Greening' Wembley Stadium – who did what?

The bulk of the management of the greening implementation work in the UK was undertaken by a partnership between The Climate Group (TCG) and SaltaSustainable, in collaboration with the LE Green Team International Project Manager in Los Angeles (John Rego). The Climate Group is a leading non-profit organization dedicated to advancing business and government leadership on climate change. SaltaSustainable is a practical sustainability consultancy for businesses and other organizations. Both organizations liaised closely with the LE production management teams in Los Angeles and the UK. Stop Climate Chaos (SCC) is a coalition of environment and development groups, faith groups, humanitarian organizations, women's groups and trade unions campaigning to stop climate change through their 'I Count' campaign. Its staff and members contributed significantly to environmental guidance, documentation, NGO liaison and support, media communications and artist briefings. The UK Green Team was very much dependent on the contributions of stakeholders, without whom none of the activities would have been possible.

The stakeholders

When undertaking any complex project, it is important to identify, consult and liaise closely with the key stakeholders – with as much advanced notice as possible. In the UK, the key stakeholders were identified as:

- WNSL management and staff;
- Delaware North Companies (DNC), food and drinks supplier to WNSL;
- Live Nation music production team;
- Events Merchandising, official merchandiser for LE;
- Freud Communications and LD Communications;
- the artists;
- the audience;
- the LE production team;
- industry sponsors;
- Ignition (activation and signage for the LE brand); and
- Harvey Goldsmith Productions for event promotion.

We also collaborated with various industry partners, such as Arup's sustainable events team and the British Standards Institution (BSI) on their new sustainable events standard, BS 8901:2007 (BSI, 2007). We met with each of these groups as and when the project schedule dictated.

Schedule

Although the global LE Green Team had previously been in place for some time, the UK Green Team was invited to participate in April 2007, 3 months before the concert date. This meant there was a lot to do in a relatively short space of time – not unusual for events management. The team focused on the 'big wins' for tackling CO_2 emissions, communicating environmental messages from Wembley and securing pledges from partners for the legacy of LE going forward.

Getting started

As a priority, leading partners were met with straightaway: WNSL, DNC and Live Nation management. At the same time, a brief environmental site review at Wembley Stadium was undertaken to assess the provision for energy, waste generation and management, transport facilities, catering and other supplies, water use and disposal. Other stakeholders were met with as required by the project priorities. For example, meetings with the merchandisers occurred early on, and discussions with the global media communications teams occurred early, as well as again immediately before and during the concert (as media interest peaked). Many of the communications relating to corporate sponsorship were handled through the LE Los Angeles office, although some local discussions were required, for example with food and drinks brands sponsoring Wembley Stadium.

An initial site review at the stadium indicated that a number of activities were already in place, most notably:

1. The waste manager at Wembley was committed to reducing environmental impact and was working with the caterers and waste contractor companies to reduce, recycle and compost as much waste from the venue as possible.
2. Early consultations had been undertaken with The Carbon Trust, a government-funded, free service for businesses aimed at auditing and reducing energy use, CO_2 outputs and associated costs.
3. Electric carts were being used by staff to get around the stadium's service road and to transport goods.
4. Fairtrade coffee and hot chocolate were provided throughout the Wembley site (although not strictly 'green' in focus, the Fairtrade Foundation certification process involves environmental criteria as well as social standards).

Nevertheless, it was apparent that there were other operational activities that could be implemented in order to help to reduce the environmental impact of the venue.

Main Greening Activities

The UK LE Green Team focused on the following main activities:

- *Management 'buy-in'*. We consulted and collaborated with the management executive teams for each of the main stakeholder groups.
- *Energy*. We focused on efficiency and reducing unnecessary use on the day. For example, the LE team developed a responsive system with the Facilities Management team so that lights around the Stadium could be turned on and off as required (rather than left on throughout daylight hours). Likewise, stage lighting was minimal during daylight hours and phased in through to darkness. The team also sought additional sustainable energy sources, such as renewable energy supply, and purchased Renewable Obligation Certificates (ROCs) for the Stadium. Biodiesel in the form of processed cooking oil was also used for Live Nation's music production generators.
- *Waste*. The Green Team worked with the environmentally focused waste manager at Wembley. We made the most of this key alliance and investigated reducing landfill waste tonnage to zero (e.g. by reducing reliance on disposal items, increasing the proportion of recyclable and compostable tonnage and sending the remainder to energy from waste – EfW). The LE team also introduced new recycling bins front of house and encouraged visitors to use them, with extensive signage and announcements via the stage during the performances.
- *Water*. We looked at the opportunities for saving water, such as use of taps with automatic sensors, reporting of leaks and reducing unnecessary use (e.g. leaving taps running when not in use). (Longer-term strategies would be to investigate the use of rainwater capture for services not requiring clean drinking water.)
- *Transport*. Audience travel is generally the largest contributor to the carbon emissions of an event, which can be up to 90%. The new Wembley Stadium was designed to discourage car use and the team at Wembley actively encourages visitors to use the excellent public transport links in place when travelling to all of their events. Wembley and Live Nation communicated the sustainable transport options even more widely to ticket holders, with as much advanced notice as possible. The number of cycle racks onsite was also increased for the event. See Box 19.1 and Table 19.1 for information on artist travel.
- *Food and drink supply*. We worked with DNC to review opportunities for reusable food and drink container options, to source sustainably sourced, compostable food containers (e.g. made from sugarcane pulp), to use recyclable drinks cups and to provide Fairtrade, Rainforest Alliance and vegetarian food and drink choices.
- *Merchandising*. We supported Event Merchandising in sourcing sustainable T-shirts made from bamboo and organic cotton and belts made from waste London Fire Brigade fire hoses. All brochures

Box 19.1. The issue of travel.

87% of global CO_2 emissions from LE were due to audience travel. Although artist travel received most attention in the media, artists were generally booked for the event because they were already on tour in the area or were based close to their event. Artists were also invited to briefings about reducing their own environmental impact going forward, such as being encouraged to use lower impact forms of travel (e.g. scheduled flights rather than private jets, lower CO_2-emitting cars, efficiency planning for tours). They were also given copies of the *Live Earth Green Artist Handbook*™ (2007), which provides environmental advice on lifestyle and tours.

were printed on recycled paper with vegetable inks.

- *Signage*. LE worked with Ignition to source sustainable materials for signage, such as recycled and recyclable card, which was reused and recycled following the event, and vegetable inks and VOC-free paints for printing.
- *Set and stage design*. LE also worked with Live Nation to source recycled, recyclable and other sustainable materials for the set (e.g. oil drums, wood), efficient (LED) lighting, and to reuse or recycle as many of their set materials as possible.
- *Training*. We provided environmental training sessions for WNSL managers and full-time staff and DNC management teams, and asked them to cascade the information to their employees. We also worked closely with environment representatives for Live Nation and held meetings with all of the key stakeholders (as above).
- *Measurement*. Data were collected on: artist, production and audience transport; venue electricity (kWh/£); waste streams tonnage; production materials; and production energy use (litres of biodiesel). This enabled the team to calculate the carbon footprint and offset the emissions from the events through reputable and independently verified schemes in alternative generation.
- *Communications*. All management teams were encouraged to communicate their greening activities, both internally and externally. We also worked closely with the LE communications teams (Freud and LD) and engaged in activities such as television and newspaper interviews for UK and international media.

It is very difficult to undertake meaningful comparisons of environmental impacts across the different LE venues and events, as like-for-like comparisons cannot be achieved. The different events in the LE global series were of different sizes (e.g. affecting audience numbers and venue operations), in different locations (e.g. affecting access to public transport) and the events themselves had different running times (e.g. affecting energy use and waste generation). It is more meaningful to look at global emissions, as shown in Table 19.1.

Table 19.1. Live Earth global emissions. (Adapted from Live Earth, 2007a.)

Entity	CO_2 emissions (tonnes)	Percentage of total
Headquarters	548	2.8
Sponsor sales	85	0.4
Production team and contractors	151	0.8
Generators	221	1.1
Facility and concerts	864	4.4
Activation contractor	29	0.1
Artist transport and merchandise shipping	529	2.7
Broadcasters	115	0.6
Audience travel	17,139	87.0
Volunteer travel	27	0.1
Total (rounded)	19,708	100

Legacy

In addition to the above, LE had a strong legacy policy: to engage as many stakeholders as possible to get involved in sustainability practices going forward. We believe that LE contributed to an emergent sea-change in the greening of music and events, and was responsible for generating discussion and raising awareness about environmental issues. A number of music industry representatives have since commented that it raised the bar for greening events. LE acted as a catalyst for new environmental initiatives, as well as providing impetus for existing greening activities in the events industry. For example:

1. At the time of LE, the Wembley Stadium Managing Director made a public declaration to commit to sustainability practices (Wembley Stadium, 2007; see Box 19.2). Wembley has since made sustainability one of the core objectives for the business, with a member of the senior management team tasked with driving forward a Corporate Green Plan. Wembley has also:

- extended its work with The Carbon Trust;
- focused on continual improvement around waste management and the avoidance of landfill (e.g. they are currently introducing trials for capturing food waste for composting – composting meat-contaminated waste offers a particular challenge);
- commenced working with a lighting consultant and other stakeholders to switch to energy-efficient lighting and other energy-efficient options over time;
- begun currently working with DNC to trial a device to reduce energy consumption in refrigerated catering rooms, walk-in freezers and bar coolers;
- installed a live organism in male toilets with urinal facilities, which improves hygiene and means only two flushes are needed per 24 hours, dramatically reducing water usage;
- registered its involvement with Green 500, the London-based carbon emissions reduction group; and
- started to implement a formal environmental management system (EMS) to measure the venue's impacts, identify priorities, set out objectives and targets, implement changes, and provide a commitment to continual review and improvement.

2. Live Nation, one of the largest music production and promotion companies in the UK, worked with the LE team on greening production for the event. Live Nation has since appointed a full-time Environmental Services Manager (who is currently working on greening 33 venues and three festivals, among other things).

3. Event Merchandising is continuing its sustainable merchandising offer to events businesses across the UK, including distributing a range of earth positive clothing and eco-bags (Event Merchandising, 2008a,b).

4. The British Standards Institute (BSI) launched its Sustainable Events Standard BS:8901 in November 2007 (the LE team contributed to the consultation rounds for this new standard).

5. UK members of the LE Green Team have established a sustainability service for the music sector – SustainableTouring (http://www.sustainabletouring.com) – and are rolling the methodology out to other sectors (e.g. http://www.sustainableproduction.co.uk).

6. DNC operates a programme called Greenpath as part of its Global Citizenship strategy. Following LE, it is planning to

Box 19.2. A quote from Alex Horne, Managing Director, Wembley Stadium.

'The Live Earth concert provided a fantastic catalyst for us to concentrate on furthering our environmental efforts and fully commit to making the new stadium as green as possible for both the Live Earth concert and beyond. The event also prompted us to engage stakeholders and staff in regards to sustainability issues ... Since Live Earth we have continued our work on greening Wembley across all fronts and I have made sustainability a core business objective, tasking a member of my senior management team with driving forward our Corporate Green Plan. Having been open for less than a year, we are not where we want to be just yet in regards to sustainability but we are certainly moving in the right direction and are committed to getting there.'

implement more of the Greenpath objectives in the UK. For example, DNC is working towards obtaining Forest Stewardship Council (FSC[1]) accreditation for food containers made from virgin pulp from sustainable forests.

7. The Ignition signage and activation team have continued to offer a green service to a number of events, thus responding to a growing demand for environmental products and services in their sector.

Overcoming Barriers to Greening

It is worth noting that implementing environmental changes can be both a highly rewarding – and a sometimes frustrating – experience. For example, most people in the many teams worked with enthusiasm and offered inspiration, ideas and additional greening suggestions. It was clear that businesses are switched on by the business case and the 'triple bottom line' (see Chapter 3, this volume), which demonstrates that business can 'do well by doing good' (Laszlo, 2008; see also Chapters 1 and 6, this volume). Nevertheless, there were times during LE preparations when there was also a certain amount of scepticism about whether some of our sustainability practices could be implemented. For example, many commented that it would not be possible to use biodiesel to power generators for a concert the size of Live Earth at Wembley. In the event, processed waste cooking oil was used for all generators at Wembley, and it proved much more straightforward than anticipated – coming in at nearly the same price and being much cleaner and safer to transport and handle.

Although resistance may occur, most people responded positively when given the right balance of information, commercial pragmatism and time to reflect. As with most things, inclusion, communication and consultation are the key to engaging stakeholders in a positive way. Often it is possible to find a small number of champions within an organization who are particularly positive, and their help is invaluable in reaching the rest of the workforce.

Key Challenges

There were a number of successes in terms of greening LE at Wembley. Most notable of these were the engagement and enthusiasm of the key stakeholders in the process, which enabled LE to introduce the range of sustainable measures described above. However, as with many new ventures, there were also challenges. These are described in the following sections.

Audience transport

Audience transport is by far the biggest percentage of CO_2 production for a major event, accounting for 87% of global emissions for LE. At Wembley, despite extensive communications of the options, a significant proportion of the audience failed to use the public transport services available.

In the UK, transport is something to be considered right at the initial stages of planning an event. Venues with good public transport hubs should be selected where possible. Visitors should be notified of the public transport options at the same time as ticket confirmation, and sent reminders with any subsequent correspondence. For major UK events, booking national train and bus tickets can be prohibitively expensive if left to the last minute, causing people to default to using their cars. The cheapest tickets are offered to those who book early, which ticket holders should be encouraged to do. For major events with long lead-in times, it is suggested that best practice would be for organizers to contact the main coach and rail operators to request discounted ticketing linked to the event. (For LE it was too late to do this as train company ticketing options had already been fixed well in advance.) Another idea is that some events could arrange coach pick-ups for ticket holders, providing a convenient and direct mode of transport to encourage uptake. As a final option, rewards can be offered for people who share lifts in preference to solo car use. For example, LE New York was at Giants Stadium, which has

[1]The FSC sets the global standard for responsible forestry and undertakes independent certification of companies and organizations that produce or sell forest products.

very few public transport links, therefore car sharing was encouraged. Those with more people in their car were rewarded with preferential car parking closest to the venue.

Lack of reusable food and drink container options at the Stadium

Like many venues, much of the food and drink equipment provided at Wembley by DNC was already established. This meant that new initiatives would take more than the 3 months' planning we had available for LE. For example, we had hoped to be able to introduce a reusable drinks cup on a deposit-and-refill discount scheme, similar to that offered in Germany for the football World Cup in 2006 (Organizing Committee 2006 FIFA World Cup, 2006). In the event, beer delivery relied on automated equipment to deliver several pints simultaneously, using plastic cups of predetermined dimensions. Unfortunately, there was no time to find a workable, reusable alternative. The opportunities for saving money and reducing waste through reusable options are immense. Every business pays for disposable items at least three times – in purchasing, in waste management and in landfill taxes. In addition, under UK law, larger businesses pay for recycling obligations. Businesses should plan reusable options into their operations as much as possible. Many venues can adapt to providing washable plates, cups and cutlery, instead of relying on items that will be used once and thrown away. For more information on better waste management, see the Waste Resources and Action Programme (WRAP) and Envirowise, both of which provide case studies and advice to businesses on saving money through waste reduction and recycling options.

Contamination of compostable waste

Another waste challenge encountered is that some disposable food and drinks containers cannot be composted or recycled due to: (i) being made from the wrong materials (e.g. it is not possible to recycle or compost card drinks cups that are lined with plastic); and (ii) food contamination – even when containers are made from fully compostable materials such as recycled card or other plant fibres, meat waste poses particular problems. We were unable to respond to these problems at the time owing to the logistical problems posed by the stadium's size. Some venues will find it easier to tackle such issues than others, depending on their size and location. In addition, planners should be aware that the environmental sector is fast-moving and new solutions are becoming available all the time. We encourage venues and events organizers to investigate these going forward, and plan well ahead (e.g. see Envirowise and WRAP for details).

Engagement of visitors in recycling opportunities

For LE at Wembley Stadium, the team actively encouraged the use of recycling bins for all plastics (drinks bottles, cups, bags) through the provision of bins, extensive signage for visitors and staff, and messages relayed through the stage during the LE concert. Nevertheless, there was significant (about 30%) contamination of the plastics recycling stream, with people using the wrong bins for recyclable and non-recyclable waste. In addition, many visitors failed to use any bin at all, and dropped waste on the ground. This demonstrates the commitment to audience engagement that is necessary to raise awareness and change habits. At the end of the LE concert, the waste manager at Wembley elected to ask his waste contractor to collect and sort all rubbish in order to maximize recycling of the plastics waste. Event planners can work with venues and waste contractors to generate innovative schemes to engage the audience in recycling opportunities. One example of good practice is use of plastic cups on deposit schemes such as that used at the Download Festival produced by Live Nation. A deposit of £0.20 per cup encourages festival-goers to collect cups and return them for recycling. Another scheme is the use of volunteer patrollers, particularly around waste bins, to educate people to use the recycling services appropriately.

Measurement

It can be difficult to garner meaningful *comparative* data across different events, as they can differ so markedly in terms of venue, location, audience numbers and timing (meaning there is no like-for-like comparison). In line with best practice, the team recommends that events managers collect data on environmental impacts before and after implementing an environmental strategy. In this way you will be able to understand your starting points, set targets for reduction and measure the effectiveness of your strategy going forward.

It may make more sense to measure comparable events over time. If you are a venue or event owner, consider measuring: (i) the impact of *similar* events over time (i.e. comparable size, venue, duration, time of year, etc.) before and after implementing your reduction plan; or (ii) your own impacts over a longer time period (e.g. ongoing monthly energy use, waste generation, purchasing) to see if your general trend is downwards.

The Principles of 'Greening' – Best Practice

In terms of implementing better environmental practices, the main principles are:

1. Buy-in from the top (i.e. board and senior management support from each organization that is implementing changes).
2. Measurement (to identify high-impact areas, prioritize and measure improvements going forward).
3. Consultation, communication and engagement (with stakeholders: people and organizations that work with you on environmental issues).
4. Development of objectives and setting targets, with timelines and roles and responsibilities allocated.
5. Implementation – e.g. policy, organization and behaviour changes for reducing wastage, improving efficiency and switching to renewable and sustainable sources where possible (in all areas: energy, transport, purchasing, waste, water).
6. Ongoing measurement and review.
7. At the end of this process, consider offsetting your remaining emissions (to aim for zero net emissions) with a Gold Standard scheme.
8. Report honestly what you are doing and what else you intend to do (for maximum commercial benefit).
9. Repeat the above for continual improvement.

Summary

This chapter has presented a practical case study of managing the 'greening' process for LE UK at Wembley Stadium. The principles outlined here can be applied to any event, whether music tours, festivals, meetings, conferences, parties, or launch and award ceremonies. Clearly it is possible to make significant greening achievements for an event, even in a relatively short timescale. The more time that is available, and the more advance planning, the more positive environmental practices can be implemented.

This chapter documents a number of successes in implementing greening practices at a major event at Wembley Stadium – not least the subsequent commitment from the WNSL management team to sustainable business practices going forward. Likewise we have documented a number of other legacy initiatives.

Sometimes introducing environmental initiatives to businesses can be viewed as a challenge – particularly among those who are new to the subject matter. There are a number of potential barriers to making a start including: a lack of awareness or knowledge; perceptions that changes may be difficult and expensive to implement; and caution about inviting sustainability practitioners in to comment on the organization in question. However, we have found that with the right combination of information and pragmatism, these barriers can be overcome. In addition, there are increasing incentives to taking action in tougher economic times because of: (i) the significant savings that can be had in terms of energy, waste and water management; and (ii) the associated reputational gains that can make a business stand out from the crowd and attract new customers.

There is an increasing number of sustainable events resources to inform those who want to take advantage of these opportunities, including: the Live Earth Carbon Assessment and Footprint Report (2007), the British Standard Institute's BS:8901 standard for sustainable events (2007); Julie's Bicycle First Step Report (2008); the Green Goal Legacy Report (2006) and the London 2012 Sustainability Plan (2007) – all of which are available for download from the web sites listed below.

Key Questions

1. What positive and negative aspects arose from greening the Live Earth concert at Wembley Stadium?
2. What potential environmental impacts do you think Wembley Stadium might have on the local community?
3. Why do you think sustainable measures were not at the core of the design of the new stadium?

References

BSI (2007) *BS 8901:2007 Specification for a sustainable event management system with guidance for use developed.* British Standards Institution, London.

Event Merchandising (2008a) Carbon Neutral Earth Positive Organic Clothing. Available at: http://www.themerchandisingshop.co.uk/shop/Carbonneutralearthpositiveorganicclothing (accessed May 2008).

Event Merchandising (2008b) Eco bags – the greener bag shop. Available at: http://www.themerchandisingshop.co.uk/shop/EcoBags (accessed May 2008).

Laszlo, C. (2008) *Sustainable Value: How the World's Leading Companies are Doing Well by Doing Good.* Greenleaf Publishing Ltd, Sheffield, UK.

Live Earth (2007a) Live Earth Carbon Assessment and Footprint Report. Available at: http://www.liveearth.org/docs/Live_Earth_Carbon_Report.pdf (accessed May 2008).

Live Earth (2007b) Live Earth Environmental Guidelines, First Edition. Green Guidelines for the Live Entertainment & Events Industry. Available at: http://liveearth.org/docs/LEGreen_Guidelines_First_edition_final.pdf (accessed May 2008).

Organizing Committee 2006 FIFA World Cup (2006) Green Goal™ – the environmental concept for the 2006 FIFA World Cup. Available at: http://www.oeko.de/oekodoc/292/2006-011-en.pdf (accessed May 2008).

Wembley Stadium (2007) Press Box. Wembley Greens up for Live Earth. Available at: http://www.wembleystadium.com/pressbox/pressReleases/Wembley+Greens+up+for+Live+Earth.htm (accessed May 2008).

Web sites

Delaware North Companies (2008) Global Citizenship. Available at: http://www.delawarenorth.com/GlobalCitizenship/GlobalCitizenship.asp (accessed May 2008).

Envirowise: http://www.envirowise.gov.uk

Freud Communications: http://www.freud.com

Goldman Sachs Group, Inc. (2007) Introducing GS Sustain. Available at: http://www.unglobalcompact.org/docs/summit2007/gs_esg_embargoed_until030707pdf.pdf (accessed March 2009).

Ignition: http://www.ignition-inc.com

Julie's Bicycle.com (2008) First Step: UK Music Industry Greenhouse Gas Emissions for 2007. Available at: http://www.juliesbicycle.com/wp-content/uploads/2008/04/jb-first-step-e-report.pdf (accessed May 2008).

LD Communications: http://www.ldcommunications.co.uk

Live Nation: http://www.livenation.co.uk

London 2012 (2007) London 2012 Sustainability Plan. Towards a one planet 2012. Available at: http://www.london2012.com/documents/locog-publications/london-2012-sustainability-plan.pdf (accessed May 2008).

SaltaSustainable: http://www.saltasustainable.co.uk

Stop Climate Chaos Coalition: http://www.stopclimatechaos.org

SustainableTouring: http://www.sustainabletouring.com

The Climate Group: http://www.theclimategroup.org

WRAP: http://www.wrap.org.uk

20 Sustainable Demand Management in Plitvice Lakes National Park, Croatia

M. Tomašević Lišanin and M. Palić
University of Zagreb, Zagreb, Croatia

The purpose of this chapter is to explore and suggest suitable ways to manage natural resources in tourism. It deals with the most important of nature's resources, National Parks, and their management. National Parks are extensive tracts of countryside selected for their natural beauty, unique nature and landscape, and serve to preserve the natural diversity of rare plants and animals. On the other hand, they must also provide educational, recreational, scientific, economic and cultural benefits to domestic and foreign visitors, the surrounding communities and society in general.

Chapter outline

- Introduction
- Relevant Background Data on Plitvice Lakes National Park
- Application of Demand Management in the Plitvice Lakes National Park
- Marketing and Sales Strategy Supportive to Sustainable Management of National Parks
- Summary
- Key Questions

Introduction

The leading trend in tourism nowadays is maintaining a symbiotic relationship between nature and those who exploit it to gain material benefits. Although the term 'sustainable development' contradicts itself, especially when discussing natural resources, exploitation and sustainable development need more tools to be able to work together. This is especially important for one of nature's most important resources, National Parks, and their management. National Parks are extensive tracts of countryside selected for their natural beauty, unique nature and landscape, and serve to preserve the natural diversity of rare plants and animals. They must also provide educational, recreational, scientific, economic and cultural benefits to domestic and foreign visitors, the surrounding communities and society in general. The problem in this case is how to manage such a fragile system and still allow people (tourists) to enjoy nature to the full. Management is a crucial element for the long-term survival of the environmental and cultural resources upon which ecotourism depends and is frequently the weak link in the connection between tourism and the environment (Eagles *et al.*, 2001).

Suitable demand management that deals with the sustainability of nature might be a solution for the main problems that concern National Parks, namely how to disperse visitors in the peak season and preserve nature. Demand management might be defined as the supply chain management process that balances the customer's requirements with the capabilities of the supply chain. With the right process in place, management can match supply with demand proactively and execute a plan with minimal disruptions (Corxton *et al.*, 2002). With the tourism industry growing rapidly, there are many possibilities for introducing the tools of demand management for improving the present state of National Parks. According to a United Nations World Tourism Organization report, market demand for National Parks is increasing because nature travel is increasing at an annual rate of between 10 and 30%, resulting in the inclusion of a cultural component for 37% of all international trips (Manz, 2007). Evidence suggests that the demand for outdoor recreation as part of the inbound tourism/travel industry on publicly owned Parks and natural areas is likely to increase further (Uysal *et al.*, 1994). National Parks all around the world are challenged with increasing number of tourists who directly or indirectly damage nature and natural habits. Consequently managers of National Parks often find it necessary to decrease the number of tourists visiting the Park, i.e. shift the demand to off-season periods. That increases Park efficiency and also the quality of visitation for tourists. But although this works in theory, in practice National Parks do not have evenly filled seasons and so the number of off-season tourists is always much lower than in the peak season. The same kind of problem can be found in the Plitvice Lakes National Park. The present state of conservation is very good but lacks many improvements; studies on carrying capacities have to be made along with strategies on how to disperse visitors and preserve nature even better. This is the reason why a National Park such as Plitvice should introduce demand management processes if it wants to compete on the market and preserve its current state. Planned marketing efforts should not just stimulate demand but should also influence demand, so that a Park's objectives are achieved. The broader view of demand management should drive Park management to better understand its visitors and markets. When there is keen insightful understanding of markets and visitors' expectations of products, services and pricing requirements, a Park can develop more accurate demand forecasts. The purpose of demand planning is to create as credible a model as possible for driving the Park's plan projections. Planning must have a sufficiently long planning horizon to allow enough time to respond to both problems and opportunities (Crum and Palmatier, 2003). In terms of sustainable development, demand management has to deal with nature preservation as a starting point of forecasting, strategy building and in satisfying customer needs. Management that wants to lead the business according to the rules of sustainable development has to find ways to ensure profitability that do not interfere with nature and its way of self-preservation. Demand management that includes sustainability has to educate about nature preservation, promote new ways of thinking about business and influence people's attitudes towards nature.

Relevant Background Data on Plitvice Lakes National Park

Croatia has eight National Parks and ten Nature Parks. They are all part of Croatian cultural, historical and natural heritage. Plitvice Lakes National Park (Fig. 20.1) is one of the most famous Croatian Parks. The Park was founded in 1949 in order to preserve the natural and cultural heritage of this part of Croatia. The Plitvice Lakes area is of outstanding universal value not only from the scientific but also from the historical and cultural points of view. Within it are places that were the former scenes of ancient and recent historical events, as well as prehistoric, classical and mediaeval archaeological sites and monuments of popular traditional architecture. The protected Plitvice Lakes area includes, as a National Park, a wide belt of very well-preserved woodland, covering a complete ecosystem, essential for the continued existence and perpetuation of its constituent material factors. The waters flowing over the limestone and chalk have, over thousands

Fig. 20.1. Plitvice Lakes National Park.

Fig. 20.2. Waterfalls at Plitvice Lakes.

of years, deposited travertine barriers, creating natural dams which in turn have created a series of beautiful lakes, caves and waterfalls (Fig. 20.2). These geological processes continue today. The forests in the Park are home to bears, wolves and many rare bird species. As a geographical phenomenon of biogenetic origin, the Plitvice Lakes with their dams, waterfalls and caves are the most beautiful and best preserved representative examples of their kind. They attract millions of visitors from all over the world, and as instructive evidence of the laws of natural processes, they also have an educational function. Plitvice Lakes National Park was inscribed on the UNESCO World Heritage List in 1979 (Bojić, 2007).

The National Park is also a main economic force in the area, as it employs local inhabitants and awards scholarships to local students. It has an impact on two counties: Karlovac and Lika-Senj. The Park is also surrounded by five municipalities. Its economic importance is shown in the fact that the Park employs around 700 people, ensuring existence for almost 3000 family members. The annual number of visitors approaches one million. There are opportunities for small family tourism and the development of tourism in private accommodations. Selling of bio-agricultural products, craft works and traditional food should boost the area (Bojić, 2007). Tourism sustains hotels, cafés, shops and attractions throughout the year. The main financial resources come from sales of Park tickets, souvenirs in craft shops, restaurants and hotels. Connections with other National Parks give Plitvice Lakes National

Park support in its work and an incentive to better conserve its natural resources.

Operational problems in Plitvice Lakes concern carrying capacities in the peak season. The peak season in the Park is in the summer months of July and August, which is also the peak season for most Croatian tourist destinations. Most of the visitors who come to Plitvice are foreign tourists (89.5%) and they mostly visit before they reach their final destination. The increasing number of tourists in the peak season results in the situation that 1% of the Park (the lakes, boat and train stops) is always cluttered. The Park management is struggling to disperse visitors to other areas. The large number of visitors has a negative impact on nature. Visitors are asked to conduct themselves according to the rules of the Park with forbidding signs, visitor education, pictograms on the tickets and a surveillance department, but still that is not enough. The Park has not yet calculated its carrying capacity but has decided to build a plan that will help to preserve and enhance the Park. There are several main decisions that the management made in order to manage crowded areas in the Park. New walking paths have been made and old ones revitalized, which should disperse visitors and open new areas of the Park. The new marketing strategy needs more promotion so that tourists can see that the Park is always improving itself. The Park promotion consists of different channels such as web pages, tourist fares, articles in different types of magazines, advertising in magazines, promotional materials (posters, flyers) and word-of-mouth. Approximately 1.5% of Park income is allocated to promotion but practice shows that the word-of-mouth technique proves most efficient. A great deficiency in Park promotional activities is not keeping in touch with their regular guests who come more than once a year. Twenty-two per cent of visitors state that they would like to visit the Park again, so the Park has to respond to these wishes with special offers. A relationship between the Park and tourists has to be introduced in order to offer visitors different seasonal activities, lower ticket and hotel prices, family programmes and other events. This will also disperse visitors and prolong tourist activity to other seasons, which creates additional benefits not only for the Park but also for local people as well. Another specificity of Croatian tourism in general – the low expenditures of tourists – is reflected in the Park's revenues in the form of low expenditures on the Park premises. On average, every tourist spends approximately €17. That would not be so bad if the structure of that expenditure was not like that shown in Table 20.1.

From Table 20.1 it can be observed that most of the money spent in the National Park is on the ticket fare. This amounts to 73% of overall tourist expenditures. Reduced ticket prices are the most wanted change demanded from visitors to Croatian National Parks (TOMAS, 2006). Park management states that the ticket prices in Plitvice Lakes are lower than in other National Parks in Europe. They conclude that for the majority of foreign visitors (89.5% in 2006) their Park ticket is a reasonable price. That is certainly correct, but there are concerns that the high ticket price prevents domestic tourists (10.5% of visitors in 2006) from coming to the Park more often. The question of the right price for both domestic and foreign visitors should be further investigated. The ticket covers the cost of parking, tourist insurance, boat and bus rides in the Park. This means that the ticket price is directly influenced by other economic and political decisions, e.g. regarding the price of oil. The money from the tickets is used for Park preservation but most of the damage in the Park comes from the boats and buses in the Park. So the real question is whether these vehicles can run on some alternative and cheaper form of fuel in order to diminish the Park's dependency on oil. The Park's management is considering use of biodiesel, ecodiesel or gas powered panoramic vehicles and electric

Table 20.1. Tourist expenditures in Plitvice Lakes National Park. (From TOMAS, 2006.)

Item	Spend (€)
Ticket	12.66
Extra Park tours that are not included in ticket price	0.07
Food and drinks in restaurants in the Park	2.54
Shopping (souvenirs, clothes, maps, etc.)	1.36
Rest	0.53
Total	17.16

boats that run on solar energy. The Park should also consider the possibility of lowering the ticket price for tourists who decide to take alternative paths to reach a desired destination without motor vehicles. It is the management's objective that tourists spend more money in the Park. But it seems there is nothing to spend it on, or perhaps prices seem a little bit too high for an average visitor. Nevertheless, most visitors who come to the Croatian Parks have incomes of approximately €1000–2000 per month (Fig. 20.3), keeping in mind that most of the tourists do not come alone but are with their friends and families.

The National Park represents a public institution and being so it cannot discriminate against any segment of population and direct its prices and activities to specific groups (Roy, 1998). This is very important when talking about domestic visitors. The Park is not obligated to make a marketing plan but still it maintains certain internal marketing guidelines. As stated earlier, the Park is not segmenting the market but has three kinds of guests who are recognized as frequent visitors: organized groups, individual guests and convention guests. Although the Park recognizes these visitors as most important, there are no specifically determined activities defined for them by the Park nor are there any special promotional activities for each of these groups.

Another alarming trend for the Park is the reduction in domestic visitor numbers that continue to fall on an annual basis (Fig. 20.4). The

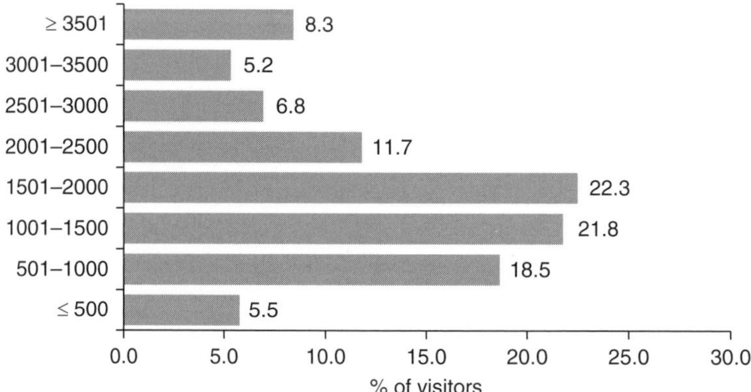

Fig. 20.3. Monthly income of visitors (€) attending Plitvice Lakes National Park.

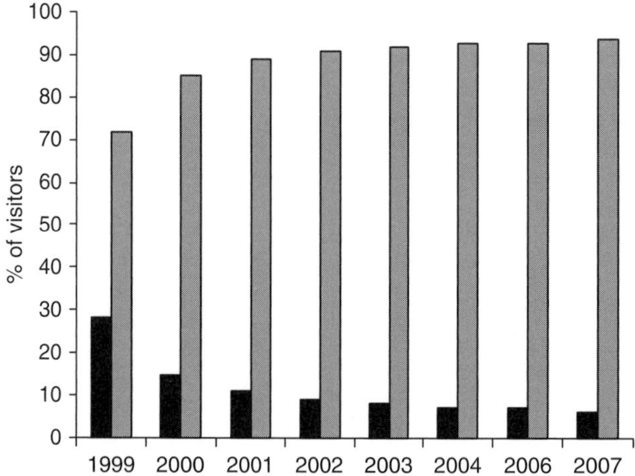

Fig. 20.4. Proportions of domestic (black) and foreign (grey) visitors to Plitvice Lakes National Park.

Park does not have any special promotional programmes for domestic visitors and it does not make any special offers that are suitable for Croatian living standards. Domestic visitors represent the greatest potential for the off-peak season, but the Park management is not exploiting that fact to the fullest. More domestic visitors throughout the year, especially in the off-peak season, would bring more life to tourist facilities and more jobs for the local community.

National Parks exist because of their special nature, but it seems they cannot offer only natural resources and beauty; other activities have to be implemented into a Park to bring guests in (Fig. 20.5). This is a very important issue for the Plitvice Lakes Park management to discuss because 42% of the total number of visitors stated they wanted more activities in the Park. Although the Park has some organized activities, they are poorly promoted and few visitors actually learn about them. Plitvice Lakes does not provide any kind of educational presentations for tourists, and bird-watching activity should be better organized. For example, Kakadu National Park in Australia gives education to tourist guides and sells them 5-year permits that allow them to guide tourists through the Park. Moreover, Plitvice Lakes does not sell 3-day passes or whole-year passes. These kinds of passes would prolong stays in the Park and encourage visitors to come to the Park more often. The group offering the greatest potential for Plitvice Lakes are organized parties of tourists: according to a survey (TOMAS, 2006) these organized groups come mostly from France and the UK (33% of tourists who come from France or the UK are in organized groups). These groups therefore present an excellent opportunity for all sorts of activities that could be arranged for them inside and outside the Park. Special proposals with discounts could be made to agencies in France and the UK that organize these kinds of trips, so they could bring more visitors.

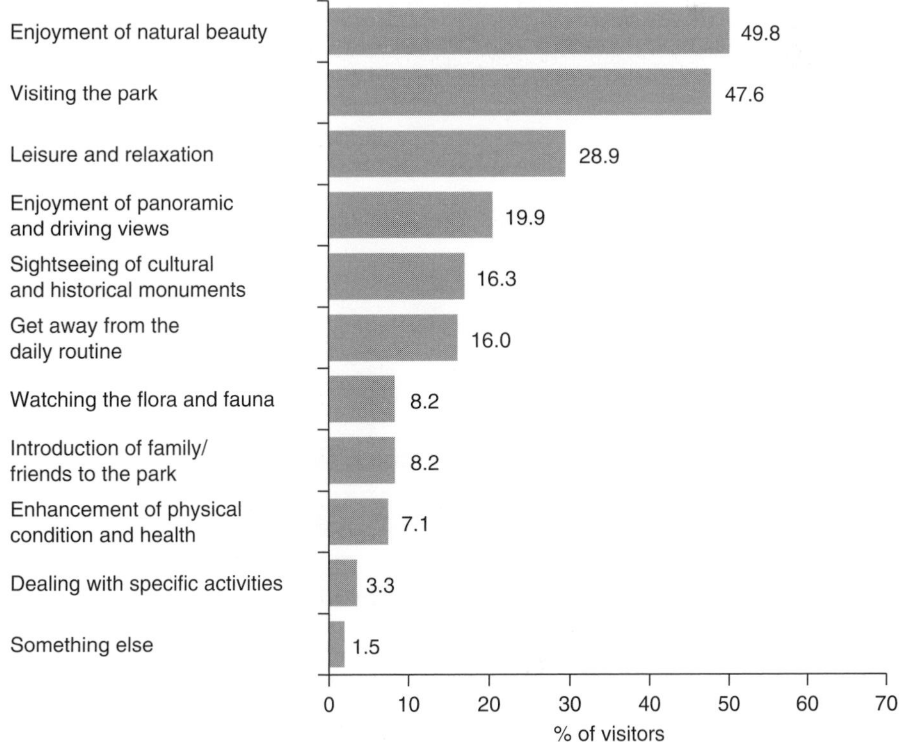

Fig. 20.5. Motives of visitors attending National Parks and Nature Parks in Croatia.

Collaboration with the local community is crucial for the Park to succeed in its work. For now the Park management is very pleased with local people and their work in the Park. Further development of cooperation should lead to new programmes that can improve Park offerings and activities. On the other hand, the Park should be more involved in the education of local people, helping them to understand the economic and natural value of the Park. The Park should be an initiator for all sorts of strategies that could preserve local culture, nature and crafts. These strategies could be the main foundations of sustainable tourism development. This would also reflect on the Park's income.

We have already discussed the price of the Park ticket and concluded that the price is very high, especially for domestic visitors. The Park derives its largest financial benefit from tickets, but that blocks other activities that could also be more profitable (Fig. 20.6). Trade seems to be decreasing along with the catering industry. This signifies that there is a lack of crafts, programmes and specific offerings that could bring more profit to the Park. We agree that the Park ticket should be an important part of the Park's financial gain; but still, we would recommend that the Park puts more effort into other ways of making profit and thereby secure its financial sustainability. Every new project or business that would tend to be profitable has to follow certain principles of sustainable development, i.e. sustainable tourism. The sustainability of the tourism industry depends largely on the region's ability to maintain product quality, ensure profitability, promote effectively, ensure safety, ensure acceptance by the local population, strengthen linkages between tourism and other economic sectors, and combine regional efforts to create a competitive force (Jayawardena, 2002).

Application of Demand Management in the Plitvice Lakes National Park

Any improvement to existing practice or knowledge cannot be properly considered until the existing condition(s) and problems surrounding it are fully understood (Abidin and Pasquire, 2005). Economic activity is dependent on a healthy environment (Common, 1998) that supports sustainability, social peace, and understanding of nature preservation. In the case of a National Park, preservation of its fragile natural resources depends on considerate conduct of

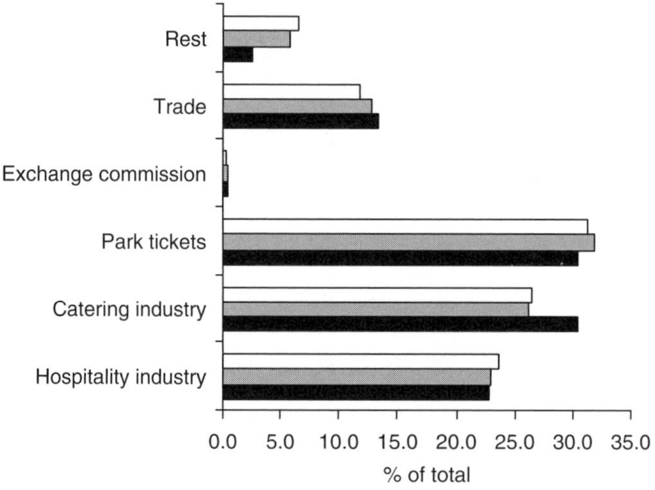

Fig. 20.6. Trend in sales activity in different segments, Plitvice Lakes National Park (white, 2006; grey, 2005; black, 2004).

all participants in its area and, furthermore, considerate conduct must be respected by employees of the Park, Park visitors and the local population. A balance between economic activity and sustainability cannot be achieved without certain measures. First, it is necessary to distinguish between sustainability management and sustainable management. Sustainability management is a way of dealing with issues occurring on strategic and operational levels, whereas sustainable management is based upon an ethical framework and considers ethically correct behaviour as the cornerstone of all its actions and considerations (Daub and Ergenzinger, 2005). As a result of literature reviews and secondary data collection, as well as conducting in-depth interviews with Parks' management, a business and marketing strategy for the National Parks was proposed (Fig. 20.7). The findings can be presented in the form of a specific model developed for application in Plitvice Lakes. Starting from the main objective, i.e. adjustment of fundamental marketing and strategy goals for the National Park, it is possible to extract four main groups of fundamental objectives influencing the development of a strategy:

- Protection of the Park's natural resources and conservation of national and world natural heritage represents the fundamental value upon which the rest of the offer is based; without preserved natural resources, the reason for the Park's existence and its offer value would cease to exist.
- Customer orientation and the creation of value based on marketing research, and alignment with financial objectives and nature protection, form the most important marketing group of factors, of which segmentation and value proposition are the key ingredients.

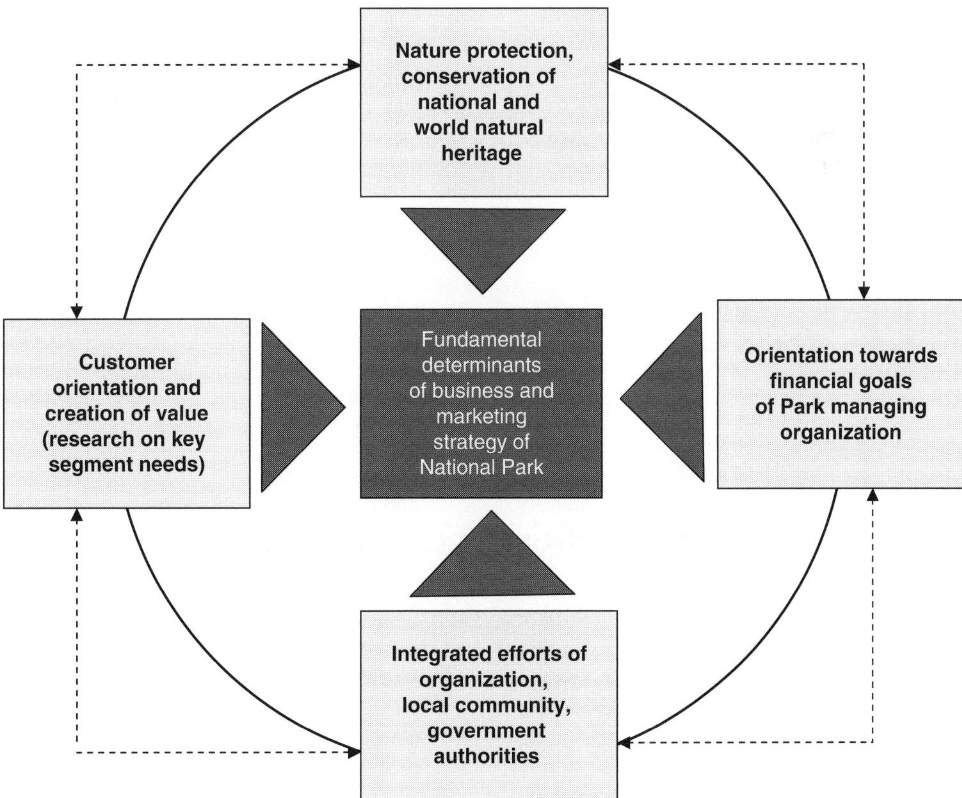

Fig. 20.7. Fundamental goals-to-strategy model for National Parks.

- Objectives concerning cooperation and benefits for the local community, Park and government agencies, which should be integrated and synergistic in function.
- Financial objectives of the Park, which are necessary for the development and protection of nature in that area.

The first objective of sustainable demand management is to find best solutions for balancing customers' requirements with the capabilities of a certain organization and implementation of these solutions to fit the ethical and sustainable patterns that have to be respected in order to maintain a healthy environment. In the case of Plitvice Lakes National Park, factors like nature conservation and ecology have to come ahead of economic factors. Demand management with its strategic and operational elements will help to find factors that do not support sustainable development and try to nullify or diminish them. Promotion of sustainable development should lead to:

- raising awareness on nature preservation;
- establishing local organizations that help generate sustainable business ideas and give information on how to finance them;
- educating local people on sustainable economic strategies for their businesses;
- involving young people in developing strategies for their future employment in the local area; and
- the National Park and the local community building strategic initiatives together, thereby making it easier for the Park to reach its goals of better nature conservation.

All of this means that there must be some serious preparations in order to start implementing principles of demand management. When discussing demand management process the Park has to focus on strategic and operational elements that fit sustainable development of the Park. Defining the Park's purposes is the main objective, in order to synchronize them with management tools. Management of Plitvice Lakes National Park has several main purposes:

- scientific research;
- protection of the Park's ecosystem;
- preservation of the Park;
- maintenance of environmental services;
- protection of specific natural and cultural features;
- tourism and recreation; and
- education.

By examining these purposes, Park management can easily implement tools of sustainable demand management to fit the Park's needs and the needs of the local community.

Marketing and Sales Strategy Supportive to Sustainable Management of National Parks

As the main steps of sustainable demand management have been examined, it is now appropriate to determine what kind of marketing and sales strategies are supportive of it. The four indicators of environment are driving force, state, reactive response and proactive response (Das Gandhi *et al.*, 2006). As a resource-dependent industry, tourism must recognize its responsibility to the environment. Tourism development which consistently ignores environmental concerns is unlikely to remain viable in the longer term (Horobin and Long, 1996). Recognizing the problems and main priorities of Plitvice Lakes National Park helps in understanding what tools should be used in order to ensure preservation of natural resources and boost visitor flow in off-season periods. These tools have to be in accordance with sustainable development rules. Park management has to decide on these elements (Magiera *et al.*, 2006), which could include:

- economic incentives such as pricing, fees and charges for Park usage;
- incentives for provision of environmental services, subsidies or rebates for more efficient water use;
- education of local people;
- recycling;
- municipal subsidies for nature-friendly businesses and crafts;
- planning of more off-season activities; and
- promotion of off-season activities.

The emphasis must be on high-volume low-impact tourism. The high volume of tourists in the peak season is causing problems for nature preservation in Plitvice Lakes Park. This means that the tourists have a high impact on the ecological system in the Park. As mentioned above, the problem is complex because tourists are mostly cluttering 1% of the Park, so leading to underutilization of the rest of the Park.

The majority of tickets are sold in the second and third quarters of the year (Fig. 20.8). Differences between quarters are immense and bring problems for the Park management because the first and fourth quarters have devastating financial results; if the Park wants to have high-volume low-impact tourism it has to deal with this problem as soon as possible. Determination of carrying capacities and Park segments has to be the first step when deciding on further ways to improve the situation. In examining the potential for improving capacity management, the following objectives have to be established (Laing and Shiroyama, 1995):

- Examine the utilization of productive capacity in terms of employment of facilities, equipment and staff.
- Identify bottleneck points.
- Examine the potential for increased organizational flexibility in terms of timing and location.

After determination of carrying capacity, the Park should keep visitor numbers around that maximum. When managing demand one must determine segments and their corresponding needs, in order to meet them. Development of the Park depends on knowledge about its visitors. The Park must decide the best ways to satisfy the visitor without harming nature and without leading the visitor to do something that is not Park-friendly. The Park has to differentiate itself from other destinations, develop high visitor understanding of the destination's unique experiences and bring value for money to the visitor. When considering what segments are the best for the Park premises, management has to think about the visitors who come now and the ones who might come in future. It is not enough to watch visitor surveys and find out what the biggest segments are. The Park has to look out and see what other segments it may serve or what other segments would be best to serve. New

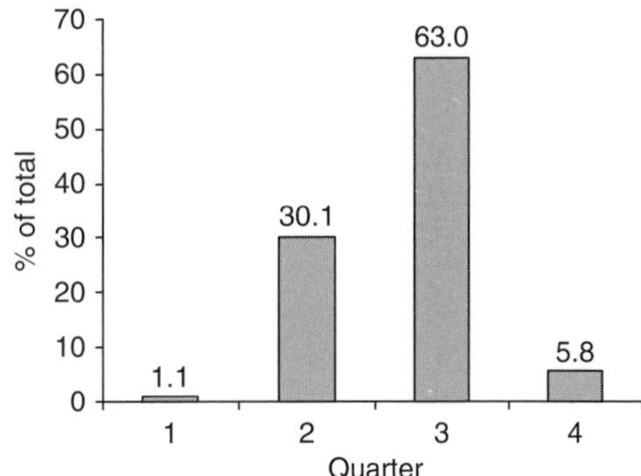

Fig. 20.8. Reported ticket sales by quarter, Plitvice Lakes National Park.

offerings should be made in order to attract new visitors, and these offerings have to be unique and original in order to stand out from other offerings from other Parks. Several interesting segments with their descriptions that could be beneficial for the Park management are presented in Table 20.2.

The Park should improve its usage of underutilized facilities, equipment and pathways. Old pathways have to be revitalized and facilities that have no use brought to life. Although the Park has plans to do these things they have to be rushed into action in order to improve quality of the service in the future. Usage of motor vehicles in the Park should be minimized. They should be used only for disabled people and when other types of movement in the Park are precluded. This would maximize utilization of the pathways and force visitors to use them more frequently. Pathways for disabled visitors should be built and kept apart from regular visitors, so they do not disturb visitors who are disabled. The Park should improve the quality of the built environment that people enjoy or use. This refers to restaurants, hotels, sitting benches, pathways, information stands and rest rooms. Sustainability requirements are easy to implement in accommodation, because hotels can make eco-efficiency gains through better management of water, waste and energy. Also this has to be carried over to local people and their accommodation and tourist infrastructures. Local residents represent a key part of the Park and this means that they have to participate in

Table 20.2. Description of segment services.

Segment	Service type	Service quality	Promotion	Distribution	Price
Domestic					
Family and friends travellers	Tour of the lake Virtual tour Theatre plays and concerts Special food offerings (family picnics, barbecue) Special mascot tour guides for children Skiing and sledging	Set quality standards Improve restaurants and hotels to be more child-friendly Build food shops Organize more fairs in off-peak season	Television Brochures and posters Internet Schools Family associations	Park centre Restaurants Hotels Camps Park premises Park skiing resort	Family ticket priced according to domestic living standards Special offerings and discounts in off-peak season
Peer group travellers	Tour of the lake Virtual tour Theatre plays and concerts Educational workshops Special food offerings (picnics, barbecue) Night sightseeing Photography and birdwatching Skiing and sledging	Set quality standards for hotels and camps Build educational facilities Ensure security for night sightseeing Build sport terrains	Internet forums Nature interest groups High schools Special stand promotion in every larger town in Croatia Buzz marketing	Park centre Park premises Restaurants Hotels Camps Park skiing resort	Ticket priced according to domestic living standards Special discounts on groups over 15
Schoolchildren	School in nature Park scout education Special mascot tour guides Photography and birdwatching Skiing and sledging	Build educational facilities Train special tourist guides Build sport terrains	Schools Internet Nature interest groups	Park centre Park premises Camps Park skiing resort	Ticket priced according to domestic living standards Special offerings and discounts in off-peak season
Foreign					
Family and friends travellers	Tour of the lake Virtual tour Special food offerings (family picnics, barbecue, special food presentations) Park concerts History and culture tour of the local countryside Day care for children Skiing and sledging	Set quality standards Improve restaurants and hotels to be more child-friendly Build food shops Organize more fairs in off-peak season	Internet Television, documentaries Travel agencies Tourist fairs Posters, stands, brochures	Park centre Restaurants Hotels Camps Park premises Park skiing resort	Family ticket price Special offerings and discounts in off-peak season

Touring travellers and retired	Tour of the lake Virtual tour Theatre plays and concerts Educational workshops Special food offerings (picnics, barbecue) Night sightseeing Photography and birdwatching History and culture tour of the local countryside Skiing and sledging	Set quality standards Build educational facilities Ensure security for night sightseeing Build food shops Build sport terrains Organize more fairs in off-peak season	Travel agencies Internet Television, documentaries Tourist fairs Posters, stands, brochures Nursing homes Religious groups	Park centre Restaurants Hotels Camps Park premises Park skiing resort	Park ticket priced according to agreement with travel agencies Travel agencies who bring more tourists in off-peak season get more discounts
Quick stop tourists	Tour of the lake Virtual tour Special food offerings (picnics, barbecue) Night sightseeing	Ensure security for night sightseeing	Internet Road maps Promotion of other seasons in the Park	Park centre Restaurants Park premises	Regular price for Park ticket, no discounts
Students and ecology groups	Tour of the lake Virtual tour Theatre plays and concerts Educational workshops Special food offerings (picnics, barbecue) Night sightseeing Photography and birdwatching Skiing and sledging	Set quality standards for hotels and camps Build educational facilities Ensure security for night sightseeing	Internet forums Nature interest groups Special stand promotion in larger student campuses Student travel agencies	Park centre Park premises Restaurants Hotels Camps Park skiing resort	Discount for off-season period Discount for larger groups in off-season period

every action that is undertaken by the National Park. Nowadays, Plitvice Lakes is attempting to level demand with lower off-peak tickets and special weekend offerings. In exchange for the lower prices, customers are restricted from using the peak times (Batra and Narinder, 1996).

This sales function is not doing well in Plitvice Lakes Park, so it has to be accompanied with other marketing attempts to increase demand in off-season periods. The Park must enhance cultural and natural features that enrich the off-season periods. This can be done by introducing new educational and historical centres that can modify their programmes as the seasons change. These centres could give information about:

- the history of Plitvice Lakes;
- a virtual tour of the lake that prepares the visitor for the most important areas of greatest value and beauty (these virtual tours would be different in every season);
- cultural heritage and the life of the people in the past, special customs that were part of everyday lives for the people of the area (also different in every season); and
- local food and beverages prepared according to the tradition of the local people, with the chance to taste and enjoy the food.

Educational centres could also connect with domestic and foreign educational facilities, schools, universities and environment organizations, to give lectures about nature preservation. Lectures could be given throughout the year and would be priced according to students' standards. The Park should prepare special workshops where young people could give their view of the Park and what could be done to ensure a more pleasant stay there. Many European Parks have young scouts that help preserve and maintain the Parks' nature. This could be a source of great potential for the local area as well, because these scouts could stay in camps or hotels around the Park. Young visitors who come to the Park should be encouraged to enjoy and value the Lakes so that they want to return later in life. Children and young adults have an adventurous spirit. They want to relax but still be active. Sports and adventures are great ways to mobilize the energy they have. For those who have an adventurous spirit and for those who feel young at heart, the Park could build exploration pathways where the visitor is able to explore wildlife to the fullest. Sport activities could be arranged if the Park builds different sport terrains along with the local community (football, skiing, sledging, running) and arrange that they stay open throughout the year.

As 30.1% of visitors to Croatian Parks are accompanied by their families, couples who have small children should be helped by offering them special tourist guides. Those tourist guides could be dressed up as an imaginary character (forest fairy, bear, etc.) and be a Parks mascot. The guide could play interactive educational games with the children, showing them the specificities of the Park and telling them about history in a fun way. Along with the government, the Park should ensure effective access to a broad range of life-long learning opportunities. These learning opportunities would consist of seminars on how to start a business whose products and services could complement Park activities, seminars on long-forgotten crafts that could fulfil tourist offerings, foreign language courses for better understanding with tourists, history courses and cooking courses. The local community should be stimulated to start growing eco-farms and gardens. They could sell their food to the hotels and restaurants in the Park area. The Park could offer this food and, along with local people, make an organic food brand that could be sold in specialized Park shops located in hotels and restaurants. By these means they could promote a healthy way of living through the organization of events such as healthy picnics and dinners. The Park would be a great distribution centre for these kinds of foods, and part of the profit could go to nature preservation. Thus local people would have more incentive to encourage visitors to stay longer and spend more on local goods and services. Promotion of healthy living could spread into hotels and restaurants, which could offer wellness arrangements for visitors who want to relax and feel free to enjoy the beauty of the nature.

In this way everybody would benefit and the Park could earn more money for nature preservation. When talking about promotion of Plitvice Lakes National Park, the local population should be more involved. They should also be able to educate visitors on basic facts about the Park. According to the TOMAS (2006) study, most visitors (37.5%) come to Croatians Parks when they hear about them from their families or friends. Local people make only 4.4% of sources who influence tourists to come to the Park. This has to be changed.

All these activities have to be properly tracked. Constant visitor surveys along with questionnaires on visitor satisfaction are needed to give answers about the accomplishment of set goals and what factors have to be improved. The Park should try to stay in touch with visitors through some kind of promotional correspondence or special offerings. Special attention has to be given to those visitors who come more than once. They should be rewarded and thanked for their loyalty. Constant tracking helps in demand management as well. When forecasting, managers will be able to be more accurate and better prepared for visitor requirements. If the Park managers would pursue all of these propositions, visitor structure could be more dispersed (Fig. 20.9). Again it is important to mention that the strategy for visitor dispersion has to be well defined and constantly tracked in order to improve certain deficiencies that may occur in time.

A well-defined and written strategy would help Park employees to know what boundaries have to be respected and how to set them for visitors who sometimes do not understand nature and the way it has to be preserved. Financial gain from new offers and diversification would help the Park to be more competitive (Tomašević Lišansin *et al.*, 2008). Although the main goal is not to compete against other Parks, Plitvice Lakes National Park must enable visitors to connect with nature. It is important to offer a unique experience of the National Park and its cultural and historical heritage. And, most importantly, visitors should learn about the delicate balance and responsibility of preserving such natural treasures.

Summary

There is no right answer on how to preserve nature or how to be fully sustainable. Every action causes reaction, and this simple law of physics means that people and organizations influence nature by their mere existence. Things get even more complicated when the economy and its laws, which are almost always in contradiction with nature preservation, become involved. Fortunately, it is possible to find solutions that reconcile the worlds of business and ecology. This chapter has explored different marketing strategies for balancing and optimizing Park visitation during high- and

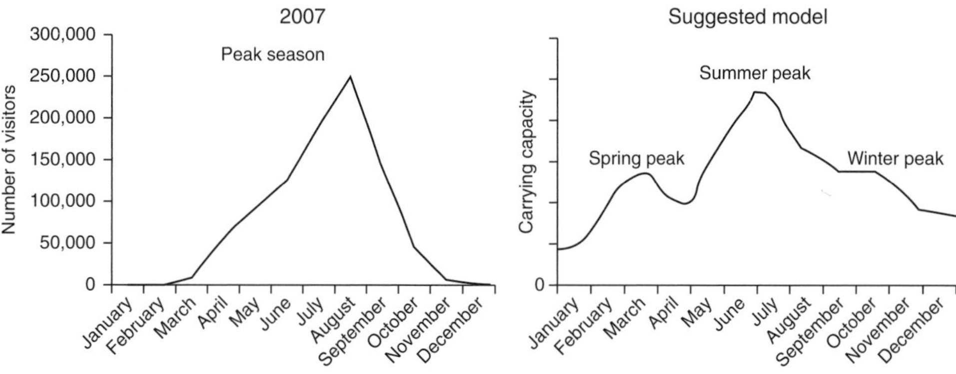

Fig. 20.9. Visitor dispersion model.

low-demand periods, in order to aid sustainable development of the Park and its resources. Knowing what sustainable development means helps people, communities and organizations to change their ethics and ways of living and conducting business. When thinking about National Parks it becomes inevitable to get involved in their salvation. National or Nature Parks are truly one of the greatest treasures of every country and their preservation depends on the right management tools. Sustainable demand management helps Parks to keep track of their visitors and their actions in the Park. Continuous data collecting, forecasting and proactive behaviour helps Park management to influence demand and preserve nature. Prioritizing demand becomes more important than just mere profit making. Nature comes first and the Park should do all the things that serve that objective. Along with the local community and their tourist offerings, the Park can easily develop strategies for dispersion of visitors in the peak season and for improving the offer value throughout the year. National Parks are specific oases for enjoyment that have a special mission: to show us that life on this planet is fragile but beautiful, and therefore priceless.

Key Questions

1. What can be done in order to disperse visits more evenly throughout the year?
2. What marketing tools should be used in order to improve value for visitors to the Park?
3. Briefly outline a marketing strategy that the Park should adopt in order to meet its strategic goals.

References

Abidin, N. and Pasquire, L. (2005) Delivering sustainability through value management. Concept and performance overview. *Engineering, Construction and Architectural Management* 12(2), 168–180.

Batra, G.S. and Narinder, K. (1996) New vistas in reducing the conflicts between tourism and the environment: an environmental audit approach. *Managerial Auditing Journal* 11(4), 3–10.

Bojić, M. (2007) Natural World Heritage in Croatia – legal and economic implications. Available at: http://www.preserveworldheritage.org/en/Training-Workshop/Plitvice/Docs_Pics/Presentations/Mirna_Bojic.pdf (accessed 16 March 2009).

Crum, C. and Palmatier, E.G. (2003) *Demand Management Best Practices: Process, Principles and Collaboration*. J. Ross Publishing, Fort Lauderdale, Florida.

Common, M. (1998) Economics and the natural environment; a review article. *Journal of Economic Studies* 25(1), 57–73.

Corxton, K.L., Douglas, L.M., Garcia-Dastugue, S.J. and Dale R.S. (2002) The demand management process. *International Journal of Logistics Management* 13(2), 51–66.

Das Gandhi, N.M., Selladurai, V. and Santhi, P. (2006) Unsustainable development to sustainable development: a conceptual model. *Management of Environmental Quality* 17(6), 654–672.

Daub, C.H. and Ergenzinger, R. (2005) Enabling sustainable management through a new multi-disciplinary concept of customer satisfaction. *European Journal of Marketing* 39(9/10), 998–1012.

Eagles, J., Bowman, E. and Tao, T. (2001) *Guidelines for Tourism in Parks and Protected Areas of East Asia*. IUCN Publications Services Unit, Cambridge, UK.

Horobin, H. and Long, J. (1996) Sustainable tourism: the role of the small firm. *International Journal of Contemporary Hospitality Management* 8(5), 15–19.

Jayawardena, C. (2002) Mastering Caribbean tourism. *International Journal of Contemporary Hospitality Management* 14(2), 88–93.

Laing, A.W. and Shiroyama, C. (1995) Managing capacity and demand in a resource constrained environment: lessons for the NHS? *Journal of Management in Medicine* 9(5), 51–67.

Magiera, P., Taha, S. and Nolte, L. (2006) Water demand management in the Middle East and North Africa. *Management of Environmental Quality* 17(3), 289–298.

Manz, K. (2007) The World Heritage Sustainable Tourism Programme. Available at: http://www.preserveworldheritage.org/en/Training-Workshop/Plitvice/Plitvice.shtml?navid=7 (accessed 16 March 2009).

Roy, K.C. (1998) Issues in resource conservation and sustainable development: Indian situation. *International Journal of Social Economics* 25(1), 16–24.

TOMAS (2006) *National and Nature Parks 2006 – Perceptions and Spending of the Visitors in National and Nature Parks in Republic of Croatia*. Croatian Ministry of Tourism, Sea, Transport and Regional Development, Zagreb.

Tomašević Lišanin, M., Palić, M. and Meštrović, R. (2008) Sustainable demand management in national parks: example of Plitvice Lakes National Park.

Uysal, M., McDonald, C.D. and Martin, B.S. (1994) Visitors to US National Parks and Natural Areas. *International Journal of Contemporary Hospitality Management* 6(3), 18–24.

21 Antalya Golden Orange Film Festival: Impacts on the Local Community

V. Altıntaş
Akdeniz University, Antalya, Turkey

This chapter aims to examine the viewpoint of local people on the Golden Orange Film Festival in Antalya, Turkey. The chapter shows the differences and similarities in the perception (sociocultural effect) of different sectors of the local community (local impact) on the film festival in terms of taking enough benefit from the event, with the organizers, local authorities and local people from urban and rural areas being the main respondents.

Chapter outline

Introduction

Antalya is at the heart of the tourism industry in Turkey. It is vital that event tourism products become an important dimension of the touristic products offered in the Antalya region in the near future, besides sea, sun and sand. This chapter uses as a case study the results of research undertaken with the aim of explaining the viewpoint of the local people on Antalya Golden Orange Film Festival. The research focuses on the differences and similarities in the perception (sociocultural effect) of different sectors of the local community (local impact) on the film festival in terms of taking enough benefit from the event, with observation and interviews being the main tools of investigation and the organizers, local authorities and local people from urban and rural areas being the main targets. This research, canvassing the locals' perceptions and views on this event and their causes, represents the first scientific study on the Golden Orange Film Festival in Antalya.

Birth and Historical Development of Antalya Golden Orange Film Festival

In recent years, festivals and special events have become one of the fastest-growing types of tourism attraction (Gürsoy *et al.*, 2004). Events are an important motivator of tourism, and figure prominently in the development and marketing plans of most destinations (Getz, 2008). Communities pursuing tourism development expect favourable socio-economic returns from it: real income, tax revenues, employment opportunities, promotion of intersectoral linkages, rejuvenation of underdeveloped community resources, enhancement of local quality of life, and positioning of the community as a desirable place to live, work, visit, invest in, relocate and/or retire to (Koh and Jackson, 2006). This reality is valid for the region of Antalya in Turkey as well.

Antalya is a city of sun, tourism and history on the Mediterranean coast of Turkey. It is the global face of Turkish tourism – it can even be called the 'tourism capital of Turkey'. In 2007, about eight million tourists visited Antalya region, a holiday destination which is the first stop-off point for one in every three tourists coming to Turkey. If one reason for this popularity is Antalya being the best and most frequent practitioner of the all-inclusive holiday system, another is its efforts in perpetuating the most long-lived film festival in Turkey to date.

During the 1950s, Antalya was a lonely city despite all its historical richness and natural beauty. Its population was only about 27,000. In those days, there were very few people who knew Antalya or its place on the map. The following narrative of Hüseyin Çimrin, famous historian-writer of Antalya, describes the history of Antalya Golden Orange Film Festival quoting from various documents:

> I remember my school years, I looked in vain for a chapter in our Geography book. Antalya was passed over with a sole sentence: 'There is a city called Antalya in the South of Turkey near Adana and İçel cities'. That was all. In those years, people of Antalya who took this to their hearts were looking for a way to make known Antalya to the world. In 1949, Osman Batur, English teacher in Antalya High School, who was an admirer of Antalya's beauties and willing to make known Antalya universally; Dr. Burhanettin Onat, another Antalya admirer, and their friends founded the Antalya Tourism and Promotion Association in 1949. Later, becoming a member of the parliament, Burhanettin Onat started to organize annual oil wrestling competitions in 1951, inspired by Atatürk's will in which he bequeathed that artistic and sports activities shall be organized for the public in Aspendos Theatre. People of Antalya, city and the country, showed great interest in the wrestling competitions.
> The competitions were lasting for a few days, attracting thousands of people to the theatre. However, these wrestling competitions were not attracting any tourists from other parts of the country or from foreign countries. We were all alone playing and dancing by ourselves. Years were passing, but we couldn't improve our efforts to promote Antalya, even within the country. One day something happened. It was 1953, the end of May. Students of Ankara State Conservatory, theatre department came to Antalya for a school trip. Their teachers had them take the costumes for the play *Romeo and Juliet* since they had heard about Aspendos theatre. When they came to Antalya, they visited the theatre. They were astonished when they saw the great Roman theatre was in excellent condition, and they decided to perform the play *Romeo and Juliet*. However, the antique theatre was covered with weeds. They immediately visited İhsan Sabri Çağlayangil, governor of Antalya, and said that they want to perform a play in Aspendos. İhsan Sabri Çağlayangil accepted their wish with the support of Antalya Tourism Association. Cleaning workers of Antalya Municipality removed the weeds on the stage building and the seats. Within a few days a wooden stage was built with the financial support of Special Provincial Administration and Antalya Municipality. People both from the centre and neighbour towns showed great interest in the play. After the performance, the administrators of the province realized the enthusiasm of people, and laid the foundation of the great festival of the future with their following efforts.
>
> (antalyabugun.com, 2007)

1953 was the start of the festival. That year, the play *Romeo and Juliet* by William Shakespeare, performed by the students of Ankara State Theatre Conservatory, became the first stepping stone of Antalya Theatre and Music Festival.

The Name of the Festival: Golden Orange

The concerts and theatre performances that came to be held from the mid-1950s were the stepping stones of Antalya Golden Orange Film Festival. The performances, held every summer with high participation from the public, became traditional and continued in the mood of a festival until the beginning of 1960s. Dr Avni Tolunay, known for his devotion to art, was the voluntary organizer of this festival.

Avni Tolunay became the Municipal of Antalya in 1963, after serving as the head doctor of the Municipality for many years. Then the festival became 'Antalya Golden Orange Film Festival', embracing the cinema as well. Dr Tolunay looked for an emblem for Antalya, and identified the orange, symbol of the region, with the sea, historical elements and the sculpture of Venus. The orange not only became part of the emblem, but also the name of the festival itself (Fig. 21.1) (Antalya Firma Rehberi, 2008).

The First Festival and Wide Interest

The first festival, held in 1964 under very difficult conditions, drew wide interest. The municipal of Antalya, Dr Avni Tolunay, declared that, with the power of people's enthusiasm, the festival would become traditional, and the organization would last forever like a relay race. He determined the mission of the festival as follows: 'To support Turkish film industry physically and morally, to lay the groundwork for promoting Turkish cinema internationally by encouraging Turkish film producers to make qualified works'. Born within this principle, the Golden Orange National Feature Film Competition took place as a part of Antalya Golden Orange Film Festival, gaining the title 'Turkey's Oscar' within a short time of its initiation owing to the enthusiasm it created. The Golden Orange Film Festival followed this route between 1964 and 1973. Selahattin Tonguc, who was elected Municipal in 1973, also followed the same format. In 1978, Plastic Arts became a part of the Festival as an international event.

Fig. 21.1. Antalya Golden Orange Film Festival logo. (From Wikipedia, 2007.)

Towards an Institutional Structure

Antalya Culture Art and Tourism Foundation (AKSAV), founded by the Municipal of the time, Yener Ulusoy, undertook the organization of the festival beginning from 1985. In the same year, Yener Ulusoy added a different dimension to the festival by starting an international music competition called 'Akdeniz Akdeniz' (Mediterranean Mediterranean), including the Mediterranean countries. This music competition lasted from 1985 to 1988 together with Antalya Golden Orange Film Festival.

Between 1989 and 1994, the festival was organized by a Festival Execution Committee consisting of assembly members of the Municipality, tourism organizations and representatives of Antalya Chamber of Commerce. In 1995, the organization became an institutional structure with the establishment of the Golden Orange Culture and Arts Foundation, with the leadership of Antalya Municipality. The foundation has been known by the name Antalya Culture and Arts Foundation since September 2002 (festivalfocus, 2008).

Opening Up to the World

After an Extraordinary General Meeting held on 29 May 2004, the Golden Orange determined its route as 'Eurasia' , defining its objective as becoming 'a world festival', and declared

2005 as 'the transition year to an international platform' (AKSAV, 2008).

The Golden Orange, defining its new perspective as the 'industrialization of Yeşilçam', 'worldwide promotion of Turkish cinema' and 'creation of cultural added value for Antalya and Turkish economy', has become a ground for the geography of Eurasia and a place for the cinema languages of this land to express themselves (Antalya Firma Rehberi, 2008).

First, the International Eurasia Film Festival started in 2005; then in 2006, the International Eurasia Film Market began. For the first time, a structure was established on the lands spanning Europe and Asia in which an International Film Festival and an International Film Market exist together. Antalya, a place where Turkish cinema opens up to the world, also became the meeting address of world cinema (Fig. 21.2). Thus, the first step was taken to set the commercial ground of the Festival with this Film Market.

The Place of the Public in the Festival

This is the short history of the festival that has been organized for over 40 years in Antalya, the capital of Turkish tourism. Considering that one-third of the tourists coming to Turkey visit Antalya, is it too much to expect that the local people of Antalya should also somehow benefit from the international activities taking place in Antalya? Coming to the 2000s, what is the latest situation of the festival which attracted viewers from not only the centre of Antalya, but also nearby provinces and cities in the 1960s? This question forms the basis of research undertaken to gauge public opinion. The comments of the public – from the people working for such a big occasion to the people living in uptown Antalya, from senior executive officers to journalists and academics – were sought, so as to learn the sociocultural effects of the Golden Orange Film Festival on the local people.

Hüsrev Özen, 76 (Fig. 21.3), is a person who knows and has followed developments in Antalya since the republican period. Hüsrev Özen said:

> In 1960s the people of Antalya were totally engaged in this organization. We used to look forward to the date on which the Golden Orange would start and gathered at the squares with enthusiasm. However, after 1980s we no longer take part at this festival, having got disconnected characteristics. The fact that the

Fig. 21.2. Altın Portakal.

Fig. 21.3. Hüsrev Özen.

Fig. 21.4. Abdullah Tekin.

Fig. 21.5. Hayrettin Duran.

> youngsters will never know what we have experienced and they have lost the chance to get the spirit of Golden Orange is what makes me sad most.

An author, instructor and critic having worked as a member of the Board of Directors for years, Abdullah Tekin (Fig. 21.4) stated that while taking the Golden Orange Film Festival into the international arena, a point disregarded was the fact that the public cannot be as involved in this process as they were in the past, which is an interesting ascertainment. While saying that a reason for the elimination of or reduction in people's efforts to see the films or cinema celebrities of the 2000s was that the festival had been moved from a partially natural environment into halls, which was the result of a desire to take the Cannes Film Festival as a model and make Golden Orange more elite, Tekin emphasized a much more interesting point. Regretting to say that the responsibility of the organizers in the divergence of the people of Antalya from the film festival should not be forgotten, Abdullah Tekin stated that we should always bear in mind that gradual divergence of the people from the festival contradicts the aim of festival.

Hayrettin Duran (Fig. 21.5), a self-employed taxi driver for 15 years, said that the Golden Orange Film festival does not mean too much to him. After first commenting in a humorous way that the emblem of the festival does not even look like an orange, the taxi driver, Hayrettin, continued that he does not know who is responsible for the fact that even taxi drivers cannot benefit from the Golden Orange Film Festival. Mr Duran said he has never been to a Golden Orange Film Festival in his life and said that many people around him do not know much about the festival and are not interested in it, either. The fact that he regards activities such as cinema a luxury for himself and his family clearly shows his viewpoint of the Golden Orange Film Festival.

Professor Dr Tuncay Neyisci (Fig. 21.6), Director of the Centre of Environmental Procedure and Research of Akdeniz University, stated that Akdeniz University, the only university of Antalya, is also responsible for the distance between the public and the Golden Orange Film Festival. Saying that as a result of the university being disconnected from the public, a significant opportunity for Antalya is being lost, Professor Neyisci underlined that there is a necessity to discuss the meaning of a film festival taking place in closed halls and luxurious places organized by a festival administration that does not want to see the public in its organization. He also emphasized that an organization not cooperating with the university will have difficulty in embracing the public.

Fig. 21.6. Tuncay Neyisci.

The editor of the turizmhaberleri.com web site, Nilgün Atar, said that one of the most essential reasons for experiencing a festival disconnected from the public was Antalya Metropolitan Municipality's idea to realize this organization together with the public but disconnected from it. She stated that the public should be informed before and after the festival, and that we have to reach the public through panels and meetings.

Finally we have the word of the organizers of the Golden Orange Film Festival. Erol Işbilir is a member of the board of directors of AKSAV and leads the Golden Orange Film Festival. According to Mr. Işbilir, the public does not have to be involved in this work and they do not expect this, either. It was surprising to hear that, although interest in the open-air cinemas in the shanty towns was low, the real objective of taking cinema to the people of shanty towns was to prevent these people from creating chaos in downtown Antalya during the festival. The authority said that from now on they have higher objectives like changing Antalya into a film plateau and added that the concerns about embracing the public would be a very simple objective compared with their higher ones. Erol Işbilir stated that the reasons for low interest in films despite the low prices specified for the local people were economic difficulties and the lack of an established cinema culture. Işbilir added that because of this current situation the festival has taken its objectives to different dimensions.

Perception of the Golden Orange Film Festival within the Concept of Event Tourism

Festivals are one of the most important tourism attractions within the concept of event tourism. Event tourism and its management, a concept that has become common since the 1990s, means the process covering planning, marketing, creation of knowledge, formation of a system, and execution of an event. In Turkey, this concept became prominent especially in the 2000s.

Event tourism is based on the facts that festivals are a part of tourism and it is possible to carry out sustainable tourism activities, creating diversity in tourism, in accordance with the importance of the processes in festival management. At this point, the economic and political effects, as well as sociocultural effects, of festivals should be taken into account. The trouble with Antalya Golden Orange Film Festival is that such a big event is carried out with the focus on economic and political concerns.

As a result of problems in festival management, if the people expected to attend a festival fall outside the process (due to either psychological reasons or reasons of the managerial viewpoint), this can cause the result that the festival is organized in spite of native people. To mitigate this situation, strong attempts to bring people together during festivals and to eliminate racism and violence have to be made.

Festivals should also serve feelings of tolerance, peace, love and sharing, yet this side seemed not to be carried out in Antalya Film Festival. In this film festival, carried from a local to a global platform, the biggest fault made in the execution is what has just been mentioned: that people relevant to the festival organization carried out this process without perceiving the important principles of event tourism, which decreased the interest of native people towards the festival.

It is known that similar troubles have been experienced in other international festivals organized in various regions of Turkey. But it is also known that native people stand at the forefront of local or regional festivals. This gap, perceived by some as a natural process that has to be lived with as the organization gets bigger, is seen as the biggest hindrance to the role that festivals can play in sustainable tourism.

Native people's attitudes towards festivals, not special to Antalya, are entwined in the attitude of management towards people all over Turkey. It is a very usual scene that when elections are about to take place in Turkey, politicians embrace their people, but afterwards they forget them. While we believe this attitude ought to be changed in festivals, the fact that native people are forgotten in international organizations causes an inexplicable situation in terms of sociology. Politics and tourism are concepts that walk side-by-side all the time. What Antalya Golden Orange Film Festival witnessed is a concrete example of this fact.

The Golden Orange Film Festival in Terms of Sustainability

It is obvious that people living in Antalya do not have a positive approach to this festival continuing for many years. The concept of sustainability is meaningful only with the concept of time. That native people, on purpose or not, are disregarded during the festival shows that event tourism principles have not become firmly fixed. Turkey, making policies that take tourism only in terms of masses, had a chance of seeing its shortcomings when it put forward its 2023 Tourism Strategy and Action Plan in the previous year.

Although in this document it is implied that various efforts will be made in terms of stimulation of activities within the concept of event tourism and inclusion of native people in the process, a concrete step needs to be taken. The main elements causing the great gap in the 2000s between the people and the festival, in which people were so much included in the 1960s, are another debated theme. But it was explained frankly that the people relevant to this event did not expect to integrate native people with the festival.

The fact that the authorities recounted that, in disregarding native people when expanding the Golden Orange Film Festival from local to the world, they followed a process used in international festivals – for example, local people were not included much in Cannes Film Festival – and our festival followed such a trend, was surprising too.

In Turkey, where economic concerns take first place, it is a problem to expect that people who do not normally go to the cinema can make a habit of it during the festival. Besides, in a city where public transportation is not used so efficiently, it is impossible for people from low-income groups to take part in the festival activities, leading us to question what this festival means, who it is for and what it brings in terms of tourism. Moreover, considering the importance of the tourism sector in Antalya, which is the locomotive for regional development, the non-inclusion of millions of tourism sector workers in the festival is another matter for discussion.

In the literature it is pointed out that all the sides of a festival should be examined to evaluate its efficiency. It is known that festivals have important sociocultural impacts as well as economic ones (Williams and Bowdin, 2007). From this aspect, it is seen that the Golden Orange Film Festival has very little effect on the native people of Antalya. Evaluating the situation within the scope of sustainability, festivals take a place on the global platform only when they merge with their own people. In terms of sustainability of the tourism sector, it is important that local governments see that festivals are created as places where native people can find their own values; then, like in previous years, the festival finds itself a place in the world with programmes which embrace its own people.

Current Situation and a Glance to the Future

Antalya is the heart of Turkish tourism. As of 2007, Antalya hosted about eight million tourists and provided one-third of Turkish tourism income. However, it is a city that perceives tourism only through the concepts of sea, sun and sand, and it cannot incorporate its own public into tourism development in the proper sense. The Golden Orange Film Festival represents an international organization on one side, offended and forgotten people of the city from past to present on the other. Some of the views from various sections of the public, quoted earlier, complement each other. However, it seems difficult for the Golden Orange Film Festival to regain the identity it used to have in the 1960s with the current perspective of the organizing committee. An organization so willing to ignore its own public in the name of opening up to the world will certainly become the target of criticism, even if it gains international success over the long term.

Until now, scientific research to understand the sociocultural effects of the Golden Orange Film Festival has not been made, nor has any support been given to such research. These are important clues to understand the current authority's perspective. The saddest aspect of this issue is to see that the festival committee, appointed by political will, also has political concerns about including the public or leaving it out while setting its sights.

What is the place of festivals in tourism? Festivals often attract serious tourists of this kind, actively consuming the familiar as an art form or socialization (Prentice and Andersen, 2003). If we take the issue from a global perspective, the truth we face is that festivals develop with the support and help of the people of their region. It is a matter of choice to become a brand without understanding and discussing this truth, and making your own people conscious of the organization (Rollins and Delamere, 2007). In this sense, the choice made in the Antalya Film Festival is to continue the process without much consideration of the feelings and preferences of the public. Thus, within this context, future expectations will not be much different than the current situation. It seems difficult for the festival to meet with its own people and to establish a meeting point; but unless these steps are taken with this consciousness, this organization will not embrace and be embraced by its own people.

Summary

The 21st century is one in which borders have disappeared; people are always in motion, travel has shifted from short distances to long ones. In this global world, owing to these facts, tourism aims to diversify tourism activities. Touristic products activating individuals and masses are produced, so that people can delight much more in the world in which they live. On this point, it would not be wrong to say that many domestic and international festivals serve this aim.

A country that connects two continents, Muslim and secular, one of the biggest economies in the world with a population of 70 million, surrounded by seas on three sides, existing in the most important geopolitical region of the world: this is Turkey. It is also one of the countries struggling in the giant's league of world tourism, hosting over 20 million tourists. Wishing to increase this importance to a great extent, Turkey has made great attempts in diversifying touristic products since the late 1990s. In addition to investments made in tourism, some initiatives in terms of employment in the tourism sector have appeared, especially in relation to native people's participation in tourism. Having started negotiations to join the EU, Turkey has tried to turn process from theory to practice in terms of tourism and its native people.

The tourism industry has an indirect influence on over 40 different sectors, so its importance is beyond dispute in terms of job creation. But there is one point to be discussed: to what extent can it carry this development without its people? This chapter has discussed one aspect of touristic diversity – festivals – and the place native people can find for themselves in this process. As a case study the chapter has explored the Golden Orange Film Festival, one of the most important festivals in Turkey, describing its development from inception to the present day and opening the debate concerning this festival's effect on native people.

The difference the festival made in the tourism capital of Turkey, i.e. Antalya, was seen from the people's point of view. This case study reveals that native people were much more involved in the festival in the past. The trouble resulting from perceiving the concept of sustainability only as a process emerges as the biggest problem of the festival Antalya is hosting nowadays. In putting forward people's opinions about direct sharing, this chapter has attempted to explain controversial themes of the festival in terms of sustainable event tourism.

As a result, in Turkey, which has a respectable place in the world tourism sector, and in Antalya, known as Turkey's tourism capital, it can now be seen how much the Golden Orange Film Festival has gone away from its people upon reaching international dimensions and how differently the 'event tourism' concept is discussed in a tourism country by the people who do not want native people to be included in this process. One of the principles of sustainable tourism – that native people should be included in the process – is apparent one more time in this result.

Key Questions

1. Antalya is the most significant tourist attraction in Turkey. What should taking part in such an important festival mean (in terms of domestic and foreign tourism) and for whom?
2. Taking into account international festivals around the world, discuss whether an international festival should be independent from the native public.
3. How should Golden Orange, a sustainable film festival in terms of time since the 1950s, open up to the sustainability debate? What are the shortcomings?

References

AKSAV (2008) Altın Portakal Film Festivali Yayınlari. Available at: http://www.aksav.org.tr/tr/81.htm (accessed 10 May 2008).

antalyabugun.com (2007) Antalya'da Zaman. Available at: http://www.antalyabugun.com/index.php?page=makale&y_id=&MID=128 (accessed 17 May 2008).

Antalya Firma Rehberi (2008) Tarihçe-Antalya'dan Avrasya'ya Altın Portakal Film Festivali. Available at: http://www.e-antalya.net/antalya/tarihce.html (accessed 12 May 2008).

festivalfocus (2008) Antalya Golden Orange Film Festival. Available at: http://www.festivalfocus.org/festival_view.php?uid=219 (accessed 12 May 2008).

Getz, D. (2008) Event tourism: definition, evolution, and research. *Tourism Management* 29(3), 403–428.

Gürsoy, D., Kim, K. and Uysal, M. (2004) Perceived impacts of festivals and special events by organizers: an extension and validation. *Tourism Management* 25(2), 171–181.

Koh, K. and Jackson, A.A. (2006) Special events marketing: an analysis of a country fair. *Journal of Convention & Event Tourism* 8(2), 19–44.

Prentice, R. and Andersen, V. (2003) Festival as creative destination. *Annals of Tourism Research* 30(1), 7–30.

Rollins, R. and Delamere, T. (2007) Measuring the social impact of festivals. *Annals of Tourism Research* 34(3), 805–808.

Wikipedia (2007) Altın Portakal Logo. Available at: http://tr.wikipedia.org/wiki/Resim:Altinportakal.jpg (accessed 10 December 2007).

Williams, M. and Bowdin, J.A.G. (2007) Festival evaluation: an exploration of seven UK arts festivals. *Managing Leisure* 12(April–July), 187–203.

22 Managing Sustainable Events: Using Kenya as a Case Study

R.N. Okech
Memorial University of Newfoundland, Corner Brook, Canada

The meetings, incentive, conventions and exhibitions industry has long been recognized as a sector that provides both a high delegate spend and a high yield (McCabe *et al.*, 2000; Lawrence and McCabe, 2001). Kenya is now being recognized worldwide for its facilities and for the professionalism of its service and operation of various events. Predominantly this is being achieved by capital city destinations and their venues and associated infrastructures. The organization of any event often comes with negative consequences: environmental, economic and social. This chapter therefore examines how Kenya is dealing with the upsurge of events management and its sustainability and to what extent this poses economic, environmental and social impacts on the country.

Chapter outline

- Introduction
- Role of Destinations in International Events Tourism
- Sustainable Events Management
- Conditions for Sustainability
- Principles that Govern Sustainable Event Management
- Case Study – Kenya School of Monetary Studies
- Summary
- Key Questions

Introduction

The meetings and conventions industry is perceived as a 'red-hot' industry (Shure, 1993) and one of the healthiest and most growth-oriented sectors within the tourism industry (Abbey, 1987). While the term 'meeting' covers all forms of meetings, conventions, conferences, exhibitions and special events (Crouch and Ritchie, 1998), the term 'convention' is described as the entire membership meetings of the sponsoring organization or association (Rockett and Smille, 1994) and a form of annual meetings (Astroff and Abbey, 1998). Currently emphasis is being placed by the Kenya Tourism Board to market and attract events business and as such boost the tourism industry. This chapter uses case studies of the Kenyatta International Conference Centre (KICC), as well as the Kenya School of Monetary Studies (KSMS), which are well-known venues for holding various types of events.

However, all sources have agreed that the association market is a potentially strong revenue source, representing two-thirds of the industry spending (Shure, 1993; Abbey and Link, 1994). Within associations there are further refinements, ranging from local, state and regional to national and international levels. Studies of the association industry focus on national and international levels. However, state and regional levels of meetings were significant contributors to the overall growth of the meeting industry, and industry statistical research on the market supported its significant expenditures and growth trends (Ja Choi and Boger, 2002).

Associations holding their meetings closer to attendees' home towns and over shorter time periods to reduce costs and improve meeting effectiveness are emerging trends. Meeting facilities/hotels in smaller cities may be positioned to meet the needs of smaller meetings because they generally provide better service with lower cost than big-city counterparts (Ja Choi and Boger, 2002). However, these meeting facility/hotel marketers as well as host cities must understand market needs before they hold state associations' conventions.

Role of Destinations in International Events Tourism

Event organizers attach greater importance to location (destination) than to any other single criterion when selecting sites. The destination has to offer:

- a suitable venue for the meetings;
- sufficient accommodation if the venue is non-residential;
- attractions for successful social and/or partner programmes;
- good accessibility to the generating markets;
- efficient transport systems within the destination;
- acceptable levels of security for delegates; and
- a price perceived to offer value for money.

According to the World Tourism Organization, there were 563 million international arrivals in 1995. The figure is projected to hit a whopping 1.6 billion by 2020. With time, cities are expected to absorb the growing numbers of international travellers, the bulk of them at conferences. They must prepare for the massive growth and position themselves to meet the needs of business travellers.

Table 22.1 reveals that security is of prime importance to event organizers as well as delegates who will be interested in attending. The cost attached to a destination is least important to many as long as the preceding factors have been sufficiently addressed. In Kenya (Table 22.2), the highest rating is on security at 90%, with cost at 60% having the lowest rating.

Table 22.1. Factors affecting choice of destination for an international conference.

Factor	Ranking
Security	1
Facilities – international standards	2
Accommodation	3
Infrastructure – airports, roads	4
Attraction and recreational facilities	5
Quality of service	6
Cost	7

Event tourism is a public–private partnership of which the primary beneficiaries are tour operators, hotels, transport providers, restaurants, curio dealers and technical equipment dealers, among others. At the second tier are secondary winners such as extra staff hired at conferences, farmers whose products fetch better prices, private security firms, translators and many more. Although the money generated in a fortnight may appear hefty, the reality is that Nairobi and other African cities can reap more profits from business travellers. There are many ways of boosting tourism earnings. Kenya must be promoted as a magical destination where tourists spend as much as possible. Business travellers spend their day in meetings and only emerge in the evening to find markets and shopping malls closed. They find the streets deserted and only venture into restaurants and social outings at night. The next day, the travellers are in meetings again and the

Table 22.2. Kenya's rating on identified factors.

Factor	Rating (%)
Security	90
Facilities – international standards	87
Accommodation	75
Infrastructure – airports, roads	73
Attraction and recreational facilities	70
Quality of service	66
Cost	60

routine is sustained for the period of the event. Due to busy and tight schedules, they usually leave immediately after the meetings with their money intact.

In conference tourism, Kenya is ranked fourth in Africa after South Africa, Egypt and Morocco. This is an improvement from 2004 when it was fifth. Revenue from conference tourism is also growing due to several factors. For instance, the rehabilitation of KICC has played a crucial role and it has hosted many international meetings. With modernization and aggressive marketing, KICC will be the nectar that attracts bees to the honey that is Kenya's tourism. Provision of first-class service is needed so that there can be repeat visits.

Events should boost the economy of host cities, countries and the private sector. It is also important to extend shopping hours, have 24-hour streets, outdoor entertainment and traditional dances, and exploit the cultural heritage by encouraging street marketing in an organized way for traders to take artefacts to travellers. Safety and security are paramount, as is good infrastructure, including easy access to toilets, resting benches and recreation facilities. South Africa's city of Durban is the number one event venue in Africa. This is attributed to conference facilities of international standards and back-up services. Aggressive marketing and good weather complete the picture. In Kenya, other than KICC, KSMS and the United Nations complex, large conference facilities that can accommodate thousands of delegates are lacking.

The International Congress and Convention Association (ICCA), the sub-sector regulator, estimates that conference tourism will double by 2013, with a predicted growth rate of 4% per annum in the coming years. According to ICCA figures, there were approximately 5315 conferences of a large magnitude in 2005, with Europe accounting for 58% of the market share. Though Asia followed Europe with a huge dividing margin at 18%, it is worth pointing out that the continent recorded the fastest-growing figures thanks to the rise in importance of the free port city of Dubai as a conference tourism destination, coupled with the rise in importance of Asian tiger cities. North America – the USA and Canada – had a share of 10.5%, while South America held on to 7% against Australia's 4%; Africa trailed with a paltry 2.5% or 132 meetings.

Recognizing the importance of conference tourism, the apex organizers of the Africities Summit, the United Cities and Local Governments of Africa (UCLGA), held a stakeholders' meeting that discussed strategies through which African cities can reap from the meteoric rise in conference tourism. Dubai is the classic case of focusing on conference tourism as an area of potentiality. Over a short period, international level conference facilities have come up in Dubai and, coupled with a no-holds-barred marketing blitz, this has led to many world organizations opting for the United Arab Emirates city for high-powered conferences. In Kenya, Mombasa city is ideal for holding large meetings because it already has sufficient bed capacity augmented by a warm climate and a variety of tourist attractions. The missing link for Mombasa is that it lacks international-level conference facilities that can cater for thousands of delegates.

Out of the 2.5% of Africa's share of global conference tourism, South Africa had a clear lead according to 2005 figures that placed the country at 43.8% or 56 meetings. Egypt was number two on the continent with 15 large meetings accounting for 11.7% of the continent's total. Morocco came third with 11 meetings that translated into 8.6%, while Kenya ranked fourth with eight international-scale meetings accounting for 6.3%. Kenya improved from position five in 2004 to number four in 2005 and has great potential for moving up the ladder if a strategic plan is mooted and implemented to specifically train focus on conference tourism.

Sustainable Events Management

Sustainability as a concept involves a number of different strands. Environmental, ecological and economic factors assume that it is applicable in the technical sciences, whereas social and political factors relate to power and values. Sustainability has emerged as a popular term and has been widely viewed as holding considerable promise as a vehicle for addressing the problems of negative tourism impacts and maintaining its long-term viability (Bramwell *et al.*, 1998; Page and Thorn, 2002; Liu, 2003).

The impacts that these hundreds of millions of tourists moving around the globe may cause on the natural environment and the social and cultural fabrics of host communities need to be anticipated, carefully studied, prevented to the extent possible and continuously monitored if events are to effectively contribute to sustainable management. This needs to be clearly understood, because there are complex and close relationships between tourism and the natural and cultural environments (Yunis, 2002a). In line with the paradigm of sustainable management, it is believed that negative effects can be avoided or minimized if events are thoroughly planned and controlled. This means that the planning and development of any event's infrastructure, its subsequent management and also its marketing should be based on environmental, social, cultural and economic sustainability criteria. Sustainability implies, to paraphrase a recommendation of the Rio Summit 1992, that tourism resources and attractions are utilized in such a way that their subsequent use by future generations is not compromised (IUCN, 1991, 1999; Priasukmana, 2001; Yunis, 2002b).

Conditions for Sustainability

Sustainable event management depends on meeting the needs of the host population in terms of improved standards of living in the short and long term, satisfying the demands of increasing visitor numbers and continuing to attract them to achieve this, and safeguarding the environment. The key elements of such approaches can be summarized as follows:

- An event policy is required at the national, regional and local levels. Governments at all levels are required to formulate policies for its orderly management.
- The event policy should be the result of a participatory process, in which all interested parties, and particularly the local community, are involved.
- A comprehensive approach should be adopted, whereby all aspects of event management are considered in the planning process, including the tourist attractions, the basic infrastructure and services, accommodation and catering facilities, transportation, management aspects, human resource development, as well as the institutional elements.
- Similarly, an integrated approach is required. Events cannot be planned in isolation; instead, they must be part of the overall development efforts of a country or area while local tourism plans must be integrated into national tourism strategies.
- Environmental impact assessment techniques must be applied from the very beginning of any event plan or project. Appropriations should be made to ensure that the cost of avoiding any potential damage to the environment as a result of such development has been taken into account in the economic and financial calculations.
- Event management companies and destinations must be managed with the environment and the local community in mind. This needs appropriate environmental and social science training of managers and employees at all levels, to enable industry-wide application of environmental management systems and corporate social responsibility criteria in all companies.
- The management of events at both the company and the destination levels requires continuous monitoring, particularly with respect to environmental and social variables. Monitoring allows managers and public authorities to take corrective actions when needed and before negative impacts become irreversible.
- As an indispensable element for the above monitoring process, indicators for sustainable event management must be developed and introduced as a normal practice at all tourism destinations. Indicators also serve to guide consumers about the environmental and social quality of the destination, and are good benchmarks to stimulate destinations to compete on sustainability grounds rather than on price.

Principles that Govern Sustainable Event Management

Consideration is now given to selected principles behind the approach to sustainable events management.

Policy, planning and management are appropriate and essential responses to the problems of natural and human resource misuse in events

From this perspective, sustainable event management is a positive approach intended to reduce the adverse consequences and to maximize the benefits resulting from the complex interactions between the industry, the visitors, the environment and the host communities. It is premised on the belief that all those involved in events have an ethical responsibility to seek to avoid the misuse of natural and human resources. This calls not only for an analysis of the impacts of event operations, but also the development and implementation of practical measures to secure more sustainable event management practices.

Long-term rather than short-term thinking is necessary

Sustainable events management is an approach that involves working for the long-term viability and quality of resources in nature and in society. This involves moving from short-term to long-term thinking and planning of events; it is no longer acceptable to exploit and exhaust scarce resource – natural, social or cultural – and then move on to new destinations. Long-term thinking to preserve resources should involve a proactive stance of policy and prevention rather than one of reaction and repair.

The concerns of sustainable event management are not just environmental, but are also economic, social, cultural, political and managerial

While the present approach to sustainable management seeks to avoid the misuse of social, cultural and economic as well as environmental resources, it also gives prominence to politics, planning and management as crucial arenas in which to secure sustainability. These crucial arenas were illustrated by Evans and Henry (1998). Political planning and management processes provide the means to achieve the desired ends of sustainable events. However, in order to achieve political sustainability it will be necessary not only to realize sustainable environmental and cultural practices, but also to do this with political legitimacy, including employing participative approaches to policy development.

Much of the current debate about sustainability focuses on the resources from which the industry draws the environmental or cultural experience. This has tended to ignore the sustainability of the service delivery itself, including the nature of the industrial structure, the ways in which human resources are employed in the industry and the character of the management practices. Given the 'non-renewable' nature of the human resources employed in the events industry, there is clearly a need to develop these resources (Burns, 1993). More generally, managerial practices appropriate for sustainable management need to be encouraged.

For example, there are many requirements for sustainable planning, such as a requirement to integrate event plans into wider national, regional and local strategic planning, which considers development and environmental management as a whole. This is important to ensure that event-related activities are in balance with other economic sectors, and with the overall economic, environmental, social and cultural priorities for development. These wider conceptions of sustainability – including environmental, economic, social, cultural, political, planning and managerial concerns – as well as the integration of these diverse elements are seen as key features of this present approach to sustainable event management.

All stakeholders need to be consulted and empowered in decision making

Sustainable management means taking account of people's views and choices on their present and future needs and welfare and on environmental, economic, social and cultural issues. The processes of consultation are central to taking account of people's views and preferences, and this should involve exchanging information, opinion, evaluation and action, as well as making the most of expertise, knowledge and resources (Drake, 1991; Ritchie, 1993; Simmons, 1994). Stakeholders who are rarely consulted in any decision making need to be more fully involved and empowered so that they have a greater influence.

Consultation between the event organizers, local communities and employees working in tourism, tourists and others is essential if they are to work alongside one another and begin to resolve conflicts of interest and identify areas of common interest. Consultation between the stakeholders also means the participants gain access to a pool of shared resources, creativity, information and expertise, and considers a broader representation of values. The community approach to the event is one illustration of wider consultation in decision making. Under this principle, residents are regarded as a focal point of event planning and management, although tourists, businesses and other interests must also be involved in this dialogue. Wider community involvement in events is clearly an important goal.

However, this may succeed only when the community has considerable control of the event management process, and when proper consideration is given to the relative power and ability of some interests to participate effectively in decision making. Achieving a wider consultation and empowering all those with an interest in the events and its consequences means giving full consideration to power dynamics. This applies within organizations, between organizations and also within local communities. The processes of agenda setting, decision making and non-decision making, and of inclusion and exclusion from decision making, need to be understood. Such an understanding will help make more successful the attempts to empower as many stakeholders as possible.

In order to empower these stakeholders, managers also need to have a sophisticated understanding not only of community development and the techniques of community involvement, but also of approaches to local governance built upon the establishment of partnerships between community, business, government and other stakeholders.

Putting feasible ideas into practice

Good intentions and idealism alone are not a sufficient basis for real advances in our understanding or for improvements in the practical management of any industry (Hawkes and Williams, 1993). There is a need to give serious attention to how sustainable event ideas can be turned into management practice. Part of this involves assessing in specific circumstances those aspects of practical initiatives that have worked well and those that have not. Equally important, it means recognizing that in the real world there are many forces influencing the operation of the economy, the culture of business environments, the power of governments and also affecting people's social relations, values and practices in the short and medium term.

The consequence of such forces is that, whatever ambitions we have for sustainability as a goal for all policies and actions, there are likely to be limits to what will be achieved in practice. Hence it is important to identify not just the ultimate goal or ideal outcome, but also what may be feasible along the path to reach that goal. It also involves recognizing that difficult choices may have to be made about the priority given to different desirable outcomes.

Events must be managed within the limits of growth

Indeed, this development is often necessary for future social and environmental investment. However, it seeks to ensure that events are sustainable in the long term, including helping to sustain the environment and the society of the areas in which they operate. Another aim for good measure is to increase visitor satisfaction, as satisfied visitors may also become concerned and care for the places they visit as well as provide long-term and repeat business.

An understanding of how market economies operate is essential

It is necessary to understand the cultures of management procedures as well as of private sector businesses and of public and voluntary sector organizations, and the values and attitudes of the public, in order to turn good intentions into practical measures. For instance, business is much more likely to respond positively if events are seen as good business sense. The bottom line is that many enterprises will themselves initiate approaches to incorporate sustainability only when it is right commercially to do so or when they have to respond to government regulation.

Case Study – Kenya School of Monetary Studies

KSMS was developed in the 1990s and made ready in 1995 to serve as a regional centre for technical conferences and workshops in finance and banking. It is located in Ruaraka, Nairobi near Thomas De La Rue and owned by the Central Bank of Kenya, but the Conference and Hospitality facility is managed by Utalii College. Similar to KICC, KSMS also focuses on meetings, incentives, conventions and exhibitions as well as private functions as their main business core.

KICC is located in the heart of Nairobi. Its mission is to be a premier global centre of excellence in conference tourism and to provide globally competitive convention facilities and services that surpass clients' expectations. KICC has a mandate in: promoting and marketing conference tourism both locally and internationally; monitoring the quality and standards of conference facilities and advising private and public investors on improvement of such facilities; and planning and implementing the expansion and modernization of existing conference facilities as well as the development of new ones.

Sustainability issues – KICC and KSMS

- *Socio-economic impacts of events.* Both KICC and KSMS bring together different personalities and nationalities, giving them an opportunity to understand each other and appreciate the differences. In terms of economic impact, most events here are meant to discuss socio-economic issues and therefore are groundbreaking for economic change. Events also create revenue for the organization and employment, as well as improve the infrastructure of the area, since the facility must be accessible and enjoy all services such as water, electricity and security.
- *Environmental issues.* KICC keeps all the rules stipulated by the National Environment Management Authority (NEMA). The ISO 9000 certification they are seeking requires a great level of compliance to environmental requirements. The operation is thus environmentally friendly. KSMS is also currently seeking ISO certification.
- *Natural operation policy.* KICC is right within the city and operates all its activities in the concrete setting. The only obligation is to keep the environment clean. KSMS, on the other hand, has a greening policy, which requires that the establishment operates in a clean natural environment. Some functions requiring breakaway groups meet among beautiful trees and lawns.
- *Managing noise pollution.* No noise resulting from functions can be heard in the streets of Nairobi except for the outdoor functions like the Motor Rally championship. Both organizations have buildings with sound-proofing. Management controls the amount of sound that can be emitted from various functions.
- *Policy on solid waste management.* KICC and KSMS are guided by the Public Health Act, and NEMA requirements also guide this practice. Management initiatives have also seen the setting up of an environment department to oversee the implementation of solid waste management.
- *Water saving programme among staff and guests.* There is a general sensitization for careful water usage by staff at both KICC and KSMS. The plumbing and end water usage system control and limit wastage of water by guests. Signs such as ones saying 'remember to close the taps' are put next to the washrooms.
- *Energy saving programme.* There is sensitization of staff to use energy carefully, especially gas, power and steam for cooking. Stickers reminding users to turn off lights on leaving a room and energy-saving bulbs are part of the energy saving programme.
- *Local community benefits.* Permanent employment is offered for career building to members of the community. Casual jobs are taken by less educated community members for labour-intensive events. Some

percentage of the profits is earmarked for building infrastructure and lighting of the neighbourhood to improve social well-being and security.

- *Employment and remuneration policy.* At KICC, the meetings and events business is a labour-intensive operation and requires a large number of staff. However, at times, these staff members become idle when business is down and one may not know what to do with them. Casual staff have been used to solve this problem but this has implications for quality of output and standardization. Both KICC and KSMS are fully compliant with the Employment Act that requires equal opportunity employment in terms of gender, race and tribe. Both facilities use guidelines and pay beyond the basic required by the Trade Union and the Employment Act. They also use performance-based remuneration to motivate hard work. Training enhances motivation and enables the organization keep its staff well informed of new changes that may affect operation, including environmental requirements. All staff are provided with orientation training upon recruitment. Senior management must attend at least one seminar or workshop per year.
- *Local community empowerment.* Purchasing of local produce is very much done at KSMS, while there is no particular emphasis at KICC. KSMS helps occasionally to feed the needy in slum residences – they claim this gives the community hope and that is part empowerment. Nothing particular is done regarding community empowerment by KICC.

Summary

The events industry in Kenya, like in its international competitors, appears to be characterized by a culture of 'casualization', with significant gender imbalances and a largely transient workforce that is relatively underpaid and underrepresented by industry unions. Research into aspects of events management is also lacking since the market is not yet saturated and hence the future of the market depends on matching the needs of the organizers with the provision of appropriate venue facilities and services. This chapter recognizes that Kenya does not yet have a mature and extensive events industry. However, there is evidence that the industry is being developed at a high rate.

Due to the continued growth of conference and meeting events in Kenya, the organizing clientele will have to become more experienced and, as a result, demand more specific responses to their needs. The quality of provision and value for money are, therefore, key factors that event organizers must recognize if they are to sustain and increase their market share. This chapter has explored the nature of the Kenyan events industry, and in particular its sustainable management practices. Using the minimal literature in the area, the chapter argues the case for a comprehensive and integrated sustainable management strategy which will effectively contribute to the events industry's productivity and profitability.

However, aspects currently being addressed by the government and industry-based associations are how other regions in Kenya might benefit from this highly attractive market. Currently a lot of emphasis is being placed by the Kenya Tourism Board to market and attract events business and as such boost the tourism industry. The organization of any event often comes with negative consequences, both environmental and social. In fact, there is a significant increase in demand for natural resources (water and energy) and added stress on the local communities (pollution and waste). On the other hand, ecological organizing enables an integrated approach towards the minimization of the negative economic, environmental and social aspects of events management.

Key Questions

1. Critically evaluate the approach towards the minimization of the negative economic, environmental and social aspects of events management.

2. Discuss and examine how Kenya is dealing with the upsurge of events management and the extent to which this poses economic, environmental and social impacts on the country.

3. Discuss the current aspects being addressed by the government and industry-based associations and how other regions in Kenya might benefit from this highly attractive market.

References

Abbey, J.R. (1987) The convention and meetings sector – its operation and research needs. In: Ritchie, J.R.B. and Goeldner, C. (eds) *Travel, Tourism, and Hospitality Research*. John Wiley & Sons, Inc., New York, pp. 265–274.

Abbey, J.R. and Link, C.K. (1994) The convention and meetings sector. Its operation and research needs. In: Ritchie, J.R.B. and Goeldner, C.R. (eds) *Travel, Tourism and Hospitality Research*, 2nd edn. John Wiley & Sons, Inc., New York, pp. 273–284.

Astroff, M.T. and Abbey, J.R. (1998) *Convention Sales and Services*, 5th edn. Waterbury Press, Cranbury, New Jersey.

Bramwell, B., Henry, I., Jackson, G. and van der Straaten, J. (1998) A framework for understanding sustainable tourism management. In: Bramwell, B., Henry, I., Jackson, G., Prat, A.G., Richards, G. and van der Straaten, J. (eds) *Sustainable Tourism Management: Principles and Practice*. Tilburg University Press, Tilburg, The Netherlands, pp. 23–71.

Burns, P. (1993) Sustaining tourism employment. *Journal of Sustainable Tourism* 1(2), 81–96.

Crouch, G.I. and Ritchie, J.R.B. (1998) Convention site selection research: a review conceptual model, and prepositional framework. *Journal of Convention & Exhibition Management* 1(1), 49–69.

Drake, S.P. (1991) Local participation in ecotourism projects. In: Whelan, T. (ed.) *Nature Tourism: Managing for the Environment*. Island Press, Washington, DC, pp. 132–163.

Evans, D.M. and Henry, I.P. (1998) Sustainable tourism projects: a trans border case study of Sumava National Park and associated Landscape Protected Area, Czech Republic. In: Bramwell, B., Henry, I., Jackson, G., Prat, A.G., Richards, G. and van der Straaten, J. (eds) *Sustainable Tourism Management: Principles and Practice*. Tilburg University Press, Tilburg, The Netherlands, pp. 201–216.

Hawkes, S. and Williams, P. (eds) (1993) *From Principles to Practice. A Casebook of Best Environmental Practice in Tourism*. Centre for Tourism Policy and Research, Simon Fraser University, Burnaby, British Columbia, Canada.

IUCN (1991) *Protected Areas of the World: A Review of National Systems*. Vol. 3. *Afrotropical*. The World Conservation Union (formerly the International Union for the Conservation of Nature). Gland, Switzerland.

IUCN (1999) *Parks for Biodiversity, Policy Guidance Based on Experience in ACP Countries*. The World Conservation Union (formerly the International Union for the Conservation of Nature), Gland, Switzerland.

Ja Choi, J. and Boger, C.A. (2002) State association market: relationships between association characteristics and site selection criteria. *Journal of Convention & Exhibition Management* 4(1), 55–73.

Lawrence, M. and McCabe, V. (2001) Managing conferences in regional areas: a practical evaluation in conference management. *International Journal of Contemporary Hospitality Management* 13(4), 204–207.

Liu, Z. (2003) Sustainable tourism development: a critique. *Journal of Sustainable Tourism* 11(6), 459–475.

McCabe, V., Poole, B., Weeks, P. and Leiper, N. (2000) *The Business and Management of Conventions*. John Wiley & Sons, Brisbane, Australia.

Page, S.J. and Thorn, K. (2002) Towards sustainable tourism development and planning in New Zealand: the public sector response revisited. *Journal of Sustainable Tourism* 10(3), 222–238.

Priasukmana, S. (2001) Forest ecotourism for rural area development. In: Bras, K., Dahles, H., Gunawan, M. and Richards, G. (eds) *Entrepreneurship and Education in Tourism. Proceedings of ATLAS Asia Inauguration Conference*. ATLAS Publication, Arnheim, The Netherlands, pp. 197–200.

Ritchie, J.R.B. (1993) Crafting a destination vision: putting the concept of resident responsive tourism into practice. *Tourism Management* 14(5), 370–389.

Rockett, G. and Smille, G. (1994). Market segments: the European Conference and meetings market. *EIU Travel and Tourism Analyst* 4, 36–50.

Shure, P. (1993) Annual spending of $75 billion supports 1.5 million jobs. *Convene* 8(6), 36–41.

Simmons, D.G. (1994) Community participation in tourism planning. Tourism Management 15(2), 98–108.

Yunis, E. (2002a) Ecotourism – a tool for sustainable development. In: *Tourism: A Catalyst for Sustainable Development*. World Tourism Organization, Madrid, pp. 7–14.

Yunis, E. (2002b) Assistance for sustainable development. In: *Tourism: A Catalyst for Sustainable Development*. World Tourism Organization, Madrid, pp. 85–90.

23 Changes in the Publicity Mode of Past Expos: a Case of Diachronic Comparison and Its Impact on Shanghai Expo

G. Jurong[1] and Z. Shichang[2]

[1]*Shanghai Jiao Tong University, Shanghai, People's Republic of China;*
[2]*Shanghai Institute of Technology (SIT), Shanghai, People's Republic of China*

The effectiveness of the publicity is of paramount significance for the complete success of Expos. On the basis of analysing changes in the mode of publicity for past Expos, this chapter makes proposals with regard to publicity to overseas countries by addressing the characteristic features boasted by the Shanghai World Expo.

Chapter outline

- Introduction
- Evolution of the Mode of Publicity of Past Expos
- Analysis of the Mode of Publicity for Past Expos
- Enlightenment from Past Expos on the Mode of Publicity for Shanghai Expo
- Summary
- Key Questions

Introduction

Being a kind of non-profit social gathering approved by Business International Education (BIE) and held by governments of host countries or various departments entrusted by governments, Expo takes as its principles to facilitate communication among people at large and the development of economy, culture, science and technology among different countries. With its incomparable importance, Expo enjoys the reputation of being the 'International Olympics' in economy, science and technology the world over. This serves as the locomotive force to encourage a hosting country to seize the opportunity of Expo, step up its efforts in terms of generating publicity and expand communication among the international community, with a view to enhancing its prestige and reputation. It is in this process that an adequate strategy and an appropriate mode of publicity have their role to play in ensuring the maximum success of this important event.

Evolution of the Mode of Publicity of Past Expos

The history of World Expos can be traced back to as early as 1851. To date, some 40-odd Expos have been held since the first one in the metropolis of London. In retrospect, the past one-and-a-half centuries have witnessed constant evolution in the format of how Expos were held and in their mode of publicity, which was performed according to changing economic and trading environments throughout the world at the time. Generally, this process of evolution can be divided into three stages, each of which bears some distinctive features (Fig. 23.1). Stage 1, which ranged from the

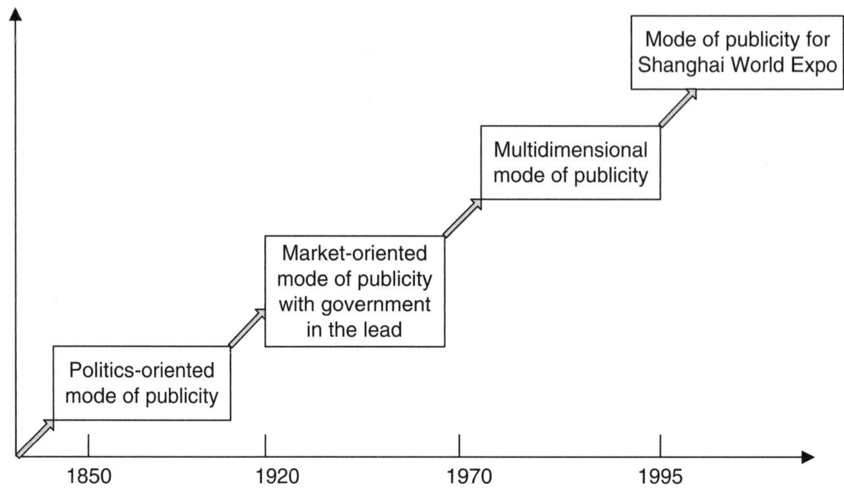

Fig. 23.1. Changes and development in publicity mode for Expos.

mid-19th century to the 1920s, had the publicity of politics-oriented development as its major purpose; thus all the publicity activities of Expos during that period bore this very striking feature. From the post-war years to the 1970s, which is termed Stage 2, the endeavour of publicity began to have the element of marketing tendency and the publicity during this stage was mainly manipulated, with much of the interference coming from government. In Stage 3, thanks to the rapid development in science and technology in recent years, an entirely new mode of publicity – the multidimensional mode – has come into being, with collaborative and unremitting efforts made by mass media, enterprises and tertiary schools, among others.

Analysis of the Mode of Publicity for Past Expos

Politics-oriented mode of publicity in the mid- and late 19th century

The mid- and late 19th century, which is often called the Second Industrial Revolution Period, saw the successful accomplishment of industrial revolution in developed countries like the UK, which was characterized mainly by mass production in its early phase with the application of machinery. Many Western countries showed keen interest in hosting Expos for they believed that Expo would be conducive to demonstrating their comprehensive power to the international community, playing a significant role in promoting the development of science and technology and facilitating trading exchanges and cultural communications. Hence the mode of publicity for Expos during this period had a strong sense of political connotation. The first World Expo held in the UK can be considered an excellent example. To enable other countries to become fully aware of the strong comprehensive power that was achieved through the Industrial Revolution, the British Government decided to hold the first Expo in London in 1851. With help from diplomatic channels, Queen Victoria herself invited over ten countries from Europe and North America to participate in this unprecedented event. The visitors were greatly stunned at such exhibits as a huge 630-ton steam-powered engine, locomotives, high-speed steam boats, cranes, the most up-to-date steel-melting approaches, and huge-size models of tunnels and bridges. In addition, when Expo was underway, visitors could participate in a variety of activities, which included the comparing and appraising of exhibits and other diversified pursuits. It was under the initiative of the former mayor of the city of Chicago, Mr Dewitt C. Gregier, that the preliminary phase of the Chicago World Expo got under way. There are more examples of this pattern of publicity, which took the publicity of political orientation as its major obligation.

Market-oriented mode of publicity with government in the lead (from post-war years to the 1970s)

When World War II ended, countries in Europe as well as North America and Japan embarked on rapid reconstruction and there appeared a flourishing situation concerning development. The Third Industrial Revolution, characterized mainly by the invention and application of computers, greatly helped to enhance social productive forces in an all-dimensional manner, hence giving rise to a great increase in production. During this period, some initial marketing approaches or methods found their way into the mode of publicity for Expos. Take the World Expo at Montreal in Canada in 1967, for example. As many as six wireless radio stations were set up, four mobile broadcasting and television units were introduced, three wireless broadcasting entities were involved in the publicity work and as many as 280 Expo guides were recruited to facilitate the publicity activities. Three years later at the World Expo held in Osaka, Japan, the publicity work experienced another high level of development, in which 18 broadcasting channels and five cable television studios were fully involved in the publicity work. In addition to these, as many as 70,000 copies of the catalogue and Expo guide and 10,000 copies of the catalogue and guide for blind visitors were published. The organizers also invited women guides with different professional levels to be engaged in the promotion of Expo. However, it should stressed that while headway was made in the marketing strategy and its process, there was still much room for further improvement – in particular, much remained to be done in strengthening the operation of the market, reducing step-by-step the interference from government and lowering the amount of its aid. At the Expo held in New York in 1964, the Federal Government of New York invested some US$24 million, accounting for two-thirds of the total amount of investment. Therefore, it can be concluded that the general feature of the publicity mode for that period was one of market orientation but with the governmental function as one of the most important factors.

Multidimensional mode of publicity from the 1970s

From the 1970s onwards, the rapid development of information technologies and a change in perception towards Expos, coupled with the increasingly important role played by mass media, enterprises and the public at large, led to the emergence of the multidimensional mode of publicity. The World Expo held in Aichi, Japan, in 2005 can be taken as the best example. In the course of applying for the right to host Expo, a committee consisting of experts, personnel from the business community and government officials played a vital role. In the course of preparing Expo, a huge number of industrial entities, mass media as well as tertiary schools were actively involved in the publicity work and its operation, thus adding the distinctive features of the multidimensional mode of publicity.

The above discussion of the three stages of modes of publicity will be conducive to our exploration of the appropriate mode of publicity for Shanghai World Expo in 2010, by fully addressing the specific conditions in Shanghai that could show the current advanced level of the world on one hand, and that could fit most appropriately with the specific situation of China's conditions on the other.

Enlightenment from Past Expos on the Mode of Publicity for Shanghai Expo

Highlighting 'marketing concept' in the mode of publicity

The year 1969 saw the appearance of the concept of 'great marketing', maintaining that the concept of marketing may be applicable not only to tangible commodities and intangible goods (i.e. service), but also to such things as organization, ideology, governmental administration, events and activities, among others. We believe that the publicity activities of Shanghai World Expo can be designed and performed by benefiting from this concept so as to maximize its effect, arouse the greatest possible interest among would-be customers, invite participation on the largest scale possible and produce the best expected results. However, considering the complexities of the potential customers at whom the marketing concept is aimed, we believe it is vital that the publicity work of World Expo be accomplished by fully taking advantage of various approaches in the course of designing specific projects. As the customers of World Expo are different from those of other events, different strategies should be therefore adopted by considering the different stages, distinctive features, strategies and their corresponding projects.

It should first be borne in mind that much is to be done to ensure maximum harmony is achieved in line with the theme of 'Better City, Better Life'. Needless to say, the beautiful appearance of a city is essential for a successful Expo, but it does not necessarily follow that rural areas could be forgotten in this aspect. We should give full consideration to the conveniences brought about by modern technology, but a great deal of effort will have to be made to produce the complete sense of balance and harmony between humans and the ecological environment. The theme of 'Better City, Better Life' will urge us to consider deeply and explore rationally the means by which human beings, nature and consideration of the future should be integrated so as to produce the most desirable result.

Moreover, much should be done to consider the budget and cost management of the publicity work. Generally, the overall expense for the publicity work of Expo may lie in two aspects. On the one hand, such a budget involves the communication and promotion activities the world over. In this aspect there will be as much as US$100 million to be used for publicity, covering various kinds of activities and publicity work by the media as well. In order to ensure the complete realization of these aims, it is strongly advisable that strict management of the budget be implemented with a view to providing a steady supply of funds for the publicity work at various phases. On the other hand, the publicity work should also exploit indistinct non-capital resources, which include such resources as the foreign relations that China has established with other countries and the publicity that both the central government and local government possess. The World Expo to be held by Shanghai Municipal People's Government is considered one of the chief events, enjoying most profound significance at both national and international levels. Therefore we have every reason to expect that Shanghai World Expo will capture maximal attention in the national framework of the publicity work and obtain various kinds of support in this regard.

Last but not least is the impact that we should strive to exert concerning Shanghai World Expo. At present, the Expo industry has been witnessing temporary difficulties. Ever since Osaka World Expo in 1970, which attracted 64.2 million visitors, people have been becoming less and less enthusiastic about attending. The hosts and organizers of Expo in Hanover have cautioned 'not to overestimate the zeal and enthusiasm of would-be visitors', as they experienced disappointment because the estimated number of visitors was reduced from 40 million to 25 million before Expo was held, while 18 million visitors were actually received during the event. Drawing on the lessons from these organizers of Hanover, the organizers of Aichi World Expo were well aware of the status quo among visitors towards Expo, putting the estimated number of visitors as 15 million. No wonder former organizers of Expo have been regretting the decline of Expo industry. In the year 2002, when the city of Seattle in the USA was celebrating the 40th anniversary of World Expo, the local media commented on the World Expo by drawing the analogy: 'World Expo: A Dying Entity'. Facing this special situation and striving to make Shanghai World Expo an excellent experience, the organizers of Shanghai World Expo should exert themselves to carry out multidimensional and multi-level publicity work both at home and abroad, so as to make Expo a most familiar event among Chinese and other overseas potential customers at large, triggering their interest and enhancing their sense of participation.

Bringing into full play the leading role by government

Successful publicity work on the theme of Shanghai World Expo would be virtually impossible were there no substantial support and powerful leadership from governments at various levels. Negligence on the part of the government in publicity work could bring very grave effects, resulting in tremendous economic loss and huge damage to the reputation to Expo. In this regard, the experience of the organizers of the World Expo in New Orleans, USA, can be cited as a most convincing example. In 1984, when the preparation work for World Expo in New Orleans was in full swing, governments at all levels in New Orleans were little involved in the publicity work. In addition, various kinds of media were not on harmonious and cooperative terms with the organizers of Expo, which greatly de-motivated would-be visitors. What was even worse was that the media carried a lot of negative reports during the preparation process and during Expo as well – inappropriate theme, insufficient funds, disqualified pavilion construction, dilatory completion during the phase of preparation, traffic congestion when Expo was being declared open, coupled with negative and repeated coverage of such issues as economy and erroneous decisions made by organizers, among others. All of these left a strong negative impact on people and made it extremely difficult for the organizers to proceed with their work. It was at that crucial moment that the US government took over the major responsibility of hosting New Orleans World Expo, which enabled it to take place as planned and also made possible the successful solution to various problems arising after Expo. Needless to say, compared with other Expos, the one held in New Orleans was by no means a success, for it had a much smaller number of visitors, and even among this limited number of visitors, as many as half of them complained that they were little aware of the theme of 'water' even after they entered the Expo. Despite the unpleasant preparations in its initial stages, the US government still earned much praise for its country because it took over the task of the preparation work.

The great success of the World Cup held in Germany in 2006 is ascribed in great deal to the publicity work in which each party assumed its own responsibility: the government working out the plan and the organizers operating by fully exploiting various resources in the form of enterprises. In 2005, advocated and initiated by the German government and working in collaboration with dozens of departments ranging from commerce and media to organizations and institutions of entertainment and recreation, the organizers proposed and hosted thousands of activities, all of which contributed a great deal to improving Germany's national image in the international community and helped to better introduce the country to football fans and newsmen from all over the world. The clear division of working among all parties concerned was important enough to facilitate the smooth operation of this event. The German government played a key role in drafting the plan, which was coordinated and implemented by Germany FC Share Co. Ltd. DPA took charge of the publicity work. With the theme of innovation and novelty, DPA introduced the event to enterprises, institutions, organizations and individuals. Those who were keen on the event provided some financial support in return for publicity. Moreover, various institutions and organizations such as the Ministry of Foreign Affairs and Gothic Research Institute, to name just two, were all actively involved in the implementation of the entire plan. The German Federal News Bureau, the News Reporters' Club and some organizations hosted introductory tours for overseas reporters to Berlin, Hamburg and other hosting cities. The visitors were much impressed and became better informed about the history, humanity, industry, culture, facilities and stadia where football matches were going to be held. Without doubt, these well-arranged activities produced a strong positive effect on the successful hosting of this event.

Based on the experience from other countries and taking into account the real situation of Shanghai, we should stress the point that much can be achieved through administrative and coordinative efforts, by providing some preferential policies, supplying some appropriate fiscal policies and making use of various essential elements in market operation, all of which aim at facilitating the publicity of Shanghai Expo. In this regard, Shanghai Municipal People's Government will surely have its role to play. In order to ensure the smooth progress and complete success of the publicity work, we set up World Expo (Group) Shanghai, which is officially in charge of the preparation and manipulation of Expo. Concerning the publicity work, World Expo (Group) Shanghai has two main divisions: Domestic and Overseas. The former has as its major responsibility to step up its efforts in marketing domestically and to introduce Shanghai Expo to the people at large. The latter, on the other hand, with help from agencies, targets the overseas market and invites China's institutions functioning abroad and foreign institutions working in China to join the publicity team for Shanghai Expo, thus ensuring cross-regional and cross-national publicity will be carried out smoothly.

Stressing coordination and cooperation among different resources

World Expo (Group) Shanghai requires that the general framework of publicity be constructed on the basis of all-dimensional, multi-level and broad perspectives, the ultimate aim of which is to pool various kinds of resources to be used for the publicity work so as to make Shanghai better known internationally.

By taking full advantage of high technology such as networking, we will ensure that the communication and coordination among governments, social organizations, industrial enterprises and the public take place successfully; this will maximize the enthusiasm and initiatives from various parties, and in the long run bring win–win success to various organizations, institutions and individuals as well. The generous support from governments will surely facilitate the full implementation of the overall plan for the publicity work for Shanghai Expo. Traditional media, networking as well as advertisements can be considered effective means by which publicity work can be accomplished. Needless to say, the active participation of mass media in the publicity work, extensive publicity and the significant role played by advertisements will work collaboratively to achieve greatest success. Generally speaking, the public are those at whom the publicity is aimed, and the sole purpose of publicity work is to invite as many people as possible to be actively involved in such a world event. On the other hand, the public may include individuals and enterprises as well as organizations. We all agree that trying to let as many people as we can become fully aware of the brand of Expo is regarded as the most important and fundamental basis for Expo; therefore, it is the most difficult aspect in terms of publicity work for Expo. Many experts have already proposed a set of criteria with which to assess the publicity work for Expo. These can be simply described in one word: 'extensive' – how many people learn about Shanghai Expo, how closely Shanghai Expo is related to every man in the street, how willing people are in general to take part in Expo, among others. Likewise, a great deal should be done to continuously give publicity to the concepts, significance and role that Shanghai World Expo assumes. Various kinds of information with regard to Expo should be released from time to time. In the meantime, we will see to it that enthusiasm on the part of would-be visitors is well displayed by inviting them to contribute their wisdom in terms of designing pavilions and in the process of construction. On the part of enterprises, we would like to take full advantage of media to organize various kinds of activities both at home and abroad. For example, we would like to supply them with some opportunities to publicize what Shanghai World Expo involves. Through providing them with some concrete examples and evidence, we will invite them to become actively involved in the development as well as the management of the world famous brand: Expo.

Highlighting the significance of the face-to-face mode of publicity

The rapid development of science and technology has made it possible for us to host events in a way that was even beyond our imagination years ago. The wide application of computers has greatly facilitated the publicity work. By just pressing buttons, relevant information can be transmitted to every corner of the world. However, we should be quite cautious in setting the limit or extent to which the latest development of information technology can be applied and how it can be used in the publicity work. The organizers of exhibitions should be very cautious when trying to use the Internet as a means of publicity. Everything – including the participants, time and the special importance of such an event – should be made explicit. We are often quite annoyed by an avalanche of e-mails in our mail boxes every day, so it is not unusual for us to delete such e-mails even before bothering to open them for a glance. Only by designing the publicity in an entirely attractive way and by providing some substantial and convincing information will would-be visitors be persuaded to show interest in the activity.

To make the publicity work quite effective, it is advisable that a great deal of face-to-face publicity work should be included in our plan, because this is likely to convey to the audience and/or visitors that the information is trustworthy.

Making steady progress in the implementation of the plan

The publicity work to the international community should be regarded as the routine work; however, as time elapses, we should have a different focus on this work during different stages. Put another way, the overall publicity work for Shanghai Expo should be performed by following the general concept of 'implementing principles along with different stages accompanied with different focuses'. Such a consideration is based on two factors: the hosting of the Olympic Games, on the one hand, and the characteristic features of Expo in terms of the stages of preparation, on the other. During 2008 the Beijing Olympics was unanimously considered as the most important event and was given top priority. However, as both the Olympic Games and World Expo are important international events that will be held within the space of 2 years and both will capture global attention, it is quite reasonable that the publicity work, taken at both national and international levels, should be accomplished step by step. Before 2008 the publicity work in China mainly addressed the issue of the Olympic Games, however World Expo has become the major focus now. Such a background has dictated the different modes of the publicity work for these two world events. In addition, the work during the preparation stages is fully shaped by the distinctive features World Expo has. The work during the preparatory stages may include such items as development of a theme, invitation of businesses and exhibitions, invitation of tourists, construction of venues and pavilions, arrangement of exhibitions and displays, operations of Expo, sustainable development after Expo, among others. Therefore it is extremely significant that the publicity work should be well matched with the general aim of Expo: to create a favourable external environment for the success of Expo in Shanghai and provide a better service to this event.

Summary

Shanghai World Expo to be held in 2010 takes as its theme 'Better City, Better Life', which fully evidences the strong desire of the hosts for harmonious development and coexistence between humans and their surroundings. The clear understanding of the connotation of the theme for Shanghai Expo can be hardly understood if it is taken out of China's context and the context of Shanghai in particular. It should be stressed that harmony should be achieved between urban and rural areas, between humans and their ecological surroundings, and on top of that among humans themselves. Therefore, the theme for Shanghai Expo not only vividly demonstrates the expectations of the appearance of pleasant views, but more importantly the upgrading of the calibre of local inhabitants and the quality that hosting cities may possess.

To attain such a goal is by no means easy, nor can it be accomplished overnight. On the contrary, it demands persevering efforts and collaborative endeavour from people of all walks of life and from government at various levels. Therefore, such an aim should be achieved in the following three aspects concerning the establishment of the publicity mode in the context of Shanghai.

By drawing on experience from World Expos from the historic perspective and by considering the realistic situation in Shanghai, we have set the aim of publicity work on the basis of the principles of multidimensional, extensive, timely and effective, so as to make the metropolis of Shanghai better known in the international community and transform it into a most important gateway to the outside world. The goal of 'letting the world know more about Shanghai and letting the city of Shanghai step into the rest of the world' will be surely attained with the unremitting and concerted efforts by government, the business community and people from all walks of life. There is no denying that well-organized publicity work will help a great deal to make our goal a reality.

Key Questions

1. Expo takes it as its principles the facilitation of communication among people at large and the development of economy, culture, science and technology among different countries. How can these goals be achieved by the organizers?

2. What are the key principles in making the metropolis of Shanghai better known in the international community and in transforming it into the most important gateway to the outside world?

3. How can the publicity work be made effective so as to convey to the audience and/or visitors that the information is trustworthy?

24 Financial Feasibility of Sustainable Events

G. Festa, G. Metallo and M.T. Cuomo
University of Salerno, Fisciano, Italy

Contributions to event sustainability are a fundamental step for the global success of any initiative; nevertheless, this can directly and indirectly affect markets and institutions ('brand' in particular). This chapter argues that enterprises will need to contribute financially to event sustainability from the perspective not of bearing further costs, but as a real investment, capable of delivering multiple benefits. The financial contribution can also be considered in terms of a portion of the value created by the event. In this context, dealing opportunely with customer relationship management concepts and tools would enable firms to monitor their investment carefully.

Chapter outline

- Introduction
- The Economic/Financial Evaluation of the Event in a Business Perspective
- The Role of Events in Branding Policies
- Customer Relationship Management as a Link between Branding and Value in Sustainable Events
- An Exploratory Survey: Health Events
- Summary
- Key Questions

Introduction

The sustainability of any kind or dimension of an event seems a difficult concept to understand because it is associated with multiple elements that are contextual to the specific initiative. In fact, 'sustainability', especially in the past, meant mainly environmental compatibility in the 'greenest' sense of the word. In more recent years, however, the concept of sustainability in a broader sense now has a multidimensional profile, where financial, organizational and production elements have their place.

However, it is evident that to reduce the environmental impact of any event from an overall perspective, a separate fund for individual events needs to be set up. This would enable the restoration, if not the development, of the environmental status existing prior to the event taking place. What is required, in effect, is to evaluate a priori the consequential expected or estimated effects of the initiative on the relative socio-environmental context in order to estimate and quantify the net value of the impact, the source of which constitutes the recovery fund. It is clear that the various firms involved in the initiative would be obliged to contribute in this respect even though they might complain about the intolerable burden of additional costs over and above those already incurred for the so-called 'normal' running of the event.

From this perspective, although the focus is clearly linked to the 'green' concept of sustainability, in the not too distant future it is more than likely that specific funds can and must be planned also for the other elements involved. An example is maintaining employment levels in a territory recently affected by a significant increase in employment (as in the case of spectacular sporting events such as the World Cup, for example) by converting investments made in favour of alternative options (such as the use of stadia for other sporting events, concerts and other initiatives).

It is of fundamental importance therefore to persuade the firms participating in the event to make an economic commitment in order to restore and possibly improve the situation existing prior to the event. This kind of commitment decidedly is to be considered an investment; and it is in this perspective that it is evaluated below.

The Economic/Financial Evaluation of the Event in a Business Perspective

The concept of sustainability has now become a driving force in terms of encouraging event-promoting organizations to consolidate this practice within a mandatory process framework, given the awareness that environmental resources will become increasingly scarce in the future. Furthermore, in a slightly more enlightened vision, this commitment becomes a clear investment in *societal marketing*, which is increasingly present in modern-day marketing strategies and communication campaigns (Guatri *et al.*, 1999).

A plan for charging the commitment only to the organizers could be considered. However, it is clear that the outlay would inevitably be a direct/indirect 'return cost' (i.e. participation fee for the exhibition or tax contribution for the development of the territory) charged indirectly to the organizations participating. Thus, it is in this direction that the different companies involved in the event would find it more convenient to contribute to the fund, even though, as suggested, they might complain of the extra burden of an additional cost beyond those already incurred for the event in the normal sense. How can these companies be persuaded to make the effort?

Taking the disadvantages into account, it seems reasonable that the following eventual benefits are available for companies willing to support the sustainability of the event as part of a strategic and more strictly operational corporate social responsibility (CSR):

- monitoring of the organization;
- increased reputation; and
- stabilization of relations with the territory.

In fact, as is easily seen in these examples of benefits, contributions to event sustainability can be compared with a risk management project; but it is fundamental also to highlight the evolutionary perspective of respect for the territory and for the community in terms of a shift from cost to investment. Accordingly, event sustainability ultimately contributes to the triple bottom line of an organization – in other words, to its general social balance sheet (Metallo and Testa, 2007).

In this respect, it would be fundamental to ask of a firm participating in the event not what might be termed a 'non-value' contribution, which in effect an additional cost would be, but rather to give up a portion of the value created (a kind of 'zero-based' sustainability). This would be possible only if the real extent of the global value that is created from the initiative could be demonstrated.

It is evident, in any case, that the value generated from the event itself will result in contributing to the greater value generated by the continuity of the enterprise. The individual event constitutes a factor of the firm's offer in marketing terms; in fact, as analysed in the following reasoning, events can be considered real marketing mix tools (at least concerning product, promotion and place, with their price also including the cost for the event's sustainability).

With this in mind, a parallel role could be envisaged, aligned with that of the 'zero-based' budget technique, that works for economic evaluations deriving from subsequent reductions, arriving at quantification of the effective financial (and in a global sense, patrimonial, economic and monetary) sustainability of the initiative, which in the end could become self-funding, or could even create, in the rosiest of perspectives, an eventual surplus. This phase, logically, plays a key role, as it requires of the management of organizations participating in the initiative the ability to plan and to verify the economic/financial benefits of the event. In effect, only by following a strict methodological approach and determining a priori the value generation matrix associated with general events, will it be possible to indicate a method of assessment for estimating the net global value produced, and consequently the concession of an eventual portion of the same on the part of the investors and/or operators. It is clear, however, that the value generated by the event tends to support the greater value generated by the enterprise as a going concern, since the single event is an element of the marketing mix of the company (product, in the case of an events management agency; communication, in the case of sponsorship; or distribution, in the case of participation in a fair and/or exhibition). In short, of course, events are tools for public relations (Kerin *et al.*, 2007).

The economic assessment of the impact associated with an event is in fact a highly complex operation, especially when the event is not directly linked with an effective generation of revenues (such as is the case for fairs or exhibitions selling directly to the public, where the volume of turnover represents merely an element, albeit the most important element, for evaluation of the initiative in economic terms). Accordingly, assessing the sustainability of an investment plan in terms of the event means calculating, or rather estimating, the differential value generated between the results obtained (calculated also in terms of costs and benefits) and the resources utilized, obviously taking into account the risks involved.

In short, the economic/financial assessment of the sustainability of an event makes the *total or global value* created the key element of evaluation, in the conviction that the wealth produced by or linked to the event is transformable and can in a certain sense be calculated in terms of monetary value. Naturally, this leads to the necessity to transform, into terms of monetary value, all the benefits and utilities that the investment in the event can generate, even in the full awareness that some benefits/utilities (such as social well-being) deriving from an event are extremely difficult to quantify in terms of monetary value.

Consequently, in this perspective, it becomes of crucial importance (and quite difficult) to estimate utility flows which the planned event will be able to generate over time and their transformation in terms of cash/income flow. It is fundamental, therefore, to identify an ulterior framework of reference for evaluating events which can and must, for the organizations participating, be identified in the greater value gained from the image of the firm and its reputation.

The Role of Events in Branding Policies

Besides merely quantitative indicators (as illustrated above, turnover in fairs and exhibitions selling directly to the public or net value created), it is possible to utilize other parameters of success – above all of a qualitative kind including 'branding', which has now become of fundamental importance.

Event participation, in effect, offers operators specific visibility, regardless of the role involving them on the different occasions:

1. Organizers (public institutions, in the case of events promoting the territory).
2. Sponsors (private enterprises, in the case of show events).
3. Entrepreneurs promoting their products or services (private enterprises again, in the case of industrial exhibitions).

The audience, in most cases, constitutes an excellent opportunity for communicating or reinforcing brand positioning in the perception of the stakeholders. This is true even more so for customers, in terms of accounts and prospects. Take, for instance, the link between Nike and Michael Jordan (probably the most famous basketball player in history): every game played by the Chicago Bulls, Jordan's team, was an event and the performance of Michael Jordan became another event, with the audience totally fascinated by a single player who was constantly identified with the Nike brand (Codeluppi, 2001).

Thus there is a very close link between events, brand image and reputation, in an interdependent vision of reciprocal influence (Fig. 24.1). This means that the modality of event proceedings, the outcomes perceived by the different sectors of the public and the judgements expressed (above all in terms of sustainability) have significant influence on the participating brand image and, consequently, on corporate reputation. However, the opposite is also true: corporate reputation and brand image can determine the value of the event and its sustainability. A major limit, however, is branding management, because it is not so easy to identify a clear cause-and-effect link between corporate brand policies (implemented in the case of events) and the related increase of corporate value (at least in its fundamental sense). Traditional components of 'benefit' in investments for events – i.e. expected flows and potential end values, together with outgoing sums, investment useful life and discount rates – are the five basic elements for investment assessment (Metallo, 2007) and consequently for investments in events.

The British Standard on event sustainability issues, BS 8901:2007 (BSI, 2007), highlights environmental importance from a general (including the socio-economic profile) perspective, even functioning as a further factor for developing corporate image and reputation. This Standard, issued in November 2007, is the first 'industrial' standard in sustainability management designed and applied specifically to the industrial event sector. It has a wider range than that of the ISO 14001, which deals 'only' or exclusively with environmental impact in the 'greenest' sense of the term. In the case of BS 8901:2007, in contrast, management is in reference to different types of capital of which 'natural' is certainly the first and the most important kind; but at the same time, certainly not the only kind (economic and social capital, etc.).

Customer Relationship Management as a Link between Brand Management and Value in Sustainable Events

Given the above considerations, it is feasible therefore to plan and develop a linking system between the sustainability of the event and the relative increase in value of the brand, which obviously constitutes greater economic value for the firm in terms of an effective asset. It should be noted that the traditional schemes for brand evaluation are divided into two broad categories (Lambin, 2008):

Fig. 24.1. Relationship between events and corporate reputation.

1. 'Goodwill-based': brand esteem is an outcome of previous investments in marketing that have increased (hopefully to a great extent) the global wealth of the firm.
2. 'Price-based': brand esteem is an outcome of the premium price (in other words, surplus of the price paid) acknowledged by the market in addition to the core essential value of the product.

It is clear that investing in a valid communication plan – which in fact an event ought to do, even more so if it is a sustainable one – should generate an increase in the value of the brand. The sustainability of the event, therefore, can and has to be financed with a part of the value gained from the firm, in whatever guise the firm participates in the event; however, inasmuch as the concept is clear, calculating the greater brand value created thanks to the event (from which to deduct a portion for sustainability) is not quite so simple.

'Goodwill-based' or 'price-based' methods in effect function prevalently in the long term, after the market (or generally the public) has assimilated the corporate image (subsequent to the communication regarding its personality and identity). As for the sustainability of the event, on the contrary, some resources need to be apportioned immediately, identifying them contextually in a perspective of economic–financial sustainability.

In this context, a fundamental contribution (Minestroni, 2002) could be provided by means of an appropriate customer relationship management (CRM) scheme. In fact, only an adequate CRM framework seems to justify, in managerial terms, the tendencies of companies (public, private or non-profit) to invest in events (also) for branding purposes. On the other hand, some scholars (Clancy and Krieg, 2002) consider an investment in branding of no use at all, unless supported (as should logically be the case) by a coherent integrated system of marketing. Furthermore, other researchers consider investment branding in the context of sustainable events inclined towards a CRM-oriented approach – albeit only in the general context of the relationship between clients and brand – a fundamental container for effective exploitation of the brand (Grönroos, 2002).

It should not be too surprising therefore that juxtaposition is created between brand (generally oriented towards all stakeholders including individual clients, present and/or potential) and CRM (usually addressed only to the latter).

CRM is the management philosophy and the operational mechanism for reaping the fruits of branding with precision and detail (one could almost say 'scientifically'). Only by means of an adequate CRM system is it possible to activate a consequent flow of strategic control and operating proposals (Ostillio and Giuliano, 2003), especially in commercial terms (Farinet and Ploncher, 2002), even though not automatically connected to the 'starting' event, which enables the constructing and reconstructing of the commercial value deriving from the event. Figure 24.2 illustrates the logical and methodological flow relative to this approach and evaluation, in a SWOT (strengths, weaknesses, opportunities and threats) perspective.

In other words, the obligation to contribute directly to the sustainability of the event seems quite natural nowadays; as detailed in Fig. 24.2, there is a shift in the perspective from threat to opportunity as this contribution comes to be considered an investment in corporate reputation. At the same time, the creation of a CRM mechanism is fundamental for evaluating the potential benefit of target loyalty resulting from the commitment to sustainability. In this sense, it becomes feasible to reserve a part of the value created in terms of loyalty (revenues) to event sustainability (costs or, better, investments).

An Exploratory Survey: Health Events

The managerial framework illustrated above finds immediate application in a specific context, that relative to the segment of events organized for health service professionals when sponsored by commercial companies (especially by the pharmaceutical industry). Reference is mainly, but not exclusively, to continuing medical education (Festa, 2003) for a very specific reason: in Italy since 1 January 2008, health professionals are now obliged by law to accrue at least 150 credits in a 3-year period, in order to continue exercising the profession. Obviously, this need boosts the perception of the overall success of a health training event, when sponsored.

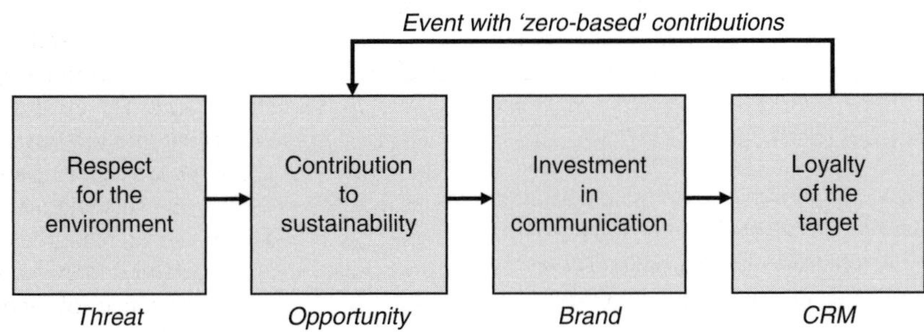

Fig. 24.2. A hypothetical link between brand, customer relationship management (CRM) and value in sustainable events.

An exploratory survey (Barile and Metallo, 2002) was undertaken in 2008 to verify perceptions of the managers interviewed on: (i) the validity of the operative link (in the context of the event) between brand, CRM and value, to guarantee avoiding the strategic failure of the economic convenience of the initiative (and hence the relative sustainability of the firm); and (ii) the overall sustainability of the event, to explore the willingness on the part of those involved to concede a portion of the value, real and/or potential, resulting from the initiative, even if or above all when participation is aimed at brand value. Box 24.1 shows the questionnaire used for the survey.

Different findings, not altogether encouraging, emerged from the survey. They revealed that managers sponsor events from quite a 'cynical' perspective, in the sense that they aim not so much at increasing brand value as should be the case in theory (Grandinetti, 2008), but above all at generating contacts, sales or customer satisfaction. Furthermore, the managers interviewed did not seem particularly sensitive to the sustainability issue in the sense that they are aware of its existence, but they are convinced

Box 24.1. The questionnaire for the exploratory survey.

1. What percentage of your budget in Marketing & Communication is intended to sponsor events?

- ❑ <20%
- ❑ 21–30%
- ❑ 31–40%
- ❑ 41–50%
- ❑ >50%
- ❑ not applicable

2. Which return do you usually expect, in economic terms, from sponsoring an event?

- ❑ sales increase
- ❑ customer satisfaction increase
- ❑ brand notoriety increase
- ❑ brand prestige increase
- ❑ not applicable
- ❑ other (if other, please explain):

____

____

____

3. Which return would you ideally prefer?

- ❑ sales increase
- ❑ customer satisfaction increase
- ❑ brand notoriety increase
- ❑ brand prestige increase
- ❑ not applicable
- ❑ other (if other, please explain):

____

____

____

4. Have you ever thought about the sustainability of the event that you sponsored?

- ❑ yes
- ❑ no
- ❑ not applicable

If YES, please go to question 5; if NO, please go to question 6; otherwise, please go to question 7.

Continued

Box 24.1. Continued.

5. Have you tried to contribute to the sustainability of the event that you sponsored?

❑ yes
❑ no
❑ not applicable

If YES, please go to question 5(ii); otherwise, please go to question 7.

5(ii). In which way?

❑ by paying cash
❑ by providing 'refreshment' services (cleaning, etc.)
❑ not applicable
❑ other (if other, please explain):
____
____
____

Please go to question 7.

6. Do you believe that the events sponsored by you have no negative impact, even generic, on the community?

❑ yes
❑ no
❑ not applicable

7. Are you aware of the certifications on event sustainability provided abroad?

❑ yes
❑ no
❑ not applicable

8. Do you consider it acceptable to give the community refreshment a part of the value generated by the event?

❑ yes
❑ no
❑ not applicable

9. Do you believe that a sustainable event, even with your contribution, could be more presentable and thus more effective in communicating towards your reference target?

❑ yes
❑ no
❑ not applicable

10. At the end of this interview, do you believe to have a deeper sensitivity for the concept of event sustainability?

❑ yes
❑ no
❑ not applicable

Thank you for your collaboration.

that the events they sponsor do not have any negative impact on the territory or the community, thus connoting the term sustainability in its 'greenest' sense. Furthermore, most of them did not seem to be aware of the existence of certification accredited for the sustainability of events contemplated outside Italy.

In any case, the survey clearly evidences the firm conviction on the part of managers as to the greater communicative impact of sustainable events, and the feasibility of financing them with a surplus of the value deriving from the event itself. These findings confirm, accordingly, the *fumus* of the perspective as to the economic convenience in terms of financial contributions towards event sustainability when there is the opportunity to transfer the cost/investment within the dynamics of a CRM perspective. In other words, communicating to your specific target that not only have you sponsored the event but also supported it in terms of sustainability, should improve the perception on the part of the user/client, increasing loyalty and, as a result, *customer lifetime value* (D'Amato and Festa, 2004).

Summary

For any organization (public, private or non-profit) it will seem increasingly more natural to associate an event to its relative sustainability, especially (albeit not only) in an environmental context, with a specific commitment to contributing to the restoration fund for the community. In the perspective of transforming threat into opportunity, it is fundamental to communicate to businesses that this contribution does not have to be considered a cost, such as an additional 'tax', but an effective investment, because within a CRM framework it can help to increase both target loyalty (probably also that of stakeholders generally) and more importantly increase customer lifetime value.

This operation could also have a limited financial impact, by linking the contribution not to disbursements (money, services, etc.) but to a percentage of the value generated by the event. It would be, in other words (almost a play on words), a sustainable contribution to the sustainability of the event. Such a vision, however, requires a substantial effort, above all in cultural and managerial terms, on the part of firms participating in the event: they should not only be aware of the issue and be committed to resolving it, but also be prepared to meticulously plan and carefully check the economic/financial outcomes of the event itself (Jobber and Fahy, 2006).

In this perspective, it is not possible to find a scheme of reference valid for each and every circumstance. However, a basic methodology for contextual application can be put in place which, on specific occasions, event organizers and participants would be able to implement. At the same time, as a result, an extremely positive image (not only necessary but also convenient) could be disseminated of the concept of event sustainability. It is hoped that this concept will be understood more fully, especially in the years to come, in culturally and environmentally aware scientific and professional communities.

Key Questions

1. How can an event be managed by a company in a marketing mix perspective?
2. Can a financial contribution to event sustainability on the part of participating enterprises be considered an investment? And if so, what benefits can it generate?
3. What is a possible approach and/or mechanism capable of creating and appraising a link between brand and value, particularly when deriving from the contribution to event sustainability?

References

Barile, S. and Metallo, G. (2002) *Le ricerche di mercato*, 2nd edn. Giappichelli, Turin, Italy.

BSI (2007) *BS 8901:2007 Specification for a sustainable event management system with guidance for use developed*. British Standards Institution, London.

Clancy, K.J. and Krieg, P.C. (2002) *Marketing scientifico*. Egea, Milan, Italy.
Codeluppi, V. (2001) *Il potere della marca*. Bollati Boringhieri, Turin, Italy.
D'Amato, A. and Festa, G. (2004) Il controllo di gestione nelle imprese della new economy. In: Antonelli, V. and D'Alessio, R. (eds) *Casi di controllo di gestione*. IPSOA, Milan, Italy, pp. 311–350.
Farinet, A. and Ploncher, E. (2002) *Customer Relationship Management*. Etas, Milan, Italy.
Festa, G. (2003) *Evoluzioni del marketing management nelle aziende sanitarie*. Giappichelli, Turin, Italy.
Grandinetti, R. (ed.) (2008) *Marketing*. Carocci, Rome.
Grönroos, C. (2002) *Management and marketing dei servizi*. Isedi, Turin, Italy.
Guatri, L., Vicari, S. and Fiocca, R. (1999) *Marketing*. McGraw-Hill, Milan, Italy.
Jobber, D. and Fahy, J. (2006) *Foundations of Marketing*. McGraw-Hill Education, Maidenhead, UK.
Kerin, R.A., Hartley, S.W., Berkowitz, E.N. and Rudelius, W. (2007) *Marketing*. McGraw-Hill, Milan, Italy.
Lambin, J.J. (2004) *Marketing strategico e operativo*, 4th edn. McGraw-Hill, Milan, Italy.
Metallo, G. (2007) *Finanza sistemica per l'impresa*. Giappichelli, Turin, Italy.
Metallo, G. and Testa, M. (2007) Etica d'impresa e governance. In: Metallo, G. and Cuomo, M.T. (eds) *Management e sviluppo d'impresa*. Giappichelli, Turin, Italy, pp. 229–283.
Minestroni, L. (2002) *L'alchimia della marca*. Angeli, Milan, Italy.
Ostillio, M.C. and Giuliano, I.A. (2003) *Interactive and Direct Marketing*. Etas, Milan, Italy.

Index

Page numbers in *italic* indicate information in figures, tables and boxes.